T0331190

Qualitative Research in Marketing and Management

This is a practical and accessible introduction to interpretive methods for doing qualitative marketing and management research projects.

Bringing together concepts of qualitative research from ethnography, digital ethnography, phenomenology, assemblage theory, critical discourse analysis, semiotics, literary analysis, practice theory, postmodernism, poststructuralism and other areas, it has a uniquely pragmatic approach. The book bridges the gap between advanced, specialised books on research traditions with more general introductory business research books. The first half of the book considers the practicalities of research and writing a research project, including the craft of academic writing, the critical literature review, the role of the independent research project as part of university courses, suggested projected structures, standards of academic scholarship, and the main techniques for gathering qualitative data. The book's second half deals with abstract concepts and advanced theory by looking at key theoretical traditions that guide the interpretation of qualitative data. This third edition has been fully updated to include new examples, insights from recent research, and an improved pedagogy for logic and clarity throughout, as well as more graphics, diagrams, chapter summaries and exercises to aid understanding.

It is perfect for advanced undergraduate and postgraduate students of Marketing, Management, Consumer Behaviour and Research Methods.

Online resources include PowerPoint lecture slides.

Chris Hackley PhD is Full Professor of Marketing at Royal Holloway, University of London, UK.

Praise for the previous edition

'This is a methods book that is easy to use. It includes all the practicalities relevant to the student, even the ones that are usually forgotten (e.g. how to work with the supervisor) – but without ever losing sight of the theoretical and philosophical embeddedness of the research process. Highly recommendable'!

Professor Søren Askegaard, *Chair of Business and Social Sciences, University of Southern Denmark*

'It is rare to find a qualitative research book that is both user-friendly and sophisticated. Chris Hackley's book speaks equally well to novices and experts. It covers the basics of how and why to do an interpretative research project and yet introduces advanced topics like introspection, literary analysis, phenomenology and discourse analysis'.

Professor Russell Belk, *Distinguished Research Professor and Kraft Foods Canada Chair in Marketing at Schulich School of Business, York University, Canada*

'I am delighted that an accessible, comprehensive and engaging text on qualitative research within an interpretative approach has finally been written! It deals with everything a novice researcher needs to know and is an ideal jumping off point for those involved with more advanced studies. I have already recommended it to my undergraduate, masters and doctoral students'!

Professor Lisa O'Malley, *University of Limerick, Ireland, and Deputy Chair of the Academy of Marketing*

Qualitative Research in Marketing and Management

Doing Interpretive Research Projects

Third Edition

Chris Hackley

Routledge
Taylor & Francis Group

LONDON AND NEW YORK

Designed cover image: DrAfter123/Getty Images

Third edition published 2025
by Routledge
4 Park Square, Milton Park, Abingdon, Oxon, OX14 4RN

and by Routledge
605 Third Avenue, New York, NY 10158

Routledge is an imprint of the Taylor & Francis Group, an informa business

First edition published by Routledge 2003

Second edition published by Routledge 2019

British Library Cataloguing-in-Publication Data
A catalogue record for this book is available from the British Library

ISBN: 978-1-032-55781-6 (hbk)
ISBN: 978-1-032-55780-9 (pbk)
ISBN: 978-1-003-43220-3 (ebk)

DOI: 10.4324/9781003432203

Typeset in Sabon
by KnowledgeWorks Global Ltd.

Access the Support Material: www.routledge.com/9781032557809

This book is dedicated to my wife Amy and my children, Michael, James, Nicholas and Dulcie-Bella. I'm so proud to say that they all have an inspiring drive to try to make sense of the world by reading, writing, thinking and scholarship.

Contents

About the author

Chris Hackley is Professor of Marketing at Royal Holloway, University of London, UK. He has published widely on topics in marketing, advertising, qualitative research methods, marketing pedagogy, consumer culture, media regulation and consumer policy.

Author's introduction to the third edition

Qualitative Research in Marketing and Management third edition provides a practical and accessible, yet sophisticated introduction to interpretive methods for qualitative research projects and dissertations. The book addresses the practical issues of doing a qualitative independent student research project as part of a taught bachelor's or master's programme of study for the first-time researcher. It also provides a guide to interpretive theory for the more ambitious student, the aspiring PhD candidate or the commercial researcher. Utilising a uniquely pragmatic approach, it bridges the gap between advanced, specialised books on specific research traditions, with more general introductory business research books that do not address interpretive theory. In particular, it provides detailed introductions to the most popular interpretive traditions that provide the theoretical basis for qualitative studies.

The first part of the book outlines the interpretive research stance with detailed introductions to deciding on the topic, writing tone and style, structuring the project or dissertation, qualitative data gathering methods and sociological paradigms and interpretive theory. The second part of the book introduces some of the most influential theoretical traditions in qualitative research, including phenomenology, poststructuralism, ethnography and digital ethnography, literary theory, semiotics, assemblage theory, critical theory and discourse analysis.

This new third edition has been selectively updated to include many new references to recent published qualitative research studies and an improved pedagogy with clearer exposition of key issues and concepts, as well as more schematics and diagrams to aid understanding. There are new and updated sections on assemblage theory, brand storytelling and textual analysis.

The book is perfect for advanced undergraduate and postgraduate students of marketing, business and management, consumer research and other related social science disciplines who are undertaking an independent research project as part of their taught master's or bachelor's degree studies. It will also be useful as a primer for PhD students and practitioners in qualitative research.

Third edition published 2025.

Foreword

Since the first edition of this book was published more than two decades ago, there have been many more PhDs, books and top journal publications in the marketing, business and management, organisational and consumer research areas using interpretive theories to analyse qualitative data sets. This reflects the growth in reach and influence of qualitative and interpretive research in the last 20 years across many disciplines of social research. In spite of the boom in qualitative research, there remains a need for an introduction to interpretive approaches for qualitative research that bridges the gap between the general research methods texts that don't really look in any depth at interpretive theories, and the very advanced texts written for PhD students in specialised interpretive subject areas. This updated third edition is a practically oriented guide for the first-time student researcher, for the more advanced master's or PhD student, and for the practitioner or academic who wants a primer on interpretive marketing and consumer research. I am gratified that the first and second editions helped a lot of students get to grips with theoretically informed qualitative research, and I hope students and their supervisors will feel that this new edition will continue to serve their needs.

2025
Chris Hackley, Oxfordshire

Introduction

This revised third edition of *Qualitative Research in Marketing and Management* continues to offer a distinctive approach that combines practical hints and insights with interpretive techniques of data analysis. The approach emphasises everyday, practical problems and issues encountered by consumers, managers and other professionals; creative, inductive research designs and the theoretically informed use of qualitative data sets. The book is designed to be accessible but also theoretically informed. The new edition has been selectively updated throughout to include reference to many new published studies, some new sections (for example, on assemblage theory, in Chapter 7, and brand storytelling, in Chapter 8) and pedagogic advances including new figures, boxes and schematics.

The book draws on interpretive traditions of social science research to show how these can be applied to qualitative research projects. It is aimed primarily at first-time researchers at any level in marketing, management, organisation and consumer research. We hope that it will also prove useful as a primer for more experienced researchers in these and other social fields who are not familiar with the wealth of philosophical perspectives, data-gathering techniques and analytical methods of interpretive research. The book offers many practical examples, and it also suggests possible topics of study for students.

Interpretive research perspectives have become highly influential in many fields of social science research, both as ways of developing rigorous constructs for quantitative research studies, and as ends in themselves for researchers seeking 'rich descriptions' of, and qualitative insights into, social phenomena of all kinds. As management, marketing and consumer research studies have grown in popularity, powerful traditions of interpretive research have emerged within these fields. In the author's specialist field, marketing, qualitative research has a long history (Levy, 2006). Today, many qualitative studies informed by anthropology, ethnography, qualitative sociology, critical theory, assemblage theory and other traditions have been subsumed under the Consumer Culture Theory (CCT) label (Arnould and Thompson, 2005, 2018) with countless methodological variations

DOI: 10.4324/9781003432203-1

amidst a growing empirical scope (Akaka, Schau and Vargo, 2022; Belk, 2006, 2017; Belk et al., 2012; Feiereisen et al., 2021; Hackett, 2016; Novak and Hoffman, 2023). Other more closely defined interpretive research initiatives include the biennial EIASM Interpretive Consumer Research Conference (Cova and Elliott, 2008) and various other conferences and workshops in management and organisation studies. The well-established qualitative approach of Grounded Theory (Glaser and Strauss, 1967) has been extended (e.g. Goulding, 2005) and is a frequently used approach to business and management PhDs, while new methods of qualitative research have emerged and grown to embrace the digital era, such as Netnography (Kozinets, 2015).

Qualitative studies have been regularly published in the top academic marketing journals such as the *Journal of Consumer Research*, the *European Journal of Marketing*, the *International Journal of Research in Marketing*, the *International Journal of Market Research*, *Consumption, Markets and Culture*, *Marketing Theory* and the *Journal of Marketing Management*, and many more are published in other top-ranking journals in related fields such as sociology, anthropology, human relations and organisation studies. There are journals that specialise in qualitative inquiry in marketing and consumer research, such as *Qualitative Market Research: An International Journal*, but qualitative studies are regularly published in general research outlets such as *Journal of Advertising*, *Journal of Business Research*, the *British Journal of Management* and the *Journal of Marketing*.

There is now a well-established book series, the *Routledge Interpretive Marketing Research* series, which brings together the work of leading international writers on diverse interpretive traditions in interpretive marketing research (e.g. Minowa and Belk, 2019; Wilson, 2019). Published studies include those providing ethnographies of management in differing organisations and cultures and in contrasting management functions; studies focusing on consumption as a major site of meaning and social identity in differing cultural and economic settings; studies examining the situated symbolic practices of management in organisations; studies focusing on consumption and the symbolism of marketing techniques and concepts. Many other studies have explored issues in gender, race and equality in the areas of management, organisation and consumption through methods such as ethnography, autoethnography or discourse analysis. These studies contribute to our understanding of cultural, social and policy issues as well as management issues.

Interpretive approaches have also become increasingly influential in management practice. For example, the fields of brand and marketing consultancy and advertising employ research techniques deriving from ethnography, semiotics and cultural studies. (Hackley, 2002, 2003a). Since the emergence of account planning as a key discipline in advertising (Griffiths and Follows, 2018) qualitative research has become identified with 'creative' advertising research, the research that is done to develop effective creative executions, as opposed to the quantitative emphasis of advertising performance metrics (Hackley and Hackley, 2021).

The intense interest in interpretive concepts, techniques and philosophies that originated in anthropology and qualitative sociology has led many more student researchers in university business schools, media departments, social studies and communication faculties to adopt interpretive perspectives for their own undergraduate or postgraduate research studies. However, student researchers who wish to find out more about interpretive social research find a vast library of texts that deal with a huge number of methodological variations, many of which are written for readerships already well versed in research practice and philosophy. Relatively few texts are available for first-time student researchers in management, communication, cultural and consumption fields who are interested in learning more about interpretive perspectives for qualitative research.

This book brings together major themes of interpretive research within a practical guide to researching and writing a research project. It is interdisciplinary in spirit in that it acknowledges the common ground and overlapping areas in the various management and business and related sub-fields and allied fields of social studies. The first part of the book reflects this inherent cross-disciplinarity as it takes a generic approach to focus largely on practical advice for the pragmatic first-time student researcher or interested practitioner. The later chapters offer informed introductions to a selection of important interpretive research traditions and suggest practical hints on how to apply these to produce a successful research project.

Part I

Doing qualitative research projects

Chapter 1

Qualitative research projects
Interpreting data

Abstract

This chapter explains the scope, perspective and structure of the book. It goes on to list just a small selection of the countless research projects for which interpretive methods could be appropriate in marketing, consumer studies, management and related areas. The chapter gently introduces some of the key concepts, assumptions and values of the interpretive research standpoint before finishing with some comments on the student research project, its educational rationale and the skills it imparts.

Chapter objectives

After reading this chapter, the student will be able to

- Appreciate the interpretive research standpoint.
- Begin to understand the scope of qualitative research projects.
- Understand some technical terms and concepts of interpretive research.
- Appreciate some of the ways in which the independent research project helps to develop the student's intellect, knowledge and employable skills as part of their higher education.

The approach of this book

This book is a practical, but theoretically robust guide for students doing a qualitative research project informed by interpretive research principles. The book's primary audience is the student researcher, from bachelor level to postgraduate, who wants to conduct an independent research project to satisfy the requirements of their bachelor's or master's degree in management, marketing, organisational or consumer research. However, it will also be useful for those with some experience of social research in business and management fields who want to learn more about interpretive theories and methods, either for academic purposes, or for practice in industry. The book

DOI: 10.4324/9781003432203-3

is written so that it can be usefully read from beginning to end, but it can also be 'dipped' into for tips on particular topics. Throughout the text there are examples and illustrations drawn from completed student research projects. The author and colleagues have supervised and conducted many successful research projects at first degree, master's degree and PhD level, as well as funded empirical projects, projects for research publication and consultancy projects. Some of these projects are referred to in this book to show new student researchers what kind of interpretive work using qualitative data sets is possible, and how it can be accomplished.

The book emphasises *qualitative* data-gathering methods and theoretical perspectives that draw on the interpretive social research traditions. This implies a creative and cross-disciplinary, yet theoretically well-founded approach to social research in marketing, management and related areas. It is hoped that student researchers can use the book and the many sources that are cited within it to make their independent research project a more satisfying, rewarding and, perhaps, less stressful experience.

The book is organised into two parts: Part 1 deals with the key practical issues of conducting qualitative student research projects, while Part 2 addresses the main theoretical traditions that are used to interpret and frame qualitative research projects. Chapter 1 introduces fundamental issues and explores the educational rationale for the independent student research project as part of the requirement for a bachelor's or master's degree. Chapter 2 looks at choosing the topic and designing the study, while Chapter 3 examines the issues in writing a research study and suggests a structure for the finished research project or dissertation. Chapter 4 introduces some of the typical approaches to gathering qualitative data sets and outlines some initial issues of data interpretation. Chapter 5 completes Part 1 of the book by elaborating on key issues in the philosophy of social research that will be important if the student researcher's analysis is to achieve the required academic standards. This chapter may also be useful for PhD students, and for academics seeking to publish qualitative work.

Chapter 6 begins the focus on theoretical traditions for framing and analysing qualitative data sets with an outline of existential phenomenology, perhaps the most influential theoretical approach (or, rather, two theoretical approaches combined) for interpretive research studies. Chapter 7 introduces another highly influential theoretical tradition in qualitative research, ethnography, including a number of other approaches that are used alongside, or as variations of, ethnography. Chapter 8 examines literary traditions of interpretive theory for qualitative research, while Chapter 9 looks at critical approaches, including critical theory. Finally, Chapter 10 rounds off the book with another important theoretical approach to qualitative research data analysis – critical discourse analysis. The topics addressed in the book are not comprehensive, but, it is hoped, they will give a strong idea of the breadth and the possibilities of interpretive research.

The independent student research project

The independent student research project (also described as a 'thesis' or 'dissertation', depending on the programme) is an entirely new experience for many students on taught bachelor's or master's degrees, and a radical departure from taught courses. It demands new skills and deeper levels of understanding compared to taught courses. University departments do provide research workshops and dedicated personal academic supervisors, but the research project must, in the end, be completed by the student as an independent researcher.

A word of caution – increasingly, essay writers offer their services to students to write their projects for them at a price. This might seem like a tempting offer if it means the student is able to pass the independent project without doing much work. But, it isn't necessarily so simple. Many universities now have software (such as Turnitin) that can be adapted to show not only plagiarised work, but work likely to have been composed by AI (artificial intelligence, such as Chat GPT). Large Language AI Models plagiarise cheerfully, so while they can be used to sketch out a structure for some types of written work, they can often be wrong, their prose can be incoherent and the work might be copied from a public source. So, they must be used with great caution.

As for commissioned work (work that the student has paid someone else to do), there are often requirements for students to engage with supervisors, so there is a recorded trail of development for the work. Students using a writer sometimes make the mistake of trying to write connecting passages to link other parts that were written to order by their writer. This can get around the problem of supervisor engagement since the work might look as if it were developing naturally. However, it is quite difficult to do this convincingly. There is a risk that the work will appear disjointed and incoherent, especially if the student does not fully understand the subject matter. Using writers, of course, is cheating and against university regulations. More to the point, the student who passes their degree having commissioned their work from a writer will not have developed the skills the project is intended to impart, and they might get found out later in their career. In this book, the assumption will be that the student is engaging sincerely in the research project process, and we will not cover the ethics of using writers or AI. Independent research projects need to be genuinely original pieces of work for them to achieve the learning effect they are designed to have on the student.

The typical research project requires students to design a study to gather data to answer a set of questions or problems that the students have identified. The student will position the study as a contribution to a given research area, write up a review of relevant academic research literature, then gather *primary data*, that is, original *empirical* data, to analyse. Increasingly, some departments are moving away from the empirical research dissertation

Three basic types of academic research project		
The empirical project or dissertation: problem/ Issue: theoretical framing: review of research literature: method: primary data collection: analysis: discussion: conclusions.	The review based project/dissertation: problem/issue: theoretical framing: extended literature review: conceptual model: discussion (no primary data).	The practice-based project: hypothetical or live problem/issue: review of practice: case-based or empirical data: analysis: managerial recommendations

Figure 1.1 Three basic types of student dissertation/project

model to adapt dissertations in two main ways (see Figure 1.1). One version is a practice-based or 'live' project focused on a specified problem, which requires a practical solution, with less theoretical context. With this type of project, there is a less demanding requirement for a thorough literature review and theoretical analysis. It would normally entail a case study (or comparative case studies), sometimes informed by a primary data gathering method such as *participant observation*, to investigate the problem at hand and suggest practical solutions. On the other hand, some other departments are prescribing dissertations based on literature reviews only, without any need for primary empirical data gathering or data analysis. Figure 1.1 does simplify the different types of independent project/dissertation offered in that some now provide quite explicit frameworks for students to follow, so that student researchers do not need to decide on every stage in the project process themselves. This book focuses mainly on the traditional empirical project so that every aspect of the process is covered, and student researchers conducting more guided projects with less empirical data gathering, or more structured literature reviews, can benefit from the sections that are most relevant to them.

This book will be of help to students doing all variations on the independent research project/dissertation. The kinds of research approaches described in the book are used in professional marketing, advertising and consumer research in various forms, and hence lend themselves well to project-based work that does not have to have an extended theoretical development. For students doing literature review-based projects, the book will help introduce them to a range of interpretive research published papers, while it will also serve as a primer in understanding the conceptual vocabulary used in such work.

The fact that the independent project is independent implies several things that demand maturity. Academic supervisors have different views on contact. Some insist on regular meetings throughout the research process. Others want only an initial meeting to establish the topic and research design. Then, once the student researcher has conducted the work and written up a full draft, they will agree to read it and offer comments and advice prior to final submission. It is important for the student researcher to meet with the supervising academic to get a feel for their personal style to judge the degree of contact required. Of course, this will also depend to some extent on the needs of the student researcher, the formal processes in the university or department, and the nature of the project undertaken. One of the most common mistakes students make is to neglect the guidance from their supervisor, thinking that they can do the project alone. By the time they realise that the task is more difficult than they thought, it can be too late. Seek guidance from the supervisor, and follow that guidance.

Even with the guidance of an excellent supervisor, an independent research project still represents a far greater challenge than taught courses. Students on master's degrees or research degrees of PhD and MPhil can find that their project planning brings them into contact with issues of research philosophy, data-gathering methods and data analysis that they have not encountered in detail in their studies of taught courses. The relative lack of research theory in the vocationally orientated curriculum of most business and management degrees means that the student then has a very wide gulf to cross to write a successful research dissertation. For many students the very idea of 'research' seems removed from their everyday experience of vocationally oriented teaching. This sense of research as a special activity distinct and separate from conventional studies can seem particularly strong in business and management courses. Indeed, some popular business and management textbooks claim that they are practical guides that can do without any theory. The truth is, they are simply unaware of or ignoring the theories that underpin every claim they make. Even for relatively non-complex practical problems, a little knowledge of social research theory goes a long way to help to design coherent research interventions that can generate insight and understanding into the problem and sometimes to suggest possible practical solutions.

Interpretive research and qualitative data sets

This book makes the assumption that qualitative data sets cannot speak for themselves. They require interpretation. The book aims to show student researchers how to conduct theory-driven qualitative research studies that will meet the criteria of scholarship and rigour required by good universities.

With this in mind, we locate qualitative research primarily in the interpretive research *paradigm* as conceived by Burrell and Morgan (1979), although we do point out that many qualitative research studies overlap with other paradigms. A paradigm in social research is a set of values and assumptions about how social research should be done in response to certain types of research problem or question. Burrell and Morgan (1979) divided organisational research into four main paradigms: the radical humanist, the interpretive, the radical structuralist and the functionalist paradigms. A research paradigm implies a standpoint on the nature of the social world (called ontology), and a set of assumptions about the appropriate methods with which to generate knowledge about this world (called epistemology). The book introduces more about research paradigms later in this chapter, and then develops greater detail in Chapter 5.

Although there has been much development since Burrell and Morgan's (1979) work (e.g. Burrell and Morgan, 2019: and, in consumer research, Cova et al., 2019: Lucarelli et al., 2023), the interpretive paradigm remains a broad label reflecting the main philosophical standpoints that underpin the qualitative research methods that are discussed in the book. The key assumption of the interpretive paradigm is that the social world is created by individuals in interaction, and the main priority for researchers is to investigate the ongoing processes of how individual actions constitute the social world. A second key assumption is that qualitative data can generate useful insights into how our language, behaviour and interactions constitute this social world. Saying that the social world is created by individuals differentiates interpretivism from realist and structuralist paradigms. These paradigms assume that the social world is created by unseen forces emanating either from human biology and psychology or from economic and social structures. The implication is that the social world can be investigated in much the same way as the material world, using the same methods and assumptions.

One criticism of interpretivism is that it invests too much *agency* and autonomy in individual actions and behaviour. One could say that our actions as social beings are agentive, that is, we are the authors of our destinies, or they are not agentive, that is, we are subject to greater forces that dictate our behaviour and even our thoughts, forces such as our social class within the economy, or our evolutionary biology. However, one could counter the criticism that interpretive approaches overstate human agency by suggesting that alternative paradigms, such as structural/functional/realist approaches, sometimes fail to capture the sense of volition or agency that characterises subjective human experience. We *feel* as if we are autonomous actors in our lives, although we also need to acknowledge the many constraints on our autonomy, such as social class, money, genetics and so forth. Interpretivist research attempts to navigate between the subjective feelings of autonomy in lived experience, and the inevitable structural constraints that impinge on our lives.

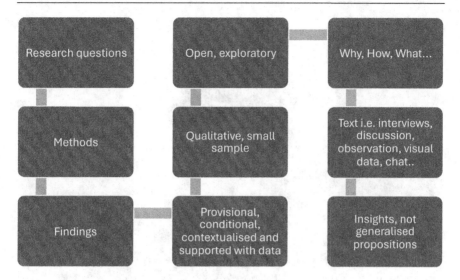

Figure 1.2 Empirical interpretive research projects

We might even suggest that the key to understanding our experience of being human is to pick apart the spaces where we seem to exercise agency within, or in spite of, the powerful constraints of class, economic status, gender, race and other aspects of social structure (Askegaard and Linnet, 2011). We can, though, set the more abstract debates aside for the present. The student project will not resolve the central sociological question of agency versus structure. What it can do is to explore a creative topic drawing on and developing skills of scholarship, analysis and organisation (see Figure 1.2). The interpretive project can be a pragmatic choice for a student project for those with a preference for exploring topics in their lived experience using qualitative rather than quantitative analysis.

Traditionally, in management and organisation studies, the interpretive paradigm has been less popular than the functionalist and realist paradigms. Nonetheless, it has retained an important place in research and, as noted earlier, many more studies working broadly in this paradigm are published today in marketing, management, and consumer research than was the case when Burrell and Morgan (1979) first published their work. Many barriers against qualitative research have been broken down in the last two decades, and qualitative PhDs and master's dissertations are now much more common in university business schools, although quantitative studies based on realist assumptions remain the dominant approach. The key to the increased acceptance of qualitative work is a greater understanding that the theory-driven approach to qualitative research demands the highest academic standards and can generate powerful and resonant findings. Many quantitative studies begin with a qualitative phase to establish the constructs to be measured.

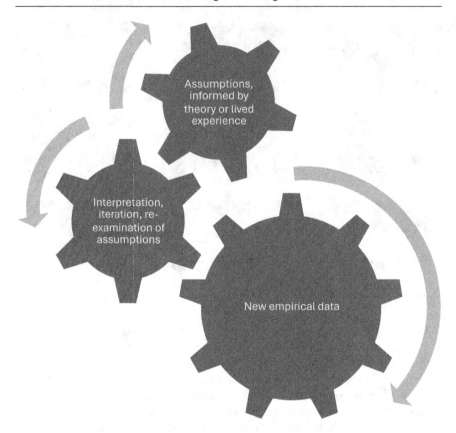

Figure 1.3 The hermeneutic cycle

Qualitative research studies can generate telling insights that would be lost if the study were to be extended quantitatively (see Figure 1.3).

Already, the reader who is new to research and tackling an independent project for the first time might be encountering new terms and concepts. The book tries to introduce these specialist terms gently and with context and places many of them in glossaries at the end of each chapter. Part of the key aim of the book is to demystify interpretive research without oversimplifying it, and it is hoped that readers will at times enjoy learning that the esoteric terms of interpretive research are not as difficult to grasp as they might sound.

One of the most exciting things about qualitative/interpretive research is that it can be used to investigate and make sense of everyday, practical activities that are within our lived experience. Far from being abstract and difficult, such studies can be highly accessible. The book advocates ways of researching that can be directly relevant to practical issues, using theoretically informed analyses of (often small sample) qualitative data sets. Interpretive studies have used qualitative data sets to investigate topics as diverse as the sub-cultural social practices of biker gangs or other consumer groups such as swap meet fans, dance clubbers or drinkers, advertising workers, religious adherents, the elderly, or white water rafters (Belk et al., 1988; Goulding et al., 2013; Hackley et al., 2015; McAlexander et al., 2014; Schau et al., 2009; Schouten and McAlexander, 1995; Svensson, 2007; Tumbat and Belk, 2011) and many more topics we will encounter as the book progresses. Qualitative research methods even include subjective introspection or autoeth-nography so that the researcher can examine their own experience as a source of data, as Professor Avi Shankar did with his record collection (Shankar, 2000), Dr Markus Wohlfeil did with his experience of being a celebrity fan (Wohlfeil, 2018), and as Professor Stephen J. Gould did with his notorious work on his personal consumption drives (which he reflects on in Gould, 2008). As the book progresses, we will encounter many more examples of in-terpretive research studies that took lived experiences and tried to understand them in everyday language, using theoretically informed qualitative data sets.

Some introductory research methods texts emphasise the construction of questionnaires, and the administration and statistical analysis of large-scale surveys. This text, in contrast, emphasises the research value of naturally occurring qualitative data sources such as conversations (on- or off-line), in-terviews and personal observations and reflections, or similar forms of quali-tative data that are elicited through participant observation, focus groups or other semi-structured data gathering approaches. The samples in qualitative/interpretive studies can be relatively small; there is no need to generate hy-potheses to be tested. The goal is to develop 'rich descriptions' (Geertz, 1973) of the social worlds investigated, not to make assertions about the world that can be generalised across time, culture, and history. Interpretive research seeks to arrive at theoretically informed and well-supported interpretations of what is really happening in social situations.

The book cannot make the research project a simple task, but it does at-tempt to provide clear signposts for students who want to do an interesting, creative, and perhaps cross-disciplinary research project that reflects their own interests and abilities.

Finding a viable research topic

More will be said about how to choose a topic in Chapter 2. However, it is worth pointing out now that new student researchers typically think in terms of big categories when they first think about what to research. They often suggest studying 'branding', 'car retailing' or 'advertising', or they suggest that they will look at, say, factors affecting brand choice in mobile phone markets, or factors affecting consumer engagement in online fashion mar-kets. These are very vague and general topic ideas. Branding, car retailing or advertising are huge topic areas, while 'factors affecting' any topic in mar-keting or management can be immensely complex and variable depending on the precise context. Such vague ideas as these need to be broken down into more specific terms. For example, investigating brand choice in mobile markets would need to focus on a specific geographical market and a specified market segment within that area. An investigation into consumer engagement in online fashion would, similarly, need to specify a fashion sector, a consumer segment, and a subset of online retail channels or other fashion platforms to make the project viable. Most importantly, the project ideas must be designed with practicalities in mind – can the student realistically get access to the data and address the research objectives within the time and resource constraints they face? It doesn't have to change the world, and it doesn't have to generate new knowledge, unless it is a PhD level study. Even if the topic and research design have been done before, a new study will be different because it will be based on a different sample frame, at a different time, in a different context.

So, originality isn't a major issue – the most important thing for the first-time independent research project student is that their proposed study must, simply, be doable. Later, many students learn that setting out a research project is both more complex and simpler than they realised. It is more complex in the sense that the way the research questions, issue, or problem are phrased is crucial for the research design. Putting a research topic in a particular form of words carries implications about the data-gathering techniques and analytical stance of the research. On the other hand, research projects are also far simpler than students often think – there is no requirement and no expectation that the project will generate a solution to a gritty management problem or that it will generate a brand new insight that could change an industry. A good student research project does not try to invent a grand theory but states a coherent question that can be investigated in a reasonably systematic and thorough way, given the time and resources available to the student researcher. The research project that is part of a taught higher degree simply needs to demonstrate that the student has acquired certain academic, intellectual and practical skills. If the project is interesting and creative, or perhaps even generates findings that could be useful to someone, then so much the better.

Incidentally, if you're wondering what was wrong with the broad project ideas outline above, well, branding or advertising are very large fields. Exactly which area would the project focus on? Marketing and management have been university subjects with published research for about 100 years – that's a lot of literature. The viable project needs to frame its scope in a less vague way. However, even the topic suggestions 'factors affecting brand choice in mobile phone markets', or 'factors affecting consumer engagement in online fashion markets', will not quite work. For example, how many factors influenced the almost 8 billion humans in the world to purchase the more than 9 billion mobile phones that exist in the world today? Clearly, a student project conducted over the course of two or three months cannot hope to engage coherently with such a huge question. What is more, a research question that begins 'what factors' really set up the student to fail, since there will inevitably be factors that the student cannot consider. Luckily, interpretive research studies are flexible enough to explore 'how' questions rather than trying to specify the unspecifiable with 'what' questions. So, if this student is interested in the mobile phone market, they could set out to explore how a given sample of mobile phone consumers choose between, say, three alternative mobile phone brands, by setting up focus groups and interviews with members of the relevant group.

The critical point when deciding on a research project is to frame the study in such a way that it is possible to succeed. There are some other examples in Box 1.1. These examples are general topic areas that could be viable studies if the student researcher settles on a specific market sector, a specified region,

---

Box 1.1   Some suggested topic areas for qualitative interpretive research studies

- Explorations of consumption practices in any sector or demographic, e.g. adoption of banking apps amongst the over 50s, tourism behaviour and attitudes, Gen X use of social media, children's computer game use
- International marketing studies, e.g. the internationalisation of fashion brands
- Cross-cultural case comparisons, e.g. movie audience behaviour in the United States and Japan
- Managerial functions in given areas, e.g. HR practices and manufacturing processes, the 'glass ceiling' and recruitment practices in a given sector such as banking or retail, or sales performance and motivation in the motor industry
- Case study examinations of business performance measurement, e.g. advertising effectiveness in the grocery sector
- Critical investigations of the social implications of business activities, e.g. advertising and inclusivity of gender/ethnicity/disability/ sexuality in given sectors
- Investigation of the consumer reception of marketing techniques, e.g. consumer use of influencer content in the cosmetics sector
- In-company ethnographic or participant observation projects
- Digital ethnographies of consumption practices
- Case studies of small business sector development, start-ups
- Management and consumption in the leisure, tourism, creative industries
- Examinations of sustainability practices in specific sectors, or explorations of consumer attitudes to sustainability in their consumption
- Studies of the ethics and regulation of areas, e.g. labour practices and/or sustainability in the fast fashion supply chain
- Studies of the role of marketing and consumption in social identity

and a specific consumer market segment to study. The list is an ad hoc selection of topics, there are many more possible, and it is not to be taken as a selection of 'good' or 'advisable' topics. Of course, an infinite number of different and possibly better topics exist, so students should absolutely explore their own interests and chosen fields.

Interpretation and the research process

All research entails interpretation, to some degree (O'Shaughnessy, 2009). Objectivity is often held up as an ideal in research, but there are choices made at every stage of a research study that will frame the findings. These choices, for example, on research questions, method, sample frame and interpretation of findings, are subjective. All *empirical research* entails looking for patterns in samples of data, and that entails interpretation of the findings, and of the implications of the findings. Calling a research paradigm 'interpretive', then, is a little nebulous, in the sense that all research is interpretive. However, the term interpretive as applied to research in general has come to be associated with qualitative methods. The implication is that *qualitative* data sets need to be interpreted, while hypothesis testing or experimental research findings based on *quantitative* studies, that is, studies that rely on statistical analysis of numerical data sets, do not, at least not in the same way. If a *hypothesis*, an assertion about the world, is being tested quantitatively, then the findings either support the hypothesis or they do not. There is no room for interpretation when a hypothesis is either supported with a significant statistical result, or it is not supported. Of course, there is an interpretive process going on here, but aspects of the interpretation are closed off and bracketed from discussion in quantitative research in ways they are not in qualitative research. Of course, all manner of interpretive judgements need to be made in quantitative studies too, and the implications of null findings have to be interpreted just as do the implications of significant findings. Nonetheless, the point is clear enough – some research designs yield findings that can be reduced to measurable outcomes, while others require a good deal of interpretation, whatever the findings may be.

Exploratory studies, access to data and 'messy' data sets

Interpretive studies based on qualitative data sets tend to be *exploratory* in nature in the sense that they are exploring a particular phenomenon without presupposing what they will find. Such exploratory studies require an interpretive process to develop a deep and nuanced understanding of the phenomenon that is being explored. Just because qualitative data are used does not necessarily mean that the research is interpretive, since qualitative data sets are sometimes used in much the same way as quantitative ones to confirm a hypothesis or proposition that might, in principle, be generalisable without there being a theoretical basis that is informing the way those data sets are understood. The term interpretive research, in this book, refers to research designs that use qualitative data sets and develop a theoretically driven interpretation of those data sets.

Interpretive research, then, tends to emphasise an approach that uses sources of data that are relatively unstructured, such as conversations, unstructured or semi structured *depth interviews*, written (textual) accounts of events or experiences, internet chat or posts, photographs and video, and observation (including participant observation). There are several advantages to this perspective. These unstructured data sets are sometimes called 'messy' data as they are not, well, neat, like survey results that can be fed into an SPSS analysis. Analysing messy qualitative data entails a more thoroughgoing interpretive process since the researcher has to decide how to make sense of it in a very fundamental way. Of course, there are qualitative research techniques designed to make the process less messy, including sorting and coding data sets, and the book discusses some of these techniques in Chapter 4.

One major issue with student research projects can be data access. Quantitative projects need to deal with poor survey response rates or integrity issues with data sets (such as whether the sample is subject to high rates of *non-response error*). Qualitative studies must deal with the question of how to get permission to access the people and places that are relevant. Student researchers cannot simply walk into a company and announce that they are conducting a participant observation study. Companies receive requests for access from students and researchers all the time, and this access must be formally granted before the researcher can begin to gather their data. The kind of *data sets* that are emphasised in interpretive research are particularly suitable for student research projects because they can often be relatively easy to access (but see below) and *samples* need not be *randomised – convenience sampling* can be fine, provided the sample is *representative* of the whole population of interest, that is, provided the sample has the same characteristics as the whole population of interest.

Of course, access to the relevant research participants can be difficult, especially for students who would ideally like to interview senior practitioners in the fields they are investigating. One of the author's former PhD students, Dr Benaliza Loo, showed great enterprise to get interviews with leading global fashion designers, and this eventually formed the basis of her PhD study (Loo and Hackley, 2013). In another example from one of the author's former PhD students, Dr Dina Bassiouni managed to gain access to children as research participants for her study on the role of video games in children's socialisation and development (Bassiouni and Hackley, 2016). Getting such access is not easy in the United Kingdom because of various laws and sensitivities around safeguarding and the ethics of using children as research participants. Dr Bassiouni had to gain signed permission from the relevant officials, from parents, and from the children themselves, and then the ethics committee of the university had to approve the entire project. Incidentally, both the above examples were published from PhD studies, but the issues they encountered would also be relevant in Master's or Bachelor's degree independent research projects. Gaining the relevant permissions and ethical approval of the university can be arduous but is essential.

All things considered, for most Bachelor's degree or Master's students, getting some friends, and/or peer group members to agree to an interview or to take part in a focus group is often enough, and a great deal easier than getting several hundred questionnaire responses (or interviewing world leading experts in their field). Students are often interested in investigating things that are relevant to their peer group. Pragmatically, it can be efficient and effective to use your own friendship and contact groups to generate interview participants.

In this book, we suggest that interpretive studies are not only useful in the pre-testing phase of large sample hypothesis-testing research, but they can also be used as a self-contained research approach for complete studies. Insight, not *generalisability*, is the goal of interpretive research. It is important to note that not only do many quantitative research studies have qualitative elements; many interpretive studies have a *quantitative* element to data gathering. The categories qualitative and quantitative are not mutually exclusive in research. Most research studies are a mixture of both with an *emphasis* on one or the other.

The interpretive standpoint, then, aims to provide a well-informed, systematically analysed, theoretically coherent, and credible interpretation of relatively unstructured or 'messy' qualitative data sets. The researcher undertaking an interpretive study will not claim that the interpretation favoured by the researcher is necessarily the only one possible. The researcher will not claim that their study has 'proved' any relationship or hypothesis. Proof is a matter for mathematicians or high court judges. What interpretive research studies can do is make a claim about the researcher's interpretation that is credible, justified empirically and grounded in careful, systematic scholarship, evidence, and reasoning.

The educational rationale for the research project

A research project conducted as part of the requirements of a taught university degree is part of the student's broader education. The work will not be judged on whether it generates new knowledge (only the PhD degree is required to do this) or whether it provides a new solution to a problem of policy. Rather, the work will be judged on the extent to which it demonstrates a synthesis of the students' learning over the course of their taught studies. The finished project should demonstrate the ability to conceive of, to articulate and to systematically investigate a coherent issue or question. It should demonstrate a high order of scholarship through a review of relevant published work, which shows that the student can conduct a literature review, and can read, understand, synthesise and critique a selection of published work in order to set the dissertation topic within a trajectory of earlier research. Students who will gravitate into employment will need to demonstrate that they have skills of research and scholarship that inform their reasoning and decision-making. They can demonstrate these skills through the process of research design, problem formulation, data gathering, analysis and interpretation.

Pragmatically, business and management students often use the research project as a 'way in' to an area of work. They can make industry contacts and acquire specialised knowledge of a key area that will be of benefit to potential employers. In addition, the research dissertation is thought to improve student employability (Sinkovics et al., 2015) through the skills and critical independent thought it develops. There are many topic areas that students can use for the dissertation that might increase their knowledge of that area with a view to future employment. In recent years, the author has supervised student marketing and management projects into communications technology, mobile telephony pricing strategies, Internet music distribution, agile systems, digital transformation, international market entry strategies, new business start-up planning, interactive advertising planning and many other vocationally motivated projects that later proved to be a useful foundation for careers in that area. The two examples mentioned above, the internationalisation and children's use of video game projects, proved to be useful foundations for the respective researchers to earn careers as published researchers and university academics.

Many students, then, choose a topic area that they feel might help them deepen their knowledge of an area they would like to work in later on. So, although vocational aims are not the main purpose of student independent projects and dissertations as part of a university course, they can often be of considerable help to students in furthering their vocational ambitions and interests by developing their employability. Many universities now place a high priority on student employability in their learning and pedagogic strategies, and the independent project or research dissertation can play an important part in the development of employable skills.

Interpretive research and the 'hermeneutic circle'

The interpretive research perspective rests on a set of assumptions about the nature of human understanding. While this book offers practical advice on how to conduct research projects throughout the range of marketing and management and other related topic areas, it is important to understand that interpretive research is based on a view of the world. This stance is informed by the *hermeneutic* tradition of social research.

Hermeneutics, the study of interpretation, derives from Biblical exegesis. For Holbrook and O'Shaughnessy (1988, p. 400), the idea of the *hermeneutic circle* is helpful in explaining the interpretive process (see also Thompson et al., 1994).

> In the Hermeneutic Circle, an interpreter's tentative grasp of the whole text guides an initial reading of its parts. The detailed reading, in turn, leads towards a revision of the original overview. This dialogue between reader and text then proceeds through subsequent iterations of a circular process that ... tends towards its own correction.

Social research is often concerned with the analysis of texts in the sense that research data are crafted into a textual representation (Hackley, 2003c) of what is being researched. A social text can be defined as anything that can be described, so, for example, a picture, a video, a screen capture of social media chat threads, an audio recording of a focus group discussion (these might be transcribed), a diary, an online interview: all can be sources of textual data. Similarly, a *depth interview* can be transcribed into a text of a dialogic exchange between researcher and interviewee. The text that results is a representation of what took place (the in-depth interview). The subject matter of the interview, the phenomenon of interest about which the interviewer was being interviewed, is also represented in the text, through the words of the interviewee. Social research is a hermeneutic task in the sense that the reader of the text (the written representation of the interview) is engaged in a cycle of re-interpretation and substantiation. The researcher engages with the text to draw meaning from it. This initial reading is loaded with prior assumptions and understandings, perhaps obtained from reading theories. The data set might challenge or change these assumptions, or give the reader reason to reflect on them. They might then revisit their assumptions, adjusting them in the light of the research data. This revised set of assumptions about the subject matter will then be brought into the process as the reader/researcher encounters next data set, and the cycle repeats, until the meanings the reader draws from the data are no longer changed by encountering a new data set (see Figure 1.3).

The final meanings that the researcher reads in the text are then communicated in the research report and substantiated with direct quotes from the interview text. Typically, in qualitative research, the researcher would engage in a process of sorting and coding (Chowdhury, 2015) of the data as they read and re-read the textual transcripts of interviews or any other data sets they have. The researcher would sort data extracts according to themes, applying a code or a title to instances of a theme they find in the data set. Eventually, after many re-readings and further sorting, the data will be collated into a series of extracts that fall under a number of over-arching themes. These themes will structure the findings and discussion in the project.

The process of hermeneutic interpretation would apply whether the researcher is analysing conversations, interviews, news clippings, pieces of elicited writing or indeed any kind of data sets that can be described. The process is often one of repeated engagement with the text and refinement of the researcher's understanding. For example, as part of his PhD, the author undertook interviews with advertising professionals, recording, and transcribing these interviews into printed texts. These texts were read, re-read and re-read multiple times before the research findings began to take shape, as the reader's interpretive understanding of the texts developed further with each re-reading (Hackley, 2000).

Interpretive strategies and the 'two cultures' of art and science

English author C.P. Snow spoke of art and science being two very different and opposing cultures of human understanding. This division is (still) reproduced in management fields such as marketing (Brown, 1996). Holbrook and O'Shaughnessy (1988) put it this way: they argued that different forms of understanding are employed in the physical sciences on the one hand, and the humanities and social sciences on the other. Humans are seekers after meaning, and we live 'embedded within a shared system of signs based on public language and other symbolic objects' (p. 400). They suggest that there is a need for an interpretive social science that does not assume that the physical and the social world are entirely analogous.

In other words, they agree that researchers should not necessarily bring the same assumptions to research in the physical and social sciences. They suggest that researchers can acknowledge that the material being researched in each case has different characteristics. The way we might understand and describe the activity of a tree and its cells reflects a different kind of reality to the way we might understand how an idea or an emotion percolates through a particular set of social practices for a given group. The assumption is that the behaviour of managers and consumers is self-determined and self-aware in a way that the behaviour of cells is not.

The division between these two cultures remains quite pronounced in social studies and management. Since the Ford and Carnegie reports on US Business School research in the 1960s, there has been a strong emphasis in American University Business School research on natural science models of business and management research (Brown, 1995; Hackley, 2009a, b, 2024). Time has broken down some of the barriers to qualitative research that this political intervention created. Management and social studies are huge academic fields, and there is unquestionably considerable plurality in research methods across many sub-fields today. Nonetheless, the division is keenly felt by many university academics and opinions are strongly held. There are still those departments where there is a clear hierarchy of research methods in which adherence to a quantitative, natural science model of research is at the top, and qualitative research is regarded as second best. There are also departments where there is a greater incidence of qualitative studies. There is a general acceptance of mixed methods studies, although the natural science model holds that qualitative investigation should normally be a route to construct development and a precursor to measurement and/or hypothesis testing, hence the hierarchical relation of quantitative versus qualitative studies in some university departments.

There is clearly room for, and indeed a necessity for, both approaches, even though each, interpretive/qualitative and quantitative/realist research study has their own specialist vocabulary and sets of assumptions (see Figure 1.4). It must be said that in some departments quantitative surveys seem to be the default research approach that is taught to students, while the case for qualitative research as a stand-alone method has to be made. Perhaps this book and the many others on the same subject will help to make this case stronger.

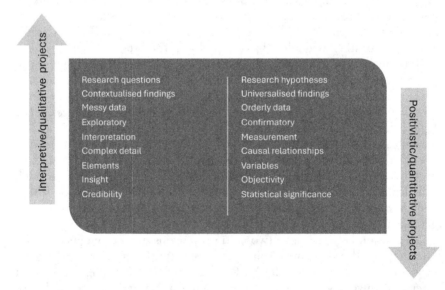

Figure 1.4 Interpretive versus positivistic research

Situated knowledge, hermeneutics and objectivity

In most quantitative research, the stated goal is to achieve an *objective* point of view and to eliminate *bias*. Indeed, the most pressing criticism of qualitative research from quantitative researchers is that it is not objective. Interpretive researchers counter with the argument that objectivity is a chimera – no researcher can stand apart from the social world they are investigating, and every research study entails choices that reflect the presuppositions of the researcher. Of course, the entire point of research is to arrive at agreements about the state of the world that are more robust, more secure than personal, subjective opinion. In this sense, both qualitative and quantitative researches have the same aim – to generate findings that are robust, transparent and well-supported by evidence. This is not about objectivity or the elimination of bias, as if that were possible – it is about good research design and strong scholarship and research practice. A softer meaning of objectivity would be not that the researcher can be eliminated from their effect on the phenomenon being studied, but, rather, that the researcher is trying to achieve a detached evaluation of the phenomenon without their judgement being swayed by their emotional feeling of what they would like or expect the findings to be. All researchers from all paradigms could probably agree that this softer meaning of objectivity is a virtue in any kind of research study.

Holbrook and O'Shaughnessy (1988) invoke the hermeneutic circle to discuss what they see as the culturally situated character of scientific knowledge (p. 433). In other words, they use the hermeneutic circle to articulate their view that there is not a science or method that can stand outside history and beyond interpretation. The hermeneutic circle is typically used in the context of qualitative data interpretation (Thompson et al., 1994, p. 433, citing Hirschman, 1990; Thompson et al., 1989, 1990). Thompson et al. (1994) suggest that the hermeneutic circle is "a general model of the process by which understandings are formed" (p. 433). They see it (citing Benhabib, 1992, as support) as a model that offers insights into the nature of human understanding:

> Personal understandings are always situated within a network of culturally shared knowledge, beliefs, ideals and taken-for-granted assumptions about the nature of social life.
>
> (p. 433)

Human understanding, then, is necessarily mediated by social context. It cannot be objective in any pure or absolute sense. We make sense of our everyday experience by deploying strategies of interpretation. These strategies can take many forms but are drawn from the cultural and social context of which we are part. Hermeneutic research seeks to elicit insights into the 'unspoken' background of socially shared meanings by which a person interprets his/her experiences (Thompson et al., 1994, p. 432). Hermeneutics, then, is the field of study that broadly informs the interpretive research perspective. It acknowledges that research is a sense-making process in which we try to make sense of the social world, and that this is a process that is conducted by human beings operating within social and cultural contexts.

Askegaard and Linnet (2011), discussing one paradigm of interpretive research, Consumer Culture Theory (CCT) (Arnould and Thompson, 2018), suggest that there can be an accommodation between the traditional emphasis of interpretive theory on the ways in which individual agents make the social world (Burrell and Morgan, 1979, 2019) and the influences of social and institutional structures of which individuals may not even be aware, what they call the context of context. They propose an *epistemology*, that is, a philosophy of knowledge, for CCT research that embraces the individual's agency and the force of social structures that both frame and impede that sense of agency:

> We ... suggest an epistemology for CCT that explicitly connects the structuring of macro-social explanatory frameworks with the phenomenology of lived experiences, thereby inscribing the micro-social context accounted for by the consumer in a larger sociohistorical context based on the researcher's theoretical insights.
>
> (p. 381)

Askegaard and Linnet (2011) situate CCT research in a hybrid paradigm that ostensibly overlaps two of Burrell and Morgan's (1979) paradigms: the interpretive and the *humanistic*. We suggest that this can be appropriate for interpretive research in general – there is no requirement that interpretive studies ignore the effects of sociohistorical structures on individual experience, and equally, there is no need to eliminate the human sense of agency from structural studies. Interpretive studies, after all, seek to achieve a rounded account of social action in its situated context.

For the first-time student researcher, all this means is that they can say what they see in the data. If the research participants raise issues that are complex, perhaps contradictory, then report the contradictions and complexities. If social phenomena appear to entail a mixture of individual autonomy (or what is experienced as such) and structural social influences, then these complexities can be part of the findings and discussion. One of the advantages of interpretive research is that the social situation under study does not have to be distorted to fit the research method. It can be reported fully, with a literary sensitivity to the lived experience of participants.

Exploratory research designs

Earlier, we touched upon the matter of qualitative and interpretive studies being used to assist in construct development as precursors for quantitative studies. At the risk of seeming defensive, a little more should be said here about quantification in social research. Many introductory research methods texts demonstrate relatively simple statistical tests that can be used in small-scale research projects, such as T-tests, Chi-squared tests, cross tabulations, Wilcoxon and other tests of statistical significance. There is value in this approach, particularly since basic statistical and numerical understanding is indispensable for students aspiring to a managerial career. However, there is also a strong case for developing intellectually rigorous research designs that do not employ statistical tests because they can form a key part of the student's education in research philosophy and critical thinking.

There are many possible reasons why a research project may not require a substantial quantitative element (see Box 1.2). It was noted above that qualitative research is often conducted in the early stages of research projects to generate constructs and hypotheses that can eventually be measured in a quantitative study. However, not all qualitative research implies the possibility or the desirability of measurement. Interpretive traditions offer means of making sense of qualitative data as an end in itself. At undergraduate and master's level, students may well wish to investigate a chosen area, question, problem, or issue to develop insights and deepen understanding of the phenomena in question. As their knowledge develops, they may wish to formulate a more specific research objective, but this may not require measurement since the student pursuing an interpretive project may not wish to generate

---

Box 1.2   Reasons for not moving to a quantitative phase in a research project

Pragmatic reasons

- Lack of researcher competence in statistical inference
- Lack of time or resources for sampling rigour/sufficient sample size
- Low survey response rates, non-response error
- To develop qualitative research skills
- Time, convenience and personal preference
- Personal preference for an exploratory project in a novel area of investigation

Theoretically driven reasons

- Theory-driven research questions/objectives
- Choice of research paradigm
- Research design demands representative not random sampling
- Seeking insight or statistical generalisation
- To research an under-investigated and/or cross-disciplinary topic

generalisable facts about the world. If a student wishes to investigate a topic that has not specifically been the subject of previous studies, then an exploratory research design based mainly on qualitative data may be the most appropriate.

Many topics that fire students' interest have arisen from their personal observations and experience of marketing and management or consumption. These interests may not fall neatly into existing theoretical categories or frameworks; hence an 'exploratory' research design may be appropriate. This does not mean that the exploratory research design would, by implication, be ground-breaking or wholly original. It might simply be that the researcher wishes to investigate, say, the social dynamics of decision-making in a local company. The empirical data set and context would indeed probably be original, in the broad sense that this problem or issue will probably not have been investigated in exactly this way using this method and in this context, but the general issue might well have been explored many other times before in different contexts with different data sets. Exploratory studies, simply, do not presuppose their findings. For example, where a confirmatory study might seek to test a hypothesis, that is, it tests a statement of putative fact about the world, such as 'eating more carrots improves the social skills of adolescents', an exploratory study might set out to explore the social skills of adolescents in particular demographics and locations.

Some students find it difficult to reconcile such an exploratory perspective with the need to have a relevant literature review as part of their work. But, even if the topic is one that has not specifically been researched before, there will inevitably be existing research that is broadly relevant to the topic in hand. From a pragmatic point of view, an exploratory study is a useful device for the first-time student researcher whose knowledge and understanding of the topic area will evolve as the project progresses. Doing an exploratory project leaves some latitude for changes, for example to the working title, to the data sample selection or to the literature review, as findings begin to emerge and the research perspective changes.

Interpretive projects and 'cross-disciplinarity'

'Cross-disciplinarity' occurs where researchers combine features from different research traditions in their research designs, like, for example, a topic that crosses psychology or anthropology with management. In other words, they work 'across' disciplines. Many students who come into postgraduate marketing, management and consumer studies have useful knowledge from their first degree they can draw upon to enhance their understanding of marketing topics. Students of literature, for example, have a range of interpretive strategies from literary criticism that they can bring to their understanding of texts in marketing (for one example of using literary theory in marketing research, see Hackley and Hackley, 2023). Psychology graduates can apply theories of psychology to consumer studies, as can graduates of many other disciplines.

In the author's experience of teaching master's courses in marketing over the course of some 25 years, often to international students from many countries outside the United Kingdom, the discipline of the student's bachelor's degree really does not matter when it comes to being successful on a marketing master's course. Indeed, some of the least likely backgrounds can be very apt. For example, students with bachelor's degrees in the arts, communication, literature, music and languages often take very well to the 'messy', creative and open-ended nature of marketing subjects. Of course, many students come to marketing from a background in science or engineering, and their numeracy skills are increasingly in demand as a basic grasp of marketing metrics, becomes essential to understanding marketing in the digital era. Marketing, though, will always be an art, as well as a science (Brown, 1996) and the 'soft' skills of imagination and creativity, insight and sensitivity to cultural trends, will be needed alongside 'hard' skills of coding and quantitative data analysis. Cross-disciplinarity, that is, looking at one discipline through the intellectual perspective of another discipline, can be highly productive in generating new ways of looking at issues in marketing, policy, strategy, consumer studies and other areas of business and management.

Cross disciplinarity works both ways. Literature searches for marketing topics can find useful sources in many research journals outside the marketing (and management, and organisation or consumer research) journals. Within social sciences such as psychology, cultural studies, youth and childhood studies, economic psychology, food studies, the sociology and anthropology of consumption, and also in some humanities areas such as social and economic history, the importance of marketing and consumption is increasingly acknowledged in research and teaching. 'You are what you buy' was a quote by sociologist Colin Campbell (2018) that has become axiomatic in many social studies. From a sociological point of view, much can be learned about society, power, and relationships by studying consumption practices. From a managerial point of view, many social scientists who are qualified in psychology, anthropology or sociology work in consumer psychology to learn what motivates and excites consumers so that advertising agencies and manufacturers can respond accordingly. Within organisations, organisational and occupational psychologists are interested in how managers manage their staff. In all these cases, it is clear that management and marketing topics and issues are accessible to a wide range of research perspectives and disciplines. While business education tends to be driven by practical management problems, it is also part of the broader intellectual tradition of the social and cultural sciences. In the second half of this book, we will look at many examples of research projects that took a cross-disciplinary approach.

The skills gained through the independent research project

The independent research project conducted as part of a taught academic course is a demanding and, at best, exciting part of a student's higher education. It is a means of teaching, and of learning, and it is thought to offer huge benefits to students in the skills developed that enhance their critical thinking, their intellectual maturity, their knowledge of a subject area, and, hence, their employability (Sinkovics et al., 2015). The skills needed to research and write a successful academic research project are both practical and intellectual. While the assessment of the research report itself is largely based on academic and intellectual standards, these standards imply many practical skills. The practical skills involved in conducting and writing a research report include gathering and organising data, planning time, and scheduling work, learning research methods, writing, selecting appropriate information, negotiating and other interpersonal skills. An intellectually persuasive research report will imply high attainment in many, or all, of these practical skills.

For example, there are many social and communication skills required in doing research (see Box 1.3). The supervisory relationship must be maintained by keeping in contact, observing deadlines, following advice, and maintaining goodwill. The student must be able to communicate his or her research ideas clearly, and he or she must also be able to listen to the supervisor's advice and act on it. The student's own life must be managed to sustain personal motivation and to plan for the required time and resources that the research project will demand. If practicing managers or other academics are asked to give time for interviews, then this access must be negotiated by the student. Busy practitioners are more likely to grant interviews to student researchers who are well organised, who can write a grammatically correct and well-structured email or letter, who can attend meetings on time, and who can strike the right tone in communications. If interviews, group discussions or other qualitative data-gathering approaches are to be conducted, then these require social, communication and interpersonal skills too. The need for the student researcher to demonstrate complex sets of skills such as these explains why the independent research project is so important in the overall assessment of taught bachelor's and master's degrees. Not only does the independent research project assess the student's ability to synthesise information and demonstrate higher order academic skills, it is also a measure of the students' personal and intellectual maturity. The independent research project is not just an outcome; it is a process.

The skills listed above are interdependent: one is often implied in another. For example, reviewing or changing existing beliefs in the light of new knowledge is an intellectual quality. It is also a feature of emotional maturity that one is able to do this. Adept negotiation skills and self-motivation are also

---

Box 1.3   Examples of research skills

Intellectual skills

- Critical reading, understanding, comparing and evaluating claims and ideas
- Synthesising new knowledge with prior knowledge
- Logical analysis, inference and deduction
- Curating the most salient points from a mess of information

Communication skills

- Communicating research ideas clearly and succinctly in writing
- Rhetorical skills, arguing, analysing, critiquing, engaging and persuading
- Writing in a scholarly style, using citations to supporting work correctly
- Listening to, assimilating and acting on advice from supervisors
- Writing, copyediting, proofreading

Interpersonal skills

- Negotiating for access to organisations, or asking for personal interviews
- Managing the supervisor, agreeing goals, meeting deadlines
- Conducting interviews and focus groups with sensitivity, tact and warmth

Practical and emotional skills

- Time management: sustaining self-motivation
- Breaking down tasks into sub-goals for scheduling and prioritising
- Self-reflection and modifying attitudes and work in response to criticisms
- Generating empathy with research participants to improve data quality

---

qualities which reflect emotional maturity, as well as demonstrating management skills. Although there is considerable blurring between skills, it is useful to set out a number of them in this way because it can show students that the research project is not just a barrier to their degree success; it is a vehicle for personal development. It does not matter if the research has not produced a striking or novel business solution or a new theoretical advance. Carrying out and producing the research project report is itself an achievement that demonstrates advanced intellectual, personal, and managerial skills.

Chapter 1 has outlined the major themes of the book. It has touched on the interpretive research philosophy and paradigms of social research, the typical qualitative methods used in interpretive research and the general types of independent research studies as part of a taught degree. The chapter has also mentioned some examples of topics and the skills demanded by, and also learned from, doing a qualitative independent research project. In the following chapter, we will begin looking at the stages of doing an independent research project, by examining how to decide on the research topic, and how to design the project.

Glossary

Agency   Individual, autonomously generated action and thought. The old sociological dilemma is between agency and structure, referring to the extent to which the social world is generated through individual action, or imposed by social structures and institutions such as class, race and economic status.

Confirmatory research design   A research design that seeks to confirm or refute a hypothesis.

Convenience sampling   A sample selection that is convenient, say, using a friendship circle or work colleagues as research participants.

Data set   The research material gathered by the researcher.

Depth interview   A long interview that explores an aspect of the world of the interviewee's experience.

Empirical   Using data that can be observed or otherwise verified by sense experience. In classical philosophy the counterpoint to an empirically based argument would be an argument drawing on pure reason, without empirical evidence.

Epistemology   A theory of knowledge, especially referring to the distinction between mere belief, hearsay or opinion, and verifiable knowledge.

Ethnographic data   Ethnography entails the scientific description of cultures through first hand observation.

Exploratory   An exploratory research design seeks insight and understanding into a novel or unfamiliar topic area or question, it does not presuppose its findings or seek to confirm generalisable facts.

Generalisability   The aim of producing a research finding that can be universally true, that is, it can be generalised across all populations.

Hermeneutics   The study of the theory of interpretation.

Humanistic   An approach to research that places lived human experience at its centre.

Hypothesis   A hypothesis is a statement of fact about the world that can be tested by observation. Hypothesis testing research usually applies statistical tests to quantitative data sets.

Interpretive research   'Interpretive' refers to a broad and diverse category of research traditions that assumes that the social world is created by individuals and employs the theoretically driven analysis of qualitative data sets.

Literature review   An extended critical discussion of previously published academic work that is relevant to the research topics under investigation. The literature review sets the context for the research project and identifies issues, research gaps and analytical concepts that may be used in the project.

Non-response error   Many quantitative studies seek random samples in order to be able to generalise their research findings. Non-response error refers to the fact that most social studies based on random samples are not in fact random because some contacted participants did not respond.

Objective   A judgement or empirical observation that is not influenced by human emotion or predisposition (*bias*).

Paradigm   A set of values and methods for research underpinned by a worldview.

Participant observation   A data generating method that entails the researcher taking part in a social process as both participant and observer. Common in *ethnographic studies*, the researcher would normally record observations in making field notes, and perhaps also by conducting interviews.

Plagiarism   Use of another author's written words without proper acknowledgement.

Primary data   Primary data are original empirical data sources that have not been previously sampled for the same purpose. This contrasts with *secondary data* sources that are already in existence, having previously been compiled for some purpose e.g. government demographic data.

Qualitative   'Qualitative' data sets are made up of material such as transcripts or audio-recordings of interviews, field notes of researcher observations, photographs, video, projective test exercises, written reflections or accounts of events, observation and any other form of research data that cannot easily be rendered into numerical form.

Quantitative   'Quantitative' data sets are any form of data rendered into numerical form, usually for statistical analysis.

Randomised   A random or randomised sample refers to a data set, each element of which had an equal chance of being selected and in which no human judgement was involved. Random samples are often generated using random number generators. A sample that is ad hoc, that is, there are no explicit criteria applied to select the sample, is not random because it entails a degree of human judgement in the ad hoc selection.

Representative   A sample that is not random, but which shares key characteristics with the whole population of interest.

Sample   Researchers cannot collect all the primary material that could possibly be relevant to their study. They must be content with a partial sample, selected according to certain criteria.

Chapter 2

Deciding on the topic and designing the project

Abstract

This chapter focuses on the choice of research topic because this important decision must be considered in the light of its implications for the project method, scope and structure. The choice of topic, and most importantly the way it is framed, has major implications for the success of the project. This chapter aims to help student researchers to think through their research project ideas and to judge whether a particular research problem, question or issue can make a viable project.

Chapter objectives

After reading this chapter students will be able to

- understand the importance of the choice of research topic
- understand the importance of how the research topic is crafted and expressed
- appreciate the need to think about the research design that is implied in the research question

Initial considerations: topic and design

As the previous chapter suggests, the choice of possible topics for a research project in marketing, management, consumer research and related fields of social research is very wide indeed. That is assuming, of course, that there is a choice. In some departments, and under some types of project, the student will be given either a set topic or a limited range of topic choices. If this is the case, there will still be choices to be made by the student, about how the research questions are framed, and, if empirical data are required, how the sample and method are chosen. In this chapter, we will assume that the student has a free choice on the topic, but even if there is not a free choice, the chapter will still be useful to students given

DOI: 10.4324/9781003432203-4

all the other choices that have to made if the project is to be completed successfully.

One point to mention is that the range of possible topics may be much wider than the student expects. It does not, necessarily, need to be a narrow business problem, such as how to increase sales in the UK toilet tissue industry, or how to increase the effectiveness of programmatic cosmetics advertising on Facebook. There are many social phenomena that can be researched from an interpretive perspective. Marketing, for example, is a functional area of organisational management but it can also be conceived as a pervasive presence in citizens' lives in developed and developing economies and a powerful influence on consumer culture. Successful marketing may be indispensable to organisations, but the institutions, values and activities of marketing have a reach and influence far beyond the organisations it serves. In many industrialised and post-industrial economies, marketing activity is seen as a source of social problems, as well as a means of generating wealth (Hackley, 2009a; Maclaran et al., 2007). While marketing increases choice and generates employment and wealth, some forms of consumption contribute to social problems including public health issues, along with environmental destruction, air pollution and more. In less developed countries, though, the relative lack of a marketing infrastructure is considered a painful absence and a major barrier to the creation of wealth and the reduction of poverty.

Marketing is a management field: practically every organisation engages with markets at some level, in some way, even if the terms of engagement may often be far from the familiar world of consumer goods transactions. People are employed to 'manage' this engagement and to manage all other organisational activities and relationships. Marketing management is not just about big organisations, executive managers and consumer goods markets. It is, crucially, about consumers and consumption in every context, since all marketing activity is premised on assumptions about the nature, needs and social practices of consumers. Therefore, student researchers should realise that it is not compulsory to conceive of a management research project as, simply, an attempt to help business sell more stuff or help them to do so more efficiently. Marketing is a ubiquitous influence in social and cultural life and any aspect of this influence is a legitimate research topic, where it concerns the marketing of alcohol to young people and the potential harms this may bring (Szmigin et al., 2011), the ideological influence of fashion magazines on gender (Minowa et al., 2019), the subtle and exploitative interplay of advertising and entertainment (Hackley, 2019) the ethical issues of deception in brand product placement (Hackley et al., 2008) or any other topic that connects to marketing and consumption.

Figure 2.1 offers a list of points to consider sequentially in deciding on a research project topic. These are pragmatic considerations of course – if the student is passionate about a particular topic or question, then that weighs the decision heavily in favour, and the other issues are secondary. However,

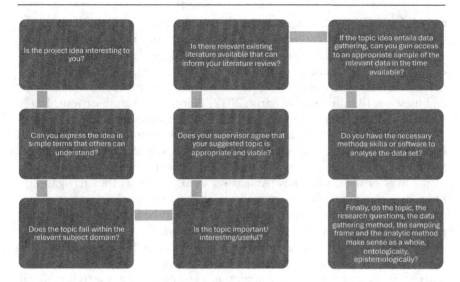

Figure 2.1 Checklist for choosing a project topic

they are all important to the successful completion of the project. The an-swer to each of the questions does depend on many considerations. In par-ticular, the 'do-ability' of the project is a question that the student researcher will be far better equipped to answer after having read this book. Do-ability is the key pragmatic issue with a project. Student researchers can probably quite easily think of topic areas they find interesting, but whether or not the project is viable, that is, whether it can be done given the time and other con-straints facing the student, is a question that requires some understanding of research methods and the research process to answer. Figure 2.1 might help with another essential aspect of the project planning. It is very useful to see all the various parts of the project listed, to see if they fit together coherently.

Marketing, management and consumer research projects

To be sure, the range of possible topic areas for a research project in this area is so great it can be daunting. The world of consumption is a vast arena of symbolic human practice that is rich in research possibilities from many perspectives. The analogy of consumption is a powerful one: we can be said to 'consume' not only perishable items such as food, drink and fuel, but also clothes, motor cars, theme parks, service encounters, even the sheets we sleep on are 'consumption' items in this sense. Any aspect of consumer experience is valid material for researchers in marketing since it all contributes towards a greater understanding of the end of marketing activity: consumption. It has been suggested that consumption has become the primary symbolic human activity in developed economies. This may take the consumption metaphor too far for some tastes, but it can hardly be doubted that marketing actively seeks to transfer meaningful values and norms from their origins in non-consumption social life to the products and practices of marketing. Hence, as consumers, we are encouraged to realise our aspirations, wishes and fantasies of fulfilment through our consumption of marketed brands, products, services and lifestyles (Bardhi and Eckhardt, 2017; Elliott and Wattanasuwan, 1998; Larsen and Patterson, 2018). On the other hand, as economic precarity faces younger generations, there has also been a movement to towards accumulating less 'stuff' and, instead, seeking fulfilment in experiences (Canniford and Shankar, 2013), such as, travel. This 'liquid' consumption can feed through to the lives of digital nomads (Atanasova et al., 2024) as they navigate the insecure economic environment while also trying to live their preferred life-style. Traditional accumulative consumption might be fading away as young people adapt to a changing economic environment.

The student's preferred research topic might evolve from a particular in-dustry issue or problem, or it might entail a more personal issue perhaps deriving from experiences as an employee, a consumer or a researcher. We all experience marketing activity as consumers and form ideas of how this activ-ity might be managed. For example, we queue in shops and banks (service delivery quality), we buy products that we like (customer loyalty and rela-tionship marketing) and products we dislike or products that were delivered poorly (relationship recovery, marketing operations). We take part in social rituals of consumption when we go out to restaurants, to see a show in a theatre or cinema, or to watch a football match. We read newspapers, eat advertised chocolate snacks, drive branded cars and wear branded goods. We follow influencers, or we don't follow them, we use social media and we navigate around the ads that constantly impinge on our viewing. Sometimes, we even buy stuff that we see advertised on social media. As consumers, our practices of consumption might generate ideas for research projects.

While the research area of consumption has a vast scope, 'Management', too, is a broad and amorphous category encompassing all manner of di-recting, coping, co-ordinating, strategising, organising, resourcing, allocat-ing, investigating and making judgements, from the executive pomp of major global corporations to the humble local store, small business or charity. Management goes on with vast resources and armies of subordinates, and it also goes on with no resources and no subordinates in small business. The management experience is vast and varied and its engagement with markets and consumers offers a fertile source of research topics, including the critical study of dysfunctional management practices (Knights and Willmott, 2017; Spicer et al., 2009).

The project topic may evolve from an interest in *functional* managerial is-sues, for example the student might be interested in examining how service quality might be improved in a particular industry context, say banking or restaurants. The interest might be motivated more by intellectual curiosity than a desire to help to solve a management problem. It may be that the student simply has an interest in an area and wants to learn how things happen, for example how advertising strategy is developed in an advertising agency. There may be a particular question that interests the student, such as how tourism destinations are influenced by the service quality of travel agents and their staff, or how tourism operator brands influence the internet purchase of 'packaged' holidays. The limit of the topics that can be explored in a qualitative management research project is the student's imagination.

The relevance of research for and to business and management

Much has been said and written about relevance in business and management studies. This chapter so far has tried to show how relevance can be conceived in a far broader way than simply in terms of a short-term solution to a management problem, such as how to make advertisements/distribution, chains/pricing strategies/service standards better and more managerially effective. This book assumes a scope of management and organisation studies that includes the social and cultural dimensions of this vast subject area. It also assumes that the focus point for many organisations is the consumer – anything that concerns the consumer should also concern the organisation that serves consumers. Consumer health and well-being, rights, ethical concerns, environmental concerns and happiness should all rightfully fall within the scope of organisations and, especially, within the scope of management education. The author has had many students worried about the adequate 'relevance' of a research project topic that interests them. They absorb the very narrow view of managerial relevance that obtains in many basic management textbooks and courses and think that research should follow the same path. Part of the aim of this book is to show that the student research project can be far more interesting, more creative and broader in scope than naïve managerial textbooks and courses suggest.

There are many traps to avoid when deciding on a project title and topic. For example, it is very important not to choose a topic merely because it seems interesting. It must also be one that can be researched easily in the available time and with the available resources. 'The impact of US Government economic policy on the level of marketing activity' might sound impressive but how would you go about studying such a broad question? Perhaps narrowing it down to a particular industry sector (motor manufacturing) and a specific aspect of government policy (say, monetary policy) might help but this remains a huge question for a 10–20,000 word Under- or Postgraduate research project undertaken as part of a taught course, that must be completed within two semesters. Even if one case study of one organisation was conducted, attributing marketing activity in the firm to US Government policy would not be easy. There could be other causes, such as shifts in consumer demand, competitor activity or internal marketing initiatives that might equally influence the level of marketing activity. And what would constitute a good measure of marketing activity? Many research projects that initially sound like a good idea to the first-time researcher come apart at the seams under more careful examination. It is essential that the research title and topic are picked apart, criticised and thought through at the very beginning. The cost of not thinking carefully enough about the title at the beginning could be a research project that runs aground when it is too late to start again. This is probably the most common failing in project design, that is, the failure to see how the various elements in the project will hang together. The research questions might be too ambitions for the sample frame, they might be answered by the data-gathering approach, the analysis might prove too complex, there might be difficulties in finding relevant literature to build a literature review: there could be many reasons why the project might fail because the whole process was not thought-through thoroughly enough at the beginning.

The exploratory project trajectory

We will return to the topic of exploratory research projects that we introduced in Chapter 1 because it is germane to the matter of how a research topic is framed and crafted in words. To reiterate, at undergraduate or master's level, research projects, especially qualitative projects, do not normally need to have a hypothesis. A hypothesis driven study would normally fall into the category of confirmatory research. Exploratory studies rather than hypothesis testing confirmation studies are often more suited to the student researcher. For example, the research question deriving from a *functional* or managerial interest can usefully be cast as a broad exploration. Say the research question is looking at the influence of travel agency staff on consumer choice of tourism destinations. An exploratory research design builds fewer assumptions into the research question and makes it less likely that the inexperienced student researcher will find the project speeding down a 'dead end'. In other words, if a research question implies that there is a relationship between two variables (in this case, travel agency staff attitudes and consumer destination choice) then the research may discover late in the study that the relationship does not hold. Tourism destinations may not be influenced by travel agency staff at all. The staff may be influential in the choice of tour operator or airline, but the destination choice may be more influenced by other factors. Too specific a research question, for example, one that postulates a direct causal relationship between variables, may be searching for a causal relationship that isn't there, setting the student and the project up for eventual failure.

The great advantage of exploratory research designs is that you are investigating a topic, and not looking for a relationship that may not be there. The student could conduct interviews with travel agency staff and customers to generate rich data on the decision process of choosing a holiday. If it turned out that the travel agency staff were not necessarily the most important element in that choice, then there would still be findings worth reporting about the other factors and the complexity of the decision process. If, on the other hand, the project had postulated a causal relationship between travel agency staff influence and customer holiday choice, and a survey did not generate a statistically significant finding, then all that remains is a null hypothesis. A functionally driven research question (i.e. one to do with managerial efficiency or effectiveness) might presuppose a link or causal relationship, say, between sales promotional activity and sales, or between celebrity endorsement and brand equity. It might proceed from essentialist categories such as 'quality' or 'strategy' or 'brand equity' that are not necessarily useful in describing or explaining organisational action in practice. An exploratory research design leaves the possible findings open and gives the student researcher the flexibility to adapt the research to new knowledge that emerges during the data-gathering process.

As Figures 2.2 and 2.3 imply, the exploratory project (beginning with a 'working' title that can be adjusted as the work progresses) takes a different trajectory to the confirmatory project. Typically, the confirmatory project will assume or propose that a fact or relationship exists in the world, and sets out to test that with a *hypothetico-deductive* study. If the anticipated relationship turns out not to be statistically significant, or the response rate to the survey/experiment falls short of expectations, the project could grind to a halt halfway down the pyramid. Of course, student projects and indeed published research studies do report null findings, that is, they report non-statistically significant findings. However, this is demotivating for the student and (usually) far less interesting to do, the student having a strong sense of trying to make a silk purse out of a sow's ear (to use an old English idiom) as they labour through the final stages of writing up their work. Of course, if a confirmatory study is well designed and based on a rigorous review of previous studies, then the chances of null findings could be reduced. The easiest way to do this would be to try to conduct a *replication study*, that is, to replicate a previously established finding with a new survey or experiment. The problem with replication studies is that (A) findings in social research are notoriously difficult to replicate and (B) it is not particularly a creative or interesting thing to do.

Being realistic about the scope of the project

There may be an assumption implied in the research question that the student with little or no experience of a particular industry can solve problems that practical people encounter every day. 'Managerial' research projects are particularly prone to this weakness. Seeking to find a solution to problems in marketing or management processes may be a laudable aim for a student

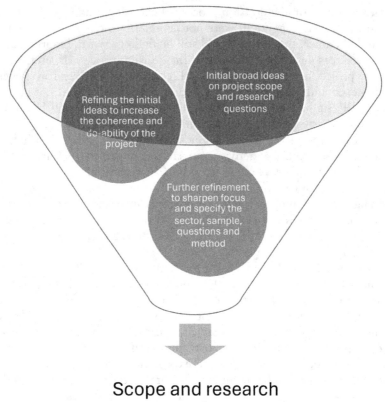

Initial broad ideas on project scope and research questions

Refining the initial ideas to increase the coherence and do-ability of the project

Further refinement to sharpen focus and specify the sector, sample, questions and method

Scope and research
questions

Figure 2.2 The development trajectory of the exploratory research project

research project, but is it realistic? If experienced people have been tackling a particular problem every day of their working lives, how likely is it that a student project can find the best way for direct entry into the Chinese motor car market for a Western car manufacturer, or any other complex and specialised managerial problem for that matter? Functional research projects may well provide new insights into problems or new ways of conceiving of the problem, but it is important for the intellectual quality and practical credibility of such projects that they are framed modestly as explorations seeking insights and understanding, rather than making grand and hollow claims about finding sweeping solutions to major industrial problems.

If the research project topic is too ambitious or unrealistic in its aims, the research is going to get side-tracked into arguments that are needed simply to defend the basic assumptions. This is a sure way to stifle research creativity. It also takes the fun out of research if you can't change your mind and

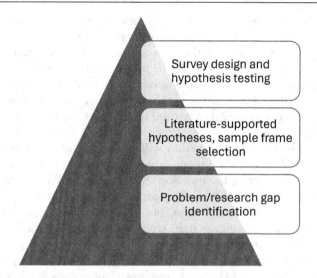

Figure 2.3 The development trajectory of the confirmatory research project

explore something unexpected but interesting that emerged from the investigation. Furthermore, it is a poor research ethos that forces researchers to ignore issues that arise because they don't fit into the *a priori* categories that were built into the research question. For all these reasons, first-time student researchers often find that broad, exploratory research questions or issues are the safest and most appropriate.

The 'working' title and student motivation

A 'working' title is statement of a research question, issue or area that is phrased broadly so that it can be made more specific at a later stage. It is useful in exploratory research that research questions have some flexibility before the final research questions are framed and before primary data are collected If a person starts out by, say, researching branding effectiveness in a particular product market and then, midway through the project, decides that communication is central to the issue, it would be an intellectually flawed exercise if they could not adapt their research to take in a change of emphasis from branding to brand communication. Research projects should not have to perform logical somersaults to defend the coherence of the question regardless of how the researcher's understanding of the question develops as their knowledge grows. This would be a little like setting out on a world back-packing trip with a bad map, then insisting that the map is right – therefore this mud patch on the left must be Copacabana Beach.

Research questions should initially be couched in broad terms even if the original interest from which they evolve is one of a *functional* managerial, *normative* nature. The term 'managerial' used in research tends to refer to research that seeks to solve a management problem, while the term 'functional' refers to one of the typical organisational management functions, such as marketing, accounting or Human Resources (HR). The term 'normative' is sometimes used to refer to managerialist texts that purport to offer such solutions; they offer frameworks for *doing* management tasks successfully. 'How can this work better?' is a natural question to ask for people attracted to marketing studies through a managerialist vein of thinking. In most cases an intellectually honest investigation will reveal the assumptions built into the question and hence lead into an exploration of the preconditions for the problem. In other words, the question 'how can we sell more stuff' would, if it is being investigated thoroughly, not simply focus on advertising, sales force management and distribution, but also on pricing, product development ('are we trying to sell the right stuff?'), HR ('are our staff any good at selling?') and, of course, customers.

In any case, in marketing and other management fields, people working in that field feel that they already know how things could work better. They feel that the hard part is trying to implement the necessary changes, because there are always barriers to organisational functions, both internal barriers such as inefficient internal systems, poor reward systems, poor sales support and so on, or external barriers such as stiff competition, difficult macroeconomic conditions or trends and fashions in consumer tastes. Self-evidently, in most cases, since implementation of managerial practices and solutions is difficult, the problem itself is not as simple as it may appear to the naïve researcher. A project entitled 'Resolving customer dissatisfaction in service encounters in the motor car hire industry' is quite likely to generate some useful insights into customer experiences in that context, but it cannot do as it claims and 'solve' the problem, because it is a complex and continuing issue of management. What is more, finding out what a problem is, is quite different to solving it. Research questions should be realistic about the limitations of research and suitably modest about their ambition. A working title that is phrased with some strategic vagueness can be useful because it can be adjusted as the researcher learns more about the complexity of the issue they are investigating.

There is also the question of student motivation. The project needs to be motivating for the student, and learning halfway through it that the hoped-for aims will not be achieved, the promised interviews will not be forthcoming, or the anticipated relationship between variables is not there, are deeply de-motivating experiences. The exploratory format, and a 'working' title that can be tweaked, allows students the flexibility to investigate a topic of their interest in ways that are satisfying to them and can, if necessary, change emphasis halfway through as the student learns more about the topic area. The choice of topic must be motivating for the student otherwise the research experience will be a chore, and commitment and performance levels

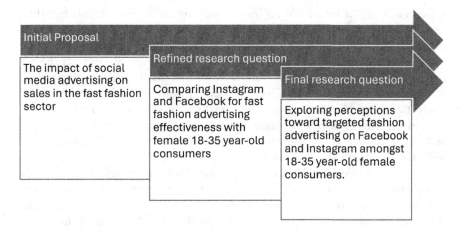

Figure 2.4 Example of refining an exploratory research question

will drop. It is by far the best course if the potential difficulties entailed in answering the original question or proposal have been identified, clarified and addressed before the project proceeds to the data-gathering stage. For example, in Figure 2.4, the original proposal is too broad to be practicable. The student needs to specify a target segment, preferably one to which they can gain access for research participants. They also need to narrow down the scope from all social media advertising to either specified types of social media advertising, or specified sources. They decide on the latter course and specify two popular platforms. This narrows down the scope to enable more effective and targeted preparatory research. It is, though, still too broad, and this would become evident as the students reads more research literature and secondary research on the topic. Finally, they arrive at a form of words that will enable them to conduct a viable project. Note that the focus is now on the 'perceptions' of those consumers, and not on advertising effectiveness, since the calculation of effectiveness cannot be made without access to proprietary data. The study can only investigate the extent to which research participants perceive the ads as effective, or not.

The student–supervisor relationship

The question of student motivation for the independent project is not unconnected to that of the supervisor's motivation. Some supervisors are highly motivated, and that can be motivating for the student, if they are supervising a committed student who is studying something that is of interest to the supervisor. Other supervisors might be supervising 30 undergraduate and/or postgraduate dissertations and need to parcel out their time carefully for the sake of their health and sanity. These overworked supervisors might be a little bit less excited by their supervisions but they will do a professional and caring job, and it is up to the student to try to make the best use of the supervisor's advice. The supervisor's feedback can be extremely useful in many ways, for example, they can help the research student to clarify issues and assumptions involved in the topic idea. Maintaining motivation is an issue of key importance to the success of the project and establishing a good relationship with the supervisor can be a big part of this. As a generalisation, supervisors tend to be more motivated and more responsive if they feel that the student is also committed and fully engaged with the process.

The student researcher's success depends a lot on their supervisor. It is always wise, and simple good manners, for students to attend meetings when requested, reply promptly to emails, listen to the advice offered, and meet deadlines when asked to do so. It is very unwise to fail to contact the supervisor for months on end, then to demand advice and guidance by the next day. In the great majority of cases, supervisors sincerely want their research students to do well, and many will go an extra mile to help a sincere and earnest student. However, students must be aware that it is a two-way street. 'Independent' research project means exactly that. Students must work independently but under the guidance of the supervisor. Too much contact, or too little, can have a negative effect. In almost every case, a little consideration and goodwill on both sides go a long way to making the experience pleasant and effective for both parties.

Many university departments set out procedures for making contact with supervisors. Some allow a good deal of flexibility. Some supervisors prefer regular meetings and updates. Others expect their students to go away and work independently once a careful initial discussion has set out just what their topic is to be and how they should go about researching it. Supervisors of this inclination would usually want to review only one draft before submission. Both supervisors and students have differing needs and preferred ways of working: the main rule is that friendly, prompt and courteous communication on both sides is important. Supervisors have a wide range of knowledge and expertise but their most important attribute for the student researchers is their experience of judging, evaluating and designing research projects. In many cases, it is not necessary that a supervisor be a specialist in a given sub-area of marketing or management for them to be able to give useful advice. Academics are often required to read and judge a wide range of papers in their work as reviewers for academic journals, research funding bodies and PhD proposals and theses. Student researchers should be aware that experienced academics have read, and in many cases written, a great many research papers, and they have developed strong research skills that enable them to help students research a wide range of topics. The research project student will become the expert on the precise topic they are investigating, while the supervisor can make judgements on the overall structure of the project, the quality of arguments, the appropriateness of the method and all other general aspects of the work.

The need to choose a topic, and stick to it

Having a working title for an exploratory project does not necessarily mean that the student researcher can change their topic entirely. What they can do is change aspects of it, such as tweaking the method, the sample, the scope or the research questions. Doing the research project entails acquiring knowledge that is new to the student researcher. This new knowledge then, obviously, changes and informs the way the problem or issue is conceived. However, there must be a clear topic area and a general perspective that cannot usually be changed once the project is underway. There may be exceptions to this, but in general, most universities do not allow students to change their project topic after a certain stage in the process in reached. It is unsettling for students and worrying for the supervisor if students change their minds about the topic they want to research halfway through the process. Research projects that are part of taught degrees are often conducted in a tight timescale and with limited resources. Supervisors are often responsible for large numbers of students. Therefore, a radical change of topic midway through the process can present special difficulties. Indeed, some universities forbid students to change the topic after the proposal has been approved. It is, again, therefore, wiser to phrase the project title in such a way that its exploratory nature is evident. Before writing the proposal, students should take time and trouble to explore different topics, different research designs and different problem formulations. This is why academics always try to encourage students to begin thinking about their research project long before it is time to submit (advice that is, unfortunately, often not heeded). Then, when the student has decided on a topic proposal in discussion with their supervisor, they need to stick to the topic area, even if they sometimes tweak the theoretical approach, method and/or the empirical scope or sample.

For example, a student might decide to investigate comparative advertising strategies for motor cars in the United Kingdom and China. As they progress in gathering data, they might decide to focus on a particular brand or class of car. They might also refine their project to focus on a specific market segment. They could even change the emphasis of analysis from a broad concern with 'advertising strategy' to some aspect of creative execution, such as the portrayal of speed in motor car ads, or the representation of masculinity that is produced through the visual imagery of the ads. They might be let down by brand managers in the car industry who had previously agreed to grant an interview but who now do not have time. In this case they might seek alternative interviewees, perhaps from the advertising agencies themselves. All this can change the emphasis of the research questions and the consequent analysis and discussion. The important thing is that, however the emphasis of the project may change, the broad topic area does not. That is why an exploratory working title for the project proposal is often, pragmatically, the best starting point.

The project proposal

The research project process often begins with a research proposal that represents the initial ideas on how the project will unfold (see Figure 2.5). Many universities require students to produce a research proposal that must be approved before they can commence the project. As mentioned above, in the initial stages of the project a 'working' title that can be slightly adjusted may be sufficient. For example, a project entitled 'The relationship between advertising and sales in the laptop segment of the UK computer retailing sector' would be rather too broad. This would be a somewhat over-ambitious project that reveals a naïve understanding of the complexity of the issues involved. Such a project would need to be radically modified at a later stage, when the student researcher realised that they could not satisfactorily

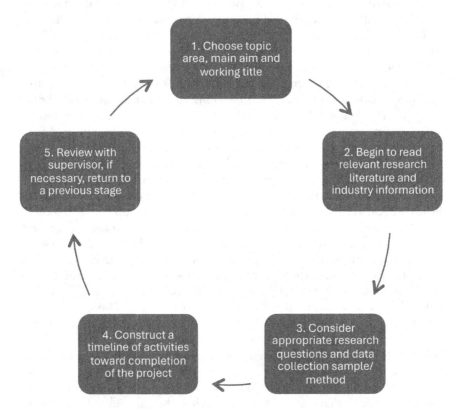

Figure 2.5 Research project proposal checklist.

establish the stated relationship. However, if the same project proposal is worded in more general terms as, say, 'An exploration of advertising strategy in the laptop segment of the UK computer retailing sector', then there is scope for the precise aims of the project to be re-appraised later, in light of the information that is gathered during secondary research and reviewing of literature. An over-ambitious, sweeping project proposal can risk setting the student up for failure. A more modest, carefully qualified proposal is usually wiser. Proposals must be interesting to the student (and, if possible, to the supervisor) and they must have a point or a question that will structure and drive the research. However, this can be phrased broadly in the initial stages because the project may then reach its full potential in an evolutionary way.

Writing the proposal

Different universities ask for slightly different things in their project proposal. They all, however, have the same general purpose. Proposals are designed to get the students to think carefully about their research project and to begin to think through and plan how they are going to complete it on time and to an acceptable standard. Many institutions try to get students to think about their proposal quite early in the year even though the project often does not have to be submitted until the very end of their course. Academic staff often find that a high proportion of students leave serious project work until rather late in the year, leading to a panic when submission time is near. The project is itself a major learning experience for most first-time student researchers and it is unreasonable to expect that they can anticipate the whole process in detail in advance. However, if students take the proposal seriously it can save a lot of stress later.

It should be unnecessary to state that the essential elements of a proposal are that it is a carefully proof-edited text that is written clearly and uses a reasonably accurate *referencing* style (Harvard, APA or another style is usually specified by the university). Some project proposals will require elaboration on each point. For example, some universities will ask students to write a 2,000-word proposal. This means that they can devote, say, 300 words to a working title and an explanation of the topic area and a list of three or four main research questions, 1,000 words to an outline literature review, 500 words to the methods and 200 words on a time-line of the research process. Leaving enough words for a list of the references used would also be a good idea, so that the marker and the potential supervisor can see that the student knows how to use citations properly and how to list them at the end of the work.

The importance of reading the academic literature

One of the best ways to prepare a proposal is by reading the academic research on the topic the student is thinking about researching. As a rule of thumb, the more reading the student does, the better the project is likely to be. This will mean taking the trouble to use the databases of academic literature that are available in most university libraries, such as 'Proquest', 'Emerald', 'ABI-inform', 'EBSCO' and ATHENS. University library staff are the experts in 'literature searching' and they are usually only too happy to advise students doing research projects, if advice is needed. Google Scholar is a useful resource although it will include student papers and theses as well as journals and books, along with un-ranked journal papers. Scopus is a more focused database of highly ranked journal articles. Being able to source research papers on a given topic is a fundamental scholarly skill and many universities will expect their undergraduate students to be fully able to do this by their final year.

Reading the academic literature has several benefits. First, students begin to understand the academic style of writing, including the use of conventions such as *Harvard citation style*. Second, acquiring a good understanding of the published research in relevant areas is a major part of the project process. For a bachelor's or master's dissertation or project the university will not expect the student to have a grasp of the entire field they are investigating, but it is a key requirement of the work that the study is contextualised by a good review of some of the main areas of work relevant to the research question. Reading research papers in a field increases the student's depth and breadth of understanding about a field of research and might even give the student ideas about a possible research topic or method.

The author studied for a taught MSc in marketing some (actually, rather a lot of) years ago. He was particularly interested in marketing and corporate communications, both to external and internal audiences. The independent research project he produced for his final (3rd) year assessment grew out of some reading on 'mission statements'. A group of researchers had collected many examples of published mission statements and had then analysed their content using a simple content analytic framework. The work was published in a refereed research journal. The author extended this work by collecting more mission statements from a particular industry sector (higher education) from the organisations' published reports, websites and other communications. He adapted the previously used frameworks by adding new categories, although what he did was essentially to replicate an earlier study, slightly modified, with a new data set. The study served for the author's MSc in marketing research dissertation (at the University of Salford, United Kingdom) and was published (Hackley, 1998a with some theoretical development that had not been present in the original project. In this example, the researcher read a journal article and thought "That looks interesting, I could do that, on a smaller scale and with a different sample". This is how research often progresses, and students new to research should not make the mistake of imagining that they must create an entirely original research question. Their own project must be entirely original, but the idea need not be if they are conducting a study using a different sample and in a different sector.

Originality of research

As hinted at above, many published research projects are essentially adaptations, extensions or replications of previous projects. Student researchers are sometimes worried about the originality of their work if they adapt or extend a previously published research study. Adapting previously published research studies should not be confused with plagiarism. It is not only entirely legitimate: it is an extremely useful way of carrying out a first research project without 're-inventing the wheel'. Student research projects must be original in the sense that they must be the student's own work. They do not have to be original in the sense of being an entirely new, never-before-thought-of idea. Indeed, no research falls into this category. Every individual researcher researching in good faith from their own particular perspective, will produce original work in the sense that it is their own 'take' on a given topic and the sample, the results, the findings and the discussions and interpretation of findings, are all likely to be somewhat different to the original study. Indeed, it is notoriously difficult to replicate studies in social research. Students should not worry about the originality of their topic because there will invariably be some things that are different if it has been conducted in good faith as a new piece of work produced entirely and wholly by the student.

In much of this book we discuss projects that use empirical data, that is, they gather their own data that has never been gathered before for that purpose. However, conceptual work that does not draw on original empirical data can also be a legitimate approach to the independent research project. *Conceptual* papers, that is, published research that does not draw on a primary data set, review previously published research to draw attention to theoretical anomalies or gaps and to suggest new lines of discussion or investigation. Review papers do much the same thing, although the conceptual paper normally generates a conceptual model to illustrate its main conclusions, while the review paper might not do so. Empirical research papers that do use primary data sets often reproduce previously used research designs and use them on new sets of data to test the findings. Such papers also often explore old data with new theory, or they explore old research problems with a new angle or concept. 'Originality' in academic research consists in the particular arguments, style and combination of ideas employed. To repeat, originality in student research projects does *not* mean never-before imagined ideas or findings. Reading published research and drawing ideas and ways of working from it is absolutely the best way for student researchers to form their own ideas about the kinds of research possible and the appropriate academic style of research writing.

'Deductive' and 'inductive' research designs

The *research design* refers to the overall design of the research method and its rationale for an empirical project. This would include details on research question(s) and/or problems, sampling, data-gathering techniques and data analysis. We will note a few broad issues on research design at this stage.

The terms 'deductive' and 'inductive' (see Figure 2.6) are often used in re-search theory. *Inductive* means reasoning from the general, to the particular. For example, if something seems true in many varied circumstances, it may also be true in specific circumstances. If, for example, you find from your lived experience that brown-eyed people tend to be generous, and green-eyed people less so, then you might form a rudimentary theory that brown-eyed people are more generous than green-eyed people. This is an example of inductive reasoning, although of course the sample size from one's own ex-perience is so small that the results cannot be extended beyond our personal experience.

Deductive means reasoning from the particular to the general. Say, for example, you wanted to test if your personal, informal theory that brown-eyed people are more generous than green-eyed people is true of the whole population of brown-eyed people in the United Kingdom, you could form a hypothesis – 'Brown eyed people are generous', then design an experiment or survey to test the hypothesis empirically on a large random sample. This would be a deductive research design. The limitation of this example is that it deals with a generalisation. Inductive interpretive research more typically does not attempt to make generalisations about the world, but, rather, it attempts to generate insights about a particular context. Figure 2.6 merely describes a way of thinking about experience, but this way of thinking is ap-plied to inductive research in specific ways.

Inductive reasoning, from the particular to the general e.g. I know two brown-eyed people who are generous. I wonder if more brown-eyed people are generous?

Deductive reasoning, from the general, to the particular e.g. Let's do an experiment with a large sample of brown-eyed people to see how generous they are

Figure 2.6 Inductive and deductive reasoning styles

In social research, exploratory studies would normally be designed on an inductive model, that is, the study would explore a phenomenon to see if any patterns or themes emerge. Strictly, inductive research looks at many cases to induce general patterns or relationships. However, major research studies can go through both inductive and deductive phases. If, say, a hundred salespeople are interviewed about their motivation, a researcher might be able to induce a general proposition about salesperson motivation that seems to be true for a large number of the interviewees. The researcher might feel that this proposition has not been considered in the previous research on sales force motivation. Perhaps some interviewees mention that having a boss with good communication skills is very important for their motivation. The researcher could then use a deductive research design to 'test' this proposition on an even larger number of cases, perhaps by means of a questionnaire. The finding would then provide material for reflection and modification of a theory of salesperson motivation. If the study is trying to find a cause–effect relationship between the sales manager communication skills and sales force motivation, then this is sometimes called an abductive form of reasoning.

A qualitative, exploratory project then would normally use inductive or abductive reasoning because the researcher would be looking at a complex situation and trying to induce conclusions from the observed patterns in the data. For example, the previously mentioned study of children and video games (Bassiouni and Hackley, 2016) sought to explore the role of video games (played on any platform or device) in children's lives. Interviewing children about their video game usage enabled the researcher to draw some tentative conclusions about this role, even though only a dozen or so children were interviewed. The findings were tentative but nonetheless, powerful, but perhaps only characteristic of this sample of children and their particular circumstances. The reasoning used was broadly inductive in the sense that the reasoning moved from the general (the interview data) to the particular (conclusions drawn about the role of video games in children's lives induced from the interview data). The conclusions were robust in the sense that the sample they came from was highly representative of the population segment of interest, but they could not be generalised from such a small sample. In the style of interpretive, qualitative research, they were offered as insights, rather than as generalised truths. One well-known example of an inductive research approach that has been used in many published qualitative studies is Grounded Theory (Glaser and Strauss, 1967).

Of course, induction and deduction both have a role in thinking and reasoning. Arguing and analysing necessarily draw on both inductive and deductive thinking. For example, if I go out of the house three days in a row and get wet because it is raining, I might take an umbrella on the fourth day. I have induced a hypothesis: 'If I leave the house without an umbrella, I might get wet'. Therefore, I carry an umbrella to prevent getting wet when I leave the house. However, if I decide to test this hypothesis deductively when I go on summer holiday to southern Italy, I will find that my hypothesis does not hold true in that situation. I could carry my umbrella around in Rome for weeks in the summer and never get wet, unless I fell into one of the fountains. In our daily life, we use deductive and inductive thinking to understand the world and to make predictions. If we relied exclusively on one or the other thinking style, we would not manage very well at all. Many large-scale research designs, as in the illustration above, move from inductive to deductive and back again as theories are refined and developed. It is therefore rather a simplification to say that a research design is either inductive or deductive. Research is usually both, to an extent.

Research philosophy and research design

We will address the topic of research philosophies in greater detail in Chapter 5. For now, we will discuss some initial considerations. Interpretive research tends to be based on a social constructionist ontology (see Figure 2.7). An ontology is a set of basic assumptions about the nature of the social world. Social constructionism is the belief that the social world is self-constituting in a way that, say, the natural world of trees or mountains are not. Trees and mountains operate to fixed laws of biology and geology that hold true for all trees and mountains on earth. They do not make up their own ways of being. The social world, according to the social constructionist ontology, is rather different – it does make up its own

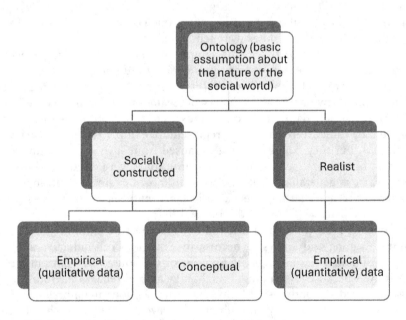

Figure 2.7 Research philosophy and research design

ways of being and does not always operate to universal laws. Human beings construct our social world through our talk, interaction and symbolic practices, according to the social constructionist ontology. They ways we do this may well be highly influenced by factors beyond our control, such as, our biology, our evolutionary behaviours and the economic and social forces that we live within. However, according to the social constructionist ontology, these influences impact our social world, but they do not necessarily determine it.

We have already mentioned positivism, a term which refers to the belief that empirical research ought only to study things that can be observed and measured. An ontological assumption that can go alongside positivism is realism, the belief that the social world can be studied as if it operates according to universal laws, just like the natural world of trees and mountains. Positivism and realism are terms that are often used interchangeably in management research books, although they are not really the same thing.

For our purposes in this book, we can say that, normally, hypothetico-deductive research studies, that is, research that proposes a hypothesis about the world and tests it, tend to be based on a realist-positivist ontology, while interpretive research studies tend to be based on a social constructionist ontology. That is, hypothesis testing studies tend to be based on the realist world view, they assume that whatever they discover might turn out to be a universally true fact or relationship between variables. Interpretive studies, on the other hand, based on a social constructionist worldview, would not make the claim that their findings have discovered a universally true fact or relationship. Rather, they would offer an interpretation of what they have found that might be more widely true of similar groups or contexts, but which also might connect with a human sense of truth, much as a novel might do the same by highlighting a truth that may hold for many people in certain situations. The insights or truths from interpretive social research might be thought of as similar to those that arise from art and literature, rather than those that arise from physical science. They are couched in contextual factors, caveats and conditionals. The assumption is that truths about the world that apply in all circumstances to all people and situations, are pretty difficult to come by, and a questionnaire survey or social experiment are very unlikely to find one.

Some university departments would expect students to understand which ontological assumptions they are making in their research design. Others would not. However, it is useful for all student researchers to understand the basic distinction between the realist ontology and the social constructionist ontology because of the implications for research design. It will also be useful for students to understand these concepts because of the kinds of claims that can be made from the findings. Each style of research design tends to follow rather different conventions. One way of really getting to grips with the differences is to read a number of published studies that fall into each category. By doing so, it would be clear that the findings from interpretive social research are neither 'proofs' nor 'generalisations' but contextualised insights, while the findings from positivistic and/or realist research studies are attempts at universal generalisation.

Hypothetico-deductive research studies based on a realist ontology tend to work best where there is already robust theory that can make strong predictions. Some interpretive researchers have argued that there are few examples of this kind of theory in the management and marketing area. Others would disagree, they would defend the state of realist/positivistic management research and would argue that, in fact, there have been robust findings, even though there are always limitations and revisions Inductive, interpretive studies tend to work best where the researcher is conducting an exploratory study to learn in greater detail about the dynamic that is operating in a given social situation.

'Empirical' and 'conceptual' research projects

The chapter will now discuss another important distinction, briefly mentioned earlier, in the kinds of projects that can be undertaken as part of taught degrees. Some research projects at taught degree level in management and marketing are based mainly on existing sources of information such as academic papers, published economic data and/or internal company records. Such projects are often termed 'conceptual' or review-based projects to distinguish them from projects that make use of original information that is gathered first hand by the research student. Projects that generate original data are often called 'empirical' projects (see Figure 2.8). The term empirical refers to primary data gathered for the specific purpose of the study. The section below will elaborate on the issues and problems of each kind of project. It will then return to important issues of what topic to research given the special demands of these two categories of research.

Empirical projects

Marketing, management and consumer research projects in higher education can be either predominantly empirical, conceptual or they can include elements of each. *Empirical* knowledge derives from experience and empirical research projects utilise first-hand experience of primary data sets from, for example, interviews, survey data, experiments or observation. The primary data sets are placed in the context of available literature (in the literature review) and are then analysed for insights or patterns. An empirical project report will represent the student's own systematic investigation into the topic. It will include a critical review of relevant research literature, perhaps including important practitioner literature (trade press, industry reports) and

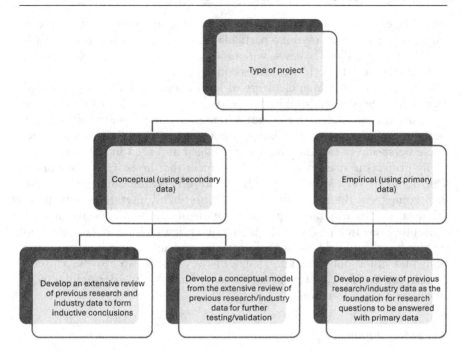

Figure 2.8 Conceptual, review and empirical research projects

published market studies too. The general findings from the review are then evaluated in the light of the student's first-hand experience of the topic area, that is, their interpretation of the empirical data that have been gathered.

The amount of primary data in the empirical project can vary greatly. In research projects that are part of taught courses, data sampling may be based on very small samples for practical reasons. Qualitative data-gathering techniques use sampling approaches that are not required to provide a basis for statistically significant generalisation. Data can be based on *convenience samples* and need not be *randomised*. For example, a student investigating the use of fashion blogs in fashion purchasing might enlist their friendship group to form three *focus groups* of six people each. This would normally be a more than adequate data set for a student bachelor's or master's independent research project. Primary data sets can be used to enhance a primarily conceptual project, or they can be used as the major basis for a project. One MSc student project the author has supervised used three focus groups, another used four *depth interviews*. The amount of primary data that might be useful depends on the research question or questions. It is important for student researchers to remember that even if small samples are representative of larger groups, that is, if they share the major characteristics of the larger groups, findings are still limited to the immediate research context and should be expressed cautiously in view of this. It is an important principle of inductive research that even if a particular fact or relationship between variables is true in millions of cases, we cannot know for sure if it will be true in every case, even if the evidence seems compelling.

Many projects combine elements of both conceptual and empirical approaches. One way of combining the two approaches is to focus on the literature review while carrying out a limited number of short 'pilot' interviews to get important practitioner or consumer perspectives on the topic. These perspectives can then be acknowledged and used in the discussion. Many projects in marketing and management that investigate a live problem, do so by reviewing relevant literature on research and practice and then comparing the major findings with first-hand interviews with practitioners. In this way, an empirical component can be added to a mainly conceptual research project. Conducting interviews with practising managers also has the added benefit of sharpening students' research interviewing skills and filling out their knowledge of the area. It can also be a useful exercise in getting contacts in an industry that might offer employment prospects after graduation.

'Conceptual' projects

Conceptual projects with no first-hand or primary data sets are also often acceptable at undergraduate and sometimes at master's level, depending on the rules at the department in question. Conceptual projects use existing published sources of information, that is, they use secondary data sets. Conceptual projects consist of an extended critical review of available research literature around a particular set of research issues, questions or problems. Students who survey academic literature will see that many published research papers in marketing, management and consumer research are like this. They report no empirical findings and have no data as such, but they explore issues or problems related to research. Many are simply a critical review of previously published literature that explores the state of knowledge in a particular area. Such a review would normally try to spot gaps or neglected areas or issues on previous research. They would then make suggestions about how future research might contribute to greater understanding by addressing these gaps or shortcomings. Other conceptual papers are more intellectually complex in that they develop sophisticated themes or conceptual models that could be used for further testing. Conceptual models are often expressed in boxes-and-arrows diagrams that indicate relationships between variables and lend themselves to further testing. Conceptual projects might, alternatively, take a more distant perspective to discuss research philosophy and methods and the scope of research in that field. Some conceptual papers offer historical analyses of certain traditions of research to show how it has developed and what influences have shaped that development.

The 'conceptual model'

Conceptual projects can induce a *conceptual model* from the literature review. A *model* in management and marketing research is a *representation* of an event or process that illustrates something important about that event or process. A critical path model of, say making buttered toast could be represented in a conceptual model. Similarly, a management process such as designing a market research project could also be represented in a conceptual model that describes the key steps in the process. Placing some related ideas in a conceptual model can be quite a powerful textual device for making certain points, or for summarising particular relationships. Models in basic management and marketing textbooks are often, simply, related concepts placed in boxes with arrows showing the supposed direction of causation or the flow of decision-making. In advertising research, for example, there are hierarchy-of-effects models of advertising effects; in marketing there are models of sales cycles and new product diffusion; in management there are models of employee motivation and decision-making. The model in the conceptual student project will be drawn from a synthesis of findings from the literature and will suggest possible implications of this synthesis for management practice or for future research.

For example, one of the author's MBA students once wrote a project on advertising ethics by first reviewing literature on the topic. She then developed a taxonomy or list of ethical problems that can arise with some advertisements. These included mis-description, overt use of negative social stereotypes, sexually provocative imagery and so on. The researcher found that, while different countries tend to have their own regulatory systems for advertising, individual advertisements often seem to succeed in by-passing these criteria with subtle use of symbolic texts and imagery. She then induced a conceptual model of criteria for evaluating the ethical status of advertisements. This conceptual model included the major criteria that could be used to judge an individual advertisement's ethical status. The research report applied the conceptual model by giving several examples of advertisements and judging their ethical status by applying the content criteria in the conceptual model. In this example the study was not purely conceptual, it did have some empirical data, but it used this to induce a conceptual model. Of course, the standards of ethics that are applied differ in different cultures, so the model could have quite limited universal application, but the student researcher tried to acknowledge this limitation and focused on more generally applicable ethical concepts, such as trust, truth, deception and honesty in advertising claims.

Another of the author's students was interested in the ways advertisers seem to target the insecurities of young women. The project was framed as a study in 'social fear'. The concept of social fear was intended to express the appeal of advertising that targets young women to sell products that exploit their fear of being unattractive or being rejected by the peer group. Products such as treatments for fresh breath, products to get rid of body hair and to prevent spots came into this category. This student conducted an extensive literature review that addressed issues such as theories of advertising effects and ethical issues in advertising. The student then collected a selection of print advertisements and creatively induced from them a typology of social fear in advertising. The typology of social fear was the conceptual model in the research project.

Other conceptual projects do not develop a conceptual model as such but, rather, develop abstract ideas and themes. One project explored the claims that research in marketing often makes to being a kind of science. The student wrote a reflexive, first-person research project expressing bewilderment at the conflicting views in marketing. They discussed the various ideas on the taught MSc in the light of their own career aspirations in marketing. A reflexive and relatively unstructured research project only reads as a credible piece of work if it is well written and well-informed. This project was based on many articles published in marketing research journals that discuss research theory in marketing. It evaluated articles that claim marketing research to be a kind of science, and articles that reject that presumption. It reflected on the implications this lack of academic consensus has on the education of aspiring marketing professionals. It did so in a lively and scholarly written style. Conceptual, literature-based projects that draw on many published articles and challenge conventional wisdom and practice in the field are a pleasure to read from an academic's point of view, at least if the academic is sympathetic to the critical view expressed. To make such a project credible the student must demonstrate that they have read and thought about a range of high-level academic papers and, moreover, understood them. Another MSc student wrote a conceptual project that entailed a critical appraisal of the literature on the sub-field of political marketing. Again, to make this piece of work credible as a research project they had to show that they were familiar with much of the current and recent literature and ideas in that field. The writing style had to be mature and elegant, and the themes developed had to demonstrate a good working understanding of research in the field.

It is wise for any student researcher considering a conceptual project to discuss it carefully with the supervisor. Projects that criticise conventional wisdom and practice need careful handling. Critical projects fit best with critically inclined supervisors. Some supervisors prefer student researchers to limit the scope of their research to exploring smaller-scale questions rather than critiquing fundamental aspects of the field as a whole. The conceptual, literature-based project is no less demanding than the empirical project – in its way, it can be more demanding, and this is why it should be treated with caution.

'What', 'why' and 'how' questions

We have already emphasised the importance of the choice of words in expressing the project proposal and title. Of particular importance is the kind of question that is implied in a research proposal. Different kinds of questions imply different methods and different analytical approaches. Students new to research are often unaware of the implications different kinds of questions have for their whole project.

'What' questions

For example, many topics entail 'what' questions. A common way of crafting a research question in marketing is to ask: 'What is the connection or link between x and y?' Very often this will be cast in terms of the possible impact of a marketing variable in a particular managerial intervention.

This could be a question of causation such as 'What is the impact of celebrity endorsement on sales of a brand of sports shoes in the UK?' or 'What is the effect of a 10% price reduction on consumers' perceptions of the quality of brand X?' Such questions, while legitimate research topics, carry assumptions that dictate the character of the research to be conducted. First, such questions assume that the categories contained in them ('celebrity endorsement', 'brand') are appropriate to the circumstances. Defining the terms in no way avoids this problem because the categories, however defined, set the terms of researcher engagement with the topic. As a result, there will inevitably be an element of logical circularity to a project in which an essential category is taken for granted.

To put this in another way, the first question assumes that 'celebrity endorsement' has an impact on sports shoe sales. In social research in marketing, management and anything else, you can always find what you think you are looking for. If you assume that 'celebrity endorsement' is what drives sales in the sports shoe market, then that is what you will 'find'. But there could be other ways of conceiving of this relation. Perhaps the brand exposure is the important thing, and the celebrity component is incidental. Perhaps celebrity endorsement is the wrong phrase to use: members of the public know very well that celebrities often 'endorse' products that they don't use. Perhaps the celebrity association with the brand is the important thing and not the endorsement as such. Clearly such questions of conceptual clarity and causal relations in marketing can and should be discussed in the research project report. However, in marketing research, in particular, it is all too often the case that they are not. Marketing research projects do need to offer a balanced justification of their assumptions, to satisfy broader intellectual criteria. In other words, research questions need to be precise and clear, and not vague.

It is useful to be aware, also, that in many cases, the academic assessing the research report may not be inclined to accept that certain concepts and relations can be taken for granted. In the above case, it would be wise for the student to pose a broader research question exploring the nature of demand for sports shoes in the UK (or other) market so that, should any causal relation become evident during the course of the research, it can be reported in an appropriate context. Alternatively, the research proposal could explore the *role* and *nature* of celebrity endorsement promotion in a national sports shoe market. That way, posed as an exploratory study, the research findings are not presupposed in the research question.

It is an important part of the ethical and the intellectual integrity of management research that conventional or given categories, phrases and relations are questioned and their use critically examined in local contexts. Marketing research does have a record of perpetuating essentialist concepts in self-confirming research exercises. For example, research that investigates the role of the 'marketing mix' in particular product markets, legitimises the 'marketing mix' as a decisive category of management activity. One may argue that the 'marketing mix' is just that: decisive in marketing success. But, research that accepts given categories and the relations implicitly, is likely to lack a spirit of creativity and critique. The possibility exists that the marketing mix, as such, was not decisive in marketing success. In any case, postulating the 'marketing mix' as a success factor in marketing management is too broad, since the marketing mix contains within it numerous sub-categories of activity each of which might have been decisive independently of the other dimensions of the mix. There are plenty of published studies that have investigated how marketing professionals actually do marketing, and some of these conclude that marketing professionals don't use text book categories such as 'marketing mix'. As an intellectual exercise, a research dissertation should be an exercise in challenging assumptions and picking apart native categories. An inexperienced researcher should not feel bound to decide what they are going to find before they start looking. So, the topic chosen can be framed initially as a working title exploring, investigating or examining an issue, problem or relationship. If the topic is cast in this way the possible conclusions are left open. The topic may change emphasis or direction depending on what the researcher finds. Initial categories (such as 'celebrity endorsement' or 'marketing mix') should be established by critical inquiry and not simply asserted by definition.

'Why' and 'how' questions

'Why' questions, as well as 'what' questions, can be inappropriately phrased in a way that implicitly presupposes the answer. For example, the research question 'Why does marketing orientation offer sustained competitive advantage for commercial organizations?' is clearly a question that has answered itself in the sense that it presupposes marketing orientation to be an important factor in achieving competitive advantage. Incidentally, this is a question that, even phrased in an exploratory style, is probably beyond the scope of a student project unless they can get access to senior executives of several organisations along with proprietary marketing data. 'How' questions also need to be used with caution. The question 'How do car salespeople maximize their sales effectiveness in customer interactions?' is a fair question to ask, but some car buyers will arrive at the franchise already knowing which car they want to buy. The salesperson's job, then, may not be to sell but to 'upsell', that is, to sell add-ons such as gap insurance and extended warranties. It would be more useful to the student who is interested in this area to explore either, (a) car sales conversations in a given market context, or (b) sales interview styles in any context. In general, it is a useful practice for first-time student researchers to pose open questions so that they are not caught out later by the presuppositions implied in certain questions.

We tend to phrase social research questions in terms of 'what', 'why' and 'how' when we first embark on an independent study project. Students new to research cannot be expected to know that they might set traps for themselves in phrasing questions in this way since they might presuppose particular ways of knowing and understanding. It is far from unusual for a student to do a conscientious research project investigating such a question (a what, why or how question) only to be told at the end that they were not awarded a better mark because their research question was too narrow or was otherwise inappropriate to the subject. 'What', 'why' and 'how' imply that there is a 'what', a 'why' or a 'how'. In social research there may be highly complex relations between an event and its consequences or antecedents. At undergraduate or master's level, an open investigation into a topic tends to be a wiser exercise for the student. It is also a more creative exercise to conduct an open investigation that is not stunted by the need to defend the assumptions implied in the question.

Chapter 2 has discussed the design of the research study, beginning with how the title of the project is phrased. The phrasing of the project title is of key importance to the successful completion of the project because of the implications it has for the research design, method and findings. The chapter has also touched on issues of research design and research philosophy. Considerable thought must be given to the way the topic title and research proposal are drafted. Getting this right and thinking it through can save a great deal of stress later in the process. The next chapter discusses the outcome of the research project process, the project report, also called the dissertation or thesis. It is particularly important for student researchers to understand that a written document, a text, is the goal of their efforts. If student researchers appreciate the likely structure, tone and style of this text at the beginning of the process, it can make research design and planning much easier.

Glossary

Conceptual project   A project that does not make great use of primary data but, rather, develops a conceptual analysis from a synthesis of published research and existing secondary data sources such as industry reports or market data.

Deductive   Normally refers to reasoning that proceeds from the particular to the general. In research, refers to hypothesis testing or hypothetico-deductive studies.

Depth Interview   A long interview with one person, lasting anything from half an hour to two hours, that probes a topic in considerable detail allowing the participant to reflect deeply on the questions.

Focus Group   A group formed to discuss a particular topic area under the guidance of a convenor.

Functional   In this chapter, 'functional' refers to research projects that seek to address a functional area of business such as business effectiveness in accounting, operations, marketing, service or manufacturing from a managerial problem-solving point of view. 'Functional' has a different meaning in sociology and cultural anthropology, often described in terms of a biological metaphor that emphasises the systemic interdependence of parts (known as functionalism).

Harvard referencing   The style of referencing used in this book. It entails citing references in the text with author and year. The full reference is placed in the references section in alphabetical order at the end of the document.

Hypothetico-deductive   A style of research that derives a hypothesis from a body of theory, tests it empirically, and uses the findings to inform or modify the theory.

Inductive   Reasoning that moves from the general to the particular. In research, usually identified with qualitative, exploratory studies.

Normative   Much managerial writing and teaching is normative in the sense that it purports to find out what a manager ought to do in a given management situation. There are implied judgements in the normative managerial tradition of thinking and writing, which may not be made clear or explicit.

Positivism   In social research, the term positivism usually refers to a set of assumptions about reality and knowledge that have some similarity to the precepts of a branch of philosophy of knowledge called 'logical positivism' (Ayer, 1936). In management research, 'positivist' often refers to research that assumes that the social world can be treated as materially real in the same way as the physical world, and can be observed and measured. Indeed, for logical positivists, if a phenomenon cannot be observed and measured, then it belongs in the realm of metaphysics.

Realist ontology   A world view that holds that the social world can be researched in the same way as the physical world.

Replication study   A research study that attempts to reproduce the finding of a previous study by using the same research design. It is notoriously difficult to replicate findings in social and psychological research.

Research design   The overall design of the research study and its rationale for an empirical project, including details on the research question(s) and/or problems, sampling, data-gathering techniques and data analysis.

Social constructionist ontology   A world view that holds that the social world is self-constituting in a profound way that distinguishes it from the natural world, therefore it requires different (interpretive) research methods.

Chapter 3

Writing high-quality research projects

From description to critique

Abstract

This chapter focuses on the structure, tone and style of the written document that must be produced for a research project. The aim in dealing with this issue early in the book is to give student researchers a rounded view of the whole text that they must eventually produce, so that they can see how the parts fit into the whole. Having this view will help with the student's confidence, research planning and time management. The chapter looks at key issues of research writing such as academic tone, style and critical thinking.

Chapter objectives

After reading this chapter students will be able to

- see both the parts and the whole of the research project structure
- plan the research knowing what kind of text must be produced
- understand the central role of writing in the production of research
- grasp some of the stylistic issues of academic writing such as 'tone', 'critique', 'reflexivity' and argumentation.

'Writing up' and the research process

'Writing up' is often considered to be the final stage in the research project and is usually treated as an afterthought in the student's research methods education. The term 'writing up' implies that all the real work has been done, and all that remains is to list the process that was undertaken along with the facts that were discovered. The reality of writing up a research project is less simple. In fact, research writing is a highly specialised genre that demands skill in the art and rhetoric of writing research texts. Writing and rhetorical skills are central to the success of professional researchers, in marketing studies areas (Brown, 2005; Brownlie, 1997, 2001; Hackley, 2009a) and equally in other areas of management and social studies. For example,

DOI: 10.4324/9781003432203-5

McCloskey (1983) pointed out the centrality of skill in persuasive rhetoric in successful economic theories, as others have done with regard to marketing texts (Brown et al., 2018; Hackley, 2003b) and ethnography (Jarzabkowski et al., 2014). The research project is not a work of literature – and yet, it is, in the sense that it is a piece of writing that is designed to take the reader on a journey that will, ultimately, be persuasive. In this chapter, we will consider the student research project as a written text that must be written with appropriate stylistic conventions and rhetorical devices.

It is strongly advised that student researchers think carefully about the written document that they must produce right from the beginning of the project process. By doing this, student researchers form an idea of the whole picture of a research project before they embark on it. In contrast, many first-time student researchers begin the project without appreciating the nature of the desired end-result. They attempt each stage without knowing why it is important and how it fits into the whole. This can result in poor planning and loss of direction. Academics are very familiar with student research projects that are flawed because they are poorly structured. Indeed, 'poor structure' is one of the clichés of academic criticism, because it is an easy one to make of a lot of student written work. If students have a holistic idea of what kind of text they must produce, then the process can be much less stressful and more successful. Later in the chapter, we will present some suggested structures for interpretive research projects.

The common idea of 'writing up' research implies that the research process is separate from the writing process, and also that 'writing up' somehow requires less attention than the research. Neither is correct. Research is constructed through writing. Research cannot be communicated unless a narrative is constructed to tell the research story. Therefore, it makes perfect sense to consider the narrative conventions of research as part of research design. This does not imply that there is one right way to write research projects. People plan and write their research in different ways. The process of writing, and the style in which the researcher writes, can differ widely. Different research genres tend to have different styles. For example, a piece of quantitative research would generally be written to different conventions than an interpretive study. As student researchers read more published research studies, they will begin to grasp the different styles that tend to be adopted.

The process of writing can be quite personal, according to preference. Some student researchers gather data and literature over time and then write up a draft of the whole project in one go. Others prefer to do their literature search first and write up the project chapter by chapter. If the project is hypothetico-deductive in style, the literature review will be the basis for the hypothesis so it will need to be written in full early in the process. If, on the other hand, the research is inductive in style there will be an initial literature review followed by a phase of data collection, followed by another more closely focused literature review (as in grounded theory studies, Glaser and Strauss, 1967). The research report will, however, be written up in the same sequence as for the deductive research project, with the literature review early in the sequence of chapters. This is because research writing does not always have to accurately represent the process of research. Indeed, it would be impossible to do this. A research study that takes several months and entails false starts and blind alleys would not make easy reading if it were described in every detail. The sequence of actual research activities depends to a large extent on the personal preference of both researcher and supervisor, and upon the nature of the project. The report itself need not necessarily reflect this sequence of activities. It is more important for a research report to satisfy some of the accepted narrative conventions of research in that field. In other words, it must look like a research report (or thesis or dissertation) for readers to accept that it is one. In a research report or dissertation, the narrative conventions are especially important in framing the way the work will be read.

Many university and business school faculties have their own conventions for style, tone and structure of such projects, typeface and references style, contents and chapter headings. Many academic supervisors have individual preferences in such matters. It is wise for students to make sure they understand exactly what conventions they are expected to observe in their research project. However, there are principles of good practice that apply to every research project. Research reports need to have certain things, like literature reviews, research objectives, findings, in-text citations, a list of references or bibliography and so on. The various sections must be presented in an appropriate sequence, and the writing style must capture the right tone or register. The next section will develop some themes on the tone of research writing.

The academic writing 'tone'

The 'tone' of a piece of writing refers to what it conveys through, for example, its grammatical conventions, sentence structure and vocabulary. Tone can be generally formal, informal, conversational, authoritative, amusing, serious, technical and so on. It is difficult to define tone since it is a matter of interpretation. The best way to address the issue for research writing is to say that the tone must seem to the reader to be appropriate for a research text. The written text produced by the student researcher needs to strike a suitably academic tone of writing, although as we discuss below there are different ways of conceiving this. Some academics criticise student work if they feel that it is too 'conversational', 'anecdotal' or 'journalistic'. Of course, all these styles can be virtues in the right context, but for many academics there is an academic tone of writing that is distinct from the tone you use when writing or talking to a friend ('conversational'), when relating an anecdote, or when a journalist writes a feature article. Precisely what that difference is, is difficult to define and no-one in academia (including this author) can tell you exactly what it is. What we can do is to mention some of the stylistic conventions that typically characterise academic writing.

Academic writing styles can sometimes seem obscure and pretentious to readers more familiar with newspapers or popular novels. Indeed, some academics argue that academic writing is generally bad writing, partly because it is so often obscure and strewn with the technical jargon of social science. Sentences are often long and carry multiple subclauses as academic writers build in contingencies and conditionals to everything they want to say. Sometimes, reading academic work, it seems as though the author has spent a whole page very elaborately *not* saying something, lest they open their work up to counterarguments. It is important to recognise that, while some writers are obscure because their thoughts are not clear, much academic writing uses technical terms and stylistic conventions because they have become part of the accepted way of writing in that field, and academic work is principally written for the approval not of casual readers, but of other academics.

A lot of the jargon used in social scientific writing is shorthand for academics to refer to issues and arguments that they feel must be stated before they move on to the next stage in the argument. It is an important part of the student researcher's task to begin to understand the purpose of this style and to write in a way that is somewhat like it, hopefully without giving in to the worst excesses of convoluted and arcane academic writing. For the many international students who will be writing in English as a second language, this will present a challenge. The challenge can be met by becoming familiar with the styles and conceptual vocabulary of social research, and that means reading books like this one. Doing so might be painful in the short term, but the pain of failing the project by neglecting such reading will be much greater. Failing to prepare properly, means preparing to fail, as someone once said.

Writing in the 'third person'

Some of the stylistic conventions of research writing are fairly easy to grasp. For example, most research papers are written in the 'third person', as when the authors refer to themselves as 'the authors' instead of simply saying 'I'. This convention can rhetorically produce a sense of detachment or objectivity. It makes the research writing sound more depersonalised, which is intended to make it seem more authoritative or credible (and less 'conversational'). It is often a good idea for student researchers to adopt this convention, but, if in doubt, ask the supervisor. Some interpretive traditions of research writing, such as autoethnography (Hackley, 2016, 2022) adopt the first-person grammar and use 'I' when referring to the author. Different academics have different preferences. If unsure, it is a good idea to write in the third person because that is the traditional approach in academic writing.

Writing in the third person can help to encourage a disciplined approach to writing up the work as a piece of systematic research rather than as a personal story. Some published researchers have, though, written very personalised accounts of their research. Holbrook (1995) has even devised an interpretive method of research he calls 'Subjective Personal Introspection' that has been used in various published interpretive consumer research studies (e.g. Shankar, 2000). Brown (1995) has produced some of the most vivid, and funniest, pieces of writing in academic marketing using a personalised style. Marketing authors have used poetry and lyricism to shed new insights on marketing as a Romantic endeavour (e.g. Brown et al., 1998, and in consumer research, Sherry and Schouten, 2002). Brown (2005), Brownlie (1997, 2001) and others have challenged the stodgy conventions of academic writing to call for livelier, more personal, *better* academic writing. It is probably fair to say, though, that you have to be a very experienced and creative scholar, and a confident writer, to produce a credible research report in as subjective a style as these authors. For most student researchers, writing in the third person is the safer option. The traditional, third person approach in social research is intended to convey a sense of formality, while writing in the first-person risks opening up the author to the charge that their work is too informal. As in all decisions around the research project, seek advice from the supervisor if in doubt.

Making 'claims' and supporting 'arguments'

Another important aspect of writing tone concerns the way 'arguments' or points of view are constructed and assertions made. The entire research report is an argument, in the rhetorical sense that the text is written to be persuasive of the author's point of view. The research project process can be seen as a test to see whether the student can develop or explore points of view of some complexity drawing on a variety of sources. In the research report he or she must show that they can sustain this for 8,000, 10,000, 12,000 or 20,000 words or more, depending on the requirements of their department and the degree being undertaken. The report will attest to the student researcher's standard of scholarship. For academics, a high standard of scholarship is difficult to define, but they know it when they see it. It consists in plausible, clearly expressed, thorough and well-supported intellectual work. Most important of all, the work must amount to an *argument*, that is, it must be persuasive. Academics argue in very stylised ways, which to the non-academic observer might not look like arguing at all. But don't be deceived – there are subtle codes of academic argument that don't involve typing in capitals or using multiple exclamation marks. Academics use terms such as academic 'rigour' (Gioia et al., 2013) or we might refer to arguments and discussions that are 'robust'. What we mean when we use these terms is that the writing is persuasive and credible, to an academic.

Credible research writing depends on not making incredible 'claims', or under-supported assertions. Academics refer to making claims when a piece of academic writing makes an assertion of fact or draws a conclusion about a topic. Such assertions are claims and they should be supported by careful reasoning or evidence from previous research or case examples. Academics are looking for a good quality argument when we read student work, and that means supporting and/or qualifying any assertions or claims carefully. The acquisition of more knowledge usually makes people less extravagant (or assertive) in their claims about their research findings, therefore more modestly styled prose suggests to the reader that the author has more knowledge. In other words, a mark of good academic writing is not overselling the author's opinion (although the popular genre of academic marketing textbooks, it must be admitted, break this cardinal rule of scholarly tone by making an art of overselling) (Brown, 1995; Hackley, 2003b).

The stance of the true researcher is that one knows enough to know how little one really knows. In fact, William Goldman's famous axiom from the movie business applies very much in business and management research: Nobody knows anything (Goldman, 1983). Knowledge progresses in very small stages, if it can be said to progress at all. Academics working in a particular field know a lot, but this knowledge shows them how much more there is to know. This does not mean that one must write only about topics that can be reduced to tiny subtopics. Neither does it mean that research writing should be excessively cautious in making assertions of any kind. There is plenty of scope for creative exploration in ideas, provided the writer is frank about what is speculation and what is a more substantive claim. Assertions, claims or suggestions should be carefully and logically supported with reasoning or evidence.

Any assertion made in a research report (such as 'Management researchers still understand relatively little about motivation in the workplace') needs to be supported very carefully with references to published authorities, to other sources or by careful reasoning. Inadequately supported assertions are probably the most common reason for losing marks in a research project report. The examiner will not normally judge the student researcher's writing on whether or not what they write about is true. Much of social science is speculative and can only be judged on its coherence or its logical connection to other bodies of theory or evidence. The examiner is, however, looking for quality of argument and discussion. Whatever the point being argued, the examiner wants to see persuasive and well-rounded argument. Authors should show that they are aware that their point of view is not the only one that may be right. Authors of research reports should show that they are aware of a number of possible points of view. A mark of good argumentation is to give suitable acknowledgement to opposing arguments, even if this is simply as a rhetorical device to dismiss them more persuasively. There is a lot of published research literature on employee motivation so the above assertion would, at least, need to be placed in a context of a careful review of a good range of that literature for the examiner to accept that the writer has sufficiently supported the claim. For picking up useful information and for absorbing the writing style of academic research, there is no substitute for reading published academic papers.

So, before embarking on the research report, read as many academic research papers as possible to grasp the academic style of writing and arguing, and to become familiar with a wide range of research in the field of interest. Second, remember that academics who have devoted their entire career to researching a specific topic often feel that, while they know a lot, they still know much less than they'd like to. Consequently, the last thing they want to read is a piece of student research from a writer who thinks they've cracked the whole problem in a semester. Popular business and management texts tend to use grammatical conventions which imply that they offer solutions: 'Managing quality better in financial services'; 'Relationship marketing, the new paradigm for business success'; 'Emotional intelligence: the key to effective management'. These are not, to my knowledge, the titles of real books, though they could be. I've made them up. They employ grammatical styles that are very (too) common in this field. Students should not be drawn in to such a sweeping writing style, as it is not appropriate for serious academic work. Students should be aware that a research project should not make too much use of the popular, consulting style of writing that is seen in many teaching texts. Write in a style that shows caution towards assertions, supports points with careful reasoning and evidence from literature and research, and shows awareness that there may be alternative points of view that have not occurred to you, the researcher.

Plagiarism: how to avoid the charge

Most university research project guides have a section on *plagiarism*, warning of dire consequences for the student if the work submitted is found to have plagiarised any other work. Many of these guides are now quite detailed and contain a lot of useful information, plus essential procedural information on how accusations of plagiarism will be dealt with in each university department, so they should be read carefully by student researchers. The growth in online businesses selling pre-written essays and dissertations has created a sense that this is now a 'problem', so universities are increasingly sensitive to the issue. Policies towards the use of Chat GPT and other forms of LLM (Large Language Models) Artificial Intelligence (AI) in student work vary from university to university. Plagiarism detection software now often includes the detection of the use of AI in writing. What students need to be aware of is that AI is (at the time of writing) not very good at writing academic research projects. Even if students use AI as a stimulus for ideas, it will need heavy editing because (A) AI based on LLM technology plagiarises all its content – it looks around the internet for relevant content and uses it without any regard for attributing sources or acknowledging copyright and (B) AI systems rarely use referencing techniques accurately. In some cases, AI machines simply write incoherent nonsense and/or they make claims that are incorrect and/or not supported by the evidence. The key principle to adhere to is that the independent research project must be entirely the student's own work. It is vitally important that the criterion of 'independence' is satisfied. However, it is also true that few ideas are truly original and research projects do contain elements that are substantially a review of previously published ideas. This is why there is often confusion over what, exactly, constitutes plagiarism. How can it be copying if the ideas are already out there in the public domain? And even more confusing, why do students get disciplined for plagiarism when they had no intention of passing off other's work as their own?

Plagiarised work is writing that is reproduced in a project report to appear that it is the author's own words when in fact it has been copied from another source. Many students, especially those working in a second language trying to understand a new educational culture, find it difficult to distinguish plagiarism from legitimate paraphrasing and quotation. The *literature review* component of the research project report describes, summarises and evaluates the published work of writers in a field. For some international students, especially those who were educated in traditions that regard rote learning and reproduction of academic work as absolutely fine, it can seem odd, and even presumptuous, to re-word the written work of published academics. However, the research project is not merely an extended paraphrase of the work of established researchers. It is the student researcher's discussion and views on this previously published work. The distinction between copying or plagiarising, and legitimate quoting and paraphrasing, is difficult to grasp for some students, but it is important to do so.

Literature reviewing demonstrates important academic skills. If a student researcher can summarise a particular piece of research or theory succinctly, it demonstrates that he or she has read and understood the work. This kind of engagement with the published work of established researchers is an important part of the Western university tradition. The biggest downside to deliberate and flagrant plagiarism, besides possibly severe penalties imposed by the university up to and including failing the degree, is that the student will have missed out on a key part of their higher education. They will have failed to develop the higher order academic, scholarly and personal skills that the independent project is designed to develop. In other words, the student who plagiarises, commissions or uses other fraudulent methods to complete their independent research project has failed to demonstrate the skills of critical analysis that they will need in their future career.

Using direct quotes in research projects

All written or graphic material that is reproduced unchanged from a source should be accompanied by the author and page citation (e.g. Smith, 2003, p. 4). Written material that is a direct quote of the work should be placed within full quotation marks, again with page number. Footnotes may be used where appropriate, depending on the convention of the student's university.

A paraphrase of a short section of work should also normally have the original author cited, even if it is not a direct quote. *It is very important to note that changing just a few words of the quote is not enough to render it into the student's own words.* This confusion is probably the single most common source of plagiarism charges – the student thinks that they do not need to represent the work as a direct quote because they have changed a couple of prepositions. Plagiarism software does not fall for this ruse, and it is clear to the marker when students have cut and pasted an extended passage of work and changed just a few words. This is still plagiarism, even if the original source is cited but there are no quotation marks and page numbers to indicate that the passage is a direct quote.

Using direct quotes can be a powerful technique of exposition, and good research projects often make liberal use of them. However, there are three things students should remember about using them. The first is that they should not normally be too long (check out published papers for guidance). Second, they should not be left to speak for themselves. A direct quote should be preceded, and followed, by extensive discussion that explains what point the quote is being used to make, and how it connects to the overall reasoning in the section. Finally, a good dissertation does not have too many direct quotes – to do so suggests that the researcher was struggling to write their own narrative.

School students of literature are often asked by the teacher to describe, criticise or discuss a particular piece of poetry or prose. Many direct quotes are useful for this purpose but there can be no mistake that the discussion must make use of the student's own original ideas and words. The student's considered views on the piece of work are being sought and their ability to demonstrate their understanding by articulating those views will be assessed by the teacher. Similarly, the independent research project requires students to engage with published research studies in an active and critical way so that the original author's words are reinterpreted by the student researcher. This is what strictures against plagiarism are designed to encourage. Plagiarism is a serious charge and, where proven, can prevent graduation, so student researchers should make every effort to ensure that they cannot be accused of it by carefully citing every source that they have used and making sure that direct quotes are cited correctly.

The use of references

The use of references in the text can seem a cumbersome device that impairs read-ability but it is essential to academic writing. If a general assertion is made (say, 'research in marketing has neglected the role of internal communications in organisational marketing effectiveness') there needs to be a citation of one or more published works that support this assertion. If a student researcher makes any assertion that they want accepted as a statement of fact, there does need to be this support from credible published research, even if the assertion seems rather conventional and uncontroversial. The published work should, preferably, come from refereed academic journals of good standing, but it is also relevant to cite websites and trade press articles when the text is discussing business conditions or case examples. As a general rule, the more references the better, provided they are relevant to the point being supported. Citing other work signals that you understand how your research is thematically linked with previous research. It is a mark of good scholarship to master a fluid style of referencing so that citations are woven elegantly into the text.

All works cited by author and date (Smith, 1995) in the text of the research report should be listed in full in alphabetical order by author at the end of the report (see Box 3.1). The term 'bibliography' is sometimes used to indicate all work read as part of the research even if it is not cited in the main body of the research report. However, the term bibliography can be seen as a list of books that the student didn't quite get around to reading, as it is sometimes used to list works that were not cited in a text. This is why the term 'references' is better for academic work. All works listed in the references list at the end of the project text must have been cited in the main body.

Box 3.1   Harvard style referencing

In-text citation

(Author, year) or Author (year)
For example, Smith (2019) or (Smith, 2019)

End-of-text reference list

Ordered by first letter of family name alphabetical order

Books

Author, initials (year) Title. Place published. Publisher.
E.g. Smith, P.J. (2019) Interpretive Research Methods. London: Routledge.

Articles

Author, initials (year) Title. Journal, Volume, Number/Issue: page numbers.
E.g. Smith, P.J. (2019) 'The role of interpretive research in improving outcomes from therapeutic psychological interventions'. Psychological Research International, 40 (2), 342–363.

Standards of scholarship

The independent research project conducted in a higher education context is a test of a student's scholarship. Scholarship consists in assimilating different sources of information into a new piece of written work. The standards required are high. Not only do research project reports have to be clearly structured with a well-defined problem or issue, logically ordered and written in appropriate and grammatically correct English, they also need to satisfy standards of good scholarship. 'Good' scholarship is not easy to define. It has many dimensions.

Some universities use tables of marketing criteria to try to itemise the different levels and different elements of good scholarship. In Box 3.2, we can see one such example. This is fairly typical of many such 'rubrics' as they can be called. This extract from a UK university rubric for master's dissertations in business and management is not intended as a template, it is just one example of how such a rubric can be constructed.

To this example of a general marking rubric for dissertations, we can add an example of a generic rubric for undergraduate written work in Table 3.1. Neither of these examples, it should be said, are particularly good – rubrics in general tend to be exercises in synonym generation for stating

---

Box 3.2   An adapted example of a Master's dissertation marking rubric

Overall mark

85–100: An exceptionally high level of understanding, and outstanding research potential
70–84: Very high competence and excellent research potential
60–69: Evidence of some creativity and independence of thought
50–59: Sound understanding of the literature but lack of accuracy
40–49: Insufficient or no understanding of the topic, poor quality of work

Marks allocated for categories of achievement

Knowledge of subject (25)

21–25: Deep understanding and comprehensive knowledge
18–20: Thorough understanding
15–17: Very good understanding
12–14: Good knowledge of the most relevant information
10–11: Basic understanding of the major issues
0–9: Little or no understanding demonstrated

Organisation of material (25)

21–25: Excellent, clearly structured work
18–20: Arguments clearly set out, fluently articulated and logically structured
15–17: Very well organised: aims met with no significant errors or omissions
12–14: Coherently organised work
10–11: Some omissions and lack of clarity, aims only partially met
0–9: Important omissions, confusion and lack of clarity

Originality, interpretation and analysis (20)

17–20: Challenging project aims and significant originality in the interpretation and/or analysis
14–16: Some originality: excellent analytical skills
12–13: Good attempt to interpret and analyse relevant literature
10–11: Minor flaws of understanding in interpretation/analysis of literature
0–9: Deeply flawed or minimal interpretation or analysis, fail to meet modest aims

Evidence of reading (10)

8–10: Thorough review of literature demonstrated
6–7: Evident reading of a good range of relevant works
4–5: Some evidence of relevant reading
0–3: Little evidence of relevant reading

Referencing (10)

9–10: Precise, accurate and comprehensive referencing of relevant work
7–8: Very good referencing, some errors of referencing conventions
5–6: Adequate range of relevant works referenced, some inaccuracy in citation style
0–4: Irrelevant, inadequate and/or inaccurate referencing

Writing style, spelling, punctuation and grammar (10)

9–10: Excellent, fluid and elegantly written work in a strong scholarly style
7–8: Very minor errors of spelling, punctuation or grammar, occasional lack of clarity
4–6: Some errors of spelling, punctuation and/or grammar, lack of clarity.
0–3: Poor writing style, many errors, incoherent in places

Table 3.1 An adapted generic rubric for written academic work

	High pass	Good pass	Pass	Fail
Content	Critical, deep, comprehensive understanding, creative interpretation	Very good understanding, some originality	Basic understanding, limited originality or insight	Limited understanding, lack of focus
Structure	Logically coherent, clear narrative progression, fully meeting the brief	Logically structured	Unclear in places, could be better organised	Lacks coherence and logical development
Reading	Fluent and insightful synthesis of secondary sources, reading beyond the set texts	Thorough and lucid coverage of relevant sources	Basic coverage of key work, some notable omissions	Little evidence of relevant reading and/or understanding
Referencing	Accurate, precise, well-integrated in the body of the text and confirming to required format	Accurate, orderly	Some errors of formatting, limited range of citations	Inaccurate, incomplete or absent referencing
Writing	Fluent and penetrating academic writing style, excellent use of supporting citations	Clear, grammatically correct, lucid writing	Clearly written but less analytically fluent and some grammatical errors	Lacking in clarity and/or coherence at times

the obvious, or, at the other extreme, some go to such lengths to display the full range of Bloom's taxonomy that it hardly seems worthwhile to do the work, such is the precision with which its features have been described. Academics often find it very difficult to describe what excellent, adequate and poor work looks like, but they do know it when they see it. Of course, it is the detail that differentiates good from poor academic work, and this book attempts to articulate some of the detail that cannot fit into a rubric when it discusses academic writing tone, style, referencing and possible dissertation structures. Both Box 3.2 and Table 3.1 do, in spite of their limitations, highlight the ways that academics attempt to be more fair and transparent to students by trying to systematise the way they assess levels of student work.

For academics, scholarship is a complex craft that is very difficult to itemise in list form. It is evident in published articles in well-established academic journals, but it is difficult to define because it comes in many styles. In an important sense, scholarship is an aspect of rhetoric because the best 'scholarship' consists in the highest quality of argument. 'Argument' in this sense does not carry its everyday meaning of acrimonious or antagonistic disputes. In academic work 'argument' is a general term that refers to all kinds of scholarships conducted in written form. All written academic work is an 'argument' in the very broad sense that it is written to persuade.

A typology of the characteristics of scholarship in Jankowicz (1991) includes careful use of evidence to support arguments, care, and accuracy in the identification of information sources, and thoroughness in the coverage of the subject matter. 'Thoroughness' implies that arguments and points of discussion are well balanced. This in turn implies that alternative points of view are acknowledged and evaluated. A further characteristic of good scholarship is integrity in the use of data in the formation of arguments and points of discussion. The data must support the argument being made. The reader must believe that the work has intellectual integrity. In other words, the reader must feel that the arguments presented represent a sincere attempt on the part of the writer to investigate and report a topic whatever the findings may be.

The project report structure

Each kind of project (empirical or conceptual/review) has similar requirements that it must follow to satisfy the intellectual standards of university degrees. The chapter headings in Boxes 3.3 and 3.4 are offered as flexible guides to the broad content of an independent research project.

Whether a research project is mainly empirical or mainly conceptual, the student researcher still needs to demonstrate an informed point of view in a carefully developed and structured piece of work. It is not enough to simply summarise a series of articles or book chapters and pass this off as a conceptual project. In both styles of project, there must be a problem/issue formulation, a set of criteria for selecting relevant literature and a way of evaluating or discussing the theories and findings in that literature. The findings of the empirical project, or the conceptual model/findings of the conceptual project, will form the basis for the analysis/discussion, so, in both, there must be a clear point of view that can be developed logically.

The structure chosen for the project can vary, but every project will contain, in whatever form, the elements of the suggested structures in Boxes 3.3 and 3.4. That is, the project must contain a clearly expressed research problem, issue or question that the supervisor has agreed is appropriate. It must contain a careful, substantial and critical review and evaluation of relevant research papers and other published sources. Finally, it must contain a careful interpretation of the data to summarise the major findings and to discuss the needs

---

Box 3.3   A suggested empirical project chapter structure

Project title: must be clear, succinct and precise

Abstract: 100–150 words summarising the project scope, aims and main findings

Contents page

Chapter 1: Introduction, overview of research issue/problem: research objectives: theoretical framing: trajectory of the project report

Chapter 2: Literature review, locating the issue/problem within a range of relevant published research, identifying key concepts and issues

Chapter 3: Method: a short literature-based discussion of methodology: explanation and justification of sampling procedure, data-gathering approach and analytical method.

Chapter 4: Report of findings from empirical (primary) research, with some contextualisation

Chapter 5: Discussion: synthesis of empirical findings with literature derived findings

Chapter 6: Concluding comments, re-iteration of research objectives, evaluation of whether they have been achieved and why/why not, conclusions/recommendations/implications for research/practice.

References: Full list of reference works cited in the body of the text

Appendices: Additional information that might have interrupted the flow of the main text, e.g. interview schedules, list of research participants by demographic information, transcripts of interview/discussion data

> **Box 3.4   A suggested conceptual project chapter structure**
>
> Project title: must be clear, succinct and precise
> Abstract: 100–150 words summarising the project scope, aims and main findings
> Contents page
> Chapter 1: Introduction, overview of research issue/problem: research objectives (based on review of existing literature and/or archive or other secondary sources): theoretical framing: trajectory of the project report
> Chapter 2: Extended literature review, locating the issue/problem within a range of relevant published research, identifying key concepts and issues
> Chapter 3: Conceptual model: inducing the main elements from the literature
> Chapter 4: Apply/evaluate the conceptual model to/in case example(s)
> Chapter 5: Discussion: synthesis of findings and case analysis
> Chapter 6: Concluding comments, re-iteration of research objectives, evaluation of whether they have been achieved and why/why not, conclusions/recommendations/implications for research/practice.
> References: Full list of reference works cited in the body of the text
> Appendices: Additional information that might have interrupted the flow of the main text, e.g. interview schedules, list of research participants by demographic information, transcripts of interview/discussion data

of future research and/or the implications for current and future practice. The following sections will discuss in more detail the particular problems and issues arising at each stage in these suggested project structures.

The project structure

The abstract and chapter one

The abstract and chapter one can, sometimes, be written last of all in the process. That is because with exploratory, qualitative research, one does not usually know how the story will turn out until the end. Hence, the abstract and chapter one, and indeed the title, could change before the final write-up. This is, to some extent, a matter of personal preference. As noted earlier, some

---

Box 3.5   Suggested structure for Chapter 1 of the empirical project report

Chapter outline: topic, main issues/problems, research approach
Introduction: elaboration/contextualisation of the research problem, statement of why it is interesting/important
Background: introduction to the key literature and empirical context
Main research objectives
Methodological stance
Brief outline of the narrative trajectory of the project report

---

researchers prefer to gather data, think about the issues, make notes and reflections, draft some sections and collect relevant research articles, until the last moment, then write a first draft of the project report in one go. Others prefer to start at the beginning and write a chapter at a time in sequence. The abstract will summarise the whole project in about 150–200 words. Chapter one will explain in more detail what the project is about, what its main aims and subject matter are. It will also set the background context and explain why the topic is of interest. Chapter one can outline the whole narrative arc of the project, to give the reader a clear steer about how the story of the research project will unfold.

The chapter can begin with a problem statement about what issues the research will seek to address. It can then set out some background to set the report issues within a broader context of a particular industry, a particular tradition of literature or a specific problem. It will need to set out two, three or four major research objectives. Finally, the chapter can outline the whole project report, indicating what each chapter deals with, how the research was conducted and briefly summarising the major findings and/or conclusions. This gives the reader a good idea of what to expect and, more importantly, shows that the report is the result of a carefully structured, well thought-through and systematic piece of scholarly research (see Box 3.5).

Research aims and objectives

It is important to remember that repeating the aims, objectives and themes of the research in the abstract, in chapter one and in the final chapter, is not only appropriate but necessary. It is necessary by convention, and also as a rhetorical device to remind the reader that what is being written is structured according to a consistent set of questions or themes. The objectives would usually be set out in chapter one, returned to at several stages during the report, and finally restated in the concluding comments. In this way, the writer clearly signals to the reader that the research was well conceived and systematic. In general, it is a good idea in research writing to make it easy for the reader to see why particular points and sections are relevant to the main theme. A degree of necessary repetition can help in this aim. In addition, 'signposting' is very useful. At regular intervals in the narrative, remind the reader why the point being discussed is germane to the research problem.

Research aims and objectives are very important, though it should be remembered that they need not be complex. It is not necessary to produce an original contribution to knowledge in a taught master's or undergraduate degree course. For this level of research project, objectives can be quite simple and straightforward. They are important because they indicate that the researcher had a focus for the research and that this focus is the basis for the narrative structure of the report. A report must tell a story of a piece of research. A story must have a plot that develops through a beginning, a middle and an end. A research report that drifts along without a point of focus will give the reader the impression that the researcher never quite thought through what it was they wanted to find out. The research objectives also provide an internal measure of the success of the research. If the final chapter can say to what extent the objectives were achieved, this is a good sign. Clear and coherent (and also realistic) objectives are a great help.

As mentioned in the previous chapter, the research report is not a temporally linear representation of the research process. That is to say, the report is not the same thing as a research diary, and does not necessarily describe the precise order of events. In exploratory research, the objectives may be crafted in final form at the end of the research process because they, like the broad research question, will be modified during the research. Some research objectives, such as 'To critically review the existing state of theory from a selection of leading journals' need not change during the process. This is a broad and straightforward objective for a conceptual project. Other, more specific objectives might well evolve and change in emphasis, although they will have been present in some form from the beginning.

For example, a research project might set out 'To find success factors in entrepreneurial marketing'. The researcher might find that this objective was too broad. Research interviews with marketing entrepreneurs might well generate interesting findings regarding the origins of the entrepreneurial mentality, but these insights may be personal, rooted in the entrepreneur's particular biography and experience. The phrase 'success factors' implies that 'factors' are the same for every entrepreneur in every entrepreneurial situation. Furthermore, entrepreneurial activity is conducted in many different industries and takes differing forms. To be entrepreneurial within a health service implies different behaviours, outcomes and priorities to being entrepreneurial in, say, a television production company or a small retail business. Hence the broad objective could be refined to accommodate the specific research context and priorities.

Many research objectives are very simple. For example, the student researcher might wish to use words such as investigate, explore, evaluate or examine a particular area or problem in an exploratory study. They might wish to craft more precise objectives if they wish to investigate relationships between events or variables, but these, too, can be phrased carefully, as in, say, 'To explore the relationship between executive pay and company financial results'. Objectives that are carefully crafted can pave the way for a good project because they signal that the student researcher understands the complexity of the issue or problem that is under investigation.

Reflexivity in research writing

Interpretive research reporting traditions often adopt a *reflexive* stance. *Reflexivity* in research means, broadly, being aware of being aware, although it must be admitted that different writers in management research tend to use the term in slightly different ways (Johnson and Duberley, 2003). In research writing, reflexivity generally implies open and transparent acknowledgement of all the circumstances of the research context, including the ways in which the researcher's personal perspective influenced their interpretation of the research findings.

Interpretive research traditions give a voice to the researcher. That is, reflexivity is more accepted and expected than it is in realist/positivist research. However, both paradigms of research require a basic reflexivity in the sense that the researcher needs to demonstrate that they are aware of weaknesses and limitations in their study. For example, it is important for the researcher to show that there is awareness of limitations of method, of sample and of ways in which the findings may have been influenced by the assumptions, beliefs and research style of the researcher.

In a reflexive research project, it is quite appropriate for the researcher to comment on how the research project evolved. There is no need to pretend that it all went without a hitch. Indeed, the examiner will normally want to see that the student researcher has developed his or her research skills and subject understanding through reflecting critically on how the project was conceived and carried out. If things went a bit wrong in some ways, it is ok to say so, and this is an opportunity to demonstrate a deeper understanding through the way that the student researcher responded to setbacks.

'Critical' thinking and the literature review

Whatever research topic is decided upon, it is essential to locate it in an appropriate body of literature. The research project should evolve out of a careful consideration of previous research in similar related areas. Some research projects (conceptual projects) consist mainly of an extended review of literature. Other, managerially oriented projects, may be based around a particular industry problem. In Chapter 1, we noted the different types of research project students might be asked to do as part of a taught degree, and on some courses this might include a practical business-focused report that addresses, analyses and presents solutions to, a business problem. For an academic research project, though, trying to solve a managerial problem is not enough. The problem, and the means of solving it, must be set within a context of previous and recent research. This entails reviewing a cross-section of published academic journal articles relevant to the research topic. The literature review must be 'critical', that is, it must employ critique, to satisfy a major criterion of higher academic accomplishment. For academics, 'critical' analysis means strong, persuasive analysis, but the types of critical thinking and writing in research and scholarly work can differ.

The word 'critical' is often used colloquially in managerial writing as a synonym for 'important' (as in, for example, 'marketing is a critical business function'). But this is not the sense in which research academics use the word. Academics feel that 'critical' thinking or critique is inherent to intellectually 'rigorous' thinking. The ability to think critically is demonstrated by the student researcher showing that they can understand research perspectives well enough to be able to evaluate the strengths, weaknesses and key assumptions of each perspective. Doing so suggests that differing theories and perspectives have not simply been accepted at face value by the researcher. Rather, the critical or rigorous researcher has compared and evaluated each theory or perspective in terms of their apparent qualities and shortcomings. Work that does this well, demonstrates a deeper level of understanding and a more penetrating quality of intellect than work that takes a passive position towards theories and merely accepts them uncritically. In other words, the literature review that merely repeats the views of several authors on a topic is not 'critical'. Research writing that is 'critical' demonstrates a deeper level of intellectual engagement than this.

However, to add to the student's confusion, writing and thinking critically does not mean simply being critical. That is, saying that a particular theory isn't very good, doesn't cut it. It would be necessary to say exactly why the theory isn't very good, and it would also be necessary to state what assumptions the writer is making to make the judgement about what constitutes a 'good' or poor theory in the context being discussed. Of course, it would be simplistic to say that a theory is either just 'good' or not so good. Theories are like cars – some are fine for popping into town, but you wouldn't want to drive across the country or tow a trailer in them. The point is, a theory needs to be evaluated against exactly what it purports to explain. There are many ways of understanding what theory means and what counts as theory (Merton, 2017). For the current purpose, we are not concerned with the

Figure 3.1 Styles of critical thinking

philosophy of science but with a basic appreciation of critical thinking and how it might appear in research projects. Figure 3.1 shows one possible way of categorising critical thinking for research to help students to incorporate it into their work.

Uncritical/descriptive thinking

Academics are fond of describing student writing that isn't very good as 'descriptive', that is, the writing merely describes ideas, theories or events. This can be ok at times, but what the academic is really looking for in student work is writing that is analytical, that is, writing that not only describes ideas but also compares and contrasts the strength and weaknesses of different ideas and evaluates them in application to different contexts. Descriptive writing is 'un-critical' in the sense that there is no element of critique – ideas are presented as if they are all of equal value and the assumptions that underpin the ideas are never critically examined. The analytical style of student writing is critical in the sense that it does compare and contrast ideas, examine their assumption and apply them in different contexts to reveal their strength and weaknesses. When we get to the analytical level of student writing, there are levels of critical analysis within this.

Uncritical or descriptive writing and thinking, then, can be exemplified by referencing a theoretical or conceptual model (an example in marketing could be E. Jerome McCarthy's (1960) Marketing Mix and the Four Ps of Price, Product, Physical Distribution and Promotion) in application to a marketing management issue without any caveats or qualifications to critically examine how useful or relevant such models are in providing a management solution in a given situation. The marketing mix, that is, the Four Ps, is still a mainstay of introductory marketing courses, but of course it is not a theory in a sociological sense because there is no empirical evidence base and no capacity for prediction. Arguably, it might have some explanatory value. Then again, normative marketing theories and concepts have been critiqued for their logical circularity and apparent irrelevance in many cases of marketing success (Brown, 1995; Brownlie and Saren, 1992; Hackley, 2009a). Of course, students on taught courses who are presented with these models in class are entitled to take them in good faith. But when the same students are writing a research dissertation, they will be expected to have thought a little more deeply about these useful classroom models and to have read at least some of the volumes of criticism they have attracted. For example, they might have grasped that the Marketing Mix is merely a heuristic or a rough rule of thumb that might have a different application in every marketing case. Hence, the idea cannot be relied upon to give managers precise operational solutions. It is, in essence, a list of factors that might, possibly be relevant in most cases of marketing management. Of course, in most organisations, the marketing manager would not have control over the Mix variables, so the idea of the Mix is primarily a teaching device and not a problem solving technique for managers.

The marketing mix framework might be represented more positively in a student project but, nonetheless, research projects that fail to acknowledge fundamental criticisms of the constructs and conceptual frameworks that they use are usually confined to the uncritical level of analysis. Whether the theory concerned is the Marketing Mix or any other, the level of thinking whereby the theory is merely described is not adequate for the independent research project. Descriptions of theories in social science must be raised to the level of analytical thinking by examining their assumptions and/or comparing, contrasting and critiquing them, and by evaluating their useful and less useful points in application to particular situations.

Levels of critique: functional critique

Critical thinking or critique, on the other hand, always entails analytical thinking. However, there are different styles of critical thinking that can be applied in student research projects in business and management. Figure 3.1 (adapted from Hackley, 2009a, b) illustrates one way of breaking down the styles of critical thinking into three categories: functional, ethical and intellectual critique. Functional critique entails analysing the usefulness of the theory in terms of how it might deepen insight into a particular management problem. There are two particularly pertinent questions entailed in this style of critical thinking:

a Does the conceptual model/theoretical knowledge add to or go beyond experiential, 'common-sense' understanding?
b Does the theoretical model work in practice? Does it fit well with the situation under investigation?

If the answer to either of these questions is negative, a third question is begged: what other theoretical frameworks could be useful? The onus is on students to explore a range of theoretical work with application to the problem. So, to extend the example, if the student researcher were to apply the Marketing Mix framework to a particular marketing management problem or issue, they would need to begin with an evaluation of the mix in their critical literature review. The review would have to address criticisms of the practical usefulness and managerial relevance of the framework, discussing weaknesses, strengths and the implicit (and explicit) assumptions that are built into it. The review would seek to move towards a frank appraisal of the mix framework as a basis for managerial problem solving. It would also acknowledge that other frameworks may offer different but equally useful insights. Indeed, most marketing practitioners make practical decisions based on no theories whatsoever but simply using their personal knowledge and experience.

Ethical critique

Criticising managerial theories and practices on ethical grounds is probably a form of critical thinking that is easiest for students to grasp. Marketing might do good in the world by increasing the efficiency with which organisations use their resources to meet consumer demand. This, in turn, would, in principle, increase the efficiency of markets while improving the quality of life and creating jobs and wealth. However, we all know that marketing can result in negative externalities, that is, unintended effects that are damaging to society and the environment. There can be excessive demand for environmentally damaging forms of consumption, while unhealthy and heavily marketed processed food has caused an obesity crisis in many Western countries. What is more, marketing, as with any business activity, might be dishonest or misleading in its communications. Ethical critique engages with the ethical or moral dimension of marketing and business practices. It is important, though, so emphasise that ethical values are not necessarily universal. An ethical critique of a business or management practice should consist of more than assertions about what may be morally right or wrong. A solid ethical critique should make clear what assumptions are being made about the ethical basis of critique.

As a level of critical thinking, ethical critique is more advanced than functional critique because it demands engagement with comparative ethics and regulatory issues. What is considered morally correct or acceptable in one country may not be in a different country. Ethical systems may be derived from religious systems, or they may be informed by moral philosophies. There are, arguably, some ethical principles that people from all over the world could agree upon, especially with regard to business and management. Most people would agree that advertising should not make false claims, that managers should treat employees fairly, that products and services should be safe to use and quality tested. There will be different views, though, on what the regulatory solutions should be for transgressions of these principles. Other issues may be more complex ethically and these might demand deeper analysis. Ethical analysis could address all manner of topics relevant to independent student projects, and it is important that where students do so, they draw on theories of business ethics to clarify their assumptions and bring complexity to their analysis.

This brings us to what is conceived as the highest level of critical thinking in Figure 3.1, intellectual critique. This entails a critical engagement with the assumptions of the model, theory or concept in question. Again, taking the example of the marketing 'mix', the review might question the social scientific basis for the model. What grounds are there for this framework? What evidence is there that it is a practically useful or intellectually viable way of categorising certain managerial marketing activities? Models in science are usually evaluated on their explanatory and predictive value. To what extent does the Marketing Mix enable us to understand marketing successes more deeply, and to what extent does it allow us to predict the outcomes of marketing strategies? This level of thinking is an advance on the previous levels of critical thinking because it not only focuses on managerial problem solving or ethical dilemmas in business, but also begins to evaluate concepts and frameworks in social scientific terms.

Intellectual critique engages with the difficult philosophical question of how it is possible to 'know' anything at all. This should not be too daunting to advanced students: after all, many primary schools find it useful to teach philosophy to very young children. The aim is not to resolve philosophical questions but to acknowledge them, to improve the student researcher's quality of thinking. 'How do you know that it is your own hand on the end of your arm?' is a classic philosophy degree exam question that forces the student to engage with the problem that we rely for our empirical knowledge on our senses, but we rely on our reason to judge whether or not we can trust what our senses seem to be telling us. The relevance of this to critical thinking in research is that scepticism towards knowledge is the mark of the mature thinker. Note that scepticism is very different to the kind of ill-informed cynicism that drives people to reject science and believe in bizarre conspiracy theories. Scepticism is the habit of not trusting our own judgements about the world until we have carefully engaged with and evaluated the various arguments and evidence behind all the differing points of view.

Many marketing academics argue that marketing has a body of theory that is *normative*, that is, it is designed to assist practical action. This, they suggest, gives it a special character that cannot be evaluated in traditional social scientific terms. Others (Hackley, 1998b) argue that this may be all right for consulting projects but that academic marketing and management research cannot claim to be a special kind of knowledge set apart from the rest of social science. Marketing and management are practical business disciplines, but academic study of them demands academic standards be applied. Words on a page or in a class case discussion can never be direct conduits to management practice, whatever some marketing texts may claim (Hackley, 2003b). Student independent research projects may be focused on management problems and solutions, but they are also designed to test the intellectual and scholarly skills that the student has developed through their course.

Intellectual critique entails a mentality that questions the 'ordinary' and the 'obvious' in social life on the grounds that what is ordinary or obvious seems so by virtue of a profoundly complex process. This level of critique asks what alternative ways the situation under investigation could be represented and questions the assumptions that underpin presumptions of knowledge. It asks this on the grounds that every way of describing something suppresses other alternatives and carries certain assumptions and interests (see the section on critical discourse analysis in Chapter 8: see also Fairclough, 2010).

This level of thinking and writing may cut across into other disciplines in its breadth of perspective and conceptual scope. Many marketing and consumer research projects engage with their subject matter in this way and ask how the consumption of goods in specific social contexts helps consumers to construct a sense of meaning and identity, hence, for example, a discussion about consumption practices in a given context might connect with psychological theories of identity. Managerial projects can ask how managers make sense of what they do by using metaphors and stories to articulate their experience of organisational work (Ardley, 2009). Managerial work and consumption need not be seen as ontologically 'fixed' or 'given' realities but can, rather, be understood as dynamic processes in which people impose meaning on to their activities through the language and social practices they employ. So, for example, a managerial project would not only ask how effective the marketing mix is in a particular problem – solving context. Rather, it would ask what managers accomplish by using the language of popular managerial marketing (if indeed they do) to articulate, rationalise or justify their actions (Ardley and Quinn, 2014; Svensson, 2007).

Theories and models

We have already mentioned the idea of the conceptual 'model' as a representation of a process or event. Many academic textbooks refer to 'theories' and 'models' (for a critical review in marketing see Baker and Saren, 2010). These terms are often used interchangeably in marketing texts, although the scope of a theory tends to be broader than the scope of a model. A model tends to be a representation of a particular process, such as a model of the life cycle of a new product (Levitt, 1965) or a model of consumer behaviour (Engel et al., 1990). Models try to show what elements are important in a process. They also try to show the relationship between elements. Students conducting a conceptual research project might try to put together a basic model to illustrate a process or the relationship between elements in a process.

Theories are attempts to explain or understand a group of phenomena. On occasion, a theory can be reduced to a representation, that is, they can be modelled. In disciplines such as biology, physics or chemistry, a theory would both explain a phenomenon and make predictions on the basis of that explanation. Theories in management and social research tend to lack the ability to predict, they more often purport to explain phenomena. Of course, some theories predict without being able to fully explain why the predictions are accurate, such as theories of economic behaviour from the behavioural economics perspective. Other findings induced from 'big' data such as Google Trends or other sources of empirical observation, sometimes also predict without being able to explain why the predictions are accurate (Stephens-Davidowitz, 2017). In other words, some theories explain without predicting, while others predict without explaining.

Writers in the business field sometimes refer to 'theory' as counterpoint to organisational 'practice'. This rhetorical use of theory is sometimes used pejoratively, as when books promoting consulting solutions claim that they are 'practical' rather than theoretical, meaning that theory implies ideas that are impractical, not relevant or self-indulgent. Another use of the idea of theory refers to speculative, as opposed to factual, discussion and thinking. 'All very well in theory' is a common complaint levelled by organisational managers at business school texts and teaching. 'In theory' it is easy to find solutions to business problems. In practice most solutions have been tried before and failed for some reason. Student researchers need to disentangle the rhetorical uses of the word 'theory' (like the use of the word 'critical') as a device of persuasion from its more substantive use as a form of carefully grounded explanation. Theories can be very practical indeed, and there is no world of practical action that is immune to the reach of theory – theories help us to explain what people regard as common sense or self-evident ways of thinking about and acting in the world.

Research 'method' and empirical projects

To conclude this chapter, we will return to the structure of the research project outlined in Boxes 3.3 and 3.4. Following the literature review, the empirical project will then move to a method chapter. 'Method' is important in social scientific research (business and management research draws on many social science research traditions for its foundations) because it distinguishes research from opinion, hearsay or intuition. The presence of a method in a research project implies that what has been investigated has been done so systematically, carefully and from a theoretically informed intellectual basis. The 'method' is central to the narrative structure of the research story. It gives the research project shape and structure. It signifies that the project has engaged with *epistemological* issues (that is, issues of what kind of knowledge can be generated) to offer insight into a particular area. In addressing the rationale for the chosen method of data gathering and data analysis, the project demonstrates that it is at the higher levels of critical thinking.

If a research project has a 'method' it implies that the research was thought about carefully, planned and executed systematically, that it proceeded according to rules, and that it satisfied some of the criteria of social scientific knowledge. If a research project at master's or undergraduate level demonstrates the ability to apply a given methodological perspective and to show some awareness of the method's limitations and weaknesses, a major outcome of the research process will have been satisfied. There must be a carefully referenced explanation and justification of the method that is chosen. The author must explain why the chosen approach was most appropriate in the circumstances, and perhaps also discuss why other methods were not chosen.

The 'method' section will explain which data-gathering approach was taken and why. It will then explain how the data were analysed. The competent use of a method, any method, is most important in student research projects that use empirical data. Social research is an enterprise that attempts to produce and/or communicate ideas, truths and insights that are more robust than everyday 'common sense' understanding, conventional wisdom or hearsay. The use of a methodological and/or theoretical perspective is what makes social research a distinctive way of trying to discover, generate, communicate or test new knowledge. Methods are never perfect. There will always be weaknesses, flaws and difficulties. But in a sense, the method is all the social scientist has. Without method, there is no scientific knowledge.

It is very important to note that the choice of method is key to the success of the project, but that choice does not stand apart from the way in which the research problem or question is framed. As indicated in Figure 3.2, the research question or problem is a key choice in the project process because the way it is conceived determines the subsequent stages of the project. The various parts of the project must fit together. For example, if the research problem is expressed as a confirmatory study intended to test a hypothesis or to establish a causal relationship between two variables, then a quantitative research design based on a positivist or realist design might be appropriate. This type of research design would then inform the sampling frame, data gathering and analysis, and the way that findings are argued and supported.

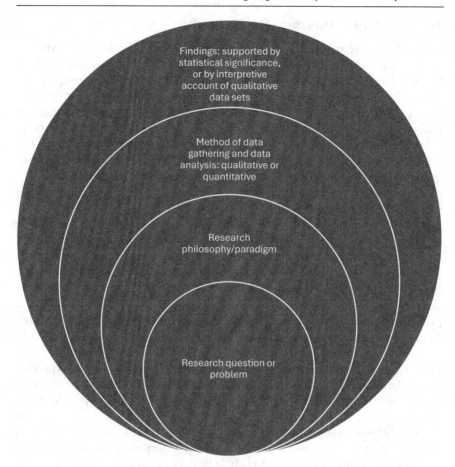

Findings: supported by
statistical significance,
or by interpretive
account of qualitative
data sets

Method of data
gathering and data
analysis: qualitative or
quantitative

Research
philosophy/paradigm

Research question or
problem

Figure 3.2 The integration of research question, method, data and findings

Specifically, there would be a statistical analysis based on a survey or experiment, and the results would be discussed regarding their statistical significance, or otherwise.

On the other hand, if the research problem is framed as an exploratory study with an open question, then a qualitative and interpretive method might be more appropriate. This would inform the sample frame, the data analysis and the way that findings are supported. So, for example, the research paradigm or philosophy would likely be a social constructionist or relativist standpoint, the sample would need to be representative rather than random, the data analysis would be some form of text-based interpretation of interviews, focus groups or other qualitative data sets, say, grounded theory or thematic analysis, and the interpretation of findings would be argued for using direct quotes from the data sets.

Triangulation in interpretive research

The findings that are generated through the research method might be subject to testing of confirmation in some way. One way of doing so is to look at findings from different perspectives. This is sometimes called triangulation. *Triangulation* is a common term in quantitative research, less so in qualitative research. It is a nautical metaphor that refers to verification of research findings by reference to more than one source. If a researcher looks at something in more than one way, say by getting two assistants to agree on the interpretation of some data sets, then that would be a form of inter-subjective triangulation. Using a method of triangulation can mean that findings are more persuasive to readers. However, the concept of triangulation is not always helpful in interpretive research.

The use of triangulation can imply that there is only one version of social truth and, furthermore, that it is available to the researcher, rather like the view that obtains in realist/positivist research. Interpretive research often proceeds on a *relativist* basis in the sense that it acknowledges the legitimacy of differing perspectives on social phenomena. Triangulation can be useful, and some qualitative research studies employ what is probably the nearest thing to triangulation in interpretive research, called inter-subjective verification, through which two or more people are asked to look at an interpretive process in the hope that they will agree. But, ultimately, interpretation is just that, an interpretation. The interpretive researcher does not claim that their interpretation is the only or the best interpretation possible. They simply argue for their interpretation of the data set using the best quality of argument and most solid standards of scholarship they can, to make their interpretive process as transparent as possible. If a reader wishes to dispute their interpretation, then at least they see the grounds for so doing. It is important to note that findings in qualitative research cannot be proven. Proof is a legal or mathematical concept. In social research, findings can be supported to a greater or lesser degree, but they cannot be proven.

The findings, discussion and conclusion

After the section on research method, the empirical project will report the major findings. 'Findings' are the results, key themes and/or insights that the researcher feels emerged from the primary data analysis. They may consist of themes, patterns, consistencies or other types of insight that seem, to the researcher's informed eye, to be evident in the data. In qualitative research reporting the findings will be supported by many direct quotes and examples from the data reproduced in the body of the research dissertation findings section. Transparency is important in qualitative and interpretive research: the reader must be able to see why the author made the interpretation of data that they made. If there are many direct quotes and the interview or other material is reproduced in the appendices, then the reader can make his or her own judgement on the quality of the interpretation. They can see how the researcher arrived at the interpretation they reached.

As we note above, the way that findings are expressed and supported depends on the research method and form of data analysis. It is important that in expressing their findings students do not make exaggerated claims. Research findings are always contingent and qualified, and subject to limitations and errors. Findings should expressed cautiously, and modestly.

The discussion

After the findings are reported they must be discussed. The 'discussion' or 'analysis' section evaluates primary data findings in the light of the concepts and issues from the earlier literature review. The discussion synthesises previous research findings in the field with the new findings generated by the project. It addresses questions such as these: Does the primary research yield findings that are consistent with the literature on that topic? Does it appear that there are shortcomings, gaps or limitations in the literature, and, if so, what new research should be undertaken? Or, were there flaws in the project that resulted in a disconnection with previous research findings?

The discussion or analysis chapter is, in several ways, the most important chapter of your project report or dissertation, since it is your chance to pull together the various strands of your research and to say what you really think, based on all the evidence you have gathered. It should demonstrate the student researcher's understanding of the method(s) used and the kind of knowledge or insight that has resulted. It should critically evaluate findings and analyse them for logical consistency and coherence with literature-based theories. It should demonstrate that the researcher has the intellectual ability to integrate primary findings with theoretical knowledge and draw logically coherent conclusions. It is here, in the discussion, that the student researcher can achieve the higher critical levels of thinking by drawing a trajectory between previous research, the present study and its findings, and possible new horizons for this area of research.

The research report will have a short section of 'concluding comments' re-iterating the research story. What did you do, why was it important, and what did you find? Again, there is some repetition involved here as the story of the research project is briefly rehearsed once again. To what extent did the research concur with previous research? To what extent were the research objectives fulfilled? What were the weaker points of the research and what did you feel worked well? You can conclude by (modestly) suggesting what implications your work might have for future practice and/or future research. The appendix and detailed (Harvard method) references sections complete your research report.

In this chapter, we have outlined the entire research project process, to try to give the student research a sense of the shape of the process. At the beginning of this chapter, we looked at what examiners are looking for when they assess completed student research projects. We then looked at the structure of a typical project and the stages it must address, whether it is an empirical project or a conceptual one without empirical or primary data. The chapter outlined some thoughts about critical analysis and how students might achieve the higher levels of analysis in their work by not merely describing theories and phenomena but by comparing, contrasting and examining the assumptions underlying different points of view. Finally, as indicated in Figure 3.2, the various decisions in the research process must fit together and make sense as a whole. Everything begins with the way the research problem is conceived and expressed, and this is why this stage in the process is key to the success of the entire project. If the student researcher has a grasp of what they must produce in the end, they will be better placed to make good decisions regarding each stage of the research process. Next, in Chapter 4, we will develop the theme of empirical research further by discussing several popular and effective methods of collecting qualitative data sets.

Glossary

'Datum' and 'data'   The research material that the researcher gathers and analyses is the data. Strictly speaking 'datum' is the singular and 'data' the plural, although the word data is often used as a collective noun for a single group of material when 'data set' would be grammatically accurate.

Empirical   Deriving from experience. In management research an empirical research project will include data gathered by the researcher. A *conceptual* research project will not, relying instead on existing published sources.

Epistemology   The philosophical study of knowledge. It addresses such questions as, how can we know what we know? What kind of knowledge counts as knowledge? And, what is knowledge?

Method   Every research project employs a systematic or theoretically informed method of investigation. In social science, 'method' usually refers to the technique of gathering data and also to the assumptions underpinning the interpretation of data. Very often in social science method and interpretive framework are implied in each other. Note that 'methodology' is the study of methods.

Normative   A 'norm' is a rule that does, or should, govern a pattern of behaviour: normative work in management and business writing and research seeks to develop norms or rules for doing management and business.

Primary data   Original data, obtained first-hand by the researcher.

Reflexivity   The experience of being aware of being aware, in other words, the ability to reflect on one's own experience. It is important in a research context because researcher reflexivity gives interpretive research reporting a special character of personal engagement, frankness, self-criticality and self-awareness. In particular, it allows the researcher to be aware of and acknowledge the influence they have on the research process.

Secondary data   Existing material that has already been produced for another reason.

Triangulation   This is a nautical metaphor that refers to checking a position from an alternative standpoint. For example, if a researcher feels that a particular finding emerges from data he or she can check that finding by seeking another colleague's opinion (also called intersubjective verification of findings).

Chapter 4

Gathering and interpreting qualitative data sets

Abstract

This chapter offers practical advice on a selection of qualitative data-gathering techniques. It introduces some basic principles of qualitative data analysis such as content analysis, thematic analysis and coding. The chapter makes the point that certain theoretical assumptions are implied in particular qualitative methods, and begins to introduce some of the themes of research theory that will preoccupy much of the rest of the book.

Chapter objectives

After reading this chapter students will be able to:

- gather qualitative data sets using well-established techniques
- understand some of the theoretical implications that are associated with particular data-gathering techniques
- appreciate some of the major difficulties of gathering primary empirical data sets
- understand the influence of the researcher in qualitative data gathering and interpretation

Introduction: interpretation, theory and 'theory'

Gathering qualitative data sets is easy. There are people out there, all you have to do to understand what they're doing, is to watch them, talk to them, ask them questions and listen to them. Everybody does this all the time, but it isn't called social science, it's called living. Of course, for academic work and science, there needs to be some sort of formality and structure to the ways in which people are watched, questioned and listened to. In life, observing people is merely part of experience. In social science, this experience becomes data. There also has to be some kind of formality to the ways in which data sets are interpreted and made into 'findings' or 'insights'. It isn't enough to

DOI: 10.4324/9781003432203-6

draw subjective conclusions from one's personal experience, although that is certainly part of interpretive research. There must be some way of making the interpretation transparent, so that other people can decide if they agree with it. After all, this book is about social science, albeit with a different way of conceiving science to the way it is conceived in natural science. Making the interpretation transparent entails three things. One is making the assumptions behind the interpretation explicit by stating the interpretive stance or theoretical approach that is being used. A second precondition for transparency is for the researcher to explain clearly to the reader what the process of data interpretation entailed. The third precondition for the researcher to reproduce some of the data set in the findings, so that the reader can see exactly what the data look like, as well as how the researcher arrived at their interpretation.

Figure 4.1 provides a slightly tongue-in-cheek image of some of the key differences between qualitative social science and life as experienced. If we draw a naïve equivalence between everyday experience and social science paradigms, we can say that watching people can be called observation, ethnography or it can even fall under practice theory. Asking people questions and listening to their answers happens when researchers conduct in depth interviews, focus groups or ask participants to complete diaries, written reflections or even photomontages. Interpreting these kinds of data might be framed as existential phenomenology, discourse analysis or thematic analysis. Social science is distinguished by the formality of data gathering and analysis, and by the inter-subjective character of findings. That is, other people are able to look at the findings of qualitative research to see if they find them plausible or well-supported by the data. Personal experience, of course, cannot be observed or inter-subjectively verified. However, there are approaches to qualitative research that attempt to draw conclusions from lived

Figure 4.1 Life and social science compared

experience, such as autoethnography, which we will look at in Chapter 7. We will look more closely at the theoretical framing of qualitative research in Chapter 5. In this chapter, we will try to set up some general principles for gathering qualitative data sets that can be theoretically analysed.

Multi-method approaches

Before detailing single approaches, it is worth noting that the data-gathering approaches in this chapter, and the theoretical stances in subsequent chapters, are not mutually exclusive. They can be used in combination in multi-method studies. In this book we will focus on a limited range of qualitative methods for the sake of clarity and to communicate key general principles. However, the variety of qualitative approaches is increasing all the time. For a selection of differing approaches to qualitative methods in business, management, marketing and consumer research (see, for example, Batat, 2023; Belk, 2006, 2017; Carson et al., 2001; Crosby et al., 2023; Diwanji, 2023; Easterby-Smith et al., 1991, 2018; Fischer and Guzel, 2023; Gummeson, 2000; Moisander and Valtonen, 2006; Novak and Hoffman, 2023; Relja et al., 2023; Schwartz-Shea and Yanow, 2012).

In Figure 4.2, we can see how different theoretical approaches can have qualitative data-gathering methods in common. *Ethnography*, for example, is noted for its use of depth interviews, field notes, observation (and *participant observation*) and other, informal data sources, as do *practice theory* approaches to empirical research. *Phenomenological/existentialist* research studies use a variety of qualitative data-gathering approaches in combination, particularly the depth interview, as do many studies framed as *discourse analysis*. Indeed, as we shall see in Chapter 5, several different interpretive

Figure 4.2 Different interpretive traditions can share the same data-gathering methods

theoretical perspectives use similar combinations of qualitative data-gathering approaches, but with differently nuanced data analysis.

It is important to remember that data-gathering techniques are not necessarily theoretically neutral: they carry implicit assumptions about the nature of the material being studied and also about the form of analysis that may be appropriate. In addition, the ways that specified data-gathering methods and analytical traditions are applied by researchers are subject to many variations. For example, practice theory and discourse analysis can be deployed in somewhat different ways and in different contexts of application (see Chapters 7 and 8). The following is intended to assist student researchers in the practical issues of data gathering, but care must be taken to check that the chosen technique is appropriate to the desired theoretical stance.

Pragmatic data gathering

First, lest theoretical framing sounds too daunting for the first-time student researcher, we should state that student researchers often use empirical data-gathering techniques in a relatively informal way, to aid and deepen knowledge and understanding in a project that is only loosely framed as interpretive research. This is ok – a student who wants to pass their course in business and management does not necessarily have to have a thoroughly worked out, ontologically grounded, epistemologically coherent method right at the beginning. That would be nice, but for most undergraduate student researchers, getting some data sets of some kind is the priority, and it can be formidable challenge. Getting access to data takes time and money, and it may require ethical approval, and even the permission of the organisation in which the data will be collected. Having a carefully worked out theoretical standpoint and gathering specific data that will address the research questions fully are necessary for a PhD or publishable research study, but data gathering can be more ad hoc and convenience-based in some circumstances for Undergraduate or Master's projects. For example, the student researcher might use ad hoc interviews with a convenience sample of consumers in the target group for material that will enrich their general understanding of the topic or research problem.

Research students might even use a pilot study before their main data-gathering phase, just to deepen their understanding of the research topic and method. On the other hand, a student researcher may wish to conduct a more theoretically driven and empirically systematic and extensive study in, say, an ethnographic style. The student researcher may use a mixture of data-gathering techniques including, say, informal interviews, naturalistic observation, some textual analysis of news articles and/or trade press information and perhaps research diaries (of course this would be a lot for a student research project) if they had decided at the outset that they wished to try to accomplish a mini-ethnographic study. The decision of whether to use multi-method data gathering normally depends upon practical constraints of time, availability of and access to data sources and the research skills of the student, as well as on the aims and theoretical framework of the research project. In student research projects conducted as part of taught courses, ad hoc methods of data gathering used to supplement critical literature reviews can be as useful as more theoretically driven data-gathering approaches. The important thing is how the data are used to enrich the analysis and discussion of a particular set of research questions.

'Interpretive' and 'quantitative' research

We have touched on this distinction earlier, but we will return to it briefly because it is the source of a great deal of confusion among first-time interpretive researchers. Interpretive research typically uses qualitative data sets, giving the rationale for this book. But, qualitative research is not necessarily interpretive research. Qualitative data sets are sometimes used in realist/ positivistic research studies. The two terms 'qualitative' and 'interpretive' are often used interchangeably. However, they imply different things. Some research looks at qualitative data sets to dig out truths that might be tested to see if they can, in principle, be *universalised*, that is, tested to see if they are universally true in all circumstances. A qualitative study is often conducted as a precursor to construct development for a quantitative statistical study, on a realist/positivist ontology. Other qualitative research studies are cast as exploratory or as creative interpretations of the data, and the findings are seen as an end in themselves and not necessarily a precursor to construct development and quantitative measurement. With a non-theoretical qualitative study, the risk for the student researcher is that the academic marking the work sees it as merely descriptive or theoretically naïve, and lacking in analytical rigour.

'Qualitative' and 'quantitative' research categories, though, are not mutually exclusive. A great deal of quantitative research has a qualitative component. As mentioned above, qualitative work (such as interviews or group discussions) can stimulate the researcher to think of 'constructs' that can then ultimately be measured in a quantitative study. To return to an earlier example, a researcher might interview salespeople to see what factors seem to influence their effectiveness. If many salespeople seem to talk about their motivation in terms of the personal qualities of their manager, then the research might generate a scale with which to measure the motivational ability of sales managers. He or she could then conduct a larger study to see if there is any statistical correlation between sales managers' motivational ability as measured by the scale and the sense of motivation felt by their sales force.

Such a study assumes that *nomothetic* (statistically generalised) findings can be useful. This term is often contrasted with *idiographic* research. The researcher seeking nomothetic insights might try to isolate the decisive motivational skill of the sales manager with the intention of making gener-alised points about all sales managers and their sales forces. The researcher seeking idiographic insights would, in contrast, conduct a depth interview with a few sales managers to establish how their approaches to sales man-agement and staff motivation evolve out of their life history and experience.

Sampling for qualitative research, or 'How many interviews will be enough?'

Data gathering for interpretive research need not be random, but it should be systematic and/or theoretically informed. The word 'interpretive' implies that data are not used to try to set findings beyond dispute or to generalise find-ings across time and social context. An interpretation is necessarily one of many possible interpretations. In interpretive research, the researcher seeks to arrive at insights for which they will offer as much evidence and reason-ing as possible. They do this to make their reasoning transparent and to try to make their interpretation persuasive, meeting high standards of scholarly exposition. Given all this, the selection of data for analysis must be purposive rather than randomised. In quantitative research, non-probability sampling is the term used to any non-random sample, whether that sample is gathered through convenience, snowballing (asking one person to refer their friends), purposive (a sample driven by the purpose of the study) and quota sampling (selecting a certain number of each category). What is important is to under-stand why particular data sets were chosen given the aims of the research. It is also important to qualify findings carefully so that they are grounded within the social context that is being researched.

Sampling issues are often resolved by necessity. In qualitative research, sampling is often based on *purposive* or *convenience* criteria. This means that the sampling decision is driven by pragmatic considerations of convenience or suitability for the problem or issue being studied. First-time researchers might ask ten people for an interview and find that three agree. That, then, has to be the sample. You can't force people to agree to be interviewed, just as you can't make people fill in online questionnaires. Quantitative research-ers and qualitative researchers alike invariably find that they are making the best of imperfect samples. There is invariably non-response error, because of surveys that are not returned or participants for whom the contact details are no longer current. This introduces an element of non-random-ness to the sampling. It is not fatal to the research though. If you can show that you have a realistic and well-informed awareness of the limitations, as well as the advantages of your sample, your research can be plausible. In some cases, qualitative researchers find that a 'snowballing' effect occurs as they get agreement from some participants who then tell others and more people agree to be interviewed. In this case, the researcher must decide when they have enough participants to stop seeking more.

It is difficult to provide a satisfactory answer to the question 'how much data shall I collect?' The answer is always unsatisfactory because it is always the same: 'it depends'. Unlike in quantitative research, there is no formula. The sample size for qualitative research depends on the objectives, the scale and the resources applied to the research. It depends on the nature of the subject matter, the kind of data sets that are sought and the quality of the data that are needed. It also depends on pragmatic consideration such as time-scale and costs. In the end, two maxims are worth remembering. For student researchers, any primary data is often better than none at all, and second, few marks are awarded for the amount of data collected. The important thing is how well the student researcher uses the data they have. A qualitative study might have one case study, or one participant, or dozens, depending on the scope of the study and the resources of the researcher.

The sample should, therefore, be decided on grounds of (a) pragmatism, (b) representativeness and (c) quality of insights generated (see Figure 4.3). The student research must be pragmatic because there isn't the time, or the need, to conduct a perfect study. You need to make the best of the time and resources that you have, and the supervisors and markers will understand that. Representativeness, we will recall from Chapter 1, is a key concept in qualitative research. It is essential in empirical qualitative research that the sample is like the wider population of interest, that is, it is representative of the wider population of interest. If the research is about the home insurance market, then the sample of participants probably need to be home insurance consumers: if the research is about teen vaping, then the research participants need to be people with some investment in and connection with the

Figure 4.3 Criteria for gathering qualitative data sets

topic, such as teenagers, retailers and/or those with parental responsibility for teenagers. If the sample is representative, it need not be large. The study is not seeking generalisable facts, just qualitative insights. This brings us to the third category in Figure 4.3: quality of insight. This depends somewhat on the quality of the analysis, and also on the quality of data. Some research respondents in, say, an interview or focus group situation, may have telling insights to offer and be forthcoming and informative, while other participants might not have much to say. Researchers need to be prepared to try to get the best out of their research participants, and we can say more about this in the next section.

Interviews – preparatory issues

Access and pilot interviews

If the project is focused on a particular industry sector, it makes sense for the researcher to learn something about the sector before engaging in the main primary data collection phase. This can be done through secondary research based on existing public sources, and perhaps also through a pilot interview with a practitioner. Interviews with expert professionals or consumers can be excellent sources of data for analysis, or for framing the study through a better understanding of the field of practice. If student researchers can gain access to relevant experts through personal or social networks such as LinkedIn, so much the better. If not, find an address and send an email. Pragmatism dictates that student researchers cannot wait months for organisations to reply to their letters requesting interviews or field access. It is, incidentally, a good idea for students requesting research access to find out the name of a person responsible and direct communications to that person. An initial email or phone call will be enough to determine whether the person has the time or inclination to grant access or interview time. Organisational staff are busy people, and some receive many such requests. Student researchers should accept this and thank the people for their time even if the response is negative. It will also be necessary to fit around the person granting the interview, in the sense that, if the student researcher wants a one-hour depth interview and the expert offers a 20 minute chat on the phone, then take what's offered and adjust the research rationale accordingly. Finally, in any communications with practitioners (or indeed with academics) make sure that emails or other communications address the intended recipient appropriately, and are carefully structured and copy edited for spelling and grammar. These things are not quaint old school concerns. They still matter, unless you play tennis with the recipient.

If there are positive responses, the technique of data gathering may dictate the amount of data to be gathered. Depth interviews are very time-consuming. Some student researchers ambitiously set out to conduct 20 or 30 interviews, until they realise how much work is involved. A one-hour interview can generate many thousands of words of dialogue. If the student researcher is to transcribe just one interview to place in the report appendix, as is good practice, this will prove a very lengthy task even if they use a transcribing programme. In general, the data sample should, on pragmatic grounds, be manageable given the time and resource constraints. In many research projects the early interviews in the project will be the longest as the researcher finds out what the major issues are. In later interviews the researcher might have a much better-informed idea of the topic and may well know what the major issues are so that they ask about these more directly.

In qualitative research, as we note above, it is more important for a sample to be representative of a larger group than for it to be random. Randomising a sample is almost an impossible task even for accomplished researchers. Students doing a project as part of a taught degree need to make sure that whoever they access for data, the insights generated will be relevant to the broader issues in their research question. For example, if you are exploring the exposure of school age young people to alcohol advertising on social media, you will need to access school age young people who engage with social media. Research access, especially to people under the age of 18, requires various permissions to earn the approval of the university research ethics committee.

Assuming access can be gained, a degree of careful thought and preparation is useful. Some researchers conduct *pilot* data-gathering sessions, that is, practice sessions before the main data-gathering phase begins. These can be very useful for refining the questions you want to ask to ensure that the main data-gathering interviews are as focused as possible on the key issues of interest. Pilot interviews are also very useful for establishing the parameters of the study, the objectives and the scope. Finally, they are also very useful for practising qualitative research skills of conducting depth interviews, or for convening and moderating focus groups.

Quality of data is often difficult to ascertain before it is gathered. Sometimes, the person being interviewed doesn't say the interesting things that they might have done. Perhaps they're having an off day, perhaps the student researcher didn't ask the right questions in the right way. At other times, unpromising participants can be fun and interesting, and they offer insights that change the direction of analysis by throwing an unexpected light on the subject matter. However, expertise in a field should never be ignored – if a request for an interview is agreed by an expert senior practitioner, then take them up on that. What they say will be useful in the discussion because of their knowledge and experience, and the experience of interviewing and making contact will be valuable even if the person may not fall directly into the original sampling frame.

Conducting the research interview

Conducting research interviews can be useful whatever kind of research design is used. In a project that is problem based rather than theoretical, interviews with practitioners can give a valuable insight into practical issues. This practical insight can then be used in discussion as a counterpoint to the more theoretically informed perspective of the literature review. In such circumstances the technicalities of the interview process are not as important as the quality of the insights generated. In other words, having a conversation with the interviewee in which they are allowed to speak freely about their experience of the industry is a valuable approach. The interview does not need to be excessively formal. In more theoretically informed research projects, the technicalities of the 'depth' interview become more important. There are some general rules of interviewing that might be useful for the first-time qualitative researcher (see Box 4.1).

Generally speaking, the more relaxed the interviewee is, the better the quality of data the interview will generate. Some researchers can strike a rapport with their interviewees so that, in the interview situation, the interviewee becomes candid and expansive. Most of us enjoy having the opportunity to talk about our work to someone who is prepared to appear interested. An interview can be a surprisingly liberating context in which to speak about such matters, since it is confidential and in a neutral setting. The interviewer should try to encourage the interviewee to be relaxed. The best interviewers can sense when to allow the interviewee to be expansive, nodding and

---

Box 4.1   Research interview checklist

- Establish the aims of the interview
- Draft some questions for a structured or semi-structured interview format. These should include initial open questions to put the interviewee at ease and to establish rapport
- Draft an ethics form reassuring the interviewee that they can withdraw from the interview at any time, they can decline to answer any question and their responses will be confidential and used only for the purpose of the research study. Ideally, print the form for interviewees to sign
- Decide how to record the interview using video, audio or just by taking handwritten notes (only video or audio record with the interviewee's explicit permission)
- Decide whether to use transcribed and printed texts of the interviews, or audio recordings only, for the data analysis

smiling at times to reassure the interviewee of their continued interest and when to interject with a question to keep the interviewee on topic.

Relaxing interviewees and learning to ask just the right kinds of questions at the right time is an art that takes time to develop. Some tips can help the novice interviewer. First, be well prepared. Think through what you want to know beforehand. Prepare a list of questions you can ask if the interviewee can't think of anymore to say about a topic. At the beginning, introduce yourself, thank the person for agreeing to the interview and explain just what it is that interests you. Reassure the interviewee that the whole process is entirely non-judgemental and confidential. Explain to them that they can end the interview at any time.

It is a good idea to maintain eye contact in interviews, stay interested and give interviewees the space to speak freely. As noted earlier, employ 'active' listening – plenty of eye contact, nodding and other facial expressions of interest really help the interviewee along. Where digression occurs, it can be used to the interviewer's advantage. The interviewee may be relaxed and expansive and could raise novel or unexpectedly candid issues and insights. If the digression becomes too tiresome the interviewee should never betray boredom or irritation but should gently redirect the topic of conversation. Once, when the author was interviewing one of the Madison Avenue advertising agency professionals mentioned earlier, the interview participant said 'just stop the recording and follow me'. The participant led the interviewer to a quiet room and, with no recording equipment in play, related a very unofficial version of the official version of his working life that he had been relating to the recording device. Without the recording device, he felt more confident in being candid and telling stories that did not necessarily reflect well on the company, or the industry. In such circumstances a research interviewer, much like a journalist, can find a scoop, a real story that will change the tone and direction of the research story (some of these stories are related in Hackley (2000) and Hackley and Kover (2007)).

It is important to remember that being interviewed can be a difficult experience for the interviewee. Many interviewees will initially feel that there are things they are expected to say, points of view they are expected to hold. For example, practising managers who are being interviewed by students doing an academic research project may imply that their everyday work is more theoretically informed than it actually is. In research in marketing, some will claim that they use marketing textbook models in their work because they feel that this makes them sound more legitimate – others concede that they do not use any formal approach and simply make it up as they go along (Ardley and Quinn, 2014). This is not dishonest: we all moderate our conversational responses according to social expectations. However, a careful research interviewer will try to anticipate and deflect expectations based on conversational conventions, in order to improve the integrity of the data that is generated. In other words, the interviewer must make judgements about the interviewee's sincerity and motives. It is important to note here that in interpretive research the goal of the research interview is not to access some version of the truth that is free from 'bias'. Their role is to interpret the structure and function of what is being said. If the researcher feels that the claims made by the interviewee are not credible, then that means the data set will not be of great quality and the researcher will need to either access better quality data, or figure out why the integrity of the interview was poor and discount certain claims. The interview text does not hint at an underlying reality in interpretive research. The interview text is the reality and must be judged as a text. We will look at the matter of data interpretation in greater detail in the second half of the book.

A questionnaire-style interview agenda is rarely necessary in a research interview. This is because the value of the research interview lies, in part, in its potential for spontaneity within the interview interaction. If the interviewer seeks to control what is said by imposing their own prewritten agenda of questions and assumptions then the interviewee's insights, thoughts and reflections might be modified to a considerable extent. The trick of qualitative interviewing is to empower the interviewee while retaining control over the broad agenda. As a researcher, you cannot know this person's job, their life, their problems at work. If you really want to understand their experience as management worker in a given context, give them the space to speak.

Structured interviews, though, can be useful in some cases. For example, in the *laddering* technique of qualitative research (Bastrygina et al., 2024; Gruber et al., 2008) the interview schedule takes the interviewee through levels of involvement in a consumption decision going from utilitarian benefits of consumption through to the more abstract emotional benefits in a structured progression. The technique, originally developed to assist in generating creative ideas for advertising (Phillips and Reynolds, 2008; Reynolds and Gutman, 1988) is essentially an interpretive method (though arguably not falling within Burrell and Morgan's (1979) interpretive paradigm) for conducting qualitative interviews based on means-ends theory. It is often used in brand and marketing research and is sometimes described as an Attributes-Consequences-Value model of qualitative interviewing (see Figure 4.4). The interviewee is asked an initial question, such as 'why do you buy brand x?'. The next question responds to the interviewee's answer. If, say, they said 'because it has the quality I'm looking for', the interviewer might respond 'why is that quality important to you?' The interviewee might then refer to a particular quality that reveals something about the self-image that buying that brand supports.

Recording the data set

Qualitative interviews or focus groups should ideally be audio recorded so that the speech can be fully transcribed to printed documents if required. When the interview has come to a close, the researcher should thank the

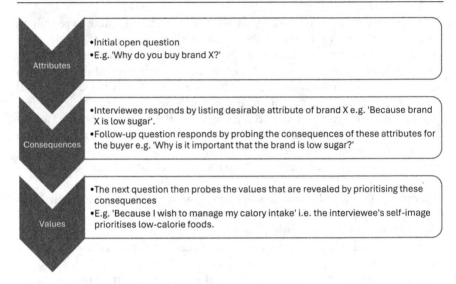

Figure 4.4 The laddering technique for qualitative depth interviews.

participant, remind them that everything in the interview will be treated confidentially and that all reporting will be anonymised. It is a very good idea to transcribe the interview into typed text soon after the interview, so that the researcher still remembers the tone, manner and intonations and gestures that gave texture to the interview responses. When transcribing, include the questions and prompts from the interviewer. In qualitative research reporting it can be useful to be able to faithfully reproduce an exchange that consisted of a conversation with several questions and/or interjections.

Audio recorded interviews can be transcribed using software or using a transcription service, but research tends to be better when the researcher who was present at the interview does the transcribing by hand, so that every word, pause, intonation and meaning is faithfully reproduced. When transcribing, it can be very useful to use *transcription conventions* (see Box 4.2) to ensure that pauses, stutters, interjections and emphases can also be reproduced in the transcribed text. The use of transcription conventions is more pertinent in the transcription of conversations in, for example, focus group discussions, but they can also be useful for adding nuance and texture to the transcription of depth interviews.

If a research interview takes one hour, it can take far longer than this to transcribe it, so do not underestimate the amount of work involved if the researcher desired to transcribe first-hand. The advantage of first-hand transcription is that the researcher has a full record of the discussion that he or she can refer to when arguing a particular point in the research report. The full transcription can be placed in the appendices of the research report so

Box 4.2   Transcription conventions

=   Indicates the absence of a discernable gap between speakers
(.)   A pause of less than 1 second
(1), (2)   A pause of 1 second, 2 seconds and so on
(...)   Some speech has been deliberately omitted
[DB laughs]   Material in square brackets is clarifying information
(DB refers to one of the participants)
They   A word or phrase underlined indicates additional emphasis
[as you can   Left square brackets indicate overlapping speech

Source: Adapted from Potter and Wetherell (1987).

that the reader can see for themselves exactly what was said and make their own judgement on the researcher's interpretation. If full transcription seems too daunting, automated transcription using relevant software or making personal notes from the audio-recording are alternatives. Direct quotes can then be used to support any point of discussion in the report, even if the full transcript will not be available for the reader to peruse. These notes can also be written immediately after the interview if the researcher feels that writing during the interview would distract the interviewee. The notes might include reflections on the manner, voice, intonation, metaphors or any other contextual feature of the interview.

The presence of accurately transcribed data extracts in the main body of the research report, supplemented by transcripts of full interviews in the appendices of the research report or dissertation, demonstrate highly committed research that the author is willing to open up to scrutiny. The presence of full transcripts (or one example with a note stating that 'data sets are available on inquiry') shows that the researcher is fully prepared to share their data and to defend their interpretation against possible alternative interpretations. If, say, ten interviews were conducted it is only necessary to provide complete transcripts of one or two in the appendices.

A further important advantage of transcribing interviews is that interviews are seldom easy to interpret on one or two hearings. In order to understand what the major themes are of a given interview, it can be necessary to hear, reflect on and reread the transcript many times. This is because what is taken-for-granted in conversation can be the most revealing, but only if it is heard so often that it ceases to be familiar. This may sound odd, but it is an important principle of interpretive research traditions that the everyday, the normal, the taken-for-granted, hides a complex social web of assumptions, codes and obscured, or forgotten, motives. In important respects, interpretive research seeks to reveal how the 'normal' is produced. This does not imply that research data generated from interviews are in some way 'biased' or even plain dishonest. The interpretive researcher takes an innocent position towards what they are told: researchers do not try to second guess 'the truth'. What they do is to try to understand where the interviewee is 'coming from' by placing their comments in the broader context of the research topic. Incidentally, having a typist copy type the interview transcript from a recording can be quite problematic. Only the most adept copy typist can capture real time conversation accurately with all its halts, false starts, ahs, ums and digressions. For truly accurate understanding of the interview, the person transcribing simply had to be there.

Focus/discussion groups

The term 'focus group' has a fairly specific meaning in some contexts of marketing research, but in this book we use the term in a general sense to refer to research data that are gathered from a small group of about three to six people, simultaneously and interactively, guided by a research convenor. Ideally, the discussion group should be physically in the same space at the same time, so they can communicate with each other as well as with the researcher. However, it is possible to convene discussion and focus groups online, although the researcher should be aware that the nature of interaction within the group will be different. The focus of discussion may be broad or narrow: the motive for the research may be exploratory, developmental, strategic or tactical (see Box 4.3).

Box 4.3   Focus/discussion group basic principles

- Group discussion sample selection need not be random but must be representative of the whole population of interest
- The group convenor's role (the researcher and/or research assistant) is to convene the meeting, ask the questions, facilitate discussion, manage the audio recording
- The group convenor should introduce the session, explain the topic and scope of interest and reassure participants of the confidentiality of the research
- Group discussions are normally audio or video recorded and then transcribed into typed texts
- The group convenor should keep interventions to a minimum if the group is relaxed, talkative and on topic. They should intervene gently to encourage the less vocal group members to contribute if they are quiet

---

Focus/discussion groups are regularly convened in marketing and advertising research to explore broad, open questions and issues. The focus group may be the most popular form of qualitative data-gathering instrument in the marketing industry, because of its convenience and potential for generating penetrating and actionable insights. In many advertising agencies, for example, getting on a train and 'doing some groups' is the first stage in the creative advertising development process (Hackley and Hackley, 2018a) when the business has been won and the agency wants to understand the relevant sector, segment and consumption practices first-hand.

The composition of the group must be *representative* of the whole population of interest. This means that it must consist of the same kinds of people as the wider population of interest in terms of age, gender, social class, interests, lifestyle or other significant variables. With this form of research, sampling is invariably purposive and convenient rather than random or systematic. If, for example, a marketing agency is investigating voter attitudes to local government policies, then clearly the group convened must be local residents of voting age. It would be useful to get a cross-section of ages in this case, but since older people are generally more likely to vote than younger people, the groups may well reflect this age imbalance. Advertising and other marketing agencies sometimes use consumer research panels that have a roster of potential interview participants of every demographic. A group of the desired demographic composition can be put together and a room hired within days. Of course, such commercially supplied groups may not necessarily yield the best quality data because the participants are self-selecting.

It is very important to understand what focus groups are good for, and what they are not good for. Focus groups are useful for exploring topics and generating ideas. They are not usually appropriate for testing concepts prior to going to market. They can be very useful for generating insights that may capture something of the character of a whole group, and there are many examples of noted advertising campaigns that were inspired by a comment in a focus group that seemed to capture the essence of a consumption practice with, say, a powerful metaphor or telling phrase. For example, if a student researcher is investigating advertising ethics, then it can be useful to convene a focus group to discuss the responses of a given demographic audience to particular advertisements. While focus group findings cannot be statistically generalised, they might well elicit a view that prevails more widely across that particular category of people, provided the group was representative of the larger population of interest.

Focus group discussions are typically audio-recorded and/or video-recorded in industrial market research settings. The researchers then replay the recordings to assess which views expressed might reflect more general positions, or which views seem to express a general insight in a particularly succinct or telling way. Contrary to popular myth, the focus group is not an appropriate way to test ideas (as we note above). Brand logos, advertisements, new product concepts, product packaging and even political ideas have all been put to the focus group test by less than rigorous market research agencies. The fact is that since focus groups are not randomised they cannot generate views or opinions that can be generalised across larger populations, hence they are not appropriate for *testing* ideas or concepts. The value of the focus group lies in its ability to generate telling insights and novel ideas at an exploratory stage of a marketing, management or consumer research issue. Focus groups offer stimulating material that can contribute to strategy discussions. The 'voice of the consumer' can then be heard in strategy and planning meetings. In research projects, the focus group can offer stimulating perspectives for further discussion and analysis in the research report.

Convening the focus group discussion

Researchers need to follow some simple rules to get the best-quality data. A focus/discussion group should ideally be comfortably seated with no noise or other distractions. The researcher needs good social skills to make the group feel at ease and to reassure members of the confidentiality and non-judgemental character of the process. The researcher also needs to have the confidence to gently intervene if discussions are being monopolised by one or two speakers, by asking quieter members of the group their view. The purpose of the research should be clearly communicated to the group. There have been cases of student researchers losing control of the theme of discussion so that the data set was not useful for the project. It is important that the researcher/focus group convenor stimulates and guides the discussion without dominating it. It can be useful to have stimulus material in the form of storyboards, pictures, role-plays or other stimuli. With focus group discussions, it is often the case that once the discussion gets going little intervention is needed from the researcher. The early stage of the group process is important in establishing the tone of the discussion, and the convenor must try to relax participants and make them feel comfortable speaking in the group, perhaps by asking them to introduce themselves if they are strangers to each other.

Recording and transcribing the discussion

Student researchers seldom need to video-tape focus group discussion, but audio-recording is always a good idea so that what has been said can be carefully examined afterwards. As with individual interviews, the task of interpreting the data is not straightforward. The transcript, or audio – recording, often needs to be read/listened to many times so that the major themes or insights become apparent. At the time of the focus group the researcher's attention is on many things so he or she cannot form insightful interpretations immediately. Transcription accuracy is important and the use of transcription conventions mentioned above can be especially useful with focus group

---

Box 4.4   A focus/discussion group transcription extract

The extract is taken from Szmigin et al. (2011) and the transcription conventions are adapted from Potter and Wetherell (1987). The conversation is about the definition of "binge" drinking (of alcohol) in the United Kingdom.

Tiffany	Yeah cos everyone's different opinion of binge drinking =
Molly	Yeah
Tiffany	= some people say oh drinking three is going on a binge
DC	mmm
Molly	See I don't drink for ages and then I'll go out and I'll get absolutely smashed off my face
Melanie	That is a binge but what about those of us that go home and have a drink every night what is that (.) binge drinking?
Dawn	[nah that's not binge drinking
Karen	[that's not binge drinking
Melanie	Well what is it then?
Karen	Just drinking
Dawn	Just drinking

Source: Rowchester FE College, March, 2006: six white British females, one Black African female; one white male, aged 18–24.

---

data because it enables accurate reproduction of interactions and conversations, such as in Box 4.4.

The data extract in Box 4.4 illustrates one way in which a focus group interaction can be reproduced using transcription conventions. Note that the data extract is fully anonymised – none of the participants' names or the college name are the real names, they have been changed to protect anonymity. Using made-up names reads better than simply putting 'Participant 1, Participant 3' and so on. Note also that demographic data are important, information such as age, gender and ethnicity help the reader to understand how representative the group was of the wider population of interest. This particular study explored the role of alcohol in the lives of young people in the United Kingdom at a time when stories of 'Binge Drinking Britain' were frequently seen in the national media, usually focusing on young people. The qualitative methods employed in the study (using focus groups, depth interviews, consumer diaries and ethnographic field notes) proved ideal for generating insights into how young people used alcohol in their social lives for purposes of friendship bonding and identity. The group discussions were especially valuable in highlighting the group dynamic within which the logic of excessive drinking played out for these young people.

The number of groups to convene depends on the topic and the nature of the research design. A master's dissertation research student of the author wanted to investigate the influence of alcohol advertising to teenagers in the United Kingdom. She convened four focus groups at three further education colleges in the West Midlands. Each group lasted about half an hour, and she used bottles of branded alcoholic drinks as physical stimuli for the discussion (for the participants to look at, not to drink!). The groups went very well, all the students had much to say about the role of alcohol, and alcohol advertising, in their social lives. The researcher loosely followed an ethnographic methodological scheme she had seen in published research literature (Ritson and Elliott, 1999) and developed a perspective that reproduced a small-scale but more closely focused version of larger studies. The focus group discussions were audio-recorded, fully transcribed and placed in the appendix of the research report. In this project, the data-gathering strategy was exceptionally thorough – it is unusual for a student researcher to be so conscientious that they gain access to focus group participants at three separate venues. It is important to note that the number of groups convened is less important than the quality of data elicited. In the above study four focus groups amounted to a very considerable data set for this topic and the participants were highly representative of the wider population of interest, that is, young people aged 18–24. In other projects, the number of focus groups convened might be fewer, or more (although more than four groups would be quite a lot for a student research project as it entails a lot of work).

Textual research and content analysis

Interpretive research traditions are well suited to textual research in which social texts of all kinds can be subject to interpretive analysis. The foregoing data-gathering techniques of research interviews and focus groups have a textual character in that they generate data sets that are converted to textual form in transcription. Other forms of text can include advertisements, emails, in-company records and documents, historical records, newspapers, visual images, television and radio, print media, course internet media and textual data elicit from research participants (Brown, 1998; Thompson, 1997). In interpretive research, a text is often defined as 'anything that can be described', that is, anything that can be rendered into words or text. For example, in advertising research, the idea of the advertisement as a social text (Stern, 1989, 1993) opened up a (then) new avenue of research that used literary theory to analyse advertising text in order to better understand the ways in which consumers react and respond to advertising (Hackley and Hackley, 2018b). Qualitative research in general has made a major contribution to advertising practice and research (Nuttall et al., 2011). Uses of literary theory in qualitative advertising research have moved on, and we develop this topic in more detail in Chapter 9.

Content analysis is a useful and flexible approach to qualitative data analysis, but it is a crude technique in some ways because the theoretical assumptions underlying content categories may not be specified. It can, however, form the basis for a more careful subsequent interpretation. The technique has a quantitative aspect in the sense that it entails counting the number of incidents of particular content in a given data set. For example, in a study of corporate mission statements (Hackley, 1998a) the content analytic framework was based on research that showed many mission statements to have similar features of content. Many made reference to the ethics of the company; many referred to the products or services that the company produced; many also referred to stakeholders in the company such as shareholders, customers or employees. These and other features of content were ticked off as each mission statement was looked at. In this way, a quantitative basis for interpretation was generated. The researcher could say that so many per cent of mission statements in a given data set displayed specific content features.

The interpretation of these features is a separate matter: why they were there, what they were intended to accomplish, what motives they implied, how effective they seemed to be, are all matters of interpretive judgement beyond content analysis. Similarly, if, say, magazine advertisements are subject to a content analysis by counting the portrayals of sexuality in a given sample and time frame, the results could inform a discussion, but the content analysis in itself tells the researcher nothing about the reasons why these portrayals of sexuality were there, or what kind of portrayals they were. The content analysis could, however, provide a basis for further reasoning and informed interpretation.

Content analyses of textual data can be expressed simply as percentages, or more colourfully as bar charts, pie charts or histograms. One researcher examining changing representations of gender in UK magazine advertisements generated graphical representations of the content analytic data set that clearly showed marked changes in the number of advertisements that showed women as independent of, or as socially dependent on and subservient to, men, over a time period. While such analyses can be stimulating and revealing, they clearly depend on a way of categorising textual data that would not necessarily be agreed upon by everyone because a degree of subjective judgement is required to decide whether or not a particular ad fulfils the category criteria set by the researcher cannot be agreed on by everyone.

There are two main ways to deal with this subjectivity in content analysis research reporting. One is to make the content categories clear to the reader and to reproduce the advertisements (or whatever data set is being used) in question in the report appendices. In this way, transparency of interpretation can be achieved so that the researcher can argue in favour of their preferred interpretation of text. The reader can then decide for themselves whether the researcher's position seems plausible to them. A second technique is to test content analytic categories to see if another person would make the same interpretation. In this way the researcher can offer evidence as to the *inter-subjective reliability* of their content analytic categories. This can never be an entirely satisfactory approach since the researcher cannot test their categories with every kind of person. It is, however, rhetorically powerful to show that the researcher's position is not purely a matter of subjective opinion but has been supported by another researcher.

Digitisation and textual data sets

There are many variations of textual research, including digital texts, some of which we will look at later in the book, for example in the section on digital ethnography. What we have tried to do here is to look at the basic data-gathering techniques without getting too deeply into the interpretive framing, which we begin to do in the next chapter. In using the category 'textual analysis' to head this section we are trying to begin with the simple principle that words and text can be subject to all manner of analysis purely according to how categories of content are defined. Researchers can look for the repeated use or incidence of single words, of phrases, or metaphors or idiomatic expressions, depending on the goals of the study.

Textual analysis cuts across all kinds of texts so that imagery can be included (as in the example above regarding print advertisements) but also digital text can be subject to the same search criteria. Indeed, such searches for content can be done with software (Humphreys and Wang, 2018) and there are plenty of software packages (such as nVivo) that are advertised as qualitative data analysis packages. Such software packages are very useful for analysing large volumes of text very efficiently, but they are essentially content analytic programmes. Digital qualitative analysis software misses the nuances of personal interaction that took place within the focus group or interview (Catterall and Maclaran, 1997) and which can be crucial for the interpretation of meaning in the data set. Software analysis tools can only be as good as the categories fed into them, and the categories in interpretive research are framed by the theoretical perspective. We would differentiate between content analysis and interpretive analysis, since the former is a matter of counting incidents (at which software is very good), whilst the latter is a matter of interpreting content according to a theoretical perspective.

Stephens-Davidowitz (2017) refers to several online sources of 'big' textual data, such as Google Trends and Google Ngrams. Cleverly conceived searches can reveal very interesting and often counter-intuitive findings by searching for particular words or phrases in all the digitised text that exists in book depositories, news story archives or social media platforms. Indeed, private emails can also be used for this, but non-Google employees have to scrape publicly available data banks since emails and other personal content are ostensibly private. Stephens-Davidowitz (2017) is undoubtedly correct when he says that Google and other search engine data banks offer unique and intriguing sources of insight into human psychology, and he offers several striking examples of prevailing or conventional opinion being soundly de-bunked by creative use of search terms in Google Trends.

However, powerful as such text-driven studies are, they suffer from two main problems. One is that they tell us little about human psychology as such because they are culturally and demographically specific. Using digital data sets is not the same as practicing digital ethnography (Pink et al., 2016). To be sure, the databases in large search engines such as Google allow for a high degree of demographic specificity when setting the parameters for a search. Nonetheless, they suffer from the same problem that afflicted one of the most famous market research failures in history, when one of the largest surveys then conducted of 2.4 million readers of the respected US magazine the *Literary Digest* failed to predict the winner of the 1936 US election by a huge margin of error of 19 per cent. The problem was, sampling error. That is, the participants in the survey, Readers Digest readers, were not representative of the wider population of US voters. Where a sample is not representative of the wider group of interest, it doesn't matter how large the sample is – the result will still be wrong. All Google surveys of text will, similarly, suffer from selection bias and non-response bias. Of course, data scientists are well aware of this limitation of their field and carefully couch their findings in caveats and conditionals whilst devising every more fine-grained forms of analysis to try to reduce the margin of error.

The second main problem with digital Big Data sources for text search is that the searches for words or phrases can be very cleverly designed but they lack a theoretical framing. Consequently, while the findings may be stimulating, counterintuitive, provocative and sometimes actionable for, say, health policy or political marketing strategies, they cannot usually inform a theoretical understanding of the world. *Empirical generalisations* give us intriguing *correlations* but tell us nothing about *causation*. The basis for this book, in contrast, is that theoretical framing for interpretive research can generate insights that can be integrated with other theoretically informed findings to build scientific knowledge.

Thematic analysis and coding

Thematic analysis (Braun and Clarke, 2006) is a way of analysing textual data sets that is not necessarily theoretically driven, but which goes beyond the content analytic search for precise words or phrases and tries instead to code data searches with more abstract concepts that might be expressed with quite different arrangements of words and phrases. Thematic analysis is

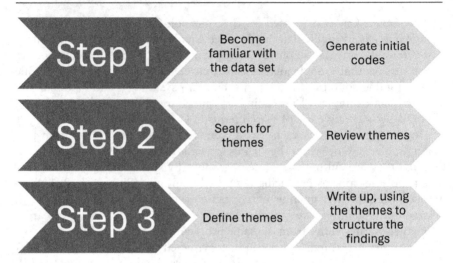

Figure 4.5 Braun and Clarke's (2006) framework for thematic analysis

often preoccupied with meaning, hence it tends to fall within the interpretive research paradigm, although it is not tied necessarily to specific theories. This makes thematic analysis particularly flexible for qualitative studies.

One possible sequence for doing thematic analysis can be seen in Figure 4.5. Figure 4.5 does not capture the qualitative evaluation of the data sets that leads to the generation of initial codes and eventual thematic categories, just the sequence of activities. Doing thematic analysis can be a creative and as-similative process that happens when the researcher becomes immersed in the data sets and begins to see patterns of meaning that structure the data sets. Maguire and Delahunt (2017) differentiate between theoretical coding, in which the researcher looks for particular themes that respond to the research question, and inductive coding, in which the researcher has no presuppositions about what they will find, and the initial codes emerge inductively from the analysis of data sets. Some researchers establish initial codes and then use qualitative data analytical software such as ATLAS or Nvivo. This is useful for large data sets but essentially reduces thematic analysis to content analysis by taking out a level of the interpretive process.

Grounded Theory (GT) (Glaser and Strauss, 1967) tends to use a version of inductive coding for thematic analysis. It seeks patterns of meaning in qualitative data sets. GT 'open' coding is consistent with thematic analysis in the sense that the researcher analysing textual data sets has the license to use some imagination as they look through the data sets and think of abstract categories that capture the sentiments, practices or other aspects of interest in the data sets. This process of coding precedes the development or the emergence of themes as an iterative process.

As noted above, thematic analysis might proceed with an idea of what it is that the data analyst is looking for, driven by a particular research question, while GT seeks to develop creative theoretical themes that 'emerge' inductively from the data analysis. In other words, the researcher looks through the data sets from an a-theoretical perspective in GT. Once the themes or categories have emerged and coding takes place to sift the data sets for incidents that contain the relevant themes, the GT researcher will look for linkages with existing theory and, if necessary, go back to the literature review to reposition the study.

GT is a well-established form of qualitative data analysis although it is not really an interpretive approach in the sense that data sets are approached with no theoretical framing. GT findings can consequently sometimes appear rather descriptive, unless they are successfully hooked into a theoretical frame a posteriori. It is very difficult to say that researchers can approach data sets with no presumptions whatsoever about the nature of what they are looking for or what they will find. It could be argued that GT essentially tries to erase the interpretive process that is, inevitably, taking place. The difference between GT and interpretive research is that interpretive research makes its presumptions, assumptions and values explicit by locating a study within a theoretical frame.

Observation as qualitative research data

Naturalistic, participant and non-participant observation

Observation is a research technique that is often implicit, informally, in data-gathering approaches. If we go to a company to interview a manager for a research study, we observe the manner and style of personnel as we walk through the organisation premises, we watch the way managers and subordinates interact, we note the quality of the furniture, how good the company restaurant is (and if there is one), we notice whether people seem happy, relaxed, aggressive, defensive, smart, depressed or whatever. We form implicit and intuitive judgements from these observations. Similarly, if we interview consumers to understand their experience of a category of consumption practice, our interpretation of what they say is influenced by our observations of their manner, tone, gesture and vocabulary. Observation is something that we cannot fail to do as people: we are all observers, and it makes perfect sense to utilise this social skill as researchers.

When we go shopping, or go to a restaurant, to the cinema or to a night-club, we observe others and their behaviour in that environment. In our own interactions with marketing, we are acting as unpaid, informal consumer researchers, forming judgements about the provision of a service or the competence of an organisation that will inform our own future consumer behaviour and that of others with whom we share our experiences and reflections. We continue to make observations and judgements when we conduct research studies. Informal observation is, then, an integral part of interpretive research. Our observations furnish the context that informs our judgements.

More formal uses of observation in social research include 'naturalistic' observation, experimental observation, 'action re – search' and 'participant' or 'non-participant' observation. Naturalistic observation entails observing people and their behaviour in their natural environment. For example, a study of the night time economy around the drug taking 'rave' club dance scene entailed participant observation as well as interviews (Goulding et al., 2009), as did a study of young people and alcohol in which research assistants were enlisted to make observations on a night out with participants and write up ethnographic fields notes as part of the data set (Griffin et al., 2009). These examples of observation were naturalistic in the sense that the group of interest were observed going about their business as they typically would. In this way, the research was lent a quality of *ecological validity*. Experimental observation, in contrast, would entail setting up an artificial situation to watch participant behaviour in an experimentally designed setting. Setting up an artificial observation for experimental purposes, for example, by asking participants to respond to questions about an advertisement viewed in a viewing booth, does not observe ecological validity since it is not the way that advertisements would normally be viewed by TV viewers who would typically watch TV in the company of friends or family (Ritson and Elliott, 1999). It is a common criticism of experimental research (both quantitative and qualitative) that research designs might lack ecological validity. That is, the contrived situation might not replicate the way that people would encounter that situation in normal social interaction.

Each of these techniques involves the researcher in the process that is being studied. For example, many researchers in the *ethnographic* tradition spend lengthy periods in the company or industry that they are researching. In some cases, they take part in the activities by fulfilling a role in the process. During and after their working day they will make *field notes* that record their observations and impressions. Later they will use these field notes as data from which they will compile their research report. We will develop more detail on ethnographic research in Chapter 7.

Observational research can sometimes take the form of intervening in a social situation to see what results. In a famous naturalistic experiment conducted by Darley and Batson (1973) seminary trainees were sent across campus to conduct a task, and some were told that they were late had to hurry. A man in distress, in a state of near collapse, had been placed on their route. The experiment was to see how many of the trainees stopped to help the man. The conclusion found that the 'good 'Samaritan' effect of people stopping to help a stranger depends on situational factors as well as personality.

Researcher/observers who are not seeking to intervene in a social situation should normally try to be as unobtrusive as possible in carrying out their non-participant observation. If they have been granted access to an organisation to shadow an employee or to watch management processes, they should at all times consider the ethical issues of confidentiality and discretion. It is a privilege to be granted research access to a company. It is inappropriate in reporting such research to report anything that may embarrass the participant or reveal commercially sensitive information. Speakers in reported dialogue should always be anonymised in the research report. The company itself should not be named or recognisable unless by agreement. The non-participant observer should act as a 'fly on the wall', present and observant but not intervening in the social processes that they observe.

Research diaries

Research diaries can be useful if the researcher is seeking an *experiential* perspective from the research participant. The participant is asked to keep a diary of their subjective thoughts, reflections and feelings relating to a particular event or experience over a given period of time. The disadvantage of research diaries is that they can generate vast amounts of data that can be difficult to interpret. Their advantage is that they offer an intimate channel into some aspect of an individual's experience, provided that people can be relied upon to fill in the diary conscientiously. If, say, a researcher can persuade a senior executive of a firm to keep a diary during a hostile takeover, this would clearly offer a very different research perspective than any other form of data gathering. It is equally clear that such data would need to be handled very sensitively and discretely by the researcher. Diaries can be kept over varying periods of time. They can be written at any time of the day, or at specific times. They can be detailed and analytical or general and personal. It all depends on the researcher's aims and interests.

The interpretation of diary data takes some skill on the part of the researcher. Comments in a diary can be fragmented and difficult to group into thematic categories. As with all qualitative data analysis, the most penetrating analyses result from having a well-informed interpretive perspective. This will give the researcher the theoretical background to generate supported insights from the data. One study conducted by an advertising agency used a *deprivation study* sometimes used by cultural anthropologists. The agency researcher enlisted music fans and asked them to give up their home audio music playing equipment for a period of time. They were asked to use the diary to articulate their experience whenever they felt the loss of the music equipment. The agency wanted to understand the roles that music played in peoples' lives, and the diaries related how some people missed it most in the mornings when they got ready for work, some missed it most in the evenings when they relaxed after work, others missed it when they were getting ready for a night out and so on. The insights generated informed the advertising strategy and creative work.

Researchers themselves can also keep research diaries. These would be supplemental to field notes and would assist in reflexive analysis of the research process. Research diaries can be useful for recording events and times, so that the chronology of events can be recorded for later reference. Subjective impressions and feelings about the research process can also be revealing in the light of information received later, so recording these carefully as the research unfolds can be useful.

Case study research

Case study research is well-established at every level of education, particularly in the business and management areas. Case studies are common as qualitative studies (Bryman, 2012), but the case study often uses mixed methods in addition to the case material. The 'case study' is a wrapper for quite a wide range of studies of differing method and ontology, focusing on either single or multiple and comparative cases. The idea of the case is that it should be bounded in some way, focusing on the business of organisation, a problem or issue or on two or more examples for comparative case studies.

For Yin (2014) the case study is not merely a data-gathering approach but a method with a distinct research design. However, although the case study can be a very useful approach for packaging a research study, particularly a practical study focused on a specified problem, it is difficult to locate in a sociological paradigm. It is, really, a kind of storytelling (Gabriel, 2017). The case study seems too often be used within an implicitly realist/positivistic framework in the sense that there is emphasis placed on verification of results, as if the case findings ought to be generalisable. Given the limited sample of the case study, generalisability in a positivistic sense is not achievable. Case studies can be used in a research design that includes a theoretical stance and this can be a useful way of organising data sets and structuring the data gathering and analysis.

Case studies are often used in qualitative studies without, necessarily, any theoretical framing. As noted earlier, 'qualitative' research in general is often conducted without an explicit theoretical framing, and whilst there is inevitably an element of interpretation as there is in all research, this does not mean that qualitative research case studies necessarily fall within the interpretive paradigm (see Chapter 5 for more on sociological paradigms). Qualitative data analysis often does apply analytical approaches that are taken from interpretive research traditions (Spiggle, 1994), but the term 'qualitative' by itself does not tell you the implicit assumptions that underpinned the data gathering and analysis. Saying that a research project is a case study leaves much unsaid, since it does not explain the theoretical assumptions that guided the choice of data sets and the analytical approach that generated findings.

Case study analysis has a distinguished pedigree. The world-famous Harvard Business School made the case study the central pillar of their teaching.

Originally, students would study the available information on a particular organisational management problem, and they would also visit the organisation to see first-hand what its methods were and to speak to its managers. In other words, there was an element of ethnography to the case method in the sense that researchers did not rely on second-hand information but gained direct personal experience of the organisation and its people. The students would subsequently return to the classroom, offer their analysis of the business issues and problems facing that company, and debate this with the students and faculty. The aim of this was two-fold. By analysing the case and then debating their analysis with colleagues and professors, student researchers might develop skills of advocacy and critique (Contardo and Wensley, 1999). Through this demanding process they sharpened their understanding of case situated business practices, along with their skills of debate and argument.

Many research studies that are labelled as using a case-study method rely on pre-existing information such as company and industry reports and other publications. Some employ an *ethnographic* style if the researcher can gain access to a company to observe processes personally, from within the organisational setting. Others draw on data from depth interviews with company managers. Some case studies use a comparative approach by taking several cases and making comparisons between them of particular managerial issues or processes, while others focus on a detailed analysis of the single case situation. Gerring (2006) refers to ideographic case analyses, which offer detailed analyses of single case situations, and nomothetic case analyses, in which many cases are analysed quantitatively to try to draw generalised conclusions. Some cases are conducted over a specified time period, others over many years, called *longitudinal* case studies. It can be very instructive to return to particular cases over time to see how the data change. Case study research can use interviews, surveys, observation and participant observation and any other of the range of qualitative data-gathering methods, they can use a sample of one case or many, and they can use descriptive forms of data analysis, or they can be used with any of the interpretive theories discussed in the latter half of this book. The flexibility of the case method is its great strength for application to a huge range of situations with a variety of methods.

This chapter, then, has taken a practical perspective to point out some of the difficulties and advantages of various qualitative data-gathering techniques. In keeping with the theme of the book as a whole, the chapter has taken the view that data-gathering techniques are implicitly theoretical in the sense that they carry assumptions about the nature of their subject of study and the kinds of analyses that are useful and appropriate. The next chapter will look in more detail at some key concepts of interpretive research, before moving into the second half of the book with an introduction to some of the most influential approaches for theoretical framing of interpretive research.

Glossary

Convenience sampling A sample frame that is convenient in the sense that participants should be relatively easy to access.

Correlation A statistical relationship between two things. Correlation does not imply *causation*, that is, just because there seems to be a prima facie statistical link between two phenomena, this does not mean that one causes the other.

Deprivation study An approach used in cultural ethnography and sociology, which entails asking a participant to go without something, an activity or an object, and then record how they feel in its absence. It is a way of generating insight into the symbolic role of a practice or object in the life experience of participants.

Ecological validity A research method that allows participants to act as they would in their everyday lives is said to have ecological validity, whereas a method that sets up an artificial situation for the purpose of research, does not.

Empirical generalisations A statistical relationship between two or more variables.

Ethnographic research Ethnography is a research technique made popular in anthropology. It entails trying to see the world through the eyes of a particular group with reference to their own cultural values and symbolic practices. Anthropologists have often lived for up to two years with the group they are researching. Management researchers tend to use quasi-ethnographic studies based on much shorter data-gathering periods (i.e. a few days).

Experiential The *experiential* perspective has evolved from humanistic psychology and phenomenological philosophy. It values the experience of the research participant and often seeks to empower research participants by facilitating constructive reflection and informed reasoning.

Field notes Term from anthropology referring to notes, observations, reflections, details and questions written down by the researcher during their period of 'field' research. Management researchers conducting ethnographic research in host organisations would usually make use of field notes.

Idiographic Research approaches that do not seek universal generalisations but, rather, seek insight into a subject's experience by taking into account all their biographical detail.

Inter-subjective reliability Reliability refers to research approaches that generate the same findings in different cases; inter-subjective means agreed upon by two or more people, so inter-subjective reliability means that an interpretation has been agreed upon by the subjective evaluation of two or more people.

Longitudinal research Data-gathering phases that are repeated over time so that a long term picture is taken of a situation.

Nomothetic Nomothetic research seeks truths that are universal and can be statistically significant.

Observation and participant observation   (discussed in Chapter 7) entails the researcher being immersed in a social group and observing the practices, behaviour and interaction of the group, either as a 'fly on the wall' non-participant, or as an active participant and member of the group.

Pilot studies   A pilot data-gathering exercise is conducted prior to the main study. A pilot interview or focus group can be useful to ensure that the sample and interview agenda are right, and also to practise interviewing or other qualitative research skills.

Practice theory   (see also Chapter 9) A theoretical stance on symbolic social practices that can be employed in qualitative research studies.

Purposive sample   Used to describe a sample frame, purposive means the same was generated according to set criteria to suit a particular purpose or objective.

Representative   Interpretive researchers seek samples that are not statistically random but are analogous to the larger research population in significant respects.

Transcription conventions   A system of indicating the pauses, tone and other quirks of natural conversation in written text.

Universalised   A concept from positivist/realist research that refers to a finding that can be regarded as true in all circumstances.

Chapter 5

Sociological paradigms and research philosophy

Abstract

Theoretically informed qualitative research studies need to be 'set up' in the sense that key assumptions about the nature of the social research task need to be clarified at the outset because they influence the way that research questions, method, analysis and findings are all conceived. Some of the key concepts and methods of qualitative/interpretive research have been introduced in Chapters 1–4. This chapter gives deeper consideration to theoretical framing for interpretive studies, particularly with regard to the location of interpretive studies within a sociological paradigm. The chapter then goes on to discuss theoretically informed interpretive data analysis.

Chapter objectives

After reading this chapter students will be able to

- grasp the key assumptions of the main sociological paradigms
- understand more of the technical vocabulary of interpretive social research
- frame a research study in the appropriate paradigm
- understand more of the philosophical principles of interpretive data analysis

The interpretive stance and empirical knowledge

We have noted earlier in the book that interpretation in and of itself is not a matter unique to qualitative research. It is an element of all research, and of all knowledge (O'Shaughnessy, 2009). For Holbrook and O'Shaughnessy (1988) 'all knowledge and all science depend on interpretation' (p. 398). It can be useful sometimes to ground the activity of research by standing back from theoretical perspectives to ask naïve philosophical questions, such as, how is knowledge about the world possible? One traditional 'problem' of Western epistemology is that we cannot know 'the world as it is': we can only

DOI: 10.4324/9781003432203-7

know it through our sense perceptions, that is, empirically (David Hume's work, *A Treatise on Human Understanding*, is a famous expression of this idea). We have no way of knowing if our sense perceptions are deceiving us. You could be dreaming that you are reading this book. You have no way of being absolutely certain that you are not. There is a further problem with this truism. We cannot 'know' the electronic impulses that are our senses. We can only interpret them, that is, we can ascribe meaning to them by finding words that seem to express what we feel or see. This problem gave form to the contrasting philosophical positions of empiricism and rationalism, empiricism being the knowledge of the world we gain through our sense perception, and rationalism being the knowledge we gain through our internal thought and reason. For interpretive researchers, knowledge of the world is gained through a combination of both empiricism and rational thought. Through our senses we gain knowledge of the world, which we interpret using our reason.

For most interpretive researchers, knowledge of the social world requires a different method of interpretation to knowledge of the natural physical world, because the nature of each is different. Empirical social research on a realist model assumes that social reality is just as concrete and stable as physical reality, at least for the purposes of social research. So, social reality can be investigated using the same methods as physical science. This is the realist/positivist ontology of social science to which we have referred earlier in the book. The 1959 Ford and Carnegie reports on American business school research and teaching lamented its un-scientific character and called for a greater emphasis on the scientific study of business and management. This was interpreted as a call to use the research methods of natural science. American University Business Schools have prioritised such methods ever since, and many others around the world have followed (Hackley, 2024).

In contrast, most interpretive researchers agree that the social world is different from the natural physical world. Social reality is seen as being constructed through social interaction in a far-reaching sense: social reality is a social construction (Berger and Luckman, 1966). This social constructionist ontology of social life is of course very different to the realist ontology, and each applies different epistemologies of knowledge. In particular, socially constructed reality has to be conveyed through rich analytic descriptions of social situations, it cannot be conveyed through generalised propositions. This is where interpretivist research, and realist research, are incompatible paradigms in the sense that their differing assumptions cannot be reconciled. Nonetheless, as we have seen, interpretation takes place in all social research, regardless of the paradigm. The difference is between, on the one hand, regarding interpretation as a source of bias and making efforts to eliminate it by seeking objectivity, and, on the other, acknowledging the inevitability of interpretation and incorporating it into the paradigmatic assumptions and methods of social research.

Interpretivism and Big Data

We touched upon the issue of digital data scraping in the previous chapter. In the age of Big Data, it is tempting to suppose that questions of social research can be answered simply by finding the right Big Data banks to scrape, and by asking the right questions. Importantly, the seductive and undeniably fascinating potential of Big Data as a research resource (Stephens-Davidowitz, 2017) does not mean that interpretation is not necessary. Some things are even beyond AI and algorithms, as Craig Thompson (2019) pointed out when he argued that Big Data myths can lead to ontologically confused opportunism;

> I argue that culturally oriented marketing researchers should promote a different ontological frame – the analytics of marketplace assemblages – to address how big data, or more accurately its socio-technical infrastructure, produces new kinds of emergent and hybrid market structures, modes of social aggregation, consumption practices, and prosumptive capacities.
>
> (p. 207)

Here, Thompson (2019) is pointing out that data scraping and algorithm-driven analytics lack the critical interpretation that is made possible by theoretical framing. He suggests a particular approach, assemblage theory (Deleuze and Guattari, 1987), to place context around the findings of Big Data. While assemblage theory is one of many possible theoretical frames for interpretive research (see, for example, Canniford and Shankar, 2013; Carrington and Ozanne, 2022; Hoffman and Novak, 2018; Molander, Ostberg and Peñaloza, 2023).

Thompson's (2019) point that taking a naïve empiricist approach to Big Data is potentially misleading, is clear. Digital data-gathering techniques and analytics have biases built into them, and they suffer from sample error and, crucially, non-response error, so the kinds of behavioural conclusions that can be drawn from Big Data) lack a theoretical grounding and are sharply constrained within a narrow cultural context. Rather like the 'nudge' theories of behavioural economics (Thaler and Sunstein, 2008), Big Data analytics can generate facts that lead to predictions, such as the fact (pointed out by Stephens-Davidowitz, 2017) that the pre-eminence of racist terms in Google searches by region seemed to predict political affiliation and voting behaviour in the United States prior to the 2016 Presidential election. However, they cannot explain the underlying reasons for the behaviour. Thompson (2019) is calling for a critical interpretive standpoint somewhat overlapping with the Radical Humanist paradigm (of which more below) and warning of the naïve reliance on Big Data without theory to guide its interpretation.

Theoretical 'framing' of interpretive research

Framing a research study means to acknowledge and be explicit about the deep assumptions upon which it is based, and being aware of the implications these assumptions have for the interpretation of findings. To put this another way, framing research studies means demonstrating that the researcher understands the ontological position they are taking with their research questions and method, and that they are also aware of the epistemological implications for their analysis. Certain research questions and philosophies fit better with one paradigm than with others. Framing a study plausibly, that is, understanding what the main paradigmatic assumptions of the research question and research design are, helps an enormous amount in interpretive research because it enables the researcher to pull together the various stands of the study into a coherent whole.

Interpretive research traditions do overlap each other, distinctions blur, there are tensions and disagreements (Alexander and Smith, 2001; Giesler and Thompson, 2016; Hudson and Ozanne, 1988; MacInnis and Folkes, 2010) even though, or because, many interpretive research traditions share similar positions on epistemology, method and scope. Some published researchers take a broad stance and frame their work as 'interpretive' (e.g. Hirschman, 1989; Szmigin and Carrigan, 2001) or 'qualitative' (Spiggle, 1994). This does not mean that their work is a-theoretical and merely descriptive, but it can mean that they have chosen not to frame their research within a specified theoretical approach. For student researchers, it often is fine to do this. Many university supervisors and departments would not expect a Master's or undergraduate student to be familiar with research philosophy for the independent research project. However, it is always best to also be able to defend the position of interpretivism by knowing what is implied in it, and likewise if the study is labelled as a qualitative study.

Many published academic authors frame their work in terms that emphasise specified theoretical traditions and/or data-gathering approaches (see Box 5.1) such as naturalistic research (Belk, 1991; Belk et al., 1988), existential phenomenology (Askegaard and Linnett, 2011; Thompson et al., 1990), anthropology (Appau and Crockett, 2023), semiotics (Chandler, 2002; Holbrook and Grayson, 1986), discourse analysis (Ardley and Quinn, 2014; Hackley, 2000), literary theory (Brown, 1999, 2016a; Hackley et al., 2013), poststructuralism (Elliott and Ritson, 1997), postcolonialism (Varman, Belk and Sreekumar, 2023), subjective personal introspection (Brown, 1998; Holbrook, 2018; Shankar, 2000), postmodernism (Brown, 1994), rhetoric (Brown et al., 2018; Miles, 2014; Scott, 1990), critical marketing (Tadajewski, 2014; Tadajewski et al., 2019), humanistic research (Stern and Schroeder, 1994), narrative analysis (Shankar et al., 2001; Stern et al., 1998), ideology (Schmitt, Joško Brakus and Biraglia, 2022; Thompson and Coskuner-Balli, 2007), practice theory (Ghaffari et al., 2019; Skålén and Hackley, 2011),

---

Box 5.1   Framing the research study

Non-theoretically informed frames

Qualitative, interpretive, thematic analysis, content analysis and case study

Theoretically informed framing

Existential phenomenology
Critical theory
Ethnography
Practice theory
Postmodern/poststructuralist
Discourse analysis/critical discourse analysis
Postcolonialism
Humanistic
Literary theory (semiotics, intertextuality)
Autoethnography/subjective personal introspection
Ideology
Assemblage theory
Philosophy (rhetoric)
Anthropology

---

social phenomenology (Svensson, 2007), assemblage theory (Preece et al., 2019) and many more, including others cited throughout this book.

Specifying the research tradition(s) in which a research project is located can be useful because of the different emphases and assumptions of each tradition about data gathering, interpretive process and epistemology. A student research project that explicitly states that it draws on a particular theoretical perspective immediately makes favourable signals to the person reading and assessing it. A defined theoretical perspective implies that the researcher has attempted to think through the implications and scope of their research questions. It also implies that the researcher is aware of the need to make assumptions explicit and to refer to previously published research. Finally, it suggests that the researcher will attempt to write a research report that is coherent: its aims, method and analysis will all 'hang together' and make sense in terms of each other.

It was mentioned earlier in this book that multi-method approaches, combining useful features of more than one approach, can be fruitful. Many research studies are innovative in adapting data-gathering methods that are typically used in one research design, for use in another. However, all such

- Paradigm
- Data gathering methods
- Research questions
- Analysis, findings, implications

Ontology, epistemology, data gathering methods

Types of data set gathered, sampling frame and analytical approach

Type, scope, aims, implied ontology

Scope of implications e.g. rich sociological description or generalised hypotheses

Figure 5.1 The role a theoretical perspective plays in 'pulling a research project together'

adaptation requires some understanding of why particular aims, methods and analyses seem to fit together while others do not. The theoretical coherence of the research study is important. Mixed method studies can be located within single paradigms, and this can give the whole a sense of coherence even where the element of the study, the data-gathering approaches and analytical methods, may be quite diverse.

Figure 5.1 indicates the inter-connectedness of research paradigm, research questions, data-gathering method, analytical approach and the implications for findings. If the student researcher has a basic grasp of the key paradigmatic assumptions discussed below, then the research design is more likely to fall into place as a coherent whole. It can be particularly useful to combine two theoretical traditions if they fall within the same broad paradigm. For example, in Ghaffari et al. (2019), the practice theory approach was embedded within an ethnographic study. The lead researcher spent more than a year in an advertising agency as a non-participant observer, conducting interviews, sitting in on meetings and making field notes. Ethnography informed the data-gathering stance whilst practice theory informed the theoretical lens through which data analysis was conducted.

Research paradigms in physical, and social, science

The idea of a scientific 'paradigm' is a term popularised by Kuhn (1970). A paradigm is a set of explicit and implicit assumptions about how research should be conducted in the pursuit of scientific knowledge. A paradigm entails a 'world view', a position on the very nature of the phenomenon being studied. Academic management and marketing researchers often argue that certain 'paradigms' or sets of assumptions are more correct or better in practice than others. Of course, the basic dispute in business and management research is between the realists and the interpretivists. The realists/structuralists make the ontological assumption that the social world can rightfully be treated the same way for research purposes as the natural world. The interpretivists argue that the social world is inherently different to the natural world, so it needs different methods to understand it. This is an oversimplification of a complex debate, but it does point to the fundamental incompatibility of some research paradigms.

An important distinction between realist/structuralist and interpretive research concerns the question of what is being sought. Realist/structuralists seek universal truths that can be confirmed under all circumstances. But, as one interpretive argument goes, life does not have to *mean* anything to an atom. Humans, in contrast to atoms, try to make sense of their world. Indeed, seeking meaning is a defining characteristic of human beings. Social research is concerned with people and their activities, including the activities of organising, managing and consuming. As such, for interpretive researchers, it is concerned with meaning since the primary activity of humans in any given context is to make sense of their lived experience, to render it meaningful.

Kuhn's (1970) classic book drew attention to the way that certain data-gathering techniques and analytical methods become taken for granted over time as the only right way to do scientific research in a particular field. What is taken for granted can become so dominant that new researchers in the field are often not even aware that other ways exist. They are simply tutored in the way that their supervisor does research, and they don't necessarily have a critical grasp of alternative methods. Alternative ways of understanding and doing research cease to be part of taught courses and texts over time. Consequently, as Kuhn (1970) suggested, it takes a 'revolution' in knowledge to make people realise that what seemed a good way of conceiving of new knowledge for a long time was not, in fact, the only way.

Business Schools are especially prone to this tendency since they began to grow their own PhD programmes in the 1960s (Hackley, 2024). The supervisors know one methodological paradigm, and they teach their PhD students the same paradigm, who then pass the same knowledge on to future generations students. It can be seen today in the research publications of the structuralist/realist paradigm in business and management area which typically focus their method section on the technicalities of sample selection and statistical technique and do not take the trouble to justify the paradigm, because its appropriateness is simply taken for granted by editors and reviewers who do not question its assumptions. Qualitative research in business and management, on the other hand, tends to have an elaborate philosophical justification in the method section, even in the journals that are relatively friendly to qualitative and interpretive research. Since quantitative research in a realist/structuralist paradigm remains the dominant research approach, every alternative contribution still needs to be justified.

This persists in spite of decades of passionate debates about the relation research in marketing and management should have to research in the physical sciences (Arndt, 1985; Hunt, 2003). Arndt (1985) suggested some 40 years ago that marketing was "dominated by the logical empiricist paradigm stressing rationality, objectivity, and measurement" (p. 11). Arndt's (1985) logical empiricist paradigm broadly falls within Burrell and Morgan's (1979) functionalist paradigm (see Figure 5.2). Arndt (1985) called for a wider understanding of other paradigms, which would benefit the academic field of marketing research. In spite of regular outbreaks of similar calls in the marketing journals, a paradigmatic imbalance remains today, even though there is a greater plurality of methods. Arguably, the consumer research field, which strangely, is treated as being distinct from the marketing research field in many faculties, has demonstrated a greater degree of plurality in its top journals than has marketing. One journal, the *Journal of Consumer Research*, regularly publishes articles based on qualitative anthropological and sociological studies (e.g. Weinberger et al., 2017) and many recent examples are cited later in the second half of this book.

Figure 5.2 Burrell and Morgan's (1979: 2019) sociological paradigms

The philosophy of science debates have, more or less, died out in the top marketing journals. Researchers forge careers in the bubble of each paradigm, and few operate across the paradigms, because this takes rare talent. This book takes the position that research is served by many differing approaches, but it is a book that focuses clearly on one paradigm: the interpretivist paradigm. Most importantly, the book takes a pragmatic view on research. Student researchers do not have to be experts in philosophy of science to understand some of the philosophical issues that are debated. If student researchers can demonstrate some understanding of the basic principles of differing paradigms, this will be of great help to them in devising creative and coherent research designs that are paradigmatically coherent.

Sociological paradigms revisited

When we write of interpretive research we are referring to a paradigm of research, roughly mapping onto Burrell and Morgan's (1979) sociological paradigms (see Figure 5.2) as mentioned in Chapter 1. Foxall (1995) suggested that no single model of science can capture the interrelation of different assumptions that act together in scientific research (p. 8). This is fair, but, nonetheless, Burrell and Morgan (1979)'s scheme is still frequently referred to as a touchpoint in discussions on research paradigms as it captures some key assumptions of the different paradigms in a way that can apply broadly to many examples of research in each paradigm. Burrell and Morgan (1979: 2019) were organisational researchers who argued that all the different ways academics research organisations were characterised by assumptions that each made about the nature of knowledge (epistemology) and the nature of social life (ontology). The different ways of looking at organisations theoretically through differing sets of assumptions, they termed paradigms. For an academic researcher, working in a particular paradigm is to work from the basis of a particular world view.

Many researchers have perfectly good careers in academic work neither knowing nor caring very much about the world view implied in their approach to research. Indeed, many would simply reject the idea that their work conforms straightforwardly to a paradigm, the world (and social research) being both too complex and too pragmatic to fit neatly into a paradigm. Burrell and Morgan (1979) felt that it was important to make the deep assumptions implied in research approaches explicit, not because every study must take sides in a philosophy of science debate, but because it is only by making the deep paradigmatic assumptions explicit in research that the coherence of the research can be fairly judged and assessed. Understanding something about social scientific paradigms is therefore essential for people who want to read social research and scholarship critically. Doing so means they can see the paradigmatic assumptions made in the work they read, and they can then make judgements about how plausible and coherent this seems, judged against their own preferred world view.

Figure 5.2 is Burrell and Morgan's (1979) graphical representation of their sociological paradigms. It is useful to understand interpretivism as they saw it by contrasting it with the other paradigms. The functionalist paradigm generally aims to improve and optimise systems, it sees the world as something that is exterior to us, knowledge is 'objective' and 'out there', waiting to be discovered. Increasing the stock of this knowledge can help to solve more problems. A lot of management (and managerial) and marketing research is functionalist in this sense, being based on a realist ontology (the social world can be understood in much the same ways as the natural world). The radical structuralist paradigm similarly feels that knowledge is objective, there is an underlying reality to the social world (structures of reality), and the *axiology* of research, its guiding purpose, is to generate knowledge that improves existing systems. However, radical structuralism is focused more on changing policies and institutions to improve the distribution of power and equity in the world.

The radical humanist paradigm also aims to change the world and re-order power structures through its research, but it assumes that social reality is created by the thoughts, language and communication of individuals, acting collectively, hence its methods and focus of research differ from those of the radical structuralists. Radical structuralism and radical humanism could both be labelled as critical research paradigms in the sense that they believe that radical change is needed in the world, and that one way of moving towards such change is through politically aware social research and education. Politically aware, in this sense, refers not to party political advocacy, but to research that focuses on power and how it plays out in social relations. So, for example, radical structuralist research might focus on, say, the laws around industrial relations and worker's rights to improve fairness in the workplace and in society, while radical humanist research might view unequal relations of power as things that are reproduced in micro-interactions to focus on, say, an ethnographic study of power and gender relations in school classrooms.

The interpretive paradigm holds that the social world is created by individuals, acting collectively. In other words, there is no underlying mechanism of causation for social life, it is produced through language and discourse, and through symbolic communication and interaction. The axiology of the interpretive research paradigm tends to be focused on rich explanations of the world to promote deeper understanding and greater individual liberty and autonomy, rather than on radical change. One criticism sometimes made of research studies in the interpretive paradigm from the point of view of radical humanists is that it sometimes pays too little attention to power structures. For example, there is a lot of published interpretive research that examines the detailed anatomy and symbolism of particular consumption practices, but without paying much attention to the overlaying structures of power that inform those practices such as race and ethnicity, nationality and social class. Interpretive researchers might counter that there is a need for greater understanding of human culture which, in itself, can act as a liberating force for individuals to empower themselves, to some extent. But can research into, say, sex workers, really claim to find empowering practices when the existence of that industry and the supply of workers to it are predicated on wider structures of inequality?

Of course, this example highlights the fact that paradigms can be logically incompatible. In another example of paradigmatic incompatibility, counselling psychology aims to empower the individual by promoting greater control and insight into their own thoughts and behaviour. This is a worthy enterprise and many people have had their lives improved by counselling interventions broadly premised on Carl Rogers's (1945: 1949) humanistic psychology principles. However, the criticism is that people who seek out counselling for personal problems of depression and mental health my often be subject to structural unfairness (such as being poor, having an unfair employer or being in an abusive relationship) that counselling can do little to address. Being encouraged to think more positively about oneself and one's own emotions is all very well, but what if one's situation in life is, really, out of one's control? Can counselling empower people to meaningfully challenge the injustice and inequity they face in their lives, or does it merely give them strategies for dealing better with their life as it is? Proponents could argue that being able to better deal with one's life, whatever the circumstances, can be a first step to changing it fundamentally. Nonetheless, it seems clear that there are tensions here between the paradigmatic assumptions of the researcher or therapist, and the social reality faced by the participant.

Many researchers would say that whilst these sociological paradigms are useful in clarifying the key assumptions of various differing research approaches, they should be treated pragmatically. It seems intuitive that the personal situation we find ourselves in life arises because of a mixture of our own personal qualities and character, and our position embedded within the structures and institutions of social life such as class, race, gender and sexuality, ethnicity, nationality and so on, over which we have no control. Interpretive research tends to occupy a space somewhere on the left of Burrell and Morgan's (1979) graphic in Figure 5.2, with some pieces focused more on describing social reality as it appears to be in that moment, and others focused more on the conditions that caused the social reality of a given situation to arise. There are tensions between the various paradigms and Burrell and Morgan's (1979) framework does oversimplify these (Alexander and Smith, 2001). Nonetheless, it is a helpful framework for an introduction to interpretive research for student researchers. One thing that interpretive and humanist researchers tend to agree on. is the assumption that social reality is produced through social interaction, and is not the result of underlying and invisible structures of reality. Hence, the framework does offer a guide to the major ontological basis for interpretive research as a whole.

Philosophical issues in interpretive data analysis

Research findings are invariably framed and constrained by the methodological assumptions researchers bring to the study. The spirit of research followed in this book is better expressed by phrases like research 'perspectives' or 'approaches' than method. In interpretive research, the researcher's reflexive and philosophically informed interpretation of the data generates findings. The findings are not cranked out of a machine: they are not generated impersonally by a research 'method'. Rather, they emerge from the embodied hermeneutic analysis of the researcher, in interaction with research participants, the research environment and theoretical influences. There is room in interpretive research data analysis for findings that are not mechanistically produced, but which are creative and emergent.

Interpretive data analysis and 'rich' descriptions

It was noted above that while interpretive research traditions hold differing emphases on the most appropriate methods of data gathering and analysis for research approaches, there are also many commonalities and overlaps between the various traditions. The interpretive stance is that social accomplishments of every kind are complex and enigmatic phenomena that cannot be represented by direct causal relations or boxes-and-arrows models without employing an extreme order of *reductionism*. Reductionism refers to the over-simplification of explanations. Such research tends to ignore contrasting perspectives to produce a simple, and simplified, process model of a far more complex process. This can be useful where models and theories provide elegant and concise representations of phenomena or relationships. However, interpretive research is more often characterised by 'rich' (Geertz, 1973) descriptions of social phenomena that attempt to confront and represent, rather than erase, the deep complexity of social worlds. These rich descriptions tend to focus on the particular social context (Askegaard and Linnet, 2011) rather than the world in general.

The idea of the rich description should not be confused with the earlier comments about academics judging student work on a continuum, from descriptive to analytic. The genuinely rich (in an ethnographic sense) description is analytical, such is the complexity and nuance with which the description is invoked. For example, Ghaffari et al. (2019) (referred to above) generated findings that fell into three broad categories of social practices around the creative advertising development process. These social practices described how power over the creative output was constituted, and represented a new way to understand advertising that could have implications for how advertising agencies organise their work and assess creative output.

Meanings in interpretive research

Another important feature of interpretive research is a focus on meanings as opposed to a focus on facts (e.g. McCracken, 1986; Puntoni et al., 2010). Interpretive researchers seek to understand how social life is actively produced by people's language, behaviour and social practices. Particular social worlds are understood from the point of view of participants. Ethnographic researchers (and qualitative 'street' sociologists) have tried to understand consumer sub-cultures by, for example, becoming a member of a crack-dealing gang (Venkatesh, 2009) or by becoming members of a bike gang (Schouten and McAlexander, 1995) to become part of the social process they are investigating. This deep participation enables the researcher to gain an ethnographic level of insight. They can understand the phenomena under investigation from the perspective of the group being investigated. In other words, the goal is to understand the meaning of this lifestyle for participants, rather than trying to understand the phenomenon at arm's length through questionnaire surveys or government statistics. For ethnographic researchers, understanding the meaning of social practices demands a first-hand, theoretically informed, qualitative engagement with the subject matter. However, such a level of deep understanding can also be gleaned from other qualitative approaches including interviews, observation and discussion/focus groups (for example, see Hackley et al., 2013, 2015).

Interpretive researchers do not seek to impose preconceived values or concepts on the people they are focusing on in their research. Researchers must seek to accept the world as it is produced by participants. Ethically, this does not mean that the researcher must agree with or encourage behaviour they think is ethically wrong. It simply means that the integrity of the research process is best served if researchers seek to empathise with research participants. The emphasis on meaning results in a focus on meanings as they are constructed by research participants, rather than imposing the meanings and values of other groups on to the group that is being studied. In this way, researchers can stand back from their research to try to understand why particular meanings become constructed and valued in a particular social setting. For interpretive consumer researchers, buying and consuming products and services and understanding advertising and branding are activities that people make meaningful by projecting symbolic values on them. These symbolic values play into consumers' senses of identity, their (and our) identity 'projects' (Elliott and Wattanasuwan, 1998; Hackley, Hackley and Bassiouni, 2018). Understanding the meanings consumption practices have for consumers is key to understanding consumer motivation and behaviour. Importantly, in the interpretivist approach, these meanings are produced by consumers in interaction with each other and the social world, they are not imposed unilaterally from above by brand managers (Gabriel and Lang, 2015) or driven from within by deep structural factors such as social class, environment or biology.

Interpretive management researchers are, similarly, concerned with management processes as aspects of human interaction in organisations. Managers are seen as thinking, feeling individuals who have a strong, subjective sense of agency, as are the people they manage. Work is an important site of meaning for human beings. Management is a class of organisational authority, but it is also, colloquially, something everyone does. We 'manage' our lives, our relationships, our embodiment, our time and our activities, as well as our work, if we have work. In managing our work, we try to bring meaning to it, and it is this meaning that interpretive researchers seek to tap into and use as a source of insight and understanding when they research organisational work and management (Watson, 1994).

Agency and situated freedom

Agency refers to the power of individuals to act and behave independently of social structures. Agency is freedom to act according to one's volition. Are your decisions and accomplishments your own and no one else's? Or are they the result of the influences under which you grew up, your social class, the culture of which you are part, the kind of family you have? Are your actions, behaviours, your very thoughts, the result of your unique personality, your experiences and your decisions? Or is this agency an illusion and our life trajectories, our decisions, our very thoughts, are in fact determined by social structures beyond our control?

Such questions as these have been the cause of much debate among social theorists and are usually referred to collectively as the agency–structure debate. The debate is important to social researchers because it influences the kinds of findings that can be produced. So, for example, researchers inclined to structuralist explanations of social life might work in the right-hand side of Burrell and Morgan's (1979) sociological paradigms, within the structuralist and functionalist paradigms. Structural explanations of social behaviour focus on the institutions and social structures that frame and constrain the behaviour and thinking of individuals. These social institutions include class, ethnicity, income, education, gender and so on. If people behave because of the forces that are imposed on them through class, culture and other outside (structural) influences, then change can only come about through large-scale social change whereby these social structures are fundamentally changed (the radical structuralist paradigm in Burrell and Morgan (1979)). This is the assumption of Marxism: individual change is only possible through the collective.

If, on the other hand, people are thought to have the power, admittedly curtailed and limited, to act, think and behave independently of the social structures around them, they are said to possess the power of agency. Some interpretive research traditions (such as the phenomenological/existentialist tradition, e.g. Thompson, Locander and Pollio, 1990) make this very assumption. They assume that people have some power, a limited or 'situated' freedom, to define their own existence and to determine their own course of action. Their freedom is situated because it is framed by the social structures and institutions within which the person lives, and which influence and constrain their thought and behaviour. The idea of agency is important in interpretive research because studies of how people produce meaning within certain social situations would have little value if the people were merely playing out destinies that have been imposed on them by their social circumstances. The very idea of interpretation implies that there is some creativity and independence to the researcher's stance: he or she has the freedom to place creative interpretations on the research they conduct, just as the research participants are assumed to be agentive (demonstrating agency) when they are creative and independent in their consumption practices. This is important, because, in interpretive consumer and marketing research, it is assumed that the actions of consumers, marketing managers and other research participants are not simply determined by forces outside their control, but are the result of their agentive action (consistent with the interpretive paradigm in Burrell and Morgan's (1979) model).

Much interpretive work assumes that the individual's power of agency is sharply constrained by institutional forces and social structures. This tends to be a standard assumption in sociological and functional approaches to social research. As a result, quite a lot of published qualitative work today is not easy to fit into Burrell and Morgan's (1979) framework. One could also say that some qualitative published work today ought to have read Burrell and Morgan (1979) because it could help achieve greater ontological clarity in the work. There is sometimes a disconnect when studies that focus empirically on a qualitative investigation of agentive individuals and their socially constructed meanings then offer structuralist explanations and solutions. But, then, academic work is all about debate and critique, and the more the student researcher knows about interpretive theory, the better they can defend their work, like academics, even if they are wrong.

Replicability and validity in interpretive research

We have touched on the notion of objectivity earlier in the book. An important principle of experimental and other quantitative research traditions has been that the researcher stands apart from the research. The people who are in the research study are called research 'subjects', denoting the authority of the researcher (the scientist) to determine what they (the subjects) should be told, to control how they are used in the experiment, and also to interpret their motives, actions and behaviour. The researcher, on this model, stands outside what is being researched and attempts to generate 'objective' findings. 'Objective' here means findings that are independent of both the researcher, and of the research design. In principle, if objectivity is achieved, then findings should be *replicable*, that is, other researchers should be able to do the same study, using exactly the same method, at another time and in another place, and replicate the original findings.

Social research is notorious for the low replicability of its findings, and the situation is becoming more and more acute. There has been recent publicity around the failure to replicate major findings in psychology, called a replication 'crisis' (e.g. Bergkvist, De Keyzer and Buzeta, 2023; Romero, 2019; Urminsky and Dietvorst, 2024). There can be many reasons for the failure to replicate published findings. They can include genuine error in research design or statistical calculation, flawed reviewing processes and deliberate researcher fraud. The point we make here is that replication is only a thing in quantitative social science, and not interpretive social science. This is mainly because quantitative social science seeks to make claims about universal truths, while interpretive social science makes claims only about a given social situation that may or may not be representative of wider groups. There is no attempt in interpretive qualitative research to make statistical generalisations.

Interpretivists assume that, in social research, findings are invariably contextual–they may, and should, resonate with wider themes and with other studies, but no one would try to replicate, say, an ethnographic study expecting to generate the same findings as in the original study. Every qualitative study is unique in the sense that it is the result of a collision of a given set of empirical events and a specified researcher's interpretation at a particular moment in time. Physical science has been shown to be a very human affair with elements of subjectivity, judgement and culture-specificity (e.g. Billig, 1987; Knorr Cetina and Mulkay, 1983; McCloskey, 1983; Woolgar, 1981, 1988, 1989). Interpretive theorists would hold that objectivity is 'worked up' as a textual production–science isn't objective, but objectivity is an aspect of the writing conventions of science.

Ethnographic studies in management, for example, seek to understand the ways in which a specified, organisational social milieu is produced. There is no attempt to reduce findings to direct cause–effect relationships or statistically supported correlations. Such studies do generate general findings in the sense that they contribute to the proposal that organisational management is a human enterprise that is produced by thinking, feeling actors who are idiosyncratic and emotional. Similar circumstances might yield similar results, and the findings from one set of participants might well be representative of larger groups with similar characteristics. But, the major emphasis of ethnographic and interpretive studies in general is on rich description, not testable cause–effect relations, or the generation of generalisable facts or relation-ships. Hence, replication as a concept in research integrity is key to the entire enterprise of realist–structuralist quantitative research in a way that does not hold for interpretive/qualitative research.

Language and the social constructionist ontology

The concept of 'bias' is sometimes invoked to distinguish between the way events are reported by interviewees or survey respondents, and the way the events 'really' happened. In much interpretive research, no such distinction is acknowledged. This is because the researcher is not in a position to speculate about a reality that lies beyond the accounts of research participants. All the researcher can do is to analyse the data sets they can obtain with as much care as possible so that the reasoning and evidence that give rise to their findings is derived systematically and presented clearly. This is not a matter of being excessively credulous towards participants who might exaggerate or lie, or who might have a particular agenda that they want to get across. For interpretive researchers, qualitative data sets are not, necessarily, an un-problematic window to underlying events and causes. Language itself is the reality that can be studied. Interpretive research is pragmatic – it focuses on what we can see as researchers, not on what we cannot see. Structuralist/realist research seeks to infer causal relationships that researchers cannot see in operation. For example, a study of senior managers' attitudes to bonus pay incentives assumes that there is something there, an attitude, which drives behaviour. We cannot see the attitude since it exists in the cognitive structures of the brain as an electrical impulse, among many such impulses that we can-not easily distinguish from each other. Nonetheless, the attitude researcher assumes that the construct of attitude has a physical reality, and that what they are measuring is, in fact, a physical entity called an 'attitude'.

Qualitative researchers, in contrast, do not assume that their data sets hint at the existence of other, deep structure of reality. An interview transcript is just a representation of what some said in response to some questions. This does not mean that qualitative researchers are credulous or naïve towards the things their research participants say. There are techniques that can be used to sift qualitative data sets to arrive at a view on the integrity of reports of events and mental states, such as variability and action-orientation in dis-course analysis (Elliott, 1996), discussed in Chapter 8. In brief, variability in accounts refers to variation in the way people describe or account for things over time. For example, some studies of racist discourse have used the tech-nique to highlight how some people who deny that they are racist then revert to racist tropes in different circumstances (Wetherell and Potter, 1992). An-other technique used in discourse analysis is to look not only at the content and meaning of words used by participants, but also to consider the function of the words (also called action-orientation), that is, the purpose expressing a particular position in a particular way might have for the speaker. Self-presentation is always an element in discourse (as it is in questionnaire surveys) and words do things as well as say things (Austin, 1962). Using concepts such as variation and action-orientation enables interpretive researchers to apply nuance and sensitivity to the interpretation of textual data sets.

This general position implies a social constructionist ontology. The *ontology* of a research study (also referred to in the previous chapter) refers to deep assumptions about the nature of the reality being studied. A social constructionist ontology regards social reality as something that people construct in interaction through their use of language and other symbolic social practices. A research setting is another social practice, it cannot stand outside the field of social practices. This contrasts with the assumption, in structuralist/realist research, that social reality is fixed, given and prior to language and social practice, and that the researcher and the research setting are ontologically distinct from the social context being investigated.

Not all interpretive research approaches assume a social constructionist ontology. For example, some traditions of *semiotics* assume that there are deep structures of communication codes underlying the construction of meaning see Chapter 8). These codes are seen as relatively stable, fixed and unchanging. However, not all semiotics researchers will agree that this is an important issue (Humphreys, 2010). The ontological position adopted by a researcher is an intellectual requirement, since high quality intellectual work demands that implied assumptions made explicit are consistent with the implications claimed for the research. The ontology of social research is a working assumption, not a fully worked-through and defensible argument about the nature of reality. Social researchers state assumptions because these have implications for the kinds of findings and conclusions that can be generated from research. They do not assume that assumptions are shared or taken for granted by all.

As noted earlier, the social constructionist ontology contrasts with the *realist* philosophical position. Social researchers invoke the philosophy of realism to support the contention that the social world of managers, organisations and consumers can be regarded as if it were like the physical world of plants, bodies and cells. This can be a rather oversimplified contrast: *realism* is a sophisticated philosophical stance that has many shades and subtleties, as does positivism, another philosophical position that is often identified with realism (hence the realist/positivist assignation sometimes used in this book). For example, *critical realists* hold that the world can and should be regarded as real in a material sense but only as a working assumption. Critical realists are agnostic on many philosophy of science questions. They take a pragmatic viewpoint. For some critical realists, social constructionist approaches to research lack a sufficiently strong sense of the *materiality* of social life (see, for an example in consumer research, Huff, Humphreys and Wilner, 2021). Human beings are embodied beings, we live in a world of materiality, with material goods, physical impulses and sensory experience – all is not text. Some who adopt a social constructionist approach might counter that social constructionism (Berger and Luckman, 1966) does not preclude an account of the materiality of a social situation.

Interpretive, qualitative research and power

A final concept that deserves introduction in this chapter is the idea of power, which is discussed in more detail in Chapter 8. Interpretive research does not necessarily seek to uncover the relations of power that frame social interaction. If one thinks of the contrast between Burrell and Morgan's (1979) interpretive research paradigm and the radical humanism paradigm, this would reflect a difference in *axiology* or purpose. Radical humanist research would normally seek to reveal relations of power with the ultimate aim of addressing unequal power relations. The interpretive research paradigm does not necessarily have this axiology, being more concerned with the delineation of the subjective experience of human actors in a social context. Interpretive studies are typically concerned with revealing how social life is produced and sustained as a 'normal' thing through language and social practice in a given context. However, an awareness of how power is reproduced and played out in social situations is implicit in much interpretive research. If researchers ask the question 'why do these meanings seem to be important to this community of people?' then they must allow that one possible answer is that meanings serve particular interests, that is, they support the power of particular interests in some way. It is, then, increasingly common for interpretive approaches to research analysis to be conducted within a 'critical' focus on power and interest. Indeed, it seems rather remiss to ignore power relations in interpretive research.

Power has two broad meanings in social research. These are defined in the glossary for Chapter 8 but are worth mentioning initially here. *Structural power* refers to the power, or lack of it, that manifests because of prevailing social structures and institutions. This kind of power is commonly understood since it is usually very apparent, being vested in economic, class, law or other social institutions. It is extrinsic to social action, being imposed from outside a given social interaction. For example, the institutional authority of the police force or other legally empowered bodies such as border force officers is a form of structural power. When a judge sentences someone who is convicted of a crime to go to jail, they are using the power invested in them by the state, and the convicted person has no ability to challenge that structural power. Another example could be the power imbalance resulting from economic or class privilege, or the lack of it. A person might, say, seek therapeutic counselling for depression, and this type of treatment normally locates the source of the depression in the person's personal history, their biology and psychology.

However, if the person is economically disadvantaged through lack of opportunity, the source of many of their problems might be their lack of structural power because of their social class. Many problems of depression, anxiety, addiction and so on would be easier for a person to address if they had a bit more money and the opportunity to find a more satisfying job. Structural power, and the lack of it, is a brute reality that defines much of our existence, but we might not necessarily acknowledge that, instead attributing our powerlessness to our own faults or mistakes. Of course, as we have noted elsewhere in the book, interpretive research assumes that humans in society have a subjective sense of agency. The effect of structural power is to set the parameters within which this sense of agency can operate.

Constitutive power is often less apparent than structural power, since it refers to the ways in which we unwittingly reproduce *ideologically* imposed values through our everyday talk and action. Constitutive power is intrinsic to a given social interaction because the language and social practice of people in interaction does not merely reflect relations of power, it actively constitutes those relations of power. In our daily lives we might reproduce constitutive power through our unconscious attitudes which, in turn, reflect larger structures of power which are ideological. Patriarchy is one example, where, say, a daughter in a family is given less freedom or less pocket money than her brother. When she questions why, her parents say 'that's just the way it is'.

For example, in many countries a way of speaking can categorise the speaker into a particular social class. This might be supported by the use of a particular vernacular and certain grammatical patterns, as in British 'working-class' or 'middle-class' speaking. Hence any interaction with a person of a different social class is immediately framed within pre-existing ideological norms that set the terms of reference for the interaction. In Britain, a regional accent was once a barrier to social and career advancement because it signified membership of a 'lower' class less worthy of responsibility and opportunity. While this is less true today (arguably), some would argue that it can still be the case in some circumstances, perhaps in certain professions. Within interaction and dialogue, people will draw (consciously or unconsciously) on ideological norms that pre-exist the interaction and they will reproduce these through language and social practice. Ideas of class membership (or ethnicity, gender, religious affiliation and so on) reflect the economic and political dominance of particular groups at certain times in history. Constitutive power often takes the form of an ideology in the sense that it is apparent in implicit assumptions and values that come to be regarded as normal, given and beyond question.

In micro-analyses of social life, researchers can look at how language and social practice confers power on individuals. For example, a study of the construction of authority in a professional relationship such as management consulting might look at the ways in which rhetoric, gesture and language produce the effect of authority in particular relationships. A study of management on the shop floor might study the play of power and authority between management and 'workers' or staff. This could be seen in terms of factors affecting the credibility of the manager, such as personal style, use of language, negotiating skills and so on. Such a study could also look at the ways in which power and authority are resisted in management–staff relations. Published studies have focused, for example, on the disconnectedness of managerial power (Munro, 1997) and on the constitutive character of managerial power in a knowledge-based, professionalised industry such as advertising (Ghaffari, Hackley and Lee, 2019; Hackley, 2000).

Consumers, as well as professionals, are engaged in power relations with not only with the vast resources and global presence of corporations, but with the capitalist economic system itself. While consumers have relatively little structural power in this relation other than that afforded by consumer protection legislation, consumers can and do resist economic forces through their own forms of co-optation and resistance. For example, consumer activism has become a vibrant source of resistance to corporate power in recent years (Chatzidikas, Maclaran and Varman, 2021; Gollnhofer, Weijo and Schouten, 2019) sometimes aided by non-governmental bodies (Nøjgaard, 2023). Consumer resistance can be overt as it challenges the legal basis of corporate power, or it can be more tacit as it is manifest in, for example, co-opting consumption practices in ways that are not sanctioned or approved by the state or by organisations (Hackley et al., 2015; Thompson and Coskuner-Balli, 2007).

Micro-studies can also employ another dimension of analysis. If physical gestures, bodily rhetoric (managers wear lounge suits, shopfloor workers wear jeans, etc.), sanctions and rewards characterise the relations between management and the workforce, then there may be historical reasons for this. In other words, there may be wider historical influences at work within the *micro-sociology* of relationships and groups. Power is clearly important in many organisational contexts. The power of large organisations to change or maintain certain market conditions through the use of large advertising budgets is highly evident in fmcg (fast-moving consumer goods) markets. Some retail organisations have considerable power over suppliers to define price and quality specifications.

On a micro-sociological level, formal management meetings are sites of the play of power from board level to shopfloor quality circles. Commercial organisations self-evidently have greater power over resources than individual consumers, but there is resistance to this power through consumer law, pressure groups and other means. Some commentators argue that the internet has changed the power balance in marketing and consumption, shifting it towards consumers who can express their wants and dislikes directly. However, as some critical theorists point out, it is clearly in the interests of commercial organisations to claim that consumers have the power of choice.

To what extent is this choice constrained or framed by commercial power? These questions and many others concerning power offer potentially fruitful lines of discussion for students doing research projects.

One very important aspect of the study of power concerns studies of gender and gender relations in organisational and consumption settings (e.g. Alvesson, 1998; Hirschman, 1993; Stern, 1993). Many student researchers have found that studies of the representation of gender relations in magazines and other media forms can provide fruitful material for speculation on the state of gender relations. Studies that, for example, content analyse advertisements and editorial of magazines from differing time periods tend to reveal striking differences in the ways that relations between genders are represented (O'Barr, 2006). In turn, the forms of representation reflect changing values and norms in the social world beyond magazines. What changing media representations of gender imply about the wider social world is a matter for the informed speculation of the researcher. Many other kinds of studies focusing on power and gender have looked at career and promotion routes for women and men in different organisations and occupations.

A focus on power, then, implies that many aspects of social action and interaction, such as language, the rhetoric of gesture and dress, the rhetoric of gender relations, can be understood in terms of the power such behaviours confer on individuals. For researchers who draw on the Frankfurt school of critical theorists, power is a ubiquitous feature of social relations (e.g. Horkheimer and Adorno, 1944). For some researchers no interpretive study is complete without a focus on the ways in which wider structures of power, such as institutions of class, gender and economics, are reproduced at the level of everyday social interaction. To be fair to student researchers, interpretive studies that are truly critical in this wide-ranging sense may be beyond the scope of most. In many cases, the aims of student research projects will be primarily managerial or interpretive/descriptive rather than truly critical. Nevertheless, the link between interpretive research traditions and critical studies that focus on power is too important to be ignored (and developed further in Chapter 8).

This chapter has developed issues first raised in Chapter 1 around where interpretive research studies fit among the other paradigms of social research. We have used Burrell and Morgan's (1979: 2019) work as a baseline for this discussion, while acknowledging that their famous approach does not necessarily fit all forms of interpretive studies. With this general discussion on research paradigms and the ontological and epistemological assumptions that carry, the book concludes Part 1 as a wide-ranging grounding in the basic issues of qualitative data gathering and interpretive research. Most interpretive research studies are, though, framed by specific interpretive traditions, and Part 2 of the book will focus in more closely on a selection of these commonly used traditions of interpretive/qualitative specific research. Chapter 6, then, will begin Part 2 by looking at existential phenomenology.

Glossary

Agency   The power of the individual to control his or her own actions, thoughts and behaviour in spite of the influence of social structures and institutions.

Axiology   The goal or purpose of a research study or paradigm.

Critical realism   Put simply, the position that the social world can be assumed to be real in a material sense for the sake of convenience. It is a pragmatic position that takes realism as a working assumption and a point of departure for research.

Ideology   In a general sense, implicit values and norms that are carried within given modes of speaking, writing and thinking. Ideology is normally regarded as having a centre from which it emanates in support of particular interests and groups. This centre is often obscured from view as ideological influences become widely taken for granted as the definitive way of regarding a subject or idea.

Materiality   The material world as an aspect of sociological thinking and research, taking account of human embodiment and the inevitability of material reality.

Micro-sociology   The detailed study of how social life is produced within a specific group. It would normally entail a close examination of language, gesture and other social practices. Micro-sociological studies are often connected to larger-scale issues through consideration of the influence of ideological norms in the wider social and historical context.

Ontology   A set of basic assumptions about the nature of social and/or material reality. The social constructionist or relativist ontology tends to be contrasted with the realist ontology in social research.

Paradigm   A set of assumptions about the best way to pursue knowledge in a field regarding data-gathering methods, philosophy of knowledge (epistemology) and analysis of data. According to Kuhn (1970), paradigms tend to become dominant and taken-for-granted until displaced by a revolution in understanding leading to a new paradigm.

Phenomenological/existentialism   Phenomenology was a branch of European philosophy associated with Brentano and Husserl that focused on the direct apprehension of experience. In modern psychology this tradition was developed into the experiential psychology perspective. In its modern form it has also been influenced by existentialists such as Camus and Sartre.

Realism   In social research, realism is often invoked to mean that the social world can be assumed to be as solid and material as the physical world, at least for the purposes of research.

Reductionism   Reducing complexity to simplicity by applying a particular form of explanation. The term is usually used in a pejorative sense to imply that the economy of a given form of explanation has been achieved at the expense of important detail.

Replicability   The ability to replicate a research study, that is, to do it again within a different set of circumstances to see if the original findings re-occur.

Representation   Social researchers can only represent the worlds they investigate, using what media are at their command (words or other representational devices). They cannot reproduce those worlds, hence what they produce is a representation of the events they investigate.

Representative   Referring to sample choice in qualitative research: if a small group has similar characteristics to a larger group it is representative of that group. Findings from research with the smaller group may, therefore, reflect the views, behaviour or norms of the larger group.

Semiotics   Simply, the science of signs. In the tradition informed by C.S. Peirce, semiotics is the study of how signs come to have meaning in a given context. The task of the semiotician is to uncover the codes through which we interpret the meaning of signs.

Social constructionism   An ontological position that holds that social reality is not fixed and given but constituted by and through language and social practice.

Part II

Working in theoretical traditions of interpretive research

Chapter 6

Practical existential phenomenology for student researchers

Abstract

This chapter begins the discussion of specific interpretive research perspectives by drawing on two linked traditions: phenomenology and existentialism. It illustrates possible applications with research studies that could be adapted for use by student researchers. It also develops some of the major ideas, themes and techniques normally associated with each perspective.

Chapter objectives

After reading this chapter students will be able to

- explain the major principles of phenomenology and existentialism
- understand the application of both to social research that focuses on apprehended experience
- apply these themes and concepts in a phenomenologically informed student research project

Theoretical framing for interpretive studies

Chapters 6–10 will offer introductions to a selection of theoretical traditions in order to make more clear to student researchers just how they might frame their work theoretically. Student researchers should note that many of the works cited in these chapters will be detailed sources designed for advanced work in specialist theoretical traditions at master's or PhD level. That is not to imply that undergraduate students cannot understand research papers – indeed, it is a requirement of many undergraduate programmes that students do read and analyse published research papers and incorporate them into their work. However, student researchers should remember not to be intimidated by published studies that are theoretically difficult, or which go through multiple phases of data collection. Chapters 6–10 are designed to offer a route into a selection of theoretical traditions. The introduction provided to

DOI: 10.4324/9781003432203-9

each theoretical tradition is not oversimplified but is a rather generic introduction. In practice, advanced studies tend to adapt these traditions, bearing
in mind that there are often debates and opposing camps within them. One
of the nice things about research is that one can innovate, combine methods,
or adapt methods for different purposes.

Some scholars use the term paradigm to refer to a theoretical tradition (or
to a combination of two theoretical traditions (as in Thompson et al., 1989,
1990). In this book we are treating the word paradigm somewhat in the way
that Burrell and Morgan (1979) treat it, as an overarching set of assumptions about epistemology, method and ontology that embrace a range of
intellectual traditions. There are quite a few different theoretical traditions
of social research and social theory that can, roughly, be placed in the same
paradigm. In this book we are taking the view that the theories discussed
in this and the following chapters *can* be placed broadly in the interpretive
paradigm, although with the two important caveats that (a) they can all be
used with differing assumptions that could place them *also* in the radical
humanist or even the radical structuralist paradigms and (b) Burrell and
Morgan's (1979) framework is useful for researchers, but it is a simplification of paradigmatic nuances and some scholars argue that the way they use
qualitative methods does not fit precisely into any of Burrell and Morgan's
(1979) paradigms.

The main foci of this book, management, marketing, organisation and
consumer studies, draw their research methods from other areas of social
scientific and human studies. For example, the techniques of phenomenological interviewing were developed in philosophical psychology before they
were applied in consumer and marketing research, the questionnaire survey
was developed by anthropologists before being enthusiastically embraced by
marketers. The approach to discourse analysis adopted later in this book (see
Chapter 10) was mostly influenced by its use in discursive psychology, while
the psychologists adapted it from the sociologists and so on. This is to say
that disciplinary areas *adapt* social scientific methods.

Management and related areas of study are somewhat new in historical
terms, many business schools in UK universities for example have only existed since the 1990s (Hackley, 2024), so the derivative character of theory
in marketing isn't perhaps too surprising. The point is that it is quite difficult to find universal agreement on a definitive account of any interpretive
methodological or theoretical area in social studies. They are all contested,
revised, evolving entities. This is why academics value the acquired skill of
critical reading and critical evaluation so highly in students. Interpretive
methods, and their accompanying theoretical frames, have to be applied
with nuance to different research questions and differing empirical contexts.
So, the accounts of specific interpretive theories in this book are aimed at
a particular level of student researcher, they are not definitive (no account
is) and they are invariably provisional. They are intended to be guides for

Figure 6.1 The relationship of paradigm, to theory, to data collection: Existential
phenomenology

student researchers, introductions for professional researchers and starting
points for academics who wish to develop advanced expertise in specialist
interpretive approaches.

Figure 6.1 offers a simple diagrammatic of the relationship between the
paradigm (interpretivism), the intellectual tradition or theory (existential
phenomenology) and the method (the phenomenological interview). As a
working model it can be useful for helping student researchers to think about
the basic assumptions they make in their research design. It should also be
helpful in assisting student researchers to adapt a suitable approach to their
research context. The key point to remember is that the three levels, the
paradigm, the theory and the method, should fit together, for the work to
make sense.

It is important to note that there are oversimplifications in Figure 6.1.
For example, in Burrell and Morgan's (1979) typology, existentialism and
phenomenology are placed in different paradigms. Existentialism is placed
in the radical humanism paradigm, while phenomenology is placed in the
interpretive paradigm. To be sure, there are oversimplifications in Burrell
and Morgan's (1979) typology too. Researchers such as Thompson et al.
(1989) have blended elements of existentialism and phenomenology to apply in consumer research, since they have areas of compatibility, each being
characterised by a focus on subjectivity rather than objectivity, and being
typically investigated through qualitative methods rather than quantitative.
Each philosophy focuses on the lived experience of human beings as it is
apprehended. Social researchers will always argue over whether or not such
theoretical combinations are valid. Our job in this book is to present student
researchers with approaches to the theoretical framing of qualitative research
that are well-established in the literature.

Box 6.1   Three of Burrell and Morgan's (1979) sociological paradigms contrasted

Paradigm	Interpretive	Functionalist/ structuralist	Humanist
Ontology	Social constructivist	Realist	Subjectivist/ relativist
Theories	Hermeneutics Phenomenology	Systems theory	Postmodernism Existentialism
Methods	Qualitative	Quantitative	Qualitative

By the same token, the characterisations in Box 6.1 can also be debated. For example, structuralism and functionalism are placed in different quadrants in Burrell and Morgan (1979), but in much published research are referred to together, as the structuralist/functionalist paradigm. Nonetheless, we present Box 6.1 here since it might help readers in classifying research paradigms with their appropriate ontology (basic assumption about the nature of the social world) and associated theories and methods. As a further complication, there is no rule against using qualitative methods to explore questions framed within the structuralist/functionalist paradigm, nor is there an iron law against investigating interpretive research questions by using quantitative methods. Indeed, methodological innovation lies at the heart of paradigm change. What this book is asserting in Box 6.1 is that the associations portrayed are widely used and accepted in social research. Generally speaking, only advanced post-doctoral researchers who are deeply familiar with the various theories would attempt innovations that challenge the prevailing paradigmatic conventions.

All social research methods have strengths and weaknesses and there are always choices to make. There is no single correct choice, but there are incorrect choices. For example, a common mistake amongst students new to research is to set up hypotheses for a qualitative study. Hypotheses are testable statements that are used in quantitative research. For qualitative research, setting up research questions would be more appropriate, since qualitative studies are not effective for testing hypotheses, given their small samples in comparison to quantitative studies.

The kind of theoretical framing referred to in this book is seen as a way to raise the intellectual level of a qualitative study by adding a theoretical perspective to the research design. Doing a qualitative study without any theoretical framing might be ok for a practical problem-solving research study, or for a lower level academic study, but if the student research wishes to conduct a higher level study in which the deep assumptions are made explicit, then it will be necessary to position the study correctly in terms of the paradigm, the theoretical frame and the appropriate data-gathering approach. Doing so is a way for student researchers to achieve clarity in pulling together their research questions, data-gathering method and analytical approach into a coherent whole under the umbrella of a paradigm. Many first-time student researchers make basic errors in mixing research questions, methods and data analysis in ways that immediately strike the person reading and marking the work as incoherent and confused. Understanding how particular methods of data gathering and data analysis fit within specific paradigms will be of great help to student researchers in raising the level of their work.

The phenomenological perspective – an introduction

One particularly important philosophical theme that has been used in many interpretive and qualitative social research studies is phenomenology, often allied with existentialism, although the two originated as distinct traditions of theory. The basic idea of phenomenological research is that the perceived reality of the participant is the focus of the researcher's attention. Phenomenology is the study of subjective experience. This marks an important point in social research because in structuralist/functionalist/realist paradigms, the assumption is that the experience of participants is caused by deeper, hidden factors, so the experience of the participant is taken to be a glimpse of a deeper reality. In contrast, phenomenological research takes the research participants' received experience as a legitimate source of research data in and of itself. Subjective experience is taken to be the social reality that matters, it is not merely the expression of deeper causative factors.

Phenomenology has served a political purpose in academic research because it has been used as an intellectual justification for qualitative and interpretive research approaches for social researchers in marketing, management and consumer research. Specifically, researchers have used phenomenology to argue that, rather than accessing research participants' inner states, reasoning and motives through experiments or questionnaires, researchers should try to find methods to access participants' direct (phenomenological) experience. Hence, terms such as the 'phenomenological interview' are used to refer to, well, an interview that regards the participants' expressed experience as valid research data, rather than using an interview to try to access deeper, hidden motivational drives, as in, say, psychoanalytic approaches or laddering (Gruber et al., 2008) techniques. Philosophical purists might say that phenomenology is used in a rather simplified way and, at times, perhaps misappropriated by business and management researchers. Be this as it may, students in business management and related fields of social research need not worry too much about what their friends in the philosophy department think of their grasp of existentialism or phenomenology. The point is to apply the philosophical frame to a practical context of research. Student researchers who find this chapter interesting should follow up some of the

Box 6.2   Key concepts of phenomenological research

Themes

A focus on the lived experience of actors
An emphasis on meaning, language, intentionality, agency and reflection
An empathetic stance from the interviewer as a research co-participant

Assumptions

People are experiencing, reflective and agentive actors who collectively product social events
The subjective experience of existence, time and death are central to what it means to be human
The integrity of the research data is paramount: there is no 'bias', since there is no single reality or truth, there are only differing interpretations

The researcher is an active part of the research process

Data-gathering methods

Qualitative, especially, the audio-recorded, transcribed depth interview. Use of reflexive researcher field notes. Representative, non-random sampling

Approach to data analysis

Thematic analysis: focus on descriptions of experience, use of metaphor, the subjective construction of meaning, existential issues

Reporting of findings

Anonymisation of participants: elaboration of major themes using direct quotes to support interpretations

cited readings and form their own view on the ways in which existential phenomenology is represented in the chapter.

Phenomenological principles (see Box 6.2) have been used in management research areas, for example, to explore tourists' aesthetic experiences (Nasiri, Kirillova and Wassler, 2024), to frame a study of marketing managers' lived experience of their working roles (Ardley, 2009, 2011), to understand customer perceptions of hotels (Alfakhri et al. 2018), they have been the basis for the use of literary theory that has been applied in consumer research (Iser, 1972; Scott, 1994a), to understand tourists' experience of Buddhism (Hwang and Park, 2021), they have been the basis for a renewed focus on consumer experience as a counterpoint to the focus on consumer's attitudes and behaviour (O'Guinn and Faber, 1989; Sherry, 1991; Wilson, 2012) and phenomenology has been particularly prominent in consumer culture theory (CCT) (Askegaard and Linnet, 2011). For Thompson et al. (1989) existential phenomenology amounts to a paradigm in itself, blending the philosophy of existentialism with the methods of phenomenology.

As with any philosophical traditions that have been adapted for social research, there are differing interpretations. Edmund Husserl's (1931, 1970) ideological phenomenology was adapted for social research by subsequent writers (Gurswitch (1974), such as Heidegger (1962), Sartre (1943, 1946) and Schutz (1932). Other strains of phenomenological research were developed, such as Habermas's (1970) interpretive sociology and the phenomenological social constructionism of Berger and Luckman (1966). These writers generally emphasised the embodied, agentive character of lived experience, placing phenomenology squarely within Burrell and Morgan's (1979) interpretive paradigm. Phenomenological social research takes the embodied, experiencing agent as a starting-point and explores the mutually constructed 'lifeworld' of participants, the world of lived experience from which all others derive. The phenomenology of Merleau-Ponty (1962a, 1962b) advocated a return to that experiential world that pre-exists science and knowledge.

Philosophical phenomenology was a development of Hegel's philosophy of knowledge: phenomenological knowledge was knowledge as it appeared in consciousness. The emphasis is placed on how people can access and describe their directly apprehended, lived experience. There is, therefore, an acknowledgement of the role of intuition, recognising that much of our understanding is not articulated but, rather, is 'felt' or intuited. Phenomenologically informed researchers attempt to draw out this understanding by being open to the various personal ways people might describe this kind of experience in phenomenological interviews.

For example, within organisations, managers are a category of person charged with a specified range of responsibilities. 'Management' has, since the 1960s, been rather mythologised in that the skills, personal attributes and tasks of individual managers are held to be the reason for organisational success or failure. Phenomenological research can reveal how managers themselves experience this role (Ardley and Quinn, 2014). Do they recognise the heroic picture drawn in many popular management books (such as Peters and Waterman, 1982)? Do managers themselves feel that they have the skills, the knowledge and, importantly, the power and authority, to enact this role? Phenomenological research approaches seek to access the subjective experience of managers to gain intimate insights into this experience. This results in what can be a distinctive and penetrating research style when the study is executed well with participants who are willing to be candid.

Phenomenology has been placed in opposition to realism/positivism in social research (Hudson and Ozanne, 1988) since the two research perspectives are usually characterised by assumptions that are mutually exclusive. Most notably, where phenomenological research assumes a socially constructed reality, positivism assumes that reality is external and objective (Easterby-Smith et al., 1991; Morgan and Smircich, 1980). As we noted in the previous chapter, the contrasting ontological positions of different paradigms imply considerable differences in the methods of data gathering and data analysis used in research projects.

Existentialism and phenomenology

Thompson et al. (1989) point out that interpretive consumer research was, then, most closely identified with ethnography, semiotics and structuralism (Hudson and Ozanne, 1988). Thompson et al. (1989) labelled their contribution to the interpretive 'turn' (Beckman and Elliott, 2001) in consumer research existential phenomenology. They point out that the dominant paradigm in research in marketing was then (and arguably remains) "logical positivism" (Thompson et al., 1989, p. 134). Arndt (1985) referred to the dominant marketing research paradigm as logical empiricism. In the philosophy of positivism (Ayer, 1936), anything that cannot be observed and measured is treated as metaphysics. In other words, the un-measurable is outside the realm of social science. The universe is treated as if it is a mathematical whole, and the goal of science is to measure everything until we have a complete mathematical picture of the universe. Hence, positivistic research studies use quantitative methods to build an incrementally more complete of the universe.

Insights about the human condition can, of course, also be gained from art and the humanities, and interpretivism in social research springs partly from this sentiment. The argument does not need to be laboured today, but Thompson et al.'s (1989) paper was part of a movement to find a place for meaning in consumer research, alongside the research that sought observable and measurable social facts. One thing that all humans have in common is that we try to make sense of our experience, we read meaning into it. Interpretive research approaches are attempts to tap into that meaning-making process, to better understand how it works. Given the subjective nature of meaning-making, the meaning-making process as it is understood by actors lies beyond the scope of positivistic or structuralist/functionalist approaches to social research.

Existentialism–phenomenology represented a new contribution in interpretive consumer research as a counterpoint to the logical empiricist/logical positivist research enterprise that drew no ontological distinction between research in the physical sciences, and research in the social sciences. The philosophy of existentialism focuses on the undeniable fact that human beings are here in the world, we live, and we will die, and in between we think and reason and make subjectively agentive decisions about our lives that shape them. We have consciousness, unlike many of the objects of physical science. Atoms don't think. This is why, for interpretivists, social research has to be different in its methods to research that studies the physical world. Our conscious experience of life matters, since it is our medium for seeking a sense of meaning in our existence. Consumer choice can be seen as an expression of existential freedom (Elliott and Gournay, 1996), that is, our freedom to make decisions, however constrained that freedom may be. Consumer research that explores the fact that we humans are thinking, feeling beings who are compelled to try to make sense of our conscious experience clearly falls within the interpretive paradigm (Burrell and Morgan, 1979) and constitutes an alternative to the dominant realist paradigms.

Phenomenology fits well with existentialism with its emphasis on the conscious experience of life as lived in the moment, in a given context. The fact that we always occupy a context is important. Logical empiricism/logical positivism focuses on decontextualised knowledge, knowledge that is distinct from the researcher, the participants and the context in which they all operate at that time. Interpretivists are agnostic on whether or not such decontextualised knowledge is viable at all in social research. As interpretivists, they wish to do social research that acknowledges the human condition, with its sense of constrained agency, the fact that our existence consists in a stream of consciousness that responds to changing contexts over time, and the fact that we strive to make sense of this conscious experience. Hence, in phenomenological research, researchers seek to acknowledge the integrity of the participant interviewee's verbatim (Thompson et al., 1989) personal expression. Research participants' expressions of their lived experience are interpreted, but they are not taken to be consequences of other, deeper, impulses driven entirely by biology or other deep structures of causation.

Interpreting the phenomenological interview

The phenomenological approach has been used in therapeutic contexts (Hackley et al. 2024) but for our purposes we focus on the academic use of phenomenological interviewing for the purpose of analytical interpretive social research. Thompson et al. (1989) refer to three criteria for interpreting phenomenological interviews – "the *emic* approach, the autonomy of the text, and bracketing" (p. 140). The emic approach requires the researcher to understand the interview participants' expressions from the participants' own frame of reference, and not from that of the researcher (in contrast to *etic* research approaches which understand groups from the outsider's perspective). The need to understand the meanings of a section of social life as the research participant understands them, echoes the priority of ethnography, which also emphasises emic understanding.

Second, the transcribed interview text is the focus of the analysis, and the text is regarded as 'autonomous' in the sense that there is no attempt to ratify the veracity of factual assertions by the participant. This does not mean that aspects of the context outside the interview text are not taken into account – the default data-gathering method of existential phenomenology is the interview, but there is also room for the researcher to take a reflexive consideration of the wider context of the situation through field notes. The autonomy of the text refers to what in positivistic research is called reliability, that is, the idea that the research data are clues to an underlying reality. The autonomy of the text is a principle also applied in other textual research approaches such as discourse analysis. The text is the reality being investigated, and the important thing is not necessarily the accuracy of participants' recollection of events and processes but the meaning the expressions of these events had for the participant.

In order to focus on the text, any ideas that the researcher has about the phenomenon being investigated must be 'bracketed' or set aside as the focus is solely on the phenomenological expression of the participant. For these to be fully apprehended by the researcher, the researcher must not approach the task of interpretation with any prejudices or stereotypical notions about the participant or the subject matter. This does not mean that the researcher is necessarily gullible or indifferent to the integrity of the research data. Indeed, the integrity of the data is of key importance, and the researcher must make a judgement about the participants' sincerity.

Figure 6.2 reminds us that the context in phenomenological interviews has two elements, according to Askegaard and Linnet (2011). The first is the context in which the speaker apprehends their lived experience, which

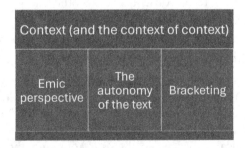

Figure 6.2 Thompson et al. (1989) three criteria for interpreting phenomenological interviews, with Askegaard and Linnet's (2011) 'context of context'

they might refer to in their interview. For example, an interviewee might express sadness in connection with a recent experience and then mention the reasons why they are susceptible to sadness because of events in their life history. Or, an interviewee might talk about a consumer service experience and how they enjoyed it so much partly because it was a reason for their family to get together. These examples illustrate that there are contextual factors that are pertinent in the way that lived experiences are apprehended by the subject.

The second kind of context which Askegaard and Linnet (2011) ask phenomenological consumer researchers to consider is the more subtle yet powerful influence of social structures and institutions. These, they argue, can profoundly influence the way that a subject apprehends their experience, often without the subject being aware of the influence of these social structures and institutions. For example, a minority ethnic person might rationalise their failure to get a better job to their personal failings in character and ability, until one day an event occurs that makes them realise that, in fact, they may have been rejected from some jobs not because of any personal inadequacy, but because of racism. In that event, their phenomenological experience was being framed by their minority ethnicity and, for some time, they didn't realise what was happening therefore they couldn't articulate it as part of their phenomenological experience. Askegaard and Linnet (2011) advocate that phenomenological consumer research should also embrace the structural and institutional influences on individual lived experience which may often not be articulated or felt but which, nonetheless, powerfully impact that lived experience and circumscribe the individual's subjective sense of agency.

Askegaard and Linnet (2011) make the point that CCT made a major contribution to consumer research by bringing existential phenomenology into the field (Thompson, 1989). As we have noted, existential phenomenology occupies the interpretive paradigm of Burrell and Morgan's (1979) matrix. However, Askegaard and Linnet (2011) suggest that there is a tension in CCT research between the grounded interpretive approaches to consumers' lived experience of consumer culture influenced by anthropology and ethnography, and the more sociologically informed examinations of the structural relationships of consumers to class, education, ethnicity, gender and other social structures and institutions. Askegaard and Linnet (2011) then argue for CCT researchers to embrace a micro-macro perspective. In effect, they are reminding readers, as Arnould and Thompson (2005) asserted, that CCT is not a paradigm, and not necessarily an interpretive paradigm, but a collection of qualitative research studies that cut across the interpretive and radical structuralist (and arguably also the radical humanist) paradigms of Burrell and Morgan's (1979) framework. A lot of interpretive research, though, regards a consideration of constitutive power as it plays out through the experiential perspective as a basic principle of critical interpretive research, and thereby does take account of wider social structures and ideologies (as discussed in Chapter 8). We will discuss CCT a little more in the subsequent chapters.

Intentionality and phenomenological research studies

Phenomenology focuses on intentional human experience. *Intentionality* concerns the sense in which experience is directed onto objects or phenomena, real or unreal. Literally, phenomenology refers to the study of appearances. Husserl was concerned with the way objects or phenomena appear to people. For researchers in management such 'objects or phenomena' could include marketed products, brands, services, consumer experiences, managerial actions and interventions, marketing communications or any other aspect of consumption, management or organisational activity. Researchers drawing on this perspective are interested in accessing the emotions and subjective reflections of research participants to better understand the processes of management and/or marketing/consumption in which they are involved and which they jointly produce.

In phenomenological research, the route to knowledge is to examine carefully what is felt, thought and perceived by the research participant(s) as expressed in phenomenological interviews (Kvale, 1983). Interpretation of phenomenological interviews is a nuanced process – it cannot be reduced to a "cookbook" (Hycner, 1985, p. 297). People ascribe meaning to the objects that present themselves in consciousness. The task of the researcher is to explore events or processes by gathering first-hand descriptions of these feelings, thoughts and perceptions. Consequently, the depth interview is an ideal data-gathering method for phenomenological research. Through this method, researchers can generate insight and understanding into marketing, management, policy and consumption issues and processes from a human perspective by acknowledging that these processes and issues are done by thinking, feeling, reflecting people.

This last sentence calls to mind the section in the previous chapter that emphasised agency and meaning in interpretive research. In phenomenological research, people are active participants in social processes. They are not merely bodies that 'behave' according to external stimuli. Phenomenology emphasises the human urge to derive meaning from experience. People are seen as actively interpreting their social worlds. Their interpretations and the meaning they ascribe to their experiences are seen as the key to understanding social events and processes, such as consumption practices, management and organisational activity. Most importantly, phenomenology sees people as independent thinkers with the power of agency. That is, people are thought to be able to initiate words, thoughts and actions. People's lives and thoughts are not simply determined by social structures and other forces.

Humanistic influences in phenomenological interpretive research

Humanist influences in social research are important to the phenomenological tradition. Humanism is an intellectual tradition that Burrell and Morgan (1979: 2019) place in its own paradigm, although it overlaps with interpretivism. Hirschman (1986), among others, has written of the humanistic influence in phenomenological consumer research, while Stern and Schroeder (1994) invoked humanism in their study of advertising imagery. Humanistic social research can be seen, historically, as a reaction to the dominance of experimental and statistical social research in the 1950s. As we have already discussed, the positivist, realist and experimental research designs place the emphasis on people as organisms that learn from and behave in response to, external stimuli. In contrast, humanism emphasises the ability of people to be aware of how their action and behaviour is based on their own reflections and reasoning. Many researchers wanted a more human level of understanding in social fields such as psychology, sociology and management studies. They felt that the model of the person in experimental research was flawed since it reduced the human being to an unreflexive organism without agency or reflexive awareness (although researchers using positivistic traditions would say that they don't minimise the agency or reflexive awareness of humans – they just don't think these capabilities are relevant for research).

The man-machine model of the person assumed in positivistic research (as a working assumption) also assumed that humans 'process' information much as computers do. For example, popular theories of mass communication are based on the transmission model from electronic engineering, that is, communication is modelled as if it were data being transmitted into a processor. This assumption is influential, for example, in marketing communications textbooks that emphasise linear models of mass communication involving encoding from the sender and decoding by the receiver (Hackley and Hackley, 2018b: 2021). By implication, the man-machine model assumes that humans have a strictly limited capacity for reflecting on their circumstances and behaving creatively in response to reasoning and emotions. In contrast, humanism emphasises the agentive capacity of humans to define our own existence and influence our own fate.

To repeat, the fact that theories and their models have assumptions that are not realistic does not necessarily invalidate them, as economists are usually quick to point out. In some disciplines, the value of a theory is not in the realism of its assumptions, but in the quality of its predictions. Of course, some would suggest that economics does not have the greatest track record in prediction either, but that is by the bye. The point is that humanistic researchers decided that, for them and their clients, having a more realistic model of the person does matter. For humanistic psychologists such as Carl Rogers (1945), the phenomenological interview enabled people to reflect on their experience and, by doing so, change their perceptions and behaviour. The goal of humanistic psychology was, and is, self-realisation. People are thought to have a capacity for reflection so that self-awareness can be increased, and behaviour changed. This is the basic premise of humanistic counselling psychology pioneered by Rogers (1945).

In social research in management and marketing and related areas, the same assumptions are made but the ends are, usually, somewhat different to those of psychology. While management researchers wish no harm on their research participants, the primary goal of the research is to generate insights and understanding about a particular issue or process, not to empower individuals with the ability to change their lives (although the happiness of research participants is certainly a part of the rationale in some consumer research studies that focus on consumer disadvantage, fairness and/or unhappiness, e.g. Husemann and Eckhardt, 2018; Labroo and Patrick, 2009; Thomas and Epp, 2019). The important thing for researchers (as opposed to therapists) is the assumption that people can stand outside their behaviour, so to speak, and reflect on it. This unique ability means that humans are more than bundles of learned responses and reinforced behaviours. We are more than machines. We are actively interpreting our experience in a search for meaning. This means that researchers must understand our experience from an emic perspective, as it appears to us, to fully understand the dynamics behind behaviour and social practices.

Experience and existence in phenomenological research

The title of one study in the *Journal of Consumer Research* shows exactly what this theme emphasises for consumer researchers: 'The experiential aspects of consumption: consumer feelings, fantasy and fun' (Holbrook and Hirschman, 1982). These researchers argued that consumption, that is, buying or experiencing stuff, is not only done on the basis of a careful and explicit comparison of product or service features in the light of rational needs. They suggested that consumption can also be indulged in for fun or to fulfil fantasies. This insight may seem profoundly obvious to student researchers reading this book who have recently enjoyed a shopping trip, a meal in a restaurant, a movie, or a night out dancing. The need for researchers to draw attention to the experiential reality of consumption arose because of the dominance in academic marketing research of theories which emphasised the economic rationality of consumers. This, in turn, arose because of the dominance of quasi-experimental and positivistic research methods which assumed a non-agentic and non-reflexive human organism responding to biological or evolutionary impulses. The publication of articles such as Holbrook and Hirschman (1982) represented a challenge to accepted research orthodoxy in consumer and marketing research.

The experiential perspective offered a radically new departure in academic business school research into buyer behaviour. Interpretive consumer research contributions developed approaches that acknowledge the emotionality (Elliott, 1998; Holbrook and Hirschman, 1982) and symbolism (Belk, 1988; Mardon, Denegri-Knott and Molesworth, 2023; Mick, 1986) of many buying decisions and consumer experiences. For example, Mardon, Denegri-Knott and Molesworth (2023) used qualitative interviews to explore the ways in which digital possessions are used in consumers' identity projects. Much consumer research in the structuralist/realist paradigm has focused on the measurement of attitudes through surveys or experiments. In contrast, phenomenological consumer researchers wish to tap into consumer experience as it appears to consumers, without the mediating influence of attitude scales or survey questions. They wish to understand the buying process as a phenomenon, as it appears to consumers. In this way, phenomenological social research seeks to understand what consumption *means* for shoppers, for example, by articulating the meaning of shopping experiences by drawing on myth (Arsel and Thompson, 2011; Brown et al., 2017).

Phenomenology, then, was adapted in social research as part of the humanistic movement to find research perspectives that employed a richer model of the person and acknowledged the influence in social events of human emotion and agency. It acknowledged the human need to make experience meaningful, and hence conceived of humans as seekers after meaning. One important part of what it means to be human is the experience of time and the certainty of death. This emphasis was incorporated into phenomenological research from existentialist writing.

Death in consumer research

Existentialism is, broadly, the study of being. We are thrown into existence, and we have to face the reality, temporality and finiteness of our own existence. Death, in fact, has been a topic of consumer research, not focusing on the fact of it, but on the consumption practices and symbolism around it (e.g. Dobscha, 2016; Hackley and Hackley, 2015a; Hackley, 2021). However, in the context of existential phenomenology, it is the fact of the inevitability of death that is important rather than the symbolism and social practices around it.

As agents of our own destiny, we make decisions about our lives. For existentialists, we are often unaware of our power to determine our own fate. Indeed, we are often scared by this power and escape from this knowledge by busying ourselves with trivial, everyday concerns and worries. This can represent a 'flight from freedom' whereby we deny our right to choose our destiny. Existentialist philosophy dwells on this extreme position on agency, suggesting that we live with choice and every moment we experience is governed by our willingness, or reluctance, to acknowledge this power of choice to ourselves. Incidentally, it is not only trivial consumption that might divert us from the terrible reality of our existential freedom. For psychoanalytic psychologist Erich Fromm (1941), those who cannot cope with existential freedom sometimes embrace the authoritarian certainties of fascism. Fromm (1941) could be writing about 2025, more than 80 years ago. Another possibility is that we escape from the terrible reality of our dismayingly finite existence through consumption (Elliott, 1997; Elliott and Ritson, 1995; Elliott and Gournay, 1996).

The themes of being, existence and death may seem out of place in a research project about, say, the marketing of garden tools or the management of fast-food service operations. The existentialist influence is important for the analysis of qualitative phenomenological research data because of the interpretive position taken by the researcher. It is a subjectivist position that focuses on our immediate experience of being and the ways in which we attempt to make sense of this experience. The ways we interpret our experiences as managers, consumers and workers can, then, be seen as ways in which we reconcile ourselves with the reality of mortality and the enigma of human existence.

Data gathering in phenomenological/existential research

Phenomenological researchers must generate verbal reports and/or written accounts of the participants' experience as their data. They must then organise and interpret this data. Clearly, the focus for research analysis here falls on language, since the route to inner thoughts and feelings lies in the accounts and descriptions that people give of their experiences. Language, written or audio-recorded, is the research data. Video and other texts (emails, letters) could also be used. This means that data-gathering and analysis have a 'messy' quality, as qualitative data sets invariably do, the data do not neatly 'fit' into categories and can be unwieldy to collect and collate. On the other hand, the value of these kinds of data set is that they can yield novel, striking and creative accounts that stimulate the researcher's interpretative imagination.

This kind of data set is also, often, intrinsically interesting in itself. When people feel relaxed and safe enough to talk about their experiences, the results can often be very engaging. When it is 'safe' to do so, we often reflect on our experience in ways which are new to us, we see things in new ways. The phenomenological interview has this quality in that it enables interviewees to access their experience in ways that may not have been clear to them before. The phenomenological interview is not designed to be a therapeutic intervention, it is intended as a data-gathering device. However, many research participants find that the interview process, conducted sensitively by the researcher, can prove to be a deeply reflective experience. People rarely have the psychological space to reflect deeply on and share their own lived experience in a non-judgemental and supportive situation. Doing phenomenological interviews can be a rewarding and sometimes surprising experience for both interviewer and interviewee.

As mentioned earlier in the book, depth interviews can have varying degrees of formality. The researcher can use a predetermined script to list topics, or they can allow the interviewee greater scope for setting the agenda of the interview. However, it can be very useful for researchers to work to an interview guide which sets out the major themes of interest. This can be useful for remembering what topics to raise and for helping to jog the memory. It is a good idea to give the interviewee some advance knowledge of the topic or issues that will be the focus of discussion. On the other hand, it is important not to be too prescriptive. Part of the excitement of qualitative research is that the researcher does not know what they will find. People are interesting, creative entities and in phenomenological research studies, the interviewee is always the expert. They have had the experiences to which you, the researcher, need to gain access. A researcher cannot know for sure what will arise; interview agenda or guides should allow for this. This implies that phenomenological and existential research principles are not usually useful for testing theories or hypotheses. They are useful for exploratory research designs that set broad terms of reference and set out to discover things about a particular issue or process. Phenomenological researchers do know what they are interested in before they conduct an interview, but they do not know exactly what they will find out about it.

The degree to which the interviewee can set the interview agenda depends to some extent on the kind of topic or research question being addressed. It also depends on the scale of and stage in, the research process. If a study entails a number of interviews, then it is likely that the researcher's interests and understanding will grow as the research progresses. This will influence the interview agenda. In many cases, research interviews become shorter as studies progress because the researcher has narrowed down the topics of interest. In many more cases the interviewee can raise unexpected and fruitful lines of thought and investigation.

Interviews that do not have a strict agenda have been used for many years in anthropology and sociology, and also in clinical and counselling psychology. Their history in marketing and management research is somewhat shorter. In humanistic psychology, the open-ended interview was devised as a therapeutic intervention by Carl Rogers (1945). In management research, the aim of the interview is not client therapy, although as we note above in most cases the interviewee does find the experience fulfilling and enjoyable. The interviewer might intervene at times to help the dialogue along, or to probe particular responses to get at more specific themes. They might also need to gently redirect the interviewee back on to the topic of interest at times. However, in general, phenomenological research gathers better-quality data if the interviewee is made to feel comfortable so that they get into a flow of uninterrupted talk in which they can be frank and insightful about their own feelings and thoughts concerning their working experience. In many cases, they will not have had such an opportunity before: good interview researchers are capable of creating a rapport or empathy with interviewees which can help to generate striking and novel research data in the form of original and creative insights.

The phenomenological researcher stance

Conducting a phenomenological interview well, demands subtle research skills. It is important that the researcher can empathise with the interviewee's perspective and suspend any judgement. The researcher must try to see the interviewee's world through their eyes (the emic perspective mentioned earlier). They must create a safe, open and confidential 'feel' for the interview. Many of the best qualitative interviews are like friendly chats: the interviewee becomes absorbed in their topic and forgets that the situation is, in fact, a relatively formal one. It helps if the interviewer has a specific interest in the topic, and a general interest in people and their thinking. It should be remembered that one-to-one interviews of this kind can be a powerful, moving and even, sometimes, a threatening experience in the sense that the participant might find some of their insights challenging. Some sensitivity is demanded of the researcher so that they know when to probe for deeper answers, and when to leave alone. Of course, at all times, the interviewee is free to terminate the interview, and they must be made aware of this at the beginning as a matter of ethical research conduct.

Ideally, the researcher should be in a physical position to maintain eye contact and to attend to what the interviewee is saying (or to 'listen actively' as discussed in Chapter 4). Even if the interview is online, the researcher can make efforts to be attentive. The researcher might find it useful to make occasional notes, but this should be done with subtlety because it can make the interviewee feel uncomfortable. It is best, in face-to-face scenarios, to ask the interviewee for permission to audio-record the interview, then place a microphone in an unobtrusive position to pick up the dialogue. In online scenarios, the interviewee should be asked to give their permission for the interview to be recorded. Later, the whole interview can be carefully replayed, listened to and transcribed. As a note of caution, it should be remembered that one interview can generate a vast amount of data. Fifteen thousand words is not unknown for one interview transcript. It is wise to keep interviews as short as reasonably possible; 30–60 minutes is more than adequate for most circumstances.

The interview tone

It is important for the researcher to be sensitive to the tone of the interview. This is an intangible thing that is hard to define, but it depends to a degree on the extent to which the interviewer can establish a comfortable rapport with the interviewee. Some interviews might be socially slightly awkward, the interviewee might be reticent or uncomfortable with giving responses. This is entirely natural. It can be difficult to create a sense of rapport. Some interviewees are simply not comfortable with the directness and intimacy of the phenomenological interview. Some other interviewees might simply be pressed for time, or they might have had second thoughts about doing the interview. In such a situation, the interviewer will have to work a little harder to generate good quality data by (gently) asking more questions and generally leading the interaction.

At the other extreme, some interviewees take some stopping once they realise that the situation is non-threatening, and they have a captive audience to whom they can relate their entire life story. In such cases, the interviewee might need to gently redirect the interviewee back onto relevant lines of discussion. Whenever possible, the tone of the interview should be friendly and relaxed but business-like, focused on the subject matter of interest. If tension emerges from the interviewee's reaction to some of the questions, it is the researcher's job to diffuse the tension, either by diverting attention to another, less problematic question, or by reassuring the interviewee that all responses are confidential.

The author once conducted a series of interviews in an advertising agency, and the first interviewee began the interaction by saying "I've been told I've got to talk to you" (Hackley, 2000). This wasn't the most promising start, but it is quite common for interviewees to be suspicious of researchers. The important thing is that the researcher tries to recover the situation by being open to and interested in everything the interviewee has to say. In the author's experience, people seldom have the chance to talk to a stranger about their work, and many people (especially the people in advertising agencies) are passionate about their work. Once they realise they have a captive, and non-judgemental, audience, they usually love to talk. Sometimes, they want to get stuff off their mind that they've been storing up, especially when it comes to ways in which their work is made less efficient or more difficult by their management. In another ad agency interview, the interviewee stopped midway and said "turn off your recorder and follow me". He led the author into another room and told a fascinating story, the real story, about how things worked there. It was very different to the official version. This happened because the interviewee realised that the researcher was sincere and decided to trust him. Sometimes, interviews in social research become a little like investigative journalism: you're being told a story, but then someone says "now, I'm going to tell you the real story". In social research, as in journalism, the researcher should always be prepared to re-evaluate just what the headline story is to be, in light of new information received.

At the end of the interview, the researcher/interviewer should thank the interviewee for their time and co-operation. They should, once again, reassure the interviewee that everything said will remain strictly confidential. Only the researcher and the readers of the research project will have access to the data. The interviewee's name will not be placed in the report unless they specifically agree to being named. In most qualitative research reports and articles, interviewees are not named. Either a pseudonym is used, or interviewees are referred to by a number or letter (interviewee A said this, interviewee B said that). Later, when the interview has been transcribed, some phenomenological researchers allow the interviewee to see the typed-up transcript of the interview to ascertain that it is a fair representation of the conversation. The interviewee might want to change some phrases, re-word some passages, or delete some parts. Some researchers even allow the interviewee to read the final research project report, so that the interviewee can see how their comments were interpreted in the findings. These practices are at the discretion of the researcher, there is no particular convention that applies, unless the institution sponsoring the research has procedures to which the study must conform which include showing the transcripts and/or the finished work to the interviewee. Generally, it would be very time intensive and cumbersome to do this. Ultimately, the researcher must own the interpretation, and the work.

Direct quotes in qualitative research reporting When reporting the findings of qualitative data sets, researchers should bear in mind the kind of research report they must produce. Most qualitative research relies heavily on direct quotes to support arguments or to illustrate particular points in the research report. The direct quote is important research material for qualitative researchers of all kinds. The quote might be indicative of a general theme that emerged in interviews. It might be a particularly pithy expression of an important issue or concern. It might illustrate something about the research issue that requires explaining to the reader of the research report.

A direct quote from the transcribed interview can often be important in showing how particular metaphors or tropes of speech are used to describe or account for actions or events. Whatever their particular purpose in a research report, direct quotes make the research tangible for the reader, and they are an important part of the scholarly goal of making the research transparent so that the reader can make a judgement on the interpretation.

Typical forms of qualitative data analysis such as thematic analysis (Braun and Clarke, 2006; Maguire and Delahunt, 2017) or Grounded Theory (Glaser and Strauss, 1967) entail grouping the data set into a selection of major themes (perhaps 5–10) that seem to structure the data. There may also be sub-themes. The data set would be read and re-read by the researcher, and codes and sorted according to the various themes. Each theme would be given a name, and the research report would explain each theme in turn, using direct quotes to illustrate each theme. In this way, the researcher is able to illustrate each theme in a nuanced and detailed way. The reader, for their part, will be able to see how the researcher interpreted the data, and the reader will be able to make a judgement on whether they feel that the researcher's interpretation was soundly based, or not. Direct quotes, then, are key not only to the revelation of the research findings, but also to the scholarly values of transparency in research reporting.

Description, empathy, metaphor and existential dimensions

The analysis of phenomenological/existential interviews emphasises several major issues (see Figure 6.2). In the research interview, there is a description of the interviewee's experience in relation to a particular object, process or event. The researcher must be careful to interpret this description with integrity by adopting an emic 'insider perspective' informed by an empathy with the interviewee's point of view. The initial description should reflect the interviewee's view of the world. Of particular interest is the interviewee's use of metaphor. When we talk or write, use of metaphor is unavoidable. The metaphors we choose are powerful in informing the meaning we draw from our experience. As mentioned earlier, there is also a concern with existential issues: how does the interviewee deal with issues of time and existence?

Such themes might seem very abstract and difficult to extract from interview texts. Indeed, the analysis of interviews as a whole, can be time consuming and difficult. The important thing is to find themes that can form the structure for the analysis/discussion. These themes may not be apparent straight away. They can come from extensive reflection on the data sets. The audio tape and/or notes and transcript might be listened/read through several times before the structure, tone and themes of the text begin to emerge for the researcher. Phrases or words might not strike you as interesting or revealing at first but may do so after more reading and thought. The researcher should think about the interviewee's 'take' on events, how they arrive at that take, what it reveals about the meaning of their experience. What metaphors does the interviewee use to describe their experience? Do these metaphors re-occur? Are they of a particular kind?

After some reflection, particular themes might emerge that can form the basis for the research analysis. Such themes would act as the organising structure for the findings and subsequent analysis/discussion in the research report. An interview or series of interviews might be characterised by distinctive metaphors. The researcher could use these metaphors as a basis for an analysis/discussion which speculates on why these metaphors and not others have been chosen, why they are powerfully expressive for the research participant, what they imply about the phenomenon being studied.

For example, one student researcher conducted a series of phenomenological interviews with entrepreneurs. The study was conducted to provide research data concerning the meaning of becoming and being an entrepreneur, so that insights could be found about the nature of entrepreneurial motivation and success. The analysis focused on the interviewees' biography, their origins and the ways in which life events had informed their entrepreneurial drive. One metaphor that seemed important was the interviewee's use of a 'no big deal' manner in discussing his transition from employee to self-employed entrepreneur. After reading the transcript many times, the researcher realised that the interviewee often played down the difficulty or unusualness of what he had accomplished. This seemed striking: having a salaried profession for 30 years and giving up that security for the risks of private business is a significant change, or at least so it seemed to the researcher. It appeared as though the dismissive 'no big deal' playing-card metaphor worked to deflect the realisation of the risk that had been undertaken. Paradoxically, the metaphor revealed exactly what the interviewee was attempting to play down: the risk of and intense motivation required for, entrepreneurship.

The interview approach was idiographic in the sense that the interviewee's entrepreneurial behaviour was considered as part of an evolutionary process tied in with his origins and life experiences. A similar interviewing approach towards a different interviewee resulted in a published paper on the 'social construction of entrepreneurship' (Mumby-Croft and Hackley, 1997).

Doing phenomenological research

Phenomenological research designs, then, normally entail first-hand descriptions and accounts of events from people who directly participate in those events. For example, a study of the effectiveness of in-store merchandising techniques in the clothes sector might generate data sets by interviewing and/or observing shoppers in stores. Interviews could also be conducted in other environments so that shoppers might reflect on their past experiences of in-store merchandising. The phenomenological interview is usually a retrospective account of events or experiences. In retrospect, interviewees can often reconstruct experience and make sense of it in ways that were not available immediately after or during the experience.

Student researchers have conducted phenomenological interviews with other students to generate insights into the experience of undergoing higher education as a mature student. Phenomenological interviewing (or similar approaches such as ethnographic interviewing) can be particularly powerful in chronicling personal change and transformation (McAlexander et al., 2014; Schouten, 1991). It often allows people to reflect on deeply personal issues of motivation and meaning that they have not reflected on before, at least not with the mediating influence of another person. The counselling psychology movement, mentioned above, is premised on the power of the interactional process that occurs when one individual is given the space and time to reflect frankly on their experience in the presence of another non-judgemental person. While the social research interview in management and marketing is not designed to foster personal change and transformation, it can be a powerful event for both parties, and researchers should remember this. The phenomenological interview is an intimate setting and should be handled sensitively by the researcher.

Shopping experiences as phenomenological research data

Other researchers have explored the experience of shopping as an aspect of consumer behaviour studies. Shopping, reduced to a price and value information processing phenomenon by many consumer behaviour models, is revealed as a rich and powerful experience by a phenomenological perspective. Brown and Reid (1997) had students in Northern Ireland, United Kingdom write down their stories of shopping experiences in short essays. Vivid experiences were recounted that revealed something of the complexity and value-laden character of shopping itself. Brown and Reid (1997) used a narrative analysis (discussed later in the book) to focus on storytelling around shopping experiences. People recounted the many meanings of their shopping experience as they appeared to them from a deeply personal perspective. The stories were frequently vivid and compelling, and shopping experiences were woven into complex narratives that encompassed relationships, identity, social positioning and other profoundly personal issues. It was apparent that people go shopping to cheer themselves up or to distract themselves from the cares of everyday life. It was also evident that shopping is an integral part of contemporary culture and forms a landscape within which everyday life takes place.

Another phenomenological study focused on the consumption practices of expectant mothers and how these practices were mediated by considerations of time. Shopping was a part of this study but more important were the insights gained into the complexity of the lives of expectant mothers and the strategies they used to manage time and their consumption behaviour (Carrigan and Szmigin, 2004). For some people, shopping becomes pathological: like drug addicts, they simply cannot stop (Elliott, 1994; Elliott and Gournay, 1996). Interpretive research approaches that focus on subjective experience, like the phenomenological approach, are able to capture just what it is in shopping experiences that many people find so compelling.

This chapter has outlined an introduction to the main philosophical and methodological assumptions behind the use of phenomenological principles in social research. It has focused on the tradition described as existential phenomenology by Thompson, Locander and Pollio (1989: 1990) since this broad tradition is highly influential in qualitative research, and especially so in consumer research. Although other theoretical traditions come in and out of fashion in different subject domains, phenomenological principles have become paradigmatically significant within interpretive qualitative research to the extent that they might remain un-stated yet taken-for-granted. However, there is another theoretical tradition that might stake a claim to being as influential as existential phenomenology in consumer and marketing/management research: ethnography, and this is discussed in Chapter 7.

Glossary

Emic and etic research In qualitative empirical research studies, the emic approach refers to understanding a group or individual from within, that is, from the perspective of the subject, while etic refers to understanding the subject from the perspective of the researcher.

Existentialism The existentialist literary and philosophical movement focused on the human experience of being and existence. It became linked with the phenomenological perspective in social research because each perspective takes the experiencing, sense-making individual as a starting point.

Humanism A movement in literature and art that has been echoed in social sciences. In social science it draws attention to the agentive, creative experiencing individual and places this model of the person at the centre of research and theorising.

Intentionality In phenomenology, the idea that consciousness is directed onto objects.

Chapter 7

Ethnography and associated methods

Digital ethnography, autoethnography, practice theory and assemblage theory

Abstract

Ethnography is another of the most important informing traditions of interpretive research. Anthropologists developed the ethnographic method in their study of indigenous populations, and it has been widely adapted to the investigation of social and cultural phenomena from an emic perspective. This chapter offers an introduction to ethnographic methods, including associated methods including digital ethnography, autoethnography and practice theory.

Chapter objectives

After reading this chapter students will be able to

- understand that the research tradition of ethnography is associated with cultural anthropology
- appreciate ways in which management, organisation, marketing and consumer researchers can adapt ethnographic approaches to suit different research questions
- grasp the role of autoethnography in ethnographic and interpretive research
- appreciate some of the ways in which ethnography can be applied to study social practices and digital practices

Introduction to ethnography

Ethnography, the preferred empirical method of cultural anthropologists, is central to the socio-cultural research approach that has characterised much CCT research (Arnould and Thompson, 2005; Arnould and Wallendorf, 1994; Giesler, 2024; Gollnhoffer et al. 2024; Grant, Canniford and Shankar, 2024; McCracken, 1986, 1989; Schouten, 1991, 2023; Schouten and McAlexander, 1995; Sherry, 1983; Tumbat and Belk, 2011; Venkatraman,

DOI: 10.4324/9781003432203-10

Ozanne and Coslor, 2024; Wallendorf and Arnould, 1988). The emic approach of trying to grasp an insider's viewpoint on group meanings, processes and practices is fundamental to ethnography (as it is to the socio-cultural approaches of CCT). Pink et al. (2016) define ethnography in this way:

> Following Karen O'Reilly (2005), we posit that ethnography is: 'iterative – inductive research (that evolves in design through the study), drawing on a family of methods … that acknowledges the role of theory as well as the researcher's own role and that views humans as part object/part subject.
>
> (p. 3)

Pink et al. (2016) offer a broad definition (borrowed from O'Reilly, 2005) that emphasises the role of theory in ethnographic interpretation, the multi-method character of ethnographic work, the evolving and iterative process of ethnographic investigation, and the human-centred approach in which humans can engage in reflexive examination of ourselves. In particular, Pink et al. (2016) argue that ethnography is not a method as such, but, rather, an interpretive process in which a set of values are applied to researching people and culture:

> ethnography is not a very meaningful practice by itself; instead, it is only useful when engaged through a particular disciplinary or interdisciplinary paradigm and used in relation to other practices and ideas within a research process.
>
> (p. 2)

Ethnographic studies tend to use a variety of data-gathering methods. These typically might include participant observation, interviews, research field notes and archival/secondary information. For example, Mardon, Cocker and Daunt (2023) employed a combination of ethnography, netnography, depth interviews and archival research to explore the impact of influencers on consumer collectives. So, for Pink et al. (2016), ethnography is not necessarily tied to a particular set of rules, it can be applied through, and together with, various alternative theoretical approaches, and we will see more examples of this multi-disciplinary approach to ethnography in the chapter.

Elliott and Jankel-Elliott (2002) describe ethnography as an improvement on the kind of 'armchair' sociology that was based on surveys and second-hand information. It was a way of entering the field to have a first-hand engagement with empirical data sets in naturalistic settings, instead of relying on the search for patterns in archival data sets. A view emerged in sociology that first-hand research might be a better way of understanding alien (that is, unfamiliar) cultures. In traditional anthropology, a prolonged immersion in a social group became the accepted method (e.g. Malinowski, 1922). At least a year of immersion was recommended so that the researcher could become truly one of the group they were studying.

In qualitative sociology and cultural anthropology, shorter field trips, involving observation, participant observation and supplemented by interviews with members of a culture, archival data and other data sources, became regarded as an acceptable approach. One famous school of ethnographic study evolved from Chicago sociologists of the 1930s, who became discontent with 'armchair' sociology and began to study sub-cultural groups in the United States as if they were studying the indigenous tribes of isolated islands. This became known as 'streetcorner sociology' as it studied the deviant sub-cultures of America (Downes and Rock, 1982, p. 36; Venkatesh, 2009). It entailed the researcher becoming a member of the group being studied, as Venkatesh (2009) did in the case of his exploration of a drug-dealing street gang. The student researcher might be relieved to hear that the application of ethnographic principles in business and management, marketing and consumer research can be achieved without that level of commitment.

Ethnography is associated with the discipline of anthropology, and the anthropological turn in marketing research has been seen as a development of *postmodern* (Brown, 1995) and *experiential* (Holbrook and Hirschman, 1982) methods that challenged the ontological and epistemological assumptions and writing conventions of the dominant neo-positivistic research reporting model in consumer, marketing and management research. For Banister et al. (1994) (see Figure 7.1) ethnographic research is characterised by multiple formal and informal qualitative data sources as the researcher becomes immersed within the group being studied using al means possible. The goal is to understand the group through an emic perspective, that is, to walk in their shoes and understand the world from their perspective. The data sources can include informal conversations, field notes based on the reflexive thoughts and observations of the researcher, non-participant and also participant observation, archival and secondary documents, photographs and film, internet sources such as chat threads or other sources of digital ethnography, participant diaries and interviews. The goal is to gain a holistic, emic understanding from the perspective of the group.

For example, Venkatesh (2009), the sociologist mentioned above, first tried to gain an understanding of a drug-dealing gang in a poor part of town by going to them with a questionnaire. He quickly realised that this was not going to generate the insights he sought. He built a relationship with the people he was talking to, developed a degree of mutual trust and rapport, and they allowed him to hang out with them for several years, observing their lifestyle. He became a nominal member of the group (he was discrete in what he disclosed to his professors). As a participant observer, he gained an emic understanding of the socio-cultural dynamics at play and, rather than taking a judgemental attitude, tried to understand the social situation the members of the group found themselves in. The group leader was in fact a

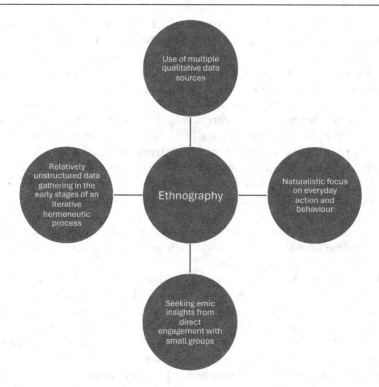

Figure 7.1 Features of ethnography

Source: Adapted from Banister et al. (1994)

college graduate but most of the group and the community in which they op-erated were poor and disadvantaged with very constrained life opportunities. Venkatesh (2009) learned that the group was part of an informal and mutu-ally supportive social system that formed spontaneously because of the lack of official mechanisms for social support in this poor and deprived area of the United States. He documented not only the criminal aspects of the group but also the ways in which it was integrated within the local community in often supportive and positive ways.

The study brings to mind one accusation that is sometimes made of ethno-graphic studies, namely that the researcher is vulnerable to taking the insider perspective so thoroughly that they lose a sense of researcher independence. The immersion in a sub-cultural group by the researcher, as noted earlier, is a common ethnographic approach that is used extensively in qualitative studies of consumption (e.g. Croft, 2013; Hein and O'Donohoe, 2014; O'Sullivan, 2016; Schouten and McAlexander, 1995). However, and we are not suggest-ing that this happened with Venkatesh (2009), the immersive aspect of eth-nography can be criticised if the researcher loses their sense of independence as a social scientist and fails to engage sufficiently critically with the subject matter and the values of the group. This criticism is more often levelled at sociological ethnographies of sub-cultural groups such as street gangs, drug addicts (Hammersley and Atkinson, 1983) or other socially marginalised groups, such as football hooligans (Armstrong and Harris, 1991).

In one sense, it is the stock criticism of interpretive and qualitative research that is often made by researchers in the structuralist/realist traditions, since objectivity is considered a mark of research integrity in those traditions, while interpretive researchers regard objectivity in social research as unobtainable, whatever the method may be. It is axiomatic in interpretive research that the presence, choices and actions of a researcher will invariably influence the results. Setting this extreme point aside, it is of course essential that the ethnographic researcher retains a sense of detachment so that, even while they are immersed in the group under study, they are able to acknowledge and articulate how the influences on their judgement might inflect and nuance their social scientific conclusions.

Ethnographers, then, seek to understand social and cultural phenomena through the eyes of the group participants, while retaining a sense of scientific detachment, so that they can understand the meanings and dynamics of a social group as well as, or perhaps sometimes better, than the participants themselves. The participants, of course, are truly immersed in their milieu and therefore less able to stand apart from it to see it as others might see it. With its emphasis on qualitative data-gathering techniques and its focus on experience and meaning, ethnography is sometimes regarded as a counter-position to traditional social scientific research approaches that focus on objective, observable facts and causation. Ethnographers normally seek rich, insightful descriptions of social phenomena as opposed to *nomothetic* generalisations that are founded on large samples and tests of statistical significance. Ethnography and quantitative, causal research share a concern with empirical data, but ethnography seeks to generate interpretive representations that derive from first-hand observation and study. It is, hence, an *applied* research tradition.

Victor Turner and liminality

One anthropological concept that has been highly influential in ethnographic social research is Victor Turner's concept of *liminality*. Turner (1967) drew on van Gennep's (1961) foundational anthropological studies on ritual process. In rituals of transformation, from child to adult, from single to married, or from follower to leader or in calendrical rites to celebrate the transition from winter to summer, van Gennep (1961) observed three main stages in the ritual process (see Figure 7.2). The pre-liminal stage entails separation from the previous life: the liminal stage refers to the mid-stage of the process when the participant is neither part of their old life and identity, nor yet part of the new one, as social status is suspended and there

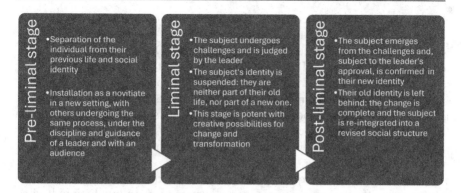

Figure 7.2 The stages of ritual process
Source: Adapted from Turner (1967).

is the possibility of great change in the midst of the flux. Finally, the post liminal stage occurs when the ritual process is consummated with the participant being confirmed in their new identity and re-integrated in their new status into the social structure. Turner's work (1967, 1969, 1974, 1982) focused on the mid stage of the process, the liminal stage and extended the theory beyond formal rites of passage (van Gennep, 1961) in pre-economic societies into realms of consumption in advanced economies.

Turner (1986) described the liminal stage as a time of "fructile chaos, a storehouse of possibilities, not a random assemblage but a striving after new forms and structures ..." (p. 42). Turner's ideas on liminality and ritual process (1967, 1969) have been adapted in many areas of social research to theorise physical and/or psychological spaces, which are characterised by a suspension of normal rules and structures and in which individuals feel a sense of the possibility of change and transformation. Roberts (2015) refers to the "liminoid zones" of urban night life areas in which young people explore alternative identities (often facilitated by alcohol (Hayward and Hobbs, 2007), while liminality has been used to theorise gender (Schau and Thompson, 2010), spiritual consumption (Husemann and Eckhardt, 2019), adventure sports (Tumbat and Belk, 2011) TV reality shows (Hackley, Brown and Hackley, 2012), cosplay (Seregina and Weijo, 2017) and wine consumption (Smith Maguire, 2010). The engineering of liminal experiences through the design of liminal physical spaces (Kozinets et al., 2004; Pielichaty, 2015) has also been the topic of empirical, qualitative research studies.

From liminal to liminoid experiences

Turner (1982) distinguished between liminal and liminoid experience. With liminoid experience, this fructile chaos can be experienced as a sense of existential liminality that is not bound to a formal and compulsory ritual process but is voluntary and impermanent. Liminoid experiences are often ludic (oriented to fun and playfulness) (Turner, 1982) and are therefore predicated on the existence of leisure as opposed to work: "One works at the liminal, one plays at the liminoid" (p. 55), thus implying that liminoid experiences are available in advanced economies. Liminoid experience can occur within groups, like sub-cultural movements such as hippies or in sports or celebrity fandom, but liminoid experience can also be manifest in individual consumption of entertainment experiences or commodities: "The liminoid is more like a commodity – indeed, often is a commodity, which one selects and pays for, than the liminal" (Turner, 1982, p. 55).

Turner (1982), then, explicitly linked liminoid experience to consumer experience. In effect, consumers in advanced economies can buy liminoid experience to experiment and play with identity and personal transformation that is never confirmed by social acceptance into a new order – this experience is engaged in symbolically and can be endlessly perpetuated through consumption experiences. For example, Hackley, Hackley and Bassiouni (2019) examined the ways in which TV advertisements promote not merely the brand, product or service they advertise, but the liminoid experience in which the consumer partakes by consuming. They propose that, among all the creative strategies advertisers use such as humour, fear, aspiration and social status, the appeal of the liminoid experience should be added, since it is so common once one begins to notice the number of advertisements that foreground this appeal. The authors argue that the ads imply that, by buying the advertised brand, consumers can experience a pseudo-transformation of identity. Turner's (1982) ideas have a wide scope of application, and they continue to bring anthropological insights to research in marketing and consumer studies.

Varieties of ethnography in business and management studies

Organisational management has long been an area of interest for anthropological researchers since the 1920s (Kellogg et al., 2006; Wright, 1994). Many classic studies of organisational management have, as Wright (1994) shows, used principles derived from ethnography to construct representations of managerial experience, with the aim of generating insights into the process and practices of organisational management (e.g. Watson, 1994). It might seem odd to the first-time researcher that a research technique devised to understand isolated tribespeople in pre-historic cultures would be used to study something as familiar and everyday as management. Management, though, as we understand it today in advanced industrial economies, may be a familiar concept, but there is still surprisingly little known about it. It tends to be a combination of skills and knowledge that are learned on the job, by doing the job, but in spite of some 100 years of research, we still cannot definitively point to which skills are most important in an effective manager, and how best these skills might be learned and taught. What is more, after more than 100 years of formalised management education in the Western world, we cannot definitively say that organisations are managed any better for all this research and theorising (Hackley, 2024). Ethnographic methods can help in revealing the internal logics of management rationality (or irrationality). In employing an ethnographic method to study familiar and taken-for-granted social practice, that social practice can be made unfamiliar, and its components more effectively revealed.

As noted, the ethnographer engages in close study of a particular social group to try to understand the cultural norms, values and behaviour of that group, usually over an extended period of time. In organisations, researchers using ethnographic approaches can utilise participant or non-participant observation, alongside interviews, reviews of internal documents and other informal data-gathering approaches. Management and marketing researchers tend to employ ethnographic approaches over shorter time-periods than qualitative sociologists or cultural anthropologists, with some exceptions. An ethnographic study as short as a week or a few days, though, can still have value. For example, Elliott and Jankel-Elliott (2002) have used shortened ethnographic research in strategic consumer research for many global brands, while Clarke et al. (1998) studied the culture of the British public house, more commonly known as the pub.

Of course, where a researcher decides to do an ethnographic study of a sub-cultural environment that they regularly occupy anyway, then they arrive at the site of study already immersed in the socio-cultural rituals and understandings of the group. Olsen (2016) is a trained anthropologist who was a partner in an international advertising agency, she made field notes and kept a diary throughout her business career and later, when she became an academic, she wrote up ethnographic accounts of her business experiences. Ritson and Elliott (1999) used ethnographic principles to research the social uses of advertising among UK adolescent advertising audiences using an ethnographic study. The first author (well-known marketing guru Mark Ritson) took a job as a teaching assistant in schools for several of months, conducting interviews with the schoolchildren during breaks.

Researchers in management have adapted ethnographic principles to enhance studies of organisational management that are theoretically framed in a variety of ways. For example, Svensson (2007) framed his doctoral study of an advertising agency as social phenomenology, although his study also made use of non-participant ethnographic observation because of the extended contact he had with the agency. Kelly et al. (2005) used access to an advertising agency to perform a "discourse analysis of ethnographic interviews" (p. 505). The ethnographic element adding to the roundedness of the discourse analytic interpretation of interview texts through an ethnographic understanding of the research context gained through time spent in the agency as a non-participant observer. The researcher's interpretation of the interview data, then, was informed by their first-hand knowledge of the organisational context about which the interviewees were speaking. Hackley (2000) took a similar approach, also famed as a discourse analysis of interviews with advertising professionals, based on a week spent in an advertising agency, and supplemented by additional shorter periods of ethnography, secondary and archival research. The main interviews for the study were conducted in the ad agency itself. They were interpreted and analysed alongside field notes, archival study of internal agency documents and informal data generated from time spent in the agency observing the activities. Hackley (2000) also gained knowledge of the agency in question through informal contact for a year prior to the main data-gathering period.

Video ethnography

Ethnographies have often made use of video as part of, or as the whole of, their data set (Belk et al., 2017; Chatzidakas and MacLaran, 2018; Jayasinge and Ritson, 2013; vom Lehn, 2014; Woermann, 2018). Video ethnography follows the same broad aims as all ethnography in the sense of gaining an emic perspective of the sub-cultural group under investigation, but they do this through a close examination of video data sets. Video ethnographies might be conducted as part of a multi-method ethnographic study, or they might be used as a stand-alone method where direct access to the ethnographic site was not possible. In addition, video can be used as a form of participant diary where members of the group under study are asked to film themselves at chosen times or at chosen events.

Video ethnography could be conducted on a social or consumption practice with which the researcher has some familiarity, to extend the scope of their study. For example, a researcher studying the social practices of working-class British weddings might use the extensive online resource of wedding video clips as additional material. Hackley and Hackley (2015a) wanted to do an ethnographic study of an East Asian ritual, the Hungry Ghost Festival. There are many hungry ghost festivals in Asia that follow differing Buddhist traditions and local mythologies. The researchers in this case set up the project by interviewing the festival organiser and some other local people online, but then could not get to the rather inaccessible region in which this particular festival takes place. Instead, they found that quite a lot of videos of the hungry ghost festival processions and rituals in this area had been put online, so the researchers were able to supplement their acquired local knowledge with accounts deriving from the video material they were able to access. As an additional ethnographic element, one of the researchers had intimate first-hand knowledge of Theraveda Buddhist rituals and Asian languages, so this ethnographic insight added to the richness with which the data could be interpreted and analysed.

Leading academic conferences in marketing and consumer research now often have sections for video ethnography and filmed scholarly work, on the basis that video can support robust ethnographic insights and contribute to theory development (Belk et al., 2017). For the student researcher, video might be a problematic medium because universities might not have the flexibility of regulations to permit student researchers to use video as a scholarly medium. However, there would, in all likelihood, be nothing wrong with student researchers using video as part of their data set, in addition to the more traditional qualitative data-gathering methods of focus groups and interviews. Other forms of imagery, especially photography, can also form part of an ethnographic data set. Student researchers should bear in mind the ethical issues entailed in using visual media as research data.

Digital ethnography

Digital ethnography has become a major subfield of ethnography. Pink et al. (2016) see digital ethnography as an important context for the inherently multidisciplinary field of ethnographic studies since human culture has extended into digital manifestations. They refer to Lupton (2014) who has suggested that digital sociologists tend to engage in four types of practices: using digital tools for data gathering, examining how people use digital media, using digital tools for data analysis and engaging in critical analysis of the implications of digital data. All of these practices can be present alongside each other in digital ethnographic studies, but there will be differences of emphasis. Pink et al. (2016) include within the scope of digital ethnography the investigation of things, experiences, social practices, relationships, events and localities and social worlds. For example, Sibai, Luedicke and de Valck (2024) analysed interactions in one online community over the course of 18 years to find out why online communities become brutal in their language and insults.

As social life becomes increasingly conducted online in various forms, there is a need for ethnography to develop techniques and principles for taking an ethnographic approach to online culture and online communities (Arvidsson and Caliandro, 2016; Schembri and Latimer, 2016). In consumer research, perhaps the best-known brand of digital ethnography is *Netnography* (Kozinets, 2015, 2019a,b). Kozinets et al. (2018) explain the basic principle of netnography as follows:

> The basis of netnography is rather simple. It is grounded by the principle that the perspective of an embodied, temporally, historically and culturally situated human being with anthropological training is, for purposes relating to identity, language, ritual, imagery, symbolism, subculture and many other elements that require cultural understanding, a far better analyst of people's contemporary online experience than a disembodied algorithm programmed by statistics and marketing research scientists.
>
> (p. 231)

Kozinets et al. (2018) position netnography as a form of digital ethnography that seeks to reclaim digital and digitised forms of understanding from naïve data science and algorithm-driven formulas and invest it with a human level of insight, seeking "a more experiential and more participative understanding of a shifting social realm" (p. 231) that is, the shifting social realm of the internet and its countless manifestations of social media platforms and communicative technologies. Netnography, like ethnography, is a flexible multi-method approach. It is designed to closely examine online consumer culture focusing on multiple dimensions of computer-mediated social interaction, taking account of the words and language used, and also the particular elements of the platform being used. That is, netnography would consider the characteristics of Instagram, Facebook, Snapchat and so on and how the design of those platforms frames and shapes interaction on the platform. It would also take account of such elements as moderator standards and behaviour, the characteristics of the various communicators making up interactions on the site, the history and evolution of each platform, the types of interaction taking place, the symbols, GIFS, images and videos deployed in the course of interactions, and so on. In effect, netnography shares some characteristics with a discourse analysis (discussed in Chapter 8) in online contexts.

Like ethnography, netnography (or other forms of digital ethnography) attempts to generate insights into the socio-cultural practices and meanings of a community or sub cultural group by immersing the researcher in the community/group and taking account of the social, symbolic and communicative practices of the group in a naturalistic way, in the sense that the researcher engages with the 'natural' ways in which people communicate and express themselves in online contexts, as opposed to setting up experiments or surveys. The process of netnographic 'entrée' occurs when the researcher first enters the site of interest, that is, the online community or group of interest, to orient themselves and immerse themselves in that context in order to absorb the tone, style, platforms and methods of interaction and communication that represent the ways in which participants produce that particular community.

Netnography, like all qualitative approaches, can be combined with others, for example, Capellini and Yen (2016) combined ethnography and netnography. Villegas (2018) combined autoethnography (discussed below) with netnography, calling it auto-netnography (Kozinets and Kedzior, 2009). Atanasova, Eckhardt and Husemann (2024), in their study of digital nomads, combined elements of netnography including interactive participation, online non-participant observation, visual analysis of screen captures and researcher's ethnographic observations and field notes. Ciampa and de Valck (2024) combined netnography with guided introspections to explore mutual gifting systems in an online community.

As we have pointed out earlier, ethnography implies a set of values rather than a method or scope, and ethnographies can be applied in many differing contexts to investigate many different kinds of situation in concert with other approaches. Netnography (non-branded typologies of digital ethnography are also available) can be especially useful for student researchers. Researchers can easily access vast tranches of publicly available data through fan forums and other online communities, social media groups and specialist websites. Online chat and comment threads and posts can be used as data. If the researchers chooses to join an online community and to interact as a member, then issues of research integrity potentially come into play. If the researcher is using online data posted by individuals, then it is incumbent on the researcher to anonymise the data (if it is not already anonymised by the poster).

Autoethnography

Autoethnography has made a small but noted contribution to marketing and consumer research. Adopting the principles of ethnography to a sample of one person, autoethnography uses the subjective and reflective perspective of the individual as a source of social research data. Denzin (2014) locates autoethnography in a tradition inspired by C. Wright Mills (1959) and J.-P. Sartre (1963) because it inspires the sociological imagination and can somehow re-connect the social with the personal. Unlike the phenomenological stance, in autoethnography, experience is not seen as a foundational category, but, rather, experience is performed and constituted through text. In other words, the act of putting words to experience constitutes that very experience. There is the phenomenological experience of, say, being outside in a lightening storm, and then there is the articulation of that experience by the subject. In autoethnography, the ontological distinction between experiencing and rendering that experience into words is moot. The experience occurs through the articulation. Deetz (1980) notes that, "Speaking speaks not only information but a tradition, a tradition which carries along that which will be recovered as thought" (p. 13). Autoethnography articulates and constitutes experience from a subjectivist position located in culture, class and race.

Autoethnographic research studies are sometimes written entirely in the first person by the researcher using their own subjective viewpoint as a sample of one (Holbrook, 1995). Alternatively, in narrative autoethnography, the first-person perspective is thrown on to an account of an experience, a phenomenon or an event (Hackley, 2022; Olsen, 2003), in contrast to autoethnographies that use the subjectivity of the person in itself as the source of data (e.g. Gould, 1991; Holbrook, 1995). Autoethnography, like ethnography, makes its points from a non-realist ontological perspective that stands in opposition to the idea of objectivity and the epistemological assumptions of positivistic/realist scientific reporting (Reed-Danahay, 1997). It would be absurd to suggest that an autoethnographic data set could render objective knowledge. In autoethnography, the very impossibility of objectivity is not only acknowledged but is treated as having great value in social research. It is the subjective experience, articulated freely in a non-judgemental setting, that can reveal insights that would be unavailable to other methods.

Different styles of autoethnographic contribution to published marketing and consumer research include Belk (1996), Brown (1998, 2012a, 2012b), Hackley (2007), Sherry's (1995) teleethnography and Olsen and Gould's (2008) ethnomusicological ethnography, Gould's (1991) introspective-praxis autoethnography and Holbrook's Subjective Personal Introspection (SPI) (1995), which is discussed below. It is possible to further subdivide autoethnographic styles into many variations. For example, Denzin (2014, p. vii) refers to collaborative autoethnography and collaborative writing (Chang et al., 2013), duoethnography (Norris and Sawyer, 2012), ethno-drama (Saldana, 2011) ethnographic fiction, polyvocal texts and mystories (Richardson, 2000), meta-autoethnography (Ellis, 2009) and sociopoet-ics (Pelias, 2011). Of these, perhaps only duoethnography (Tiwsakul and Hackley, 2012) has been deployed in marketing, in a study of cross-cultural consumer identity.

Autoethnography foregrounds not only the subjective experience of the writer, but also the writing craft that can draw the reader in to understand the emotional texture of what is being expressed. In this sense, autoethnog-raphy's emphasis on writing reflects Brown's (2005) insistence that writing, as the key representational form of research, is not merely a neutral medium through which researchers communicate their research findings about a 'real' world beyond the text. Rather, the social reality being described is brought into being through text. Some forms of autoethnography have something in common with creative nonfiction writing (Gutkind, 1996) in that they offer a first-person account of histories, experiences and events. In this regard, autoethnographies have considerable critical potential since they can offer deeply personal accounts that are sometimes written with emotional force, giving voice to the marginalised (Pratt, 1992).

For example, racism in British Universities is given deeply personal ac-counts in one autoethnographic collection (Gabriel and Tate, 2017). Alsop (2002) emphasises the self-reflexivity of autoethnographic writing in a study of the way immigration changes the notions of being home or not home, while Tiwsakul and Hackley (2012) take the same theme of immigration/emigration in a collaborative autoethnography to explore the shifting sense of identity of the immigrant and how that marginalisation is expressed and identity re-ordered through selective consumption.

Holbrook's (1995) SPI approach is probably the most well-known mani-festation of autoethnography in marketing research (Shankar, 2000). In-trospection strictly entails observing oneself, examining one's own internal responses to stimuli, rather than commenting on the world from the first-person perspective. The latter is referred to as extrospection by Gould (1995,

2008), or sometimes as narrative autoethnography (Olsen, 2003). Narrative autoethnography consists in first person accounts of experiences and reflections, which bring the personal and biographical within the scope of social research.

Like all interpretive approaches to research, autoethnography has its critics. Some regard the subjective viewpoint as inherently un-scientific and not worthy of serious consideration as a social research method (Wallendorf and Brucks, 1993; see Gould, 1995). Other criticisms in the field of autoethnography take in the ontology, epistemology, tone of voice and choices of subject matter. Autoethnography, say critics, has no hypotheses and does not have systematic data sets, it celebrates bias as a virtue (Denzin, 2014, p. 70) and it can be a self-indulgent platform for self-indulgent, egoistic writing. There are no glib answers to these criticisms, what constitutes science is an ongoing debate. For the converted, autoethnography liberates the critical voice, mobilises minority viewpoints and liberates the authentic and creative voices of researchers and research participants, and hence acts as an important corrective and antidote to prevailing objectivist scientific ideologies.

There are also many instances of published studies in marketing that are not labelled as autoethnographies as such, but which use elements of biographical or autobiographical data in their analysis. These might use first-person vignettes and/or direct quotes to use the subjective perspective to illuminate various topics. Examples include the life history method used by McLeod et al.'s (2009) study of advertising creatives' professional lives, in which advertising agency creative professionals described not only their work but their personal life journey to becoming a creative, in which their social class turned out to be an important feature. Other examples include the use of personal subjective vignettes to give reflexive context to a study of top advertising agencies' working practices (Hackley, 2000), or Wohlfeil et al.'s (2019) study of celebrity fandom. In these works, autoethnographic vignettes form a significant part of the data set, along with quotes, field notes and observations. Autoethnography's contribution to academic marketing studies was reflected in a 2012 special issue of the *Journal of Business Research* edited by Stephen Gould with papers including Brown (2012b), Wohlfeil and Whelan (2012), Minowa et al. (2012), Patterson (2012) and Roberts (2012).

Practice theory

We include a brief note on practice theory here because it has been used in tandem with ethnography in a number of published qualitative studies (e.g. Ghaffari et al., 2019; Thomas and Epp, 2019). Ghaffari et al. (2019) followed a number of ethnographic studies of advertising agencies (e.g. Alvesson, 1998; Kelly et al., 2005; Moeran, 1996; Svensson, 2007) in conducting an ethnographic study but supplemented the theoretical framing with a version of the practice theory approach that has become well established in management and organisation studies (Schatzki, 1996, 2002, 2012) and which has been adapted to marketing communications (Ots and Nyilasy, 2017). The ethnographic approach generated the data sets in these studies, through participant and non-participant observation. The data sets included reflexive field notes, recorded observations and interviews. The theoretical perspective of practice theory informed the observations and the data analysis.

Practice theory is a broad school (Skålén and Hackley, 2011) of thought deriving from the work of Pierre Bordieu (1977). The approach attempts to capture the situatedness of human beings as we work through everyday activities always being constrained by our reliance on symbolic communication and our place in the social structure designated by our social class, ethnicity, gender and citizenship. The idea of a social practice embraces the multi-faceted character of human activity as we do things that often have a ritualistic and performative aspect. Practice theory therefore seeks to capture something of the culturally and socially contextualised character of subjectivity, as called for by Askegaard and Linnet (2011). Human beings operate in the interstices of social structure, exercising agency and trying to shape events, but often constrained by structural and constitutive power. Practice theory approaches attempt to capture the full context of how social relationships and happenings are constituted through this complex dynamic.

For example, Ghaffari et al. (2019) conceived advertising creativity not as a thing or as a process, as many previous studies had done (e.g. Hackley and Kover et al., 1995), but as a set of social practices constituted through the linguistic and symbolic interaction of the various parties, the creatives, the account executives and the client. What emerged as creative output was therefore not simply an idea that was 'owned' by whoever claimed it, but a set of practices through which the creative output was constituted, which Ghaffari et al. (2019) labelled control power, knowledge power and persuasive power. Using direct quotes from the data sets, they described how these practices came about.

Ots and Nyilasy (2017) highlighted five key elements of social practices in the constitution of Integrated Marketing Communications (IMC) plans, listed in Figure 7.3. The five concepts in Figure 7.3 amount to a framework for practice theory analyses of ethnographically informed qualitative data sets. The routines roughly echo Bordieu's (1977) notion of habitus, the relatively un-reflexive routines into which organisational workers (and everyone else) falls, through the unquestioned acceptance of tacit values and routines. The material set-ups reflect the materiality of social practice, the fact that it is invariably contextualised in a material world full of objects and scenes that can have an effect on how people think and behave. The rules and procedural knowledge are explicit ways of operating that organisational members are expected to know, because the organisation insists on them, while the cultural templates are the implicit and unspoken rules and values that obtain in any social interaction that people are expected to absorb and enact without

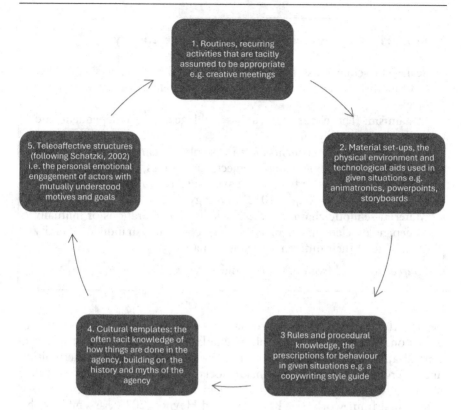

Figure 7.3 Five social practices of advertising creativity in an advertising agency
Source: Adapted from Ots and Nyilasy (2017)

being told. Finally, teleoaffective structures refer to the personal emotional engagement actors have with motives and goals. For example, in advertising agencies, creative professionals are highly emotionally involved in the creative ideas that they pitch to clients. These categories act as ways of thinking about and interpreting the ethnographic observations that are made in a study.

The example in Figure 7.3 merely illustrates one of many possible ways of conceiving social practices in a given social context. This one just happens to be about advertising creativity, but ethnographic study could potentially reveal the practices of any social process or activity.

Assemblage theory

Along with practice theory, assemblage theory is often associated with multimethod qualitative research. Indeed, in recent years assemblage theory has

---

Box 7.1   Characteristics of assemblage theory

Scale: The scope of assemblage theory is broad, there is no specific unit of analysis since the causative features can inter-connect in various ways

Dynamism: The elements in an assemblage are interdependent and their relations dynamic

Heterogeneity: the elements of an assemblage can be quite different in nature, including material objects, discourses, people, institutions and no elements individually have causative priority – the assemblage has a 'flat' (Bajde, 2013) ontology

Material-semiotic character: the particular configurations of mutually dependent elements in an assemblage constitute an individual entity in spite of their different ontological nature

Source: Adapted from Bradshaw and Haynes (2023) p. 972.

---

become the theory du jour for consumer researchers. There are many variations on, and interpretations of, assemblage theory. Broadly, it is a conceptual approach that allows social scientists to acknowledge the multiple and heterogeneous causal elements in social phenomena in a way that does not require them to shoehorn these elements into an ill-fitting and over-determined framework. For Bradshaw and Haynes (2023), assemblage theory draws on the work of various influential writers, especially Deleuze and Guattari (1987), DeLanda (2006:, 2016), Roffe (2015) and Buchanan (2021) and highlights five key characteristics: scale, dynamism, heterogeneity and material-semiotic (p. 972). These features, referring to the scale, heterogeneity, dynamism and material-semiotic character of assemblages, are outlined in Box 7.1.

Assemblage theory tends to be easier to define by what it is not, than what it is. It is not focused on a single unit of analysis, it is not a static analysis but attempts to describe processes that are in perpetual motion, and it does not easily conform to traditional paradigmatic criteria as regards ontology or epistemology. Its elements can include anything that might have a role in the production of a social phenomenon, whether that is a person, a material artefact or its symbolic reception by a group, a historical event, a social practice, a discourse or an institution. Its scale its broad, since it is an attempt to describe configurations of events that lead to certain phenomena. It attempts to straddle the two extremes in social science between the extreme reductionism of the way structuralist/realist positions conceive of social causation, and the extreme relativism of anarchist or some postmodernist positions. In effect, assemblage theory tries to account for the complexity of social causation.

It tends to be used in marketing and consumer research with a focus on a single case. Molander, Ostberg and Peñaloza (2023), for example, used a variety of data sources that included ethnographic field observations in a range of settings, archival data, individual and paired interviews and photographs to study a Swedish fashion brand's evolution over time. Preece, Kerrigan and O'Reilly (2019) also studied the longevity of a brand, the James Bond movie franchise, using an ethnographic content analysis approach which entailed watching all 24 of the movies, reading all the books on which the movies are based, and scouring media coverage and other archival artefacts dating from 1953 when Ian Fleming's first James Bond book (Casino Royale) was released. Note that Preece et al.'s (2019) approach does not explicitly include traditional ethnography but applies its key principle as regards immersion in the group (of Bond viewers/readers/consumers) to try to understand the brand's reception among heterogeneous audience groups across many decades.

Bradshaw and Haynes (2023) draw on assemblage theory to analyse one iconic advertising billboard and its effect on British political culture. The billboard (called 'breaking point') was a political advertisement. Much advertising research simply focuses on the finished ad as a causative artefact. In contrast, Bradshaw and Haynes (2023) examine the institutional and personal context of the ad's emergence, that is, the people and organisations who commissioned, created and consumed the ad, along with an analysis of the prevailing political, cultural and media events that might have influenced the consumer reception. Again, there is a focus on immersion in a wide range of archival data sets. In other examples, Weijo, Martin and Arnould (2018) use a combination of ethnography and assemblage theory to analyse a Nordic consumer movement, while Carrington and Ozanne (2022) apply assemblage theory in their investigation of the relationship between consumers, social media and celebrity using a combination of individual and group interviews and mobile digital data.

'Doing' ethnography

Ultimately, ethnography is something researchers must do, it is a practice, and arguably less theoretically bound than existential phenomenology. The researcher must, simply, give themselves up to the group under investigation to try to see the world through their eyes. Arnould (1998) suggests that ethnography aims to 'clarify systematically the ways that culture (or sub-culture) simultaneously constructs and is constructed by the behaviours and experiences of members' (p. 86). He suggests that this entails four main principles, illustrated in Figure 7.4: ethnographic description: experiential immersion within a cultural context: a focus on particular, rather than general, insights: and the use of multiple data collection methods.

'Doing' ethnography, like doing any interpretive research, entails specific (normally, qualitative) methods of data collection and analysis. But,

Figure 7.4 Principles of ethnographic practice

Source: Adapted from Arnould (1998, p. 86)

more importantly, it entails using a set of broad principles that inform the researcher's whole engagement with the subject matter. Interpretive researchers draw on a theoretical perspective: they do not mechanistically apply a 'method'. Ethnographic description entails multi-faceted detailing of a social context in which interactions and behaviour take place. The material for such a 'rich' or 'thick' ethnographic description is gathered from the qualitative data sets gained through the researcher's experiential immersion in the social context being studied. The focus is placed on particular insights that obtain in the social and cultural context being studied. These are not generalisable in a positivistic sense, but they may resonate with the human experience of the reader of the ethnography, much like a work of poetry or literature. Another way of summarising key elements of practical ethnography is listed in Box 7.2 under the categories Assumptions, Methods of Data Gathering and Approach to Data Analysis.

The ethnographic research study involves, first, gaining as much 'insider' knowledge as possible about the subject in question. For management researchers, this might initially entail reading all the available published information about a particular organisation or brand before the primary research is begun. It may mean establishing links with a particular organisation to try to engage members in discussion. A research study into a particular consumption practice or a specific consumption group would begin with a thorough investigation of secondary sources. The research would then progress to a first-hand engagement with the contexts of consumption (see Figure 7.5).

For most student researchers in management and marketing, a prolonged period of field research is impractical. Even if access is granted, the time and resources are rarely available to students. But this need not rule out the application of ethnographic principles. Indeed, many management and marketing research studies apply the principles of ethnography to much shorter periods of field work. If a period of immersion in the group of interest is not possible, then other means can be used to try to gain a degree of ethnographic insight,

---

Box 7.2   Key elements of ethnographic research studies

Assumptions

Social and cultural life is created by people through symbolic interaction

To truly understand a social milieu a researcher must experience it directly

Qualitative research data sets are interpreted through a frame of presuppositions

Ethnographic interpretation is informed by an intimate understanding of the local cultural context

Methods of data gathering

Multiple qualitative methods including observation, interviews, informal conversations and exchanges, group discussions, field notes, audio and visual media, archival records, online methods

Approach to data analysis

Creative interpretation based on researcher knowledge of the social and cultural context in question

Focus on deep analyses of particular phenomena, not generalised truths or hypotheses

The researcher creates an imaginative representation of the social life in question in an attempt to convey something of the meanings, motivations and experiential understanding of participants

Focus on 'repairing' the indexicality of language and gesture

---

such as informal sources and online sources, as mentioned above. As a general principle, anything the researcher can do to increase their understanding of the social context in which their research is located, is a positive asset. A degree of intimacy with the social context of the subject matter will improve the integrity of data interpretation.

For example, if the principal data-gathering instrument is to be focus/ discussion groups, then the researcher should gain as much knowledge as possible of the social milieu of the participants. In Hackley et al. (2015), the research team were investigating young people's drinking. This was not a student project but a funded study, and, clearly, if middle aged professors were to go out drinking with a group of undergraduates for research purposes, it might not end well. Besides, middle aged professors are usually getting ready

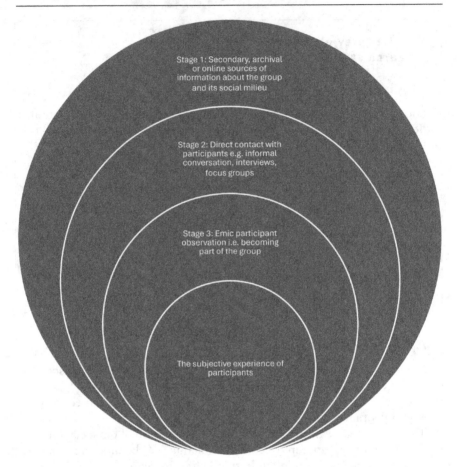

Stage 1: Secondary, archival
or online sources of
information about the group
and its social milieu

Stage 2: Direct contact with
participants e.g. informal
conversation, interviews,
focus groups

Stage 3: Emic participant
observation i.e. becoming
part of the group

The subjective experience of
participants

Figure 7.5 Achieving the ethnographer's insider perspective

for bed just when their undergraduates are beginning their night out. The research team relied mainly on the reports of the sample, but also employed depth interviews of individuals and informal data sources including informal conversations with their students to increase the ethnographic integrity of the data interpretation. They also employed younger research assistants who were personally closer to the social milieu of the group being studied. In this way, the internal sense-making logic evident in the data sets was made accessible to the researchers.

Ethnographic data analysis entails a creative interpretation of the data sets. Creative interpretation lies at the heart of interpretive research, and it is important to nuance what this means. The data analysis is a social scientific process, there must be clear evidence for any interpretation. The ability to read insights into the data sets, though, is to some degree creative, in the sense that not all researchers will be able to see what is there, just as some journalists are better than others at seeing the story. The scholarly integrity of ethnographic social science lies in the extent to which the researcher can convey their interpretive process, that is, the extent to which they can show their workings by drawing persuasively on the evidence in their data. The reader of the research will not have the researcher's first hand insight into the process being studied, so ethnographic researcher's task of communicating their findings to readers is a challenging one.

Indexicality in ethnographic research

As we have seen, an important ethnographic principle is that of seeking to understand social phenomena in their social and cultural context from the point of view of group participants. This principle can also prove fruitful in interpretive studies that are not necessarily framed as 'ethnography'. The interpretation of, say, a depth interview is always conducted within a frame of presuppositions. The researcher can only understand what an interviewee is talking about to the extent that he or she understands their work, their idiom of expression, and the organisation they work in. The researcher must understand enough about the context of research to know just exactly what the interviewee is talking about.

This touches on the issue of *indexicality* of language and gesture. In a famous example, if a person winks their eye, this can mean different things depending on the context (Geertz, 1973). A wink of an eye can be complicit, seductive, friendly, sexual, patronising, funny, even threatening. Without an understanding of the context, a winking eye cannot easily be interpreted. Indexicality refers to the contextualised meaning of spoken words, tones and gestures, the things people say and do. Language has a context: if an engineer uses the technical phrases and concepts of engineering in talking about their work, then an interviewer who does not have any knowledge of engineering will not fully understand what is being said. In the same way, ethnographers feel that interviewers must have first-hand knowledge of the social context of which a research participant is part, so they can better understand what they are referring to in their interview. Ethnographic principles dictate that we cannot take this understanding for granted. We must go into 'the field' and get to know something of the shared meanings and symbolic social practices in a particular social realm if we are to properly understand what people are talking about. Taking account of 'ethnographic context' means interpreting ethnographic research data in the light of a broader understanding of that social context gained from first-hand immersion in the field (also note that indexicality is an important concept in semiotics; Grayson and Shulman, 2000). We discuss indexicality in semiotics in Chapter 8.

Comments and gestures may carry subtle shades of meaning that are not apparent to an outsider who has no knowledge of the group culture of the interviewee. Language, gesture and social practice have an 'indexical' property in that they refer to a particular social setting for their meaning. The principle of indexicality derives from the *ethnomethodological* sociology of Garfinkel (1967). The researcher carrying out an interpretive analysis of interview transcripts or other primary data cannot 'repair' the indexicality of comments and gestures without this knowledge. Social understanding and the appearance of social competence are far more complex than they may often appear to the casual observer. The ethnographic researcher generates insights into social life by understanding the meaning that language, gestures and other social practices have for participants. This might sometimes entail making the familiar strange. Sociologist C. Wright Mills (1959) used this term, making the familiar strange, when he spoke of the social scientist's task of revealing the complex symbolic and interactional processes that underlie the normalness of everyday life. What we take for granted in social processes can be rich material for sociological analysis, and ethnography can be a useful tool for picking apart the familiar and the everyday.

The important thing for ethnographers is to generate a 'thick description' of social behaviour, which seeks to understand, and then describe, the complexity of social life (Geertz, 1973). Elliott and Jankel-Elliott (2002) refer to the distinction between 'inductive' ethnography and 'interpretive' ethnography (citing Alvesson and Skoldberg, 2000). The former research style tries to ground findings very securely in a detailed analysis of empirical data. The latter 'interpretive' style of ethnography attempts to render bold or striking creative interpretations of limited data sources. The best ethnography, arguably, falls part way into each camp with detailed and systematic data gathering providing the basis for creative insights that go beyond logical induction into the realm of imaginative representation.

Sampling, timescale and access issues

As already discussed, data gathering for traditional anthropological ethnography requires a long immersion in the social context under investigation, but this is curtailed to a few weeks or even a few days in commercial applications of ethnography or in its application in business and management studies. 'Quasi-ethnography' (Elliott and Jankel-Elliott, 2002) makes use of shorter, often opportunistic periods of data gathering. The key principal at stake is that any degree of first hand familiarity with the social milieu under investigation is likely to deepen the integrity of the researcher's data interpretation. For example, Rust (1993) describes a commercial study in which researchers loitered in supermarkets waiting for families with children to enter. They would then record some information about the family and follow them (discretely, one supposes) around the store. After the family left the store, the researcher would make notes on what they had said and done to generate insights into shopping practices and family interaction. This would take place over just a few days, until the researchers had a good sense of the social dynamic of family grocery decision making. In some families, one of the adults would determine what was to be purchased, but in others there was more negotiation and the children's influence on the family grocery buying process became more evident.

The researcher-as-voyeur position may imply some ethical issues that would need to be addressed on a study-by-study basis. Privacy is important to many people, and personal safety is important for researchers. If a student researcher is thinking of conducting a study like that of Rust (1993), then the explicit permission of the organisation in which the research will be conducted must be obtained. If permission is granted, then great care must be taken in gathering the data. It may be possible to simply informally 'hang-out' at places of interest, as a silent observer. This was done in many famous sociological studies into youth sub-cultures conducted by Chicago-based sociologists in the 1960s. As part of their method, researchers would make it their business to be where the group of interest would be, so they could observe behaviour and listen to talk and observe behaviour unobtrusively in a naturalistic setting. This would deepen the researcher's understanding of the social milieu. This kind of casual ethnographic style is sometimes employed by marketing professionals. In one interview the author conducted with an advertising agency creative professional, the creative (as they are known) said that if he received a brief for a brand of tea bags, he would hang out in supermarkets to watch people buying tea bags. It was his way of getting a sense of his audience and its behaviour and approach to shopping. Armed with this insight, he felt better equipped to communicate with this group in ways that might resonate with the group.

In consumer research applications, researchers have adopted ethnographic principles by, for example, spending time in kindergartens and primary schools to understand how infant children become aware of and recognise brands. In one study, the researcher convened 'focus' groups in which he showed pre-school children brand logos and elicited recognition. In another, concerning teenage school children, the researcher got a job as a school assistant and hung out with the children at break times to interview them about how they talked about advertisements (Ritson and Elliott, 1999).

Bassiouni and Hackley's (2016) study entailed the first author spending time helping at a primary school children's after school club, in order to understand the role that computer and video games played in the children's lives. As the children played their computer games, the researcher chatted to them, sometimes joining in with the games. This style of ethnography demands a warm interpersonal style and, of course, since the subject group were children, detailed ethical permissions had to be obtained. This was a piece of academic research – commercial researchers also seek to understand how children recognise and understand brands, for commercial purposes. Academic researchers usually have broader terms of reference, driven by intellectual curiosity, theoretical relevance or policy implications. In the case of Bassiouni and Hackley (2016) the lead researcher was interested in the ethical question of how computer and video games affected children's lives, given that, at that time, there was a lot of negativity about the effect of such games on children.

Whether the terms of reference for research are commercial and by implication potentially exploitative, or ethically informed and investigative, the ethnographic principle of simply hanging out with group members in the places where they hang out is a powerful one for the generation of insights into group meanings and actions.

Formal and informal ethnographic data

Part of the goal of ethnographic research, then, is to provide a rich description of a social process or phenomena by acquiring a thorough first-hand understanding of that social process or phenomena. This would normally imply multiple methods of data gathering since ethnographic researchers can acquire insights about a cultural context from many sources. Typically, ethnographers combine formal data-gathering methods such as observation, field notes, interviews, archival research and so on, with informal methods. Our understanding of social contexts is often acquire intuitively through things we overhear, accidental observations we make, casual phone conversations or off-duty encounters and unguarded comments from people who live and/ or work in that particular social context. All such sources are potentially useful for the ethnographic researcher.

For example, it is far from unknown for an interviewee to say one thing in a formal interview then to offer a much more candid opinion in the pub afterwards. Indeed, informal social settings, such as staff restaurants, the bar or pub after work or other work-related social gatherings, can be particularly valuable for the ethnographic researcher. It would hardly be appropriate for a student researcher to take an audio-recording device along if they were invited to the bar or pub at lunchtime with work staff. However, the off-duty comments, jokes and ways of talking about work issues and personalities can offer important routes to understanding what happens in more formal work settings.

Researchers have confirmed that the formal research interview held, say, in an office of the host company might yield very different insights to a subsequent interview that is conducted in a less formal setting off-site (Easterby-Smith and Malina, 1999). Such informal settings can 'round out' a researcher's understanding of a topic because the research participant may be more relaxed and less defensive. The author has conducted many interviews with marketing professionals and has had several experiences of people taking him aside to a quiet corner of the office to offer a franker viewpoint than could be offered in a more formal setting. The ethnographic stance gives researchers the license to use this kind of insight (anonymised in the research report, of course) actively as research data.

High-quality informal data often emerges if the researcher has established a good rapport with the research participants/interviewees. Indeed, in ethnography as in most qualitative research, the quality of this rapport often dictates the quality of insights generated (Agar, 1996). Easterby-Smith et al. (1991, p. 90) refer to the importance of establishing trust between researcher and participant. The research participant is more likely to be candid and spontaneous if they trust the researcher to use their discretion and not to reveal the sources of any potentially embarrassing quotes or opinions. In many research contexts in which employees or managers are the research participants, they do worry that the researcher might name them as the source if they express a criticism of organisational policy or scepticism towards organisational aims and methods. It is important for the researcher to develop sensitivity for organisational politics and to establish an informal sense of rapport with the research participants.

Field notes as research data

The ethnographer will take field notes of their observations, thoughts and reflections as they conduct fieldwork. They might take these notes at the time, or later, when they are no longer in the company of the group. Clarke et al. (1998) explored the cultural meanings of the British 'pub' by using a combination of depth interviews and questionnaires administered in pubs. They also drew on semiotic influences to interpret the audio-recorded data. *In-situ* studies such as this allow researchers to utilise rich sources of field data. 'Field notes' are the impressionistic and relatively un-formalised reflections and ideas of the ethnographic researcher. In a service industry context such as a public house, researchers can make great use of such first-hand observation to enrich their understanding of the dynamics of social interaction within that space. It is important that these observations are recorded in the form of field notes. For Spradley (1980), field notes can include comments on such things as the physical space in which interactions take place, descriptions of the people involved, the things they are doing, and the objects that are present, and the timing and sequence of events and the feelings expressed or indicated. Researchers can draw on field notes as they seek interpretations of formal data such as interview transcripts. They can interpret data in the light of their understanding of the social context that is reflected in the field notes.

Revisiting reflexivity in research reporting

A feature of interpretive research that has been mentioned previously in the book is critical reflexivity. Reflexivity is sometimes defined as being aware of being aware, that is, being able to examine one's life as if from an external perspective. In research, reflexivity refers to being able to comment on the way that the research evolved, including being aware of the assumptions brought to it by the researcher, and it is often labelled as critical reflexivity to indicate that one can be critical of the assumptions one brings to one's own research just as one tries to be critical of the assumptions made in other research perspectives.

There are different forms of reflexivity (Johnson and Duberley, 2003) and it is not confined to researchers, for example it is a noted feature of some forms of consumption (Thompson et al., 2018). Reflexivity has two main practical implications for the researcher. One is that the researcher should try to be consciously aware of the values, assumptions and perceptions they bring to the research process. This critical reflexivity is brought into the research report through a self-conscious, and self-critical, writing style. In other research styles it is conventional for the researcher to write and behave as if they are detached and independent and that the research report is a neutral channel for conveying the findings. The research report is written to minimise the identification of a thinking, feeling, interpreting individual as author, and any doubt, any dilemmas that the researcher faced, and any digressions that the study took, are erased from the research report text. Interpretive research studies are particularly associated with reflexive writing styles, while research in the functionalist paradigm, especially realist research based on experiments or survey data, tend to conform to more formal reporting conventions in which reflexivity is less important than the performance of objectivity.

Interpretive research studies are often written-up in the 'third person' (although sometimes not – see the section on autoethnography) but nonetheless they should have a reflexive, that is, self-aware, tone and self-conscious style. They can be written in the first person, that is, using the personal pronoun 'I' to represent the author. It can be more difficult to create an impression of rigorous scholarship in this style and student researchers are advised not to use it unless they are very confident about their writing and analytical skills. Even then, it is strongly advised to obtain the opinion of the research supervisor on whether the work should be written up in the third person, or the first person.

Alvesson and Deetz (2000) suggest that, in interpretive research, "people are not considered to be objects … but are active sense makers like the researcher" (p. 33). The researcher's part in the interpretive process is, then, openly acknowledged. Researchers seek to use this involvement to deepen their understanding of the research process and they express it in their research reporting through a *reflexive* research reporting style that is open to self-criticism, honest about influences and biases and frank about limitations.

Representation and reflexivity in research writing

Alvesson and Deetz (2000) remind readers that interpretive research reports are *representations* of a slice of social reality. That is, when the researcher writes about a management issue or set of consumption practices, they cannot claim that the research report is ontologically the same thing as the reality of what has happened. The written account of a slice of life in the world, is, self-evidently, an interpretation of that world, written down in text. For Brownlie (2001) "interpretive marketing research [is] a highly coded and situated form of representation ... that works to legitimize and privilege certain kinds of knowledge" (p. 48). Brownlie's (2001) point is that the representation of the world in text is inflected by the interests of the writer. But, of course, all social research has this rhetorical character. After all, the researcher is attempting to persuade the reader of the rightness of their interpretation of the data. Research writing adopts certain forms of rhetoric and writing conventions to privilege certain forms of knowledge or claims about knowledge. Brownlie (2001, p. 50) points out that research does not merely "reproduce a pre-existing world of marketing managers or consumers" but "constructs the research domain" through "scholarly artifice". For example, it is not correct to assume that because ethnographic research seeks a rich and detailed description of a social phenomenon, that this in some way produces a representation that is closer to reality. Ethnography is just another representational practice (Brownlie, 1997; van Mannen, 1995).

'Representation' implies that whatever is written in research represents a viewpoint that is selective and reflects the educational, cultural and political influences on the researcher. It is appropriate, therefore, for the researcher to reflect on the interests that may underlie any given form of representation. In other words, it is incumbent on the ethnographic researcher to employ critical reflexivity in their practice. For Alvesson and Deetz (2000), representation is political in the sense that any representation of reality will concur with some interests, and conflict with some others. Most obviously, an ethnography carries the assumption that the researcher has the power and authority to act as interpreter of this group's world. Perhaps less obviously, the interpretation of data favoured by the researcher will carry presumptions about what is important, and what is not.

For example, much consumer research uses the concepts of consumer 'satisfaction' and 'choice'. However, there are circumstances in which consumption can be a source of dissatisfaction and a restriction of choice. A reflexive piece of interpretive consumer research would acknowledge the conflicting interests that may be invested in the use of given representational strategies, such as framing consumer experience in terms of constructs like 'choice' and 'satisfaction'. As an example, some interpretive studies of management have painted a picture of organisational management as chaotic and stressful, and managers as unhappy, unfulfilled and stressed (e.g. in parts of Watson, 1994).

Other studies celebrate managerial tasks and, by implication, they celebrate managerial skills, reproducing a representation of the organisational manager as a folk hero (e.g. in Peters and Waterman, 1982). In the case of Watson (1994) the author was representing management in a way they he saw as having integrity, by showing it as a sometimes chaotic and conflicted practice. For Peters and Waterman (1982), they, too, were seeking to portray the role of manager with integrity but in a different way, by drawing attention to the positive difference that effective management can make in organisations. Both accounts had their own integrity, but in writing, and reading ethnography, it is important to understand that what is being portrayed is a point of view which, in itself, can be subject to critical analysis.

Styles or modes of representation do tend to become accepted and conventional over time. For example, popular marketing management textbooks have developed distinctive rhetorical strategies that have become so familiar that it is difficult to articulate marketing issues through alternative representational strategies (Hackley, 2001, 2003b). This presents a difficulty for researchers. A good researcher will not want to present a picture of the world that relies solely on conventional, and perhaps stereotypical, ways of representing the world. The challenge to interpretive social researchers is to see the worlds they research through the eyes of the people in them while also retaining a distance from that world, so that what is familiar to participants remains unfamiliar to the researcher.

This chapter, then, has discussed another of the most important and influential qualitative research approaches, ethnography. It has outlined the general principles of ethnography and introduced a number of variations, including digital ethnography and autoethnography. In addition, the chapter has outlined practice theory as a theoretical approach sometimes used in tandem with ethnography. In discussing the roles of reflexivity and representation in ethnographic writing, the chapter has pointed to the ways in which ethnographies and practice theory are often concerned not merely with agnostic description of life experience, but with the dynamics of power that impinge on and form experiences of powerlessness and disadvantage. In some ways, ethnography lies at the centre of the interpretive research paradigm, since its core ethos is to understand the world as others see it. This insight demands the ability to read qualitative data sets in an informed yet also creative way. The chapter has referred to many examples of published ethnographic studies to which student researchers can refer. Chapter 8 will introduce another important set of connected intellectual traditions that have been influential in the interpretive analysis of qualitative data sets – literary theory, in which we include semiotics and semiology.

Glossary

Applied research As opposed to theoretical or 'blue skies' research, applied research seeks to solve a specified problem.

Assemblage theory An approach to social science reflecting the heterogenous and multiple causative elements in social phenomena.

Ethnography A method of qualitative cultural research adapted from anthropology that emphasises the researcher's full participation in the lives of the group being studied.

Experiential To do with apprehended subjective experience.

Indexicality In semiotics and philosophical linguistics, indexicality is the idea that language points to or refers to something, hence repairing indexicality means understanding the context of a piece of speech or talk in order to fully understand its meaning.

Liminality Victor Turner's work on liminal process and rights of passage has been highly influential. Liminality refers to a state of being in-between one position in social structure, and another, during liminal ritual. Turner's work was originally based on rites of passage from adolescent to adult among indigenous peoples, but he extended the concept to apply to contemporary society. So, for example, an undergraduate student is neither a child under the care of their family nor an independent member of adult society until they graduate. Liminality indicates a rich potentiality for experimentation and creative change.

Postmodern Often used with the term *post-structural*, postmodernism was an architectural movement that became a term variously used to express an epoch, a style or a philosophy in literature and social theory.

Post-structural Anthropological studies that reject the structural approach of a fixed reality underlying social life.

Nomothetic Associated with quantitative research designed to produce generalisable truths and relationships.

Netnography A version of applied digital ethnography adapted for consumer research by Kozinets (2019a,b).

Chapter 8

Literary theory and qualitative research

The analysis of text, narrative and stories

Abstract

Literary criticism has been a fruitful source of interpretive theory for qualitative research in marketing and related areas. This chapter outlines some of the key approaches deriving from literary criticism, including reader-response theory, narrative analysis, rhetoric and semiotics/semiology. The focus falls on the communicative dimensions of marketing, management and consumer research, and the qualitative analysis of text.

Chapter objectives

After reading this chapter students will be able to

- appreciate the contributions of literary theory to social research
- apply some literary concepts to theoretically informed analyses of qualitative data sets such as interview transcripts or other forms of text
- understand the concepts of symbolism, polysemy and intertextuality for application in research studies

Literary theory, marketing and consumer research

Contemporary marketing practice often hints at its literary character when commentators speak of marketing 'discourse' (Skålén, Fougére and Fellesson, 2008; van Laer and Izberk-Bilgin, 2019), brand 'storytelling' (Moin, Hosany and O'Brien, 2020), brand 'narratives' (Russell and Schau, 2014; van Laer et al., 2014, 2019), consumer imagination (Martin, 2004), consumer 'engagement' and 'emotional' branding (Brown, 2016b). Commercial applications of literary theory are also common, especially semiotics and, more unusually, discourse analysis (Magenta Research, 2023). Yet, mainstream textbooks and research methods in marketing, management and consumer research seldom offer an exposition of literary methods for research projects. As has been pointed out earlier in the book, a research study

DOI: 10.4324/9781003432203-11

is ultimately a piece of literature, a written document, and we have touched on the role of textual analysis in social research. Not only are literary principles important in social research – marketing and management practice are working fields in which communication is central to professional practice. Management and marketing practitioners write emails, reports and presentations, and they use written texts in countless other ways, in addition to the verbal texts of meetings and interviews (Brown, 1999). Much of management is the task of verbal and/or textual communication and persuasion. These are inherently rhetorical tasks (Nilsson, 2019). Marketing has become a popular academic discipline partly through the rhetorical force of the metaphors, tropes and conventions that have come to characterise the field, most significantly in the popular marketing management genre of textbooks (Kotler, 1967; analyses in Brown, 2005; Hackley, 2003b). Literary theory can provide useful routes into the understanding of marketing and consumption practices, experiences and processes, in both the academic and practice contexts.

Advertising research and literary theory

Literary theory as a research perspective first became noted in academic consumer research around the 1990s (e.g. Brown, 1999, 1999; Brownlie, 1997; Easton and Aráujo, 1997; Hirschman and Holbrook, 1992; Holbrook, 1990; O'Donohoe, 1994, 1997; Sherry and Schouten, 2002; Stern, 1989, 1990, 1993; Stern and Schroeder, 1994). The use of literary methods has continued to flourish in both consumer research and marketing research (e.g. Brown, 2016a, b; Hackley et al., 2013; Hackley and Hackley, 2022; Humphreys and Thompson, 2014; Miles, 2013, 2014; Phillips and McQuarrie, 2004, 2008; van Laer et al., 2019). Since Stern (1989) introduced the analysis of the social text into consumer research, reader-response theory (Iser, 1972) has been used to understand how consumers 'read' and respond to advertisements (Scott, 1994a). Reader-response theory originated in literary criticism as a counterpoint to formalist literary criticism, but Stern's (1989) perspective allowed researchers to theorise consumers not as behavioural machines who unreflexively react cognitively and biologically to advertising stimuli, but as active readers who interpret and reason communications, either accepting or rejecting what they see as the implied or desired interpretation cued into the message by the brand and its advertising agency.

Ritson and Elliott (1999) had pointed out that most academic advertising research lacked ecological validity – that is, it asked individual consumers questions after they'd viewed an advertisement in the controlled and artificial conditions of a viewing booth. In fact, consumers view advertisements in a socio-cultural context. Our opinions on the advertising we view are mediated by the context of viewing and the opinions of the people with whom we discuss and/or view the ads. The notion of advertisements being understood as social texts has been extensively developed in qualitative and conceptual research studies (e.g. Brown et al., 1999).

Stern and Schroeder (1994) pointed out that research into advertisements has often focused on the 'information' (price, quality, positioning) that is available to be 'processed' by consumers. Such research has neglected the view that consumers draw meaning from advertisements as a whole, rather than focusing on distinct parts of the ad in isolation from the other parts. We do not look at advertising text, sound and imagery as distinct sources of information. All three wash over us holistically as we are exposed to advertising. Literary researchers focused on a holistic understanding of advertising in its socio-cultural context and on how aspects of the advertisement, including the visual imagery and sonic effects, acts as sources of meaning that can influence the meaning of the other components of an ad. Stern and Schroeder (1994) drew on literary and art criticism to develop an approach to the analysis of visual imagery in advertising.

Reader-response, intertextuality, polysemy and paratextuality

Student researchers often want to investigate something about advertising, but usually lack the theoretical background to articulate exactly what it is they want to explore. Literary theory approaches such as reader-response (Iser, 1972; Scott, 1994a) allow researchers to analyse how consumers read and interpret advertisements. The assumption is that consumers do not only 'process' advertisements as cognitive stimuli, consumers can also be said to read an ad as a social text, assessing the text and reading meaning into it. In this way, using interviews, researchers can probe into the meanings of, and the discourses around (Cook, 2001; Ritson and Elliott, 1999) advertisements to generate insights into how consumers draw meaning by reading and interpreting them. Naïve managerial models of advertising affect conceive of an advertisement as a univocal message, the meaning of which is independent of the medium and the receiver (Hackley, 2010). In contrast, literary theories of advertising acknowledge that advertisements can be understood as social texts that are read and interpreted by consumers, hence the meaning of an advertisement is mediated by the interpretation of the receiver. In turn, the receiver will interpret the meaning of an advertisement with reference to their own cultural context, the other discourses surrounding the ad including other advertisements, and the medium (Cook, 2001). The implication is that the meaning of an ad, and its message, cannot be unilaterally controlled by the brand or the ad agency without reference to the interpreting consumer.

Literary concepts such as *polysemy* (Puntoni et al., 2010, 2011) and *intertextuality* (O'Donohoe, 1997) can be useful in analysing consumer responses to advertising. Polysemy refers to the potential for a communication to have mor than one meaning. Intertextuality refers to the inter-dependence of meaning, since the meaning of one text invariably depends on its reference to other texts. For example, many Nike advertising campaigns have tapped into current cultural priorities, news events and currently newsworthy individuals, one example being their 2018 'Dream Crazy' campaign featuring former NFL player Colin Kaepernick. Kaepernick had a huge media profile because of his association with the Black Lives Matter movement, and Nike chose to intertextually reference and leverage this cultural meaning in their campaign. The audience responses to the campaign were polarised, reflecting the freedom of consumers to read and interpret advertisements in different ways. Specifically, using sociologist Stuart Hall's terminology (discussed in Wood, 1998) audiences might give the ad a 'hegemonic' reading if they were inclined to agree with the progressive political values implied in the ad, or a 'resistant' reading if they did not. While intertextual references are a feature of any communication, they are often used strategically in advertising to deepen the audience engagement or to signal specific intended target groups. Intertextual references can advertising campaigns emotional resonance evoked by the consumer's knowledge of the cultural context.

Polysemy, similarly, can be used strategically in advertisements (Puntoni, Schroeder and Ritson, 2010; Puntoni, Vanhamme and Visscher, 2011). Polysemic ads are open interpretation since they do not have a clear and unambiguous meaning. If a consumer sees an advertisement and is intrigued about what it might mean, then that is a win for the brand since the ad has succeeded in attracting the consumer's interest. Polysemic advertising can draw the consumer in to the game of interpretation, because the creative execution intrigues the consumer/reader. We feel an urge to complete the story when we see polysemic communication. This literary concept can show us that advertisements without a clear message are not necessarily poorly designed ads but, in contrast, can be the most creatively ingenious ads of all, since they invest the ad with strategic ambiguity that invests the brand with significance.

These literary concepts allow interpretive researchers to analyse textual data sets (such as advertisements or other bran communications) in ways that allow for latitude in their interpretation. This acts as a counterpoint to research methods that assume a hegemonic interpretation of a univocal and unambiguous message.

Paratexts, epitexts and peritexts

For Hackley and Hackley (2019, 2022), the literary concept of intertextuality can be supplemented by a different unit of analysis for the investigation of marketing communication – the paratext. The paratext (Genette, 2010; Genette and Maclean, 1991) is a secondary text that acts as a threshold through which the primary text is brough into existence. The literary analysis of advertisements in consumer research since the 1980s since Stern (1989) has taken the position of classical literary criticism in positioning the primary text, the book, artwork or other text under analysis, as a dominant source of meaning. In contrast, Genette (2010) demonstrated that the primary text depends for its meaning on secondary or paratexts. In printed literary works, the secondary or paratexts include the footnotes, the chapter titles, the artwork, the preface and foreword, the title, contents pages and index. It is these, Genette (2010) showed, that give the primary text its meaning.

Genette's (2010) work focused on literary texts, but his ideas have been widely adopted in media, film and television studies research (Gray, 2010). Hackley and Hackley (2019) adapted the idea for research in marketing communication and showed that the brand can be regarded as a notional primary text, one into which meanings are inscribed by its paratexts including all its brand communications, the packaging, the promotion and the advertising. Paratexts comprise peritexts and epitexts. Peritexts are paratexts within the work and attributable to the author, for example, in the case of a brand, the packaging, the advertisements, the brand name. Epitexts are paratexts that refer to the work but are not within it. To continue the previous example, brand epitexts would include customer reviews, independent media comment and customer word of mouth. Some brands create paratexts that seem to be independent, but in fact are not – the face that may be perceived as independent lends authority to the way they inscribe the brand with meaning. An example could be the use of influencers to endorse the brand, or the use of third-party produced video content on social media.

Paratextuality, like intertextuality and polysemy, are underpinned by reader-response theory in the sense that they assume audiences to have the power to interpret brand texts, in contrast to the idea that brand texts are controlled by the brand and its agencies and received hegemonically by audiences. Hence, these concepts are part of an interpretive approach to consumer and marketing research.

Advertising, brands, ideology and rhetoric

Another literary idea used in the analysis of advertisements is ideology (Eagleton, 2007). At least, Eagleton (2007) has treated ideology not just as a concept of political science but as a communicative phenomenon that can be understood through the literary lenses. Elliott and Ritson (1997) postulated that advertising collectively carries considerable persuasive force as what they termed a superideology promoting the consumer lifestyle. Other researchers adopted versions of the ideological perspective to analyse advertisements for their ideological character (e.g. Barthes, 2000; Wernick, 1991; Williamson, 1978). Conceiving of advertisements as ideological in character hints at the rhetorical dimensions of all advertising and marketing – that is, it is all designed to be persuasive, and the study of rhetoric is the study of persuasion, in linguistic forms or in other forms, including visual or aural rhetoric (McQuarrie and Mick, 1992, 1996; Scott, 1990, 1994b). Consumer ideologies sometimes tap into myth to mobilise and articulate brand meanings for consumers (Luedicke et al., 2009).

Of course, ideology is a term more commonly associated with political forms of persuasion, and Zhao and Belk (2008) analysed the ideological effect of advertising in reversing the strong antipathies in China that existed towards market values before the Chinese government embraced markets. Although the ideological effect of advertising is not necessarily political (unless it is political advertising) it does have a connection with political attitudes to market capitalism. In addition, in the contemporary environment, political advertising has become more like commercial advertising, while commercial advertising has taken on more of the techniques of ideological propaganda, so it is sometimes hard to see the distinction between the political and ideological rhetorics of persuasion in mediated communication, and their commercial counterparts (Cronin, 2018; Davis, 2013). Indeed, some analyses would hold that commercial advertising is inherently political in the sense that it reproduces values and norms that mask narrow interests and seek to exploit power differences between corporations and consumers (Elliott and Ritson, 1997).

Holt (2002) and Holt and Cameron (2010) looked at ideology from a managerial perspective. Holt's (2004) cultural branding approach conceives of brands as ideological vehicles in the sense that they need to tap into prevailing sub-cultural values and trends and identify with those. By so doing, successful brands resolve ideological dilemmas, for example, as the iconic advertising image the Marlboro Man tapped into myths of American masculinity and, for its consumers, symbolically resolved the tension between traditional masculinity and the modern world. In more recent advertising, Nike's Dream Crazy campaign (also mentioned above) made intertextual reference to ideological tensions in American politics, positioning the brand clearly in a politically progressive camp. This is consistent with Nike brand positioning since the 1970s when it associated with legendary middle-distance runner and counter-cultural hero Steve Prefontaine, and, later, in 1987, when it was the first brand to use an original Beatles track in its iconic TV ad, Revolution (Bradshaw and Scott, 2018). The cultural branding perspective (Holt and Cameron, 2010) focuses on brands as socio-cultural phenomena and not as bundles of attributes and associations that reside in the consumer's cognitive apparatus, hence it stands in direct opposition to the more cognitively nuanced theories of branding that tend to be more popular in the managerial marketing and branding literature.

Advertising ideology can be understood not as an unintended consequence of commercial activity but as a fundamental part of its operation (Elliott and Ritson, 1997; Hackley and Hackley, 2021). Brands and advertising 'work' as ideological forces that normalise brand consumption practices (like smoking cigarettes, driving cars that will go at 150mph, buying food in plastic packaging, eating breakfast 'cereals', wearing fur, eating bacon and eggs) and universalise the values of consumption. In addition, consumers' political ideology can frame their consumer behaviour (Crockett and Wallendorf, 2004; Lisjak and Ordabayeva, 2023; Shepherd, Chartrand and Fitzsimons, 2015). Note that there is not necessarily a moral judgement in the above – advertising operates ideologically, but this does not mean that what is promoted is necessarily bad or wrong. It is simply a way of understanding how marketing 'works'. Consumers are fully enabled to exercise choice and to resist the blandishments of consumer ideology, such as where sub-cultural consumption practices emerge that subvert brand ideologies (Schouten and McAlexander, 1995). However, these resistant readings of consumer culture are sometimes quickly co-opted back into the service of corporate marketing (Thompson and Coskuner-Balli, 2007), for example, through cultural branding strategies (Holt, 2002).

Rhetoric in organisational and academic practice

Rhetoric, the art of persuasion, is typically regarded as a literary art, although as we point out above, other forms of representation such as visual art and music can also be seen to have a rhetorical character. Brown et al. (2018) have commented upon the rhetorical character of marketing research and practice and the need for more detailed rhetorical analyses of marketing practices. Brown (2005) has also noted the rhetoric styles of noted marketing academics and 'gurus', while Hackley (2003b, c) drew attention to the rhetorical tropes by which mainstream marketing text books produce a sense that they are a-theoretical and focused on practice (as if they were practical marketing activities in themselves rather than books about practice). Marketing, as the science of persuasion, seems a prime candidate for rhetorical analysis, yet the topic of rhetoric has been neglected in research in the field, notwithstanding a special issue of the *Journal of Marketing Management* (Brown et al., 2018; Miles and Nilsson, 2018; Nilsson, 2019).

The word 'rhetoric' is often used in a pejorative sense to mean insubstantial or empty. Tonks (2002), writing of marketing rhetoric in consumer contexts, dates this pejorative usage of the term back to Plato who criticised the Sophists' teaching of rhetoric for being 'mere cooking' associated with 'trickery, deceit, immorality and superficiality' (Kennedy, 1963, p. 15, in Tonks, 2002, p. 807). Aristotle took a rather more benign view, and the study of rhetoric became a key part of the school curriculum right through to medieval times. Rhetoric, in fact, became regarded as the overarching intellectual discipline, unifying the sciences because of its integrative 'epistemic' (Tonks, 2002, p. 810) character. It was studied as part of the school and university curriculum throughout the medieval era and, in the United Kingdom, up to the 1800s.

The interest in rhetoric has returned in many studies that consider it not only as a part of literary analysis, but more fundamentally as an organising principle for thought and argument. There is no necessary implication that to use rhetoric is deceitful or cunning. It is, simply, the means through which humans argue and persuade. Language and, hence, thought itself, are rhetorically organised to produce certain (rhetorical) effects. For some psychological theorists, rhetoric is more than simply a literary craft of persuasion. It is an important organising principle of human psychology (Billig, 1987, 1991). In a sweeping sense, we can be seen to depend on accounts of events and experiences to make sense of the world. We have explanations for our behaviours that seem, to us, to justify them. We understand our beliefs and actions in terms of accounts we construct of our lived experience.

The rhetoric of absence

The literary study of rhetoric, then, focuses on the persuasive character of written language. It is important to note that rhetoric is not simply about what is written, or indeed, what is said. It is also about what is excluded. Expressing a view or idea in a persuasive or plausible way distracts attention from other possible ways of expressing that idea. Alternative forms of expression with quite different implications might seem equally plausible. Forms of expression tend to privilege certain ways of seeing the world and accounting for events while, by default, silencing alternatives. Social psychological researchers Edwards and Potter (1992) note that a major feature of rhetorical analysis is 'the demonstration of how, in order to understand the nature and function of any version of events, we need to consider whatever real or potential alternative versions it may be designed to counter' (p. 28, citing Billig, 1988, 1989).

In accounting for events, mental states or actions we are, in effect, arguing a point of view to others, and also to ourselves. As we construct accounts (of events, actions or experiences) we make sense of them: we fill in the account with implied motivations and explanations. Other accounts or explanations then become rhetorically less forceful or persuasive: they become 'alternative' rather than accepted 'common sense'. In this way the rhetorical use of language is highly significant in not only describing, but also in constitutively forming our psychological states.

Rhetorical strategies of writing or speaking invite the question: what potential threat or criticism was this way of putting things designed to counter? If my son comes home, opens the door and says 'it wasn't me, Dad' I immediately wonder what he's done wrong. What potential accusation or criticism is his denial intended to counter? If a marketing text proclaims that 'This book is focused on practical marketing management', a focus on rhetoric might prompt questions like 'why write that? In what way is marketing management not practical? What does the text accomplish by saying this?' Rhetorical strategies seek to exclude possible alternative accounts or claims (such as the claim that marketing management text books fail to adequately explain marketing practice). Marketing is a textual genre in the sense that marketing ideas, research and thought are produced, sustained, perpetuated and defended through writing. These words and phrases then become the instruments of managers and others in organisational settings.

Rhetorical analysis is inherently a critical method since it seeks to reveal the mechanisms by which consensus and agreement are produced. The study of rhetoric is therefore bound up with the issue of power. The power of rhetorical devices and strategies to persuade can be seen to have a historical basis in particular social structures and institutions. 'It's only rhetoric' is sometimes a comment levelled at political or commercial claims and discourse that suggests that rhetoric is trivial and reflects a mendacious, half-truth approach to accounts and claims. In social research, rhetoric is far more than this. The study of rhetoric is the study of how meaning and persuasion are mobilised through language and social practice.

For example, Brown (1999) drew on literary analysis to compare the rhetorical styles of two leading marketing writers and consultants, Professors Theodore Levitt and Morris Holbrook. Such critical rhetorical analysis is not always well received by business academics who feel that a focus on rhetoric demeans their work. They write as if they are offering solutions that can be applied in the practical worlds of business. Many do not wish attention to be drawn to the rhetorical skills that enable them to write persuasively. The study of rhetoric is based on the truism that all knowledge is mediated: we cannot convey experience except through language and writing. Many business consultants have won influence and credibility through the ability to write and speak as if they are offering homespun wisdom deriving from direct experience of organisational management. This ability itself is a mark of high-order rhetorical skill, as Brown (1999) points out. Other researchers have critiqued the rhetoric of management buzz-words and fads as Case (1999) did with business process re-engineering (Hammer and Champy, 1993), while Hackley (2003b) and Furusten (1999) have critiqued the rhetoric of popular management text books (such as Kotler, 1967; Peters and Waterman, 1982). McCloskey (1983) drew attention to the rhetorical character of economics, a discipline that still succeeds in selling itself as a science.

Student researchers considering a rhetorical analysis for their project or dissertation could do worse than to take a look at Nilsson (2015), which is a PhD thesis that is available open access. Nilsson (2015) undertook a close study of classical philosophical studies of rhetoric and applied those principles to an analysis of the sales conversations of business professionals in B2B contexts in order to understand how expert professionals deployed rhetorical strategies in order to be persuasive (see also Nilsson, 2019). As we have noted earlier, it is also possible to conduct studies of visual and aural rhetoric to understand the persuasiveness of marketing and other corporate communications (Schroeder, 2002; Schroeder and Borgerson, 2015; Scott, 1990, 1994b).

Narrative analysis

Narrative analysis is another literary influence that has been drawn on in interpretive marketing, management and consumer research. A 'narrative' is a linguistic account of an event or events that is organised into a sequence or structure so it can be understood and connected. Some literary studies of narrative have focused on the structures of narrative and how these come to be imbued with meaning. Other approaches have emphasised the interpretation of narrative by focusing on the reading strategies that people employ to draw meanings from narrative accounts. Narrative analysis in qualitative research often focuses on personal accounts, stories of events or experiences related from the first-person perspective, and in that sense has something in common with autoethnography (discussed in Chapter 7) as it does with discourse analysis (discussed in Chapter 10). There are also studies of narrative that use mixed interpretive methods. For example, Yang, Ozanne and Phipps (2024) conducted an iterative hermeneutic analysis of consumer cultural repertoires, while Beverland, Fernandez and Eckhardt (2024) used mixed ethnographic methods to investigate consumers' sense of agency in pursuing technologically retro forms of consumption.

In this short section, we focus on narrative analysis as a distinct analytical style of interpretive research, while acknowledging that it overlaps with many other styles of the qualitative, interpretive analysis of text (see Figure 8.1). Narrative analysis in qualitative research is often conducted to analyse the personal stories and accounts of individuals, but it can also refer to third-person textual narratives. For example, academic research into management fields can be seen in terms of 'narrative projects' since it consists of literary texts that construct narratives, or stories, about, for example, marketing (Shankar et al., 2001; Stern et al., 1998). In most popular marketing

Figure 8.1 **Key elements of narrative analysis**

management books, the text is organised persuasively to give marketing a sense of narrative. There is a familiar story of the evolution of marketing as a constantly improving technique (Brown, 1995; Brown et al., 1996; Keith, 1960; Kerin, 1996). Marketing management theory is given origins (normally placed in the late 1950s in the United States), there is a time of struggle (the 'production' and 'sales' eras of business orientation) and it achieves great popular success in the modern era.

Marketing has its pantheon of management guru-heroes and there are the trials and tribulations of misunderstanding and mistakes along the way (Hackley, 2001). The historical accuracy of these claims is not important: the textual organisation of marketing management texts gives the discipline a striking and persuasive narrative character. But literary theory also gives us a critical antidote to modernist progressiveness. Lyotard (1984, p. xxiv) writes that 'I define postmodern as incredulity towards metanarratives'. For Lyotard, the narrative form is a highly significant cultural artefact that frames the way we think. He seems to position postmodernism as an antidote in that it seeks to recover these narrative forms and, by questioning their unstated assumptions and exposing their rhetorical techniques, undermine their effect.

Narrative studies in management disciplines

There has been much critical scholarship in marketing that has challenged these narrative conventions, such as in Brown and Patterson (2000) and many other examples (e.g. Brown, 2006; Drummond, 2018; Holbrook, 1990; Sherry and Schouten, 2002). Literary tracts of all kinds have a narrative character, they have a story arc, and a beginning, a middle and an end. And, to some extent, so do brands (Russell and Schau, 2014; van Laer et al., 2014). Narrative analysis focuses on how the narrative is structured, what purposes the story might serve, what is the content of the story, and how it is performed.

Of course, marketing is by no means the only business and management discipline that has question its own popular narrative conventions. Referring again to textual narratives, we are used to scientific research being presented as if it stands outside narrative because it is represented as if it were a discourse separated from storytelling by its objectivity and rigor. Science is supposed to be about facts, not about stories. Yet (even) scientific research tracts can also be seen to have narrative characteristics (Latour and Woolgar, 1979; McCloskey, 1983). Scientific research and development, for example, can be seen as an enterprise that invents narratives to interpret compounds and substances in terms of new 'uses' for need satisfaction. The effects of the drug that became marketed as Viagra, for example, were known for a long time as an unacceptable side-effect, before somebody connected the drug to the narrative of male sexual performance enhancement and made it into a huge marketing success (Letiche, 2002).

Narrative and brand storytelling

Brand 'storytelling' has become a highly fashionable idiom for consultancy and practice in advertising and marketing communication, and much of it is based on narrative analysis. Narrative and storytelling are fundamental to human mental organisation and brands can leverage considerable consumer resonance by tapping into consumer narratives and stories around brands (Feiereisen et al., 2021). We are acculturated into narrative forms from the stories we read and hear from infancy. We learn narrative structures and expect the accounts we read and hear as adults to conform to these narrative characteristics that we have learned. Our preconceptions about which narrative forms are appropriate in given contexts frame our interpretations. However, brand communication often disrupts narrative convention. For example, hero myth stories, drawing on the work of Joseph Campbell (Campbell, 2020; Ganassali and Matysiewicz, 2021; Holt and Thompson, 2004) are foundational in certain sectors, such as tourism (Moin, Hosany and O'Brien, 2020). The idea that the consumer is the hero in their own story, enabled on their heroic journey by brands and consumption, is a powerful device in advertising (Hackley, Hackley and Bassiouni, 2019). Brand storytelling sometimes plays with the traditional narrative structures, referencing them but subverting or abbreviating them, so that the brand storytelling genre leaves out many of the traditional stages in the myth of the hero's journey while maintaining some of the key elements.

For example, contemporary social media allows individuals to launch themselves into celebrity status without the infrastructure of intermediaries and without observing the traditional narrative of heroic struggle and triumph (Hackley and Hackley, 2015b; Mills et al., 2015). Many brand communications today consist in fragmented intertexts and vignettes that have little in common with traditional narrative conventions or classical poetics but generate meanings through polysemic intertexts (Hackley, 2018; Hackley and Hackley, 2018b, 2022). What is occurring when consumers respond emotionally to brand paratexts, arguably, is not so much narrative transportation (van Laer et al., 2014), but a form of intertextual semiosis.

However, while the idea that brands tell 'stories' needs to be reconfigured for the social media age, it still makes sense to use versions of narrative analysis to understand how consumers receive and interpret brand communications of differing types. Human beings seem to have a fundamental need for narrative (van Laer et al., 2018). Narrative analysis is a well-established qualitative research approach (e.g. Brown and Reid, 1997; Grayson, 1997; Shankar and Goulding, 2001; Stern et al., 1998). Olsen (2003) used narrative analysis in an ethnographic study, while van Laer et al. (2019) used a form of narrative analysis to understand how online consumer reviews generate consumer engagement. Shankar and Goulding (2001, p. 1) adapt a table of narrative characteristics from Gergen and Gergen (1988).

These authors suggest that narratives have some important characteristics that make them emotionally compelling (see Figure 8.2). Narratives have a structure, they have a beginning, middle and end, and events are selected and causally linked to lead up to and support the main point or moral of the story. The story might have components of drama, such as protagonists, divergence or disruption and resolution. Of course, there is an argument that brand stories are not stories in a true sense, since they all have the same point – to sell the brand, unlike literary stories, poems or movies which are created to entertain and/or to persuade the reader to sympathise with the values or moral of the story. Understanding narrative structures helps brands to understand their poetics, that is, the ways in which narrative structures tap into the human need for narrative to generate emotional engagement.

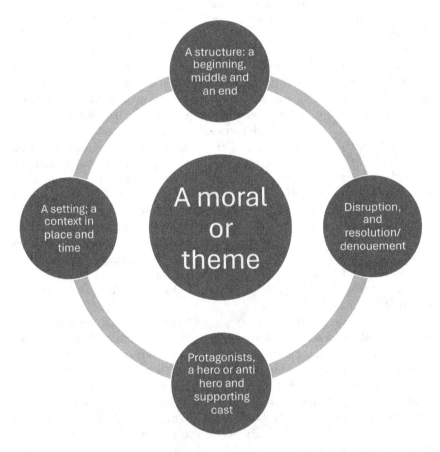

Figure 8.2 Elements of story narratives

Literary journalism and creative nonfiction

In Chapter 7, we discussed autoethnography as a genre of social research deriving from ethnography and based on written, first-person accounts of lived experience. Autoethnography has commonalities with literary journalism, also termed creative nonfiction (Gutkind, 1996). This genre of writing prioritises the value of writing in and of itself as a threshold to heightened experience, self-knowledge and critical understanding. It can include narrative accounts of events or phenomena, and subjective introspection. The common factor is that the authorial voice is not suppressed, as it is in third-person research writing, but projected into the writing.

The focus on writing also highlights the fact that good quality writing is fundamental to good research, whatever the paradigm, although the craft of writing is seldom in taxonomies of research skills or in research methods taught courses. In Chapter 7, we also pointed out that even though social research and management practice are founded on words and communication, there has been very little focus on the communication. This is, perhaps, a by-product of the dominance of the structuralist/realist paradigm, since the assumption there is that social reality lies beneath the surface and the role of words is merely to describe that reality.

The ontological assumption of interpretive and qualitative research paradigms is that social reality is produced and sustained through language and discourse. This, social constructivist ontology, acknowledges that the words we choose have a significant influence on the ways in which we understand the world. They are not merely describing an underlying reality – they constitute that reality.

All this means that words, communication and writing, shift from the background of social scientific practice, to the foreground. After all, social research is the pursuit of truth, and great writing has truth at its heart. When we write social research we are not merely 'writing up' findings: we are writing findings into existence. This can be hard for a student to grasp if they are schooled in realist research paradigm, but although seldom expressed in social research methods books, the fact remains that an interpretive research report is telling a story, and at its heart is a point of view about the world based on the data set. Students of research who are conducting an interpretive project for the first time need to embrace this perspective – it is their point of view that they need to communicate, persuasively and with strong scholarly values that ground the point of view in the data set.

There has also been a heightened focus on writing given that the great majority of published social research papers are seldom read (Brown, 2005). Better writing not only brings greater integrity to social research, it communicates that to a wider readership. Brown (2005) has projected this ethos with a publication initiative in marketing research that foregrounds the quality of writing and personal perspectives, with the *Journal of Customer Behaviour* (e.g. Brown, 2024; Brown and Ponsonby-McCabe, 2022).

There are other social research initiatives focused on the critical intellectual potential of autoethnography to expose power relations and foreground personal perspectives (e.g. Hackley, 2020; Herrmann, 2022). Reading can be a powerfully transformative experience, especially when reading personal accounts of lived experience. Social science as the pursuit of truth can transport the reader into a deeper appreciation of the topic, if it is written in an engaging and vivid style. For the student researcher, this style of writerly research must be approached with caution since it often uses the first-person perspective, when the traditional writing style for research projects is third person. Student researchers should always discuss using the first person with their supervisor before embarking on such an endeavour for their research project.

Semiotics/semiology: origins and scope

Many students wish to explore the visual imagery of branding and advertising in their research projects. To do so, it is useful to know something of the conceptual vocabulary of semiotics. Semiotic has been around in marketing and consumer research and practice for a long time and its concepts are still invoked in published research studies (e.g. Castilhos, 2023; Humphreys, 2010; Roux and Belk, 2018) such is their explanatory power (Danesi, 2004, 2016). Semiotics is, broadly, the study of signs and their meaning in communication. A sign in this sense is something that can stand for something else. 'Semiotics' or 'semiology' is etymologically derived from the Greek *sema*. It can be traced back to the ancient Greek medical techniques of Hippocrates and Galen who inferred medical conditions from the symptoms reported or presented by patients.

The word semiology is usually associated with the study of linguistic signs. The tradition of semiology deriving from European linguistics is associated with Ferdinand de Saussure (1974). The North American tradition (known as semiotics) reflects work by philosopher C.S. Peirce (1953–66, 1986). Scholars have borrowed indiscriminately from each tradition so the distinction between the two is blurred in many research studies. This chapter will emphasise the concepts and terminology of the North American tradition. In 'semiotics' the focus of study is on any signs whatever with regard to their capacity for communicating and generating meaning. That is, the focus can be on visual, aural, word-signs, written or non-written signs. 'Semiosis' is the process of extracting messages and significance from signs, and thereby generating meaning. In human semiosis, the central problem is to understand how signs come to have meaning. Some traditions of semiotic analysis attempt to reveal the codes through which humans draw meaning from signs in particular cultural contexts. However, such codes need not be stable or enduring: they may not pre-exist the relation of sign and *interpretant*. The meaning of signs, according to Peirce (1986), is arbitrary. In principle, anything (an image, an utterance, an object) could stand for anything else. It is the cultural context that frames the interpretation of signs and imbues signs with localised meanings.

Danesi (1993) explains how the colour red can have many different meanings, depending on the cultural context for semiosis. A red traffic light, a blushing cheek, a red armband can all communicate different messages. Red faces in Western cartoons often signify anger or, alternatively, embarrassment, while in China red is a lucky colour. An open window, footprints in the snow, a bloodied knife are classic signifiers in detective stories (Hackley, 1999, p. 137). The Marlboro man, a classic marketing sign, stands for 'American culture, independence and self-reliance, but may also stand for rebellion, chauvinism, fatalism, ill-health or the genocide of Native American Indians, depending on the communication context and the particular interpreter' (Mick, 1997, p. 251). National flags are such powerful signs that some are revered in one country and regarded with contempt in another. The variation in cultural contexts means that people can bring quite differing interpretive strategies to the same signs.

Semiotic studies have been developed in a wide range of human fields. For Mick (1997), semiotics is 'one of the richest sources of principles, concepts and tools for studying communication and meaning' (p. 260). There have been studies of the semiotics of cinema (Metz, 1974), communication (Fiske, 1982; Fry and Fry, 1986), theatre and drama (Elam, 1988) and language (Barthes, 1968; Eco, 1976, 1984), not forgetting the semiotics of emojis (Danesi, 2016). For some semioticians, semiotic study can form a superordinate human science of communication (Sebeok, 1991), ranging from the communication of single cells to the communicative codes of entire cultures. *Semiosis* in marketing and consumption occurs through language (both spoken and printed) and other visual and aural signs. Marketing communications and brands can be seen as a system of 'strings of signs' (Sebeok, 1991, p. 146) that communicate values through brand imagery, packaging design, prices, advertisements and a plethora of other signs.

While marketing has, in the past, been a fertile site for semiotic analysis (e.g. see Larsen et al., 1991; Umiker-Sebeok, 1987; Umiker-Sebeok et al., 1988; *International Journal of Research in Marketing*, special issue 1988, vol. 4, nos. 3 and 4) two marketing fields have proved especially interesting for semioticians. These are advertising and consumer research. Researchers such as Williamson (1978), Tanaka (1994) and Bertrand (1988) have explored the semiotics of advertising in depth. Sherry and Camargo (1987) developed a semiotic analysis of the use of English language words in Japanese advertising. Consumer research has also proved important in stimulating semiotic analysis (Holbrook and Grayson, 1986; Holbrook and Hirschman, 1993; Mick, 1986, 1997; Mick and Buhl, 1992) although, as we note above, more recent studies tend to invoke semiotics terminology or semiotics as a part of their analysis (e.g. Kozinets, 2019) since it has been absorbed into the basic vocabulary of interpretive research.

The symbolic character of human communication is seen as a 'central and differentiating aspect of the species' (Mick, 1986, p. 196) and nowhere is this more evident than in the worlds of marketed consumption. The world of consumption is replete with signs, as Mick (1997) notes: 'Examples of signs in the consumer world are everywhere a person wished to look, listen, smell, feel or taste: brand names and logos, lyrics, melodies and tempos in music; deodorants and perfumes; wool sweaters and silk pillows; pizza and whiskey ...' (p. 251). The semiotic arena of marketing reflects and constitutes the wider cultural setting for semiosis. Anthropological researchers such as Leach (1976), Belk et al. (1988) and Wernick (1991) emphasise the revealing nature of consumption and promotional and marketing culture. They show that marketing appropriates values and signs from non-marketing culture and attaches them to marketed entities to serve corporate aims. Your ownership of branded goods can signify much about you, such as your social status, the groups to which you claim membership and your aspirations and fantasies about yourself (Belk, 1988; Roux and Belk, 2018; Thompson et al., 2018).

Themes and concepts of semiotics

There may be many ways in which signs signify (66 for Peirce, according to Mick, 1997, p. 253; also see discussion in Leach, 1976, p. 10). Three forms of semiosis are often used as the basis for analysis. These three forms of semiotic relation are not mutually exclusive: they do overlap but nonetheless can be useful organising categories for researchers. That is, a sign can act as an index, a symbol and an icon (see Box 8.1). As an index, the sign points to something: as a symbol, it stands for something, and as an icon, it is identified with something. So, for example, a religious icon such as a status of a holy figure is treated by adherents as if it is holiness manifest in the object: an example of an index could be a silhouette image of a man on a bathroom door, and an example of a symbol could be a Nike Swoosh that stands for the sportswear brand Nike.

Semiosis 'takes place on a boundary of cultural, historical and sociological analysis' (Hackley, 1999, p. 141). This cultural dimension has been neglected in some studies that over-emphasised the individual, private aspect of interpretation and the putatively fixed relation of sign to signifier. As Wernick (1991) has pointed out, many studies of advertising 'eclipsed attention both to the historicity of promotional texts and to their contextual dimension' (p. 25). In other words, our interpretation of signs is culturally mediated. We must learn the cultural codes that predetermine particular modes of interpretation. These cultural codes may be culturally specific and they may change over time, so this is not the same as saying that there can be only one culturally correct interpretation of a sign, since signs and interpretants are necessarily embedded in a given (and highly specific) cultural context.

Box 8.1   Features of semiotic analysis

Themes

Semiotics is the study of signs and their meaning
Focus on semiosis as meaning-making in a given cultural context
Humans are interpreting creatures: the universe is suffused with signs.
Semiotics is an inter- and cross-disciplinary field
Important concepts include the sign, icon, index and symbol

Assumptions

The symbolic interpretation of signs is a defining characteristic of human understanding
The relation of sign and signifier is arbitrary: in principle, anything can stand for anything else. It is the cultural context of communication that frames semiotic interpretation

Methods of data gathering

Semiotic studies have often used judgement samples of advertisements or other visual data such as brand logos
The ways in which consumers interpret particular signs could be investigated through focus groups or other qualitative data-gathering techniques

Approach to data analysis

Focus on revealing the semiotic codes that cue particular interpretive strategies in a given context
Any kind of sign can in principle be subject to semiotic analysis such as marketing brand logos, packaging, advertising, the spaces of consumption such as shopping malls, other media texts such as movies, radio jingles, etc.

Dyadic and triadic semiotic relations

The context of interpretation is important because of the differing cultural codes that may be drawn on for interpretive cues in differing cultural contexts. Seen in this light, meaning is something that authors attempt to control or influence, but texts are subject to unpredictable interpretations. Consequently, imposing authorial meaning on the interpretation of a text is a delicate balance and a complex achievement. Advertising agencies that understand this know that they must take great care to isolate the right groups of consumers and to understand them as an 'interpretive community'. Agencies must also create ads that attempt to impose particular meanings in powerfully suggestive but subtle ways by drawing on the semiotic codes that are used within a given interpretive community.

The process of interpretation can be seen as a dyadic or triadic relation. For Peirce, semiosis has a *triadic* character since it depends on a relation between the sign, the object and the interpretant (i.e. the interpretation). This contrasts with de Saussure's ideas about semiosis as a *dyadic* relation between the sign and the signified. As Mick (1986) suggests, the interpretant refers to the interpretation placed on the sign and not to the entity (such as a person) doing the interpreting. The interpretant (interpretation) will vary depending on the cultural context. It will also be influenced by the extent to which its meaning in a particular context is dependent on previous interpretations of the same object.

A dyadic model of semiotic interpretation (see Figure 8.3) has two elements: the sign and the signified. So, for example, the sign might be an outline of a male figure on the door of a public toilet, and the signified is a toilet designated for males. The sign in this case would be operating as an index (much like a road sign signifying a sharp bend ahead or a speed limit). The sign could also operate as a symbol, as in the aforementioned example of a brand image that consumers have become acculturated into interpreting as the brand. This interpretation of course is culturally and historically specific. The Nazi symbol of the swastika existed for perhaps thousands of years as an East Asian symbol of peace and religious piety before Adolf Hitler appropriated it, and for many people today it can only signify the Nazi party. Finally, an iconic sign, such as a religious symbol, signifies the religion or piacular aspects of it.

The variability of interpretive possibilities is perhaps easier to conceptualise using Peirce's triadic model of semiotic interpretation (see Figure 8.4). There are three rather than two elements in Pierce's triadic model: sign, object and interpretant. This model allows for flexibility and change in the meaning of a sign, depending on the perspective and context of the interpretant, or the person who is doing the interpreting. For example, some

Figure 8.3 Ferdinand de Saussure's dyadic model of semiotic interpretation

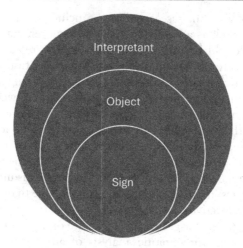

Figure 8.4 Charles Sanders Peirce's triadic model of semiotic interpretation

years ago, the Skoda motor car brand first entered the UK market, it was portrayed in UK advertising as a cheap alternative to mainstream brands. However, negative reports about the car's reliability and engineering quality resulted in media stories and jokes in the United Kingdom that poked fun at the brand. The Skoda brand and its associated signs (the word-sign Skoda and the brand badge on the cars) were interpreted in terms of a communicative code that denigrated the brand. However, a reorganisation of the brand, re-engineering of the car and a re-launch with new advertising changed this code in the United Kingdom. The Skoda brand signs are now interpreted much more positively because of favourable quality reports in motor trade magazines and generally positive media coverage. The advertising campaign intertextually (and humorously) referred to Skoda's old negative image so that people bought into the new interpretation of Skoda. The relation between the object (Skoda motor cars), its various signs (the word-sign 'Skoda', the brand badge, the advertising) and the interpretant (the interpretive reaction the sign elicited) changed as a result of a change in cultural understanding. For people to understand the new meaning of Skoda from the new advertising, they had to understand the references the ads made to the old meaning of Skoda. The interpretation of the Skoda band signs changed as a result of consumers' exposure to contradictory signs in the media.

Doing practical semiotics

As evidenced by the published work cited above, semiotics can be a useful approach in empirical research studies that seek insights into the arbitrary and culturally mediated character of human understanding in communication. It is particularly so when the research data set includes pictures or other kinds of visual images, such as advertising images. However, many other contexts of consumption could be useful areas for semiotic research, provided the aim of the study is to uncover meanings and their relation to signs.

Practical semiotics entails the deconstruction of meaning in given contexts. In semiotics as with all interpretive research the obvious, everyday and taken-for-granted must be made strange and unfamiliar. The object of the researcher is to understand the complexity and arbitrariness of taken-for-granted modes of meaning-making. To do this, researchers must try to understand the world view of particular groups while also standing outside those groups. This is precisely because much of our everyday understanding is unreflexive. We are not aware of the assumptions and cultural knowledge that are built into our common-sense, subjective understanding. The task of the social researcher is to go beyond the taken-for-granted to speculate on its implications.

As a starting-point for semiotic analysis of advertising, the checklist in Box 8.2 is offered, adapted from Hackley (1999, p. 145). This is an informal and simplified framework for beginning to think like a semiotician – if

---

Box 8.2   A simple approach to semiotic deconstruction

Questions to ask:	What does X signify to me?
	Why does X signify this to me?
	What might X signify for others?
	Why might X signify this for others?
Possible sources of X:	
Objects (visual semiosis)	For example, clothes, hairstyles, make-up styles, the ways objects are used by people, use in press ads of printed copy, typeface, use of logo/pictorial symbolic image, the spatial inter-relationships of objects
Gesture (bodily semiosis)	For example, body types, facial types, expressive gestures, facial expressions, posture, gaze, juxtaposition of bodies, juxtaposition of bodies with products
Speech (verbal semiosis)	For example, use of idiomatic expressions, regional or national accent or dialect, use of metaphor/metonymy, tone and volume of speech, pace of delivery, use of voiceover, use of humour, emphasis on particular words/ phonemes

students and researchers wish to conduct more advanced studies they might like to refer to the frameworks in one of the cited works in this chapter, for example the semiotic square (Cian, 2012; Corso, 2014; Greimas, 1988) is used as a framework for analysis in several studies (e.g. Humphreys, 2010; Kozinets, 2008; Varman, Belk and Sreekumar, 2023; Williams Bradford and Sherry, 2015).

This checklist is designed to help student researchers to deepen their semiotic analysis of visual material such as advertising. Many first-time researchers find that beginning the process of deconstruction of an advertisement is difficult. Until one acquires the habit of deconstruction, meanings can appear to have a 'given' and 'common-sense' character. Box 8.2 focuses on specific aspects of an advertisement. If the student researcher can begin to understand the complexity of apparently simple advertisements as 'strings of signs', then they have taken a step towards deconstructing the way in which an advertisement seeks to tap into cultural codes of communication to frame and privilege specific interpretations over others.

The way in which advertising semiosis occurs can be spontaneous and unreflexive. We take for granted the meanings that we read into symbols. Without careful reflection, it is easy to overlook the extent to which the mechanisms of semiosis become silent when we are immersed in the cultural context. In this sense, semiotic analysis is an attempt to achieve the sociological goal of 'making the familiar strange' (Mills, 1959), or, in other words, revealing and making explicit the tacit nuanced symbolic interpretations that we take for granted in our everyday lives. The empiricists since David Hulme pointed out that human beings are constantly responding to environmental stimuli, through our senses. Our interpretations of the sounds, images and other signs that surround us are our attempts to render these signs meaningful. Semiotics attempts to reveal the underlying structures of this meaning-making process.

This chapter has introduced various concepts from literary criticism, and it has given examples of their application in marketing, management and consumer research. Concepts such as intertextuality, paratextuality, polysemy, reader-response and semiosis have been introduced as some of the tools of literary analysis that are most readily applied to topics in advertising, branding and consumer research. Semiotics, and literary theory more generally, offer social researchers ways of understanding marketing and consumer culture that generate very different types of insight to the ones generated by quantitative and positivistic research studies. Literary concepts are well suited to qualitative and interpretive research studies, and student researchers are urged to look into some of the published studies cited in this short introduction to this rich area of research. Chapter 9 will discuss the applications of critical theory in interpretive, qualitative research studies.

Glossary

Narrative   The organisation of writing or language to portray accounts of events in a way, which seems sequential and connected.

Polysemy   A message or entity is said to be polysemic if it displays not one but many possible meanings.

Dyadic   Relation with two dimensions, as when one interviewer interviews one interviewee (a dyadic interview).

Icon   A sign that is similar in some ways to its referent, in the way that a photograph bears a resemblance to the image it portrays, or an onomatopoeic word resembles a sound, such as in 'plop' or 'roar'.

Index   A form of semiosis in which a sign points to or indicates something else, such as where the word 'TAXI' lights up on the top of a yellow car.

Interpretant   The entity (usually human) that interprets the sign. The word 'interpretant' is also used to refer to the interpretation.

Semiology   The study of linguistic signs and their relation to concepts.

Semiosis   The process of semiotic interpretation.

Semiotics   The study of signs and their interpretation.

Sign   For C.S. Peirce, a sign is anything that can stand for something else.

Structuralist   The term is often used in social research to imply a realist ontology. That is, explanations for social phenomena can reveal universal structures of meaning that underlie social processes.

Symbol   A form of semiosis in which something acts as a symbol of something else, such as when a clenched fist symbolises aggression.

Triadic   A relation with three dimensions, e.g. Pierce's model of semiosis.

Chapter 9

Critical research

Power, ethnicity and gender

Abstract

Research in the interpretive research paradigm has sometimes been accused of lacking a critical edge, although this criticism becomes less telling over time as increasing numbers of critical interpretive studies become published. In this chapter, we review the idea of critical research in the light of traditions of critical management studies and critical marketing. The chapter discusses some approaches to criticality in research, and it examines how critical perspectives on power, gender and ethnicity can be incorporated into qualitative research projects.

Chapter objectives

After reading this chapter students will be able to

- explain some of the key aims and values of critical social research
- understand distinctions between the colloquial usage of the word 'critical' and the more specific usages associated with research
- critically discuss issues of power in social research in relation to ethnicity, gender, sexuality and disability

The aims of 'critical' research

The idea of 'critical' intellectual work has been introduced earlier in the book. This sense of critical reflects an intellectual commitment to rigorous thinking and analysis, a level of analysis that rises above the merely descriptive to compare, contrast and evaluate ideas. In this chapter, we examine the notion of the critical in a different sense to simply meaning intellectually and critically engaged. As we noted earlier in the book, in many management texts the word 'critical' is used as a synonym for 'important', as in 'marketing is a critical business function'. In educational contexts, 'critical' intellectual work refers to a deep engagement with the subject matter, an uncompromising

DOI: 10.4324/9781003432203-12

examination of the assumptions of any given point of view or theory, and an independent stance that acknowledges that versions of the truth in social science may serve some interests more than others. In this sense all research writing should have a critical dimension since it should rigorously evaluate the intellectual and moral grounds for claims. Intellectual work that is critical in this general sense engages with the explicit and implicit assumptions of any given research perspective.

In social research, 'critical' can have a much more specific meaning focusing on structural and constitutive power (introduced earlier in the book) and the implications of power imbalances for individuals and groups. Critical research in this sense engages with the inequalities and inequities of class, ethnicity, disability, sexuality and gender. The theoretical stances, though, from which critical studies engage with their subject matter can differ. For many researchers, 'critical' research implies a particular theoretical stance that is informed by Marxist theorists such as Horkheimer and Adorno (1944) and the 'Frankfurt school' of writers and developed by writers such as Althusser (1971). Critical historical sociology (e.g. Foucault, 1977) has also been an important influence.

The aims of critical research in business and management

In marketing, management and consumer research, critical research traditions have been invoked with two broad aims. One has been to contribute to an intellectually viable management education agenda that moves away from 'how to' consulting prescriptions and develops the wider critical intellectual awareness of managers, students and researchers. This commitment to intellectual rigour has largely been agnostic on matters of patriarchy, gender equality, class inequality and other issues of social and economic justice. One criticism of business and management education, as a whole, has been that it acts as an ideological fig leaf for the injustices and inequities of capitalism (discussed in Hackley, 2024; also see Bradshaw, 2023). The marginalisation of critical research has been seen as a key part of this ideological role. Today, though, there are many research outlets that resist this marginalisation by foregrounding critical perspectives in general social science (e.g. Boylorn and Orbe, 2021) and in management outlets specifically.

There has been a growing canon of work that takes a more fundamentally critical stance and engages in a far-reaching reappraisal of the aims, methods and ideologies of both management education and organisational, marketing and consumer practice (e.g. Ellis et al., 2011; Hackley, 2009a, b; Maclaran et al., 2007; Tadajewski et al., 2019, 2014; Tadajewski and Maclaran, 2009). From a managerial perspective, critical theorists point out that much management theory is inherently *ideological* in character, and this tends to place limits on the intellectual scope of representations of theory in the field. One argument is that one cannot faithfully evaluate the use or truth of a theory or model unless one asks whose interests are served by this form of representation. From a broader ethical standpoint, critical theorists seek to critically reappraise the ways in which practice and representation impose narrow values and reproduce narrow interests. Critical research questions the moral conduct of organisational marketing and management and attempts to put forward alternative agenda from the point of view of less powerful parties, i.e. consumers, citizens and employees.

For example, Henderson et al. (2016) examine the extent to which inequalities and inequities are reproduced through consumption, while Foster Davis (2018) explores race in the 'whiteness' of the marketing research canon. There are academic initiatives that examine racism in academia and academic research (e.g. 'Race in the Marketplace', in the United States, and Gabriel and Tate, 2017, in the United Kingdom) that have emerged as part of wider attention being given to racism in society (e.g. Akala, 2019; Eddo-Lodge, 2018). Critical gender studies have also begun to appear in marketing and consumer research literature (e.g. Bettany et al., 2010; Eckhardt et al., 2021; Enck and Morrissey, 2015; Gurrieri et al., 2022; Martin et al., 2006; Mclaran and Chatzidikas, 2022; Thompson and Ustunier, 2015), including some major edited works (Dobscha, 2019). Such work reappraises how assumptions about race and gender are often institutionalised in the values and priorities of academia and research, and these works seek to reveal the inherent inequalities and inequities of power that result. A central aim of critical research is to pick apart the assumptions and values underlying world views, so that prevailing power relations are not uncritically reproduced by and for researchers and the users of research, but, rather, are revealed and held up to critical examination.

Critical perspectives in management research are by no means new, but there has been a renewed awareness and scope of the role race, class, sexualities, disabilities and gender play in constituting power relations through academic research, writing and teaching. Older work that began the critical perspective in management areas includes Hirschman and Stern's (1994) work on women as commodities in prostitution, while Alvesson and Deetz (2000), Alvesson and Willmott (1992) and Murray and Ozanne (1991) (see also Murray et al., 1994) were among those who established the critical (as opposed to the managerial) perspective in management and consumer research respectively.

Interpretive research and critical approaches

Alvesson and Deetz (2000) draw attention to the common ground between interpretive and critical research and suggest that critical perspectives can often usefully be conjoined with interpretive approaches, such as ethnography and discourse analysis. They cite critical ethnography (Thomas, 1993) as a useful approach and offer examples of work that have combined ethnographic principles with varied data-gathering approaches such as direct observation and interviewing to powerful effect as with Kunda (1992). Critical research, like interpretive research, tends to focus on the particular, rather than the general. It is situational in that its main concern is to conduct microsociological studies of power in a given organisational or other context, but which also connect to wider discourses and ideologies of structural power. In the discussion and analysis of such studies it may sometimes be possible to go beyond the particular social context to trace the historical and cultural origins of a particular form of social relations or interactional practices, such as where local asymmetries of power result from a history of class relations.

Marketing, it is generally accepted, has been largely dominated by a non-critical style of managerial research which ignores (or silences) issues of power and inequity. Arguably this may be because the marketing management point of view is widely accepted and propagated as an ideology heavily informed by consulting and other financial interests. In addition, the case method and its un-critical managerial aims have become heavily identified with marketing research and education. In other words, the marketing 'philosophy' and attendant concepts are often put forward as unquestionable organisational and managerial virtues the sole aim of which is to support managerial and organisational goals (e.g. Brownlie et al., 1999; Hackley, 2001, 2003b, c, 2009a).

However, more and more published research has emerged that provides critical perspectives (e.g. Mahoney, 2015; Tadajewski et al., 2019; Varey and Pirson, 2014) with a critical focus falling on many aspects of marketing, such as postcolonialism (Varman, Belk and Sreekumar, 2023), feminism (Maclaran, Stevens and Kravits, 2022), marketing and disability (Beudaert, Mason and Nau, 2023; Salomonson and Echeverri, 2024), the ethics of care (Chatzidikas et al., 2020; Preece and Rojas Gaviria, 2024) and many other areas in need of critical investigation by marketing, consumer research and management scholars. Interpretive research is ideally placed to advance a critical agenda in business and management studies (Dobscha and Lee, 2014).

The critical research 'stance'

Language and power

Critical research, broadly conceived, can be characterised by certain priorities and precepts. In this introduction one particularly important precept deserves special mention. This is the social constructionist (or constructivist) position that language is assumed to be *constitutive* in the sense that it constructs, or constitutes, its objects. That is, language does not merely refer to entities and concepts like 'marketing' or 'management' that subsist in a different ontological plane: it actively constructs them. This 'linguistic turn' in (critical and interpretive) research (Alvesson and Kärreman, 2000;

O'Shaughnessy and Holbrook, 2015) is reflected in a concern with language, texts, discourse and narrative in research approaches. Because of this concern with language and representation, interpretive approaches to social research in management fields fit particularly well with critical analyses.

Critical research in marketing and management does not focus solely on the managerial problems of how to do marketing/management more effectively. Rather, it focuses on the ways in which language is used to construct marketing/management phenomena. Large, global commercial organisations, in whose name much academic business research is conducted, are powerful entities. An important part of their power lies in the ability to define what is normal, taken-for-granted and of value, through their communications and influence. It is this power that is placed under scrutiny in critical research. This does not necessarily mean that critical research is anti-capitalist or anti-organisations, although much critical social research is indeed critical of neo-liberal aspects of capitalism (e.g. Felix and Fuat Fırat, 2019; Khare and Varman, 2017; Schöps et al., 2019; Tadajewski et al., 2014; Varman et al., 2011; Zwick, 2018). Critical research acknowledges a political reality, that is, the interests of large commercial organisations, reflected in the values of university research, may not always coincide with those of all citizens, consumers, employees or minorities.

Critical research practices

Critical research is not a method as such but an intellectual standpoint for social research. The intellectual criticality that is the benchmark of excellent academic work is taken to its next logical step when not only does the researcher examine the deep assumptions that underlie taken-for-granted values and priorities, but also examines the social and cultural conditions that led to those deep assumptions becoming taken-for-granted. The critical researcher does not settle for easy, conventional or superficial explanations but 'unpacks' concepts and develops a reflexive dialogue with the reader. This is accomplished by using the research data (whether primary or secondary) as material to develop lines of discussion, argument and investigation that do not simply accept the apparent order of things but question it to reveal obscured relations of power and control. Box 9.1 is necessarily over-simplified but attempts to capture some of the major concepts and practices of critical qualitative research studies.

Qualitative data sets are often the basis for critical empirical research studies. However, the critical stance applies to the interpretive strategies and representational practices that the researcher brings to their objects of study, regardless of whether the study includes quantitative or qualitative data sets, or both. The critical perspective informs research design but can also be applied in the literature reviewing and analysis/discussion aspects of any research study.

Box 9.1   Some key themes of critical interpretive research

Themes

Power; exclusion: equality and social justice: sustainability: discourse and language: ideology: emancipation: class: gender: class: neoliberalism: disability: patriarchy: neo-colonialism: globalism: anticapitalism: ethnicity: sexuality: race

Assumptions

Social constructionist or critical realist ontologies

Language actively constitutes its objects, it does not merely refer to them

Social relations are infused with power: social structures and institutions exercise deep influence over the ways in which people talk, think and feel

Agency is strictly constrained by social structures and institutions

Indeed, a sense of agency may be illusory if people have simply internalised values and norms that reflect asymmetrical relations of power

This sense of agency may unwittingly serve narrow interests rather than self-interest, for example in some management initiatives to 'empower' workers that in fact do the opposite

'Normality' and 'common sense' are taken-for-granted as are the values of things that are produced in social life under the influence of social structures and institutions that have a historical basis

Critical perspectives are thought to have moral force as they might generate practical change and individual liberation

Methods of data gathering

Qualitative, naturalistic, ethnographic, phenomenological, observational

Approach to data analysis

Interpretive approaches (such as critical discourse analysis, thematic analysis) are used to draw categories, metaphors and other themes from data. These are used to develop lines of discussion that seek to generate insights into the ways in which interests and values are reproduced in 'normal' and 'everyday' interactional practices

Social critique, discourse and power

Researchers familiar with the work of the Frankfurt school of political/ economic theorists understand critical research as a more radical approach than one that demonstrates (only) intellectual values. For those researching in the Frankfurt school tradition, it is capitalism itself in its many forms that is the object of critique. Capitalist *discourses* are considered to be repressive in the sense that they exclude and rule out ways of talking, thinking and being that may be more fulfilling of human potential. Discourses of marketing (that is, ways of talking and writing about marketing) are said to reproduce structures of control and domination, especially the domination of corporations and allied political and governmental institutions over the social and psychological life of citizens. Critical social research, then, has a role in revealing, through critique, how these structures of domination are reproduced in everyday working and consumer life. By so doing, critical research aims to create discursive space for resistance, thereby making possible a form of *emancipation* (Murray and Ozanne, 1991). Critical perspectives aim to promote a reflexive awareness of how language and discourse construct particular relations, subjectivities and ways of being and working.

Much managerial research is decidedly non-critical in the sense that it seeks to provide organisational managers with solutions to business and policy problems based on the blanket assumption that what is good for organisations, managers and shareholders is necessarily good for individual citizens, social groups and societies. It reproduces a social order assuming it to be a natural, unquestionable thing. The authority of managers, the social benefits of organisational marketing and the desirability of ever greater levels of consumption are assumed as given.

Marketing discourse, for example, stands accused of excluding or playing down consideration of other interests such as environmental concerns, gender and race inequities, the ability of citizens to resist the power of corporations, and the legality and fairness of organisational policies and practices (Maclaran et al., 2007; Skålén et al., 2008). Critical research seeks to overturn the apparently 'natural' or 'given' order of things to explore how these have become taken-for-granted. The aim is to achieve a greater integrity in research by openly revealing the interests bound up with ways of knowing and describing. The assumption is that all representations of knowledge are political in the sense that they serve some interests more closely than others.

Ideology and critical research

Ideology is a central concept in critical social research and cultural studies, as we have seen earlier in Chapter 8. The topic might be more commonly seen as part of political science, English or communication studies (Eagleton,

2007), but the study of ideology applies aptly in management and business topics, including marketing (Elliott and Ritson, 1997; Hackley, 2009b; Marion, 2006; Patterson and Elliott, 2002; Tadajewski, 2014). The reason, put simply, is that ideology inflects many areas of life and business schools, and business and management studies, have been accused of acting as ideologists for capitalism (discussion in Hackley, 2024). Ideology is a critical form of research since it entails revealing and examining the implicit assumptions and values that underpin ways of seeing the world. In this section we will outline some key principles of the study of ideology as they might apply to selected areas of business and management and related subjects.

Althusser (1971) broadened the Marxist notion of ideology as a system of *structural power* by drawing attention to its *constitutive power* to form *subjectivities*. He suggested that social institutions such as schools, religions, the law and the media perpetuate values, practices and interests that serve the state in ways which become so taken-for-granted that they form our very subjective system of values and presuppositions, and hence inform our thought and behaviour in subtle and penetrating ways. Edgar and Sedgwick (1999) suggest that the word 'ideology' derived from French educational philosophy that associated ideas with some underlying cause in biological, social or material conditions. Napoleon ridiculed the *idéologues* and ideology became a pejorative term. For Marx (Marx and Engels, 2011), ideology referred to the ideas of the economic ruling class that define class structures, permeate subjective consciousness and perpetuate the power of the elite. For Marxists, there is no individual subjectivity other than the false consciousness created by class ideology.

In later social theory, ideology becomes a more subtle notion that manifests in the micro-practices of everyday life and is continually reconstructed and renegotiated through social practice and interaction. Ideology does not necessarily refer to a delusion or false subjectivity, as it did for Marx. In contemporary social research, ideology cannot be counterposed to an absolute truth of which it is a distortion. Ideological beliefs are simply part of the socially constructed world of ideas that reflect differing perspectives. Ideology can be relatively benign, for example, brand management can be seen as an inherently ideological practice (Holt and Cameron, 2010; O'Reilly, 2006) in the sense that it entails the manipulation of the public reception of ideas. Of course, quite how benign this is open to debate: consumerism has many negative outcomes, socially, economically and environmentally. The point here is that the study of ideology should be central to branding and advertising because it simply reflects the way that ideas are communicated and accepted in society.

The ideological influences in marketing and consumption, and in academic research, have been understood for many years (Crockett and Wallendorf, 2004; Firat Fuat and Venkatesh, 1995a; Holt, 2002; Levy and Luedicke, 2013; Lisjak and Ordabayeva, 2023). For example, Hirschman (1993) adopted Eagleton's (2007) definition of ideology in her investigation of the influence of masculine ideology in consumer research. Ideology refers to the ways in which a 'world-view or value-and-belief system of a particular class or group of people' (Hirschman, 1993, p. 538) is reproduced through certain kinds of representational strategies. Writing tropes, metaphors and styles are primary forms of ideological representation in marketing (Hackley, 2003c). Advertising has been a fruitful source of ideological analysis (Wernick, 1991), and Williamson (1978) famously analysed the ideology of advertising using a Marxist frame of reference.

The notion of ideology is sometimes used in marketing, management and consumer research to refer broadly to sets of ideas and implied relations that have become taken-for-granted. Since ideas are always political in the sense that they emerge from specific sets of historical circumstances, they may serve interests that are not immediately apparent. The use of the term ideology in social research does not necessarily have pejorative implications even though it is often used in a highly critical context. Alvesson and Deetz (2000) note that academics in management studies are often viewed as ideologists (p. 84) in that 'they serve dominant groups through socialization in business schools, support managers with ideas and vocabularies for cultural – ideological control at the workplace level, and provide an aura of science to support the introduction and use of managerial domination techniques'. While Alvesson and Deetz (2000) do not intend this as a compliment, many management academics suggest that they are entirely satisfied with the role of being an ideologist in university business schools, promoting pro-business values as a good in and of itself. Prominent researchers in marketing who claim no critical agenda readily concede that marketing, alongside the other business and management sub-disciplines, is particularly ideological in character (e.g. Brownlie et al., 2013; Deshpandhe, 1999; Gronhaug, 2000; see also Hackley, 2024).

If we mention ideology, we should also mention propaganda, since the two are related. Indeed, they intersect (see Figure 9.1). Edward Bernays (2004) who originally wrote his famous book *Propaganda* in 1928 became notorious for his approach to marketing publicity. Bernays (who was Sigmund Freud's nephew) worked for the US Government as a propagandist during World War 11. After the war he wanted to apply his skills to commerce, but he realised that propaganda had unpleasant associations with lies, authoritarianism and deceit. He coined the term Public Relations, and opened his practice on Madison Avenue. Bernays felt that there was little meaningful difference between Public Relations (or PR) and propaganda, but he understood that telling outright lies was not in the commercial interests of his clients. Instead, he chose to exert a softer form of ideological influence in the sense that he framed information in ways that benefited his clients. For an early client, a cigarette brand, Bernays contrived an event that was covered in the cinema newsreels in which socially prominent ladies lit up cigarettes (Bernays felt

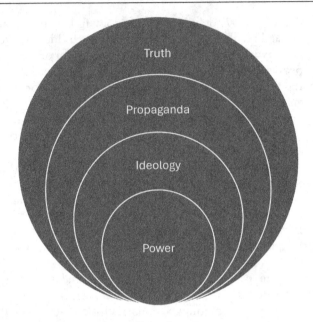

Figure 9.1 Truth, ideology, propaganda and power

that news and information media were far more influential than advertising). This event was seen by huge audiences and helped to break the social taboo against women smoking cigarettes.

This story hints at the distinction between propaganda and ideology. Propagandistic art, advertising and publicity is typically exercise by totalitarian states and founded on untruth. The objective is either to obscure the truth, or to get audiences to believe the untruth. The aim is to exert power over public opinion. The aim of ideology is the same, but the means are normally more subtle. Rather than communicating untruths, which can be undermined if the right information is accessed, ideology is concerned with framing truths in such ways that benefit the interests of a specific group. Bernays's publicity initiative for his tobacco client was not an explicit lie, but it was not a true record of a spontaneous event either. It was contrived to make cigarette smoking not only look acceptable for women, but to make it look deeply attractive, almost as if cigarettes were a source of independence and power for women.

In other settings, ideology works more subtly. For example, some critical theorists consider advertising to be a powerful form of ideology that ultimately promotes one thing – consumption. The fact that advertising is a ubiquitous presence in advanced economies makes its ideological force more compelling, since we take it for granted. These critics point out that this ideology benefits capitalists, shareholders and industry, but has negative effects on the environment and on society since it creates false desires and results in inequality.

It might be thought merely pedantic to draw a distinction between ideology and propaganda, as Bernays apparently thought, and perhaps it is. But the study of propaganda tends to be confined to distinct forms of communication, especially communication in war, and communication from and by authoritarian states, while ideology can have an effect throughout almost any kind of discourse and in any area of life.

Ideology critique in organisational management

In critical organisational research, ideology critique focuses on 'worker's self-understanding of experience' (Alvesson and Deetz, 2000, p. 83, citing Burawoy, 1979; Gramsci, 1971). Workers, a category into which most of us fall one way or another whether we are a CEO, an intern or a managerial trainee, articulate the experience of being a worker in ways which reflect the ideological norms we have assimilated. In business schools, and through our reading of popular texts, we may have absorbed ideas that are not necessarily in our interest, but which we take for granted, nonetheless.

For example, we might take for granted that it is our responsibility to go out to work as an employee, to earn a living and to do our best to be a good worker, pay our taxes and be independent. These ideas inform our preconceptions and values which, in turn, underlie our values and behaviour as workers, but there are other, alternative ideologies in play Some people might think being an employee is for suckers, and the wiser path is to either be a criminal, or to be a business owner and capitalist, and therefore earn (or take) money for ourselves instead of earning it for our employer. An important thing to note regarding the comment on 'self-understanding' is that it is the subjectivity of workers that is formed by ideology. That is, as workers we deeply internalise values of self-control and a work ethic because we accept the assumption that they are consistent with our own interests. In this sense, ideology critique attempts to dig deep into our 'self-understanding' as workers to see where our internalised values came from, and to recover the implications these have for our subjective sense of identity and personal realisation.

As an example, it has been suggested that marketing management students are used to assimilating sets of ideas that are presented in many introductory texts as unquestionable and ethically neutral. Marketing students and managers often feel that the marketing curriculum produced through popular texts consists of normative problem-solving techniques (Hackley, 2003b; 2009b) that don't stand up to rigorous examination. These techniques and concepts are presented as if they are in the interests of all: marketing activity creates wealth for society, promotes opportunity and growth for individuals and corporations, and confers expertise and privilege on the managers (and academics) who learn and espouse them.

However, these ideas can be seen in an entirely different light. For some critical commentators, managerial-(ist) social research tends to be loaded with un-stated presuppositions and lacks intellectual rigor. Such work tends to reproduce, rather than challenge and expose, narrow interests and relations of power that serve certain consulting and corporate interests at the expense of other groups. Marketing management concepts are derived from historical conditions. They emerged during a huge rise in wealth in Western Europe and North America after the Second World War. They were popularised by a growing group of management 'gurus' with origins in business consulting. Many of these gurus then took their ideas into the academic world as business schools became established in universities. Through publishing and the huge growth in interest in marketing studies (Hackley, 2009b) these ideas became widely accepted as authoritative and taken-for-granted. Marketing management assumed the characteristics of an ideology that is perpetuated through the use of particular rhetorical strategies (Hackley, 2003b, 2009a; Yang, Ozanne and Phipps, 2024 and see also Firat, 1985; Firat and Venkatesh, 1995a; Furusten, 1999; Meamber and Venkatesh, 1995).

Whether or not marketing management textbook frameworks are managerially useful, socially beneficial or intellectually sustainable is not the main issue here. The suggestion that they are ideological in character has implications for how they are judged as intellectual products. It also has implications for how we understand the ways in which people draw on marketing and management discourses to account for and justify events and practices in the contexts of work, management and consumption and social policy. Of course, how they are judged as intellectual products may well, in turn, have implications for how people view their managerial usefulness and social value.

Constructing managerial authority in organisations

Critical research normally assumes a social constructionist ontology. That is, it assumes that social life is constructed in interaction through language and social practice. Interaction and social practice are, in turn, framed by the context given by social structures and institutions (Askegaard and Linnet, 2011). Our power to act freely and in our own interest in local interactions is constrained by social realities of economics, social class, gender, ethnicity, education and other social structures and institutions. The social constructionist ontology implies that there is an important distinction between two kinds of powers. On the one hand there is *structural power*: structural power derives from a particular arrangement of social institutions and allows certain individuals to demand co-operation from others. Structural power is wielded by those who have legal authority, such as legally sanctioned officials like police, customs and immigration agents and so on, those that have organisationally sanctioned power such as managers who have authority to fire or sanction junior staff, or those with authority invested in them by custom and practice, such as teachers or, in some cultures, parents. Constitutive power, on the other hand, is a more subtle concept, since it alludes to the ways in which power is manifest in and through language in interaction in ways that are not necessarily obvious or explicit.

To offer an example, a manager might have structural power over an employee because they can impose sanctions for non-compliance on that employee, such as pay deductions, the denial of promotion opportunities or disciplinary action. However, it might be the case that the employee is better educated than the manager and is a member of the social class of more senior managers even though they do not hold that rank in the organisation. In such circumstances, it may be difficult for the manager to negotiate their authority against the background of class superiority that frames interaction with the subordinate.

In the United Kingdom, as in other countries, some people who have been educated in elite institutions can convey this confidence through their speech and manner, and some people who have a less prestigious and/or wealthy background can sometimes feel intimidated by such displays of social status. One could also assume that BAME (Black and Ethnic Minority) managers who are promoted to their positions may sometimes find that white subordinates undermine their authority, or that national citizens undermine the authority of promoted non-nationals and so on. Even legal structural power can be undermined by the social institutions of race, ethnicity and class.

Managerial authority is sometimes regarded as a given, a taken-for-granted aspect of organisational life. Books such as *In Search of Excellence* (Peters and Waterman, 1982) have shown management in a powerful light as the class of worker that can make or break an organisation through their skills of analysis, leadership and problem-solving. Other academic studies have shown management in a different light, as a group of people trying to cope with enormous organisational pressures in difficult circumstances (Watson, 1994). Still other studies have shown how the idea of managerial power is itself highly questionable: in some contexts, managers don't really have any power (Munro, 1997). Some studies have suggested that managerial power within some organisations can be seen as a discursive effect produced not by explicit sanctions and rewards but by expropriating certain forms of language and imposing certain values on employees (Hackley, 2000).

At the centre of managerial marketing normative theory is the marketing mix, the idea that marketing managers hold the key to organisational success through their judicious use of the four Ps of Product, Price, Place (distribution channels) and Promotion (Kotler, 1967). This ideology of marketing management retains considerable influence in marketing education, yet, the marketing manager is seldom if ever in control of these variables in real organisations, notwithstanding the highly simplistic framing of the marketing task that the mix implies (Brownlie and Saren, 1992). The marketing manager is given a heroic status in managerial marketing texts (Hackley, 2003b) that does not square usually with organisational reality because in practice the price is set by the accountants, the product is designed by the designers, the promotion is handled by the advertising department and the distribution is controlled by logistics. The poor marketing manager can be left wondering where they fit in.

Constitutive power, then, refers to the ways in which power is manifest in particular ways of talking and acting that have historical, social and cultural origins. A particular manager might, say, wear a dark lounge suit to work and exhort the workforce to be more 'customer-facing'. The lounge suit carries with it overtones of authority because of its class-based history. In many countries the suit (still) signifies membership of a non-manual class of workers that has access to education and wealth. A manager might feel that they would be taken less seriously if they wore casual clothing to work (although this convention is increasingly challenged today).

Language is another important rhetorical aspect in constructing managerial authority. Invoking management buzz-phrases such as 'customer-facing' or 'customer-focused' has become a particularly powerful resource for managers to extract compliance from workers in organisations. The jargon of managers is important in producing managerial authority since it can imply that managers have technical knowledge and, therefore, hold power over subordinates. Much management jargon also implies that individual action is part of a collective enterprise that cannot be questioned. If a call-centre worker is disciplined for not being sufficiently 'customer-sensitive', it can be very difficult for them to defend such charges because the notion of being 'customer-sensitive' is so widely accepted as an unquestioned virtue in itself. Managers have the power to define exactly what terms like this mean in terms of behaviours in the organisational context.

Gender studies and feminism in research

Research into gender studies and feminism has a well-established record of publications in consumer research going back many years (e.g. Catterall et al., 2001; Hirschman, 1993; Hirschman and Stern, 1994; Stern, 1993). For example, the extent to which marketing images mediate the social construction of gender has been a recurring topic of gender research (Borgerson and Schroeder, 2018; Patterson and Elliott, 2002; Schroeder and Borgerson, 2015), as have feminist perspectives on management (Martin, 2004) and marketing, reflected, for example, in major research collections (e.g. Catterall et al., 2000; Dobscha, 2019; Hearn and Hein, 2015; Maclaran,

2012, 2015; Maclaran and Chatzidikas, 2022; Maclaran, Stevens and Kravets, 2022).

A major concern of such research is the way that social identity formation and relations of gender are informed by marketed images (Borgerson and Schroeder, 2018; Schroeder and Borgerson, 2015) and values. Marketing is a pervasive influence in developed economies. Do the values and norms implicit in marketing activity reproduce relations of power and domination? For example, do magazine images reproduce male dominance as a norm? (Patterson and Elliott, 2002). Much consumption is visual, in the sense that we 'consume' marketed images on a vast scale in advertising, packaging, movies and other media replete with marketing imagery, yet the practices of visual consumption are still under-theorised and the visual remains relatively under-recognised in research (Schroeder, 2002). However, visual imagery offers a fruitful source of material for research. For example, some student researchers have found that, by analysing the visual imagery and/or editorial content in popular magazines over a period of time, they have been able to develop critical analyses of gender representations in such magazines. This might entail a focus on the portrayal of gender relations, or a focus solely on the construction of ideologies of masculinity or femininity in media representations.

Interpretive analysis of gender representation must engage at some level with the issue of power when the researcher asks why certain forms of representation are popular or prevalent and others are not. For example, Alvesson (1998) studied the ways in which gender relations were produced through the discourse of an advertising agency. Workplaces are important sites in the play of gender relations. Issues of equal opportunities and the 'glass ceiling' phenomenon of male-dominated promotion procedures can be investigated through such gender-based research perspectives.

Researchers could employ a phenomenological approach in seeking to understand the experience of gender, race or class in the workplace, as Gabriel and Tate (2017) did with BAME academics' experience of race in universities. Such autoethnographic accounts of the lived experience of being a member of a minority in white and male dominated institutions generate powerful testimony and give voice to minority views that are often crowded out of mainstream academic discourse. Continuing with racial imbalance but in a very different context, notoriously, the UK and US prison populations have a disproportionately high representation of black and ethnical minority prisoners. In the United Kingdom in 2019, 13 per cent of the general population identified as non-white, but 27 per cent of the prison population did so (Sturge, 2019). In the United States, the disparity is even more striking. According to Pew (2023) Black inmates make up almost 50 per cent of the 2 million prison population even though only 13 per cent of the general US population identifies as black. The reasons for these disparities are complex, but can we be sure that marketing does not contribute to the perpetuation of negative racial stereotypes through the images it uses and the values it reinforces? This kind of topic clearly falls within the scope of a critical marketing research project.

Some professions, especially caring professions such as primary school teaching and hospital nursing, are predominantly female occupations, even though most senior medical positions and head teacher positions tend to be occupied by males. Other professions, such as stock broking or civil engineering, are predominantly male. It cannot be denied that progress has been made in race and gender equality in many countries in many fields of employment. Yet, there remains much to be done. Again, it falls to the researcher to ask what is the role of universities, academics and organisational management in perpetuating, or addressing and challenging, negative stereotypes that limit the life chances of individuals? Gender-based studies can elucidate these and many related issues in marketing and management.

The postmodernist critique of marketing 1990–2007

Postmodernist themes (Harvey, 1989) (often linked, or conflated with, post-structuralism) have been singularly influential in developing the critical interpretive stance in marketing and consumer research (Holt, 1997; Thompson, 2002; Thompson and Tambyah, 1999) and, arguably, remain relevant although perhaps now of mainly historical interest. Firat and Venkatesh (1995a, 1995b), Firat et al. (1995), Featherstone (1991) and Brown (1994, 1995) have each set out themes of postmodernism in consumer research and in marketing respectively. Postmodernism in marketing and consumer research became a label for a set of precepts and positions which, collectively, challenged modernist notions of progress, unity and coherence. Postmodern influences have been important in art, architecture and literature (for a 'genealogy' of post-modernism see Firat and Venkatesh, 1995a, p. 241). Epistemologically, postmodernism indicates a reaction against modernist notions of epistemological unity, objective truth and linear historical progress.

Prominent in postmodernist themes is a sense of the fragmentation of meaning into multiple contested meanings (or 'polysemy') and a break in the reliance on 'grand narratives' or organising themes that, in previous historical eras, were thought to have ordered social structure and, hence, private thought (Lyotard, 1984). Postmodernist writing often emphasises a 'de-centring' of knowledge so that what might once have been unified, absolute, progressive and consensual is now fragmented, relative, temporally indeterminate and contested. Postmodern writing stands for experimental narrative forms, challenging prose styles and (purportedly) new ideas. It tends to be irreverent and sceptical, questioning norms and challenging convention.

Much postmodern writing remarks on the curious character of marketing institutions such as 'shopping centres, department stores, advertising campaigns, package designs, new product development and the entire con-sumption experience' (Brown, 1995, p. 8). Indeed, marketing has been iden-tified as the quintessential site of postmodernism (Firat and Venkatesh, 1995a, b). Postmodernist reflections on marketing point to the simulated character of vaunted consumption experiences as in the 'hyperreality' of Dis-neyland. It indicates the pastiche of differing styles and genres in advertis-ing text and visuals, brand names and product design. For example, 'Retro' design in furniture, popular music and motor cars combines modern styles with classic designs to produce a new effect that rehabilitates the old (Brown, 2001; Dam, Hartmann and Brunk, 2024). The culturally trivial nature of popular marketing phenomena and the privileging of style over substance is also addressed by post-modernist writing that refers, for example, to 'reality' TV shows and 'designer' clothes labels. Postmodern critique in marketing in-cludes Brown, Stevens and Maclaran (1999) using postmodernism and liter-ary theory to critique gender bias in advertising (also see Stern, 1993), while Üstüner and Holt (2007) referred to postmodern consumer acculturation in their study of poor migrant women living in a Turkish squatter camp. There are few topics that cannot fall within the scope of a critical marketing and consumer research treatment.

In postmodernist writing, the text is a major focus of attention, and the media is a major source of social texts. Postmodernist writing is often highly critical of conventional practice and beliefs and uses irony to undermine 'grand narratives' of belief and practice. Marketing, a 'narrative project' as noted above, has become part of the media complex with its big-selling text books, web-based resources and video-star management consulting gurus. Not only have marketing phenomena provided a showground for the literary talents of postmodern commentators: marketing writing has itself attracted the critical attention of postmodernists. As noted above, popular marketing writing's relentless progressivism (the drive to universalise marketing orienta-tion) and essentialism (the 'core' concepts of marketing) make it particularly vulnerable to postmodernist critique.

Some of the telling criticism comes from Brown (1995): 'I don't think mar-keting has all, or even many, of the answers: I don't think the marketing concept can be applied to everything under the sun ... and I suspect that ... marketing theory seems resolutely stuck in a modernist time-warp' (p. 181). The certainties of marketing management texts never seem to change while postmodernism 'reminds us of the reflexive or circular nature of social knowledge, where the very existence of a concept influences and alters the phenomena to which it pertains' (Brown, 1995, p. 178). In mainstream mar-keting writing, the text refers to a 'real' world of marketing practice that lies beyond the text. Postmodernist and poststructuralist writers indicate that marketing as object is constructed through and by the text. Marketing real-ity is, therefore, not merely referred to by marketing texts. It is constituted through texts.

Postmodernism and student research projects

While the postmodern tendency in marketing writing is avowedly critical of the verities of mainstream marketing management, it also points to the novel insights and intellectual vigour that can derive from postmodernist perspectives. Nevertheless, from the student researcher's perspective, a postmodern empirical research project is probably a risky undertaking, at least in most university business schools. Empirical postmodern marketing research might be quite implausible, or at least highly problematic (Brown, 1995, p. 172) so the student researcher interested in postmodernism is largely confined to a conceptual project that engages in a postmodern critique of a branch of theory or practice. Postmodernist themes lend themselves aptly to critique of marketing culture and practices, especially writing and other text-based practices. Some of the most penetrating, critical and witty scholarship in the marketing field has been produced under the postmodern brand.

Students considering wading into the swirling waters of postmodernism for their student project would be well advised to discuss this carefully with their supervisor. They should be advised that mention of postmodernism can provoke heated (and heatedly negative) responses from some business school academics. For many academics, postmodernism is a byword for obscurantism, literary self-indulgence, aimlessness and inaction. Postmodernism loftily critiques everything without having a position itself on anything. Even those student researchers who gain approval for such a project should not congratulate themselves too quickly. They have a difficult task ahead of them. It could also be a rewarding one to the diligent and open-minded student researcher who is prepared to read a large number of difficult books and articles. The researcher could begin by reading some of the texts cited here (especially Brown, 1995). Student researchers can go from there to make their own observations on marketing culture, texts and practices. They can do this from their vantage point as consumers of products and services and aspirants to the status of marketers, and also as consumers of marketing itself.

Mainstream managerial marketing is an example of commodified knowledge that is produced (by management consultants), distributed (by academics, publishers and trainers) and consumed (by all the above plus citizens and students). A critique of one's own experience of consuming marketing education would make a distinctively postmodern research project, although much of the critical marketing work cited in this chapter has now moved beyond using postmodernism as a label. To the extent that postmodernism is, or rather, was, hugely important in inspiring major movements in marketing and consumer research that remain influential, it deserves at least some recognition if only, as mentioned earlier, as a historical note in the development of critical perspectives in the field.

This chapter has discussed critical research as it is understood in social science, mentioned some of the noted critical perspectives. It has outlined some principles of critical research, focusing on the idea that words are presentations of reality that can be influenced by power structures, and leading to ideological elements in communication. The chapter drew attention to some areas of ideology critique in business and management studies, including studies of advertising and branding, and studies of workplace management. The topics of critical research focus on structural and constitutive power and how these can play out in relations of gender, class, disability and race. Critical research, though, is not a method as such, it is a theoretical position that informs the research questions, and the possible answers. In doing critical research the researcher needs to draw on other interpretive methods and among these is discourse analysis, which we will look at in the final chapter.

Glossary

Constitutive Language is said to constitute its objects rather than merely refer to them. Language actively constructs the meaning of terms and concepts. In the context of power, constitutive power refers to power that is reproduced in and through specific discourses. Language and discourse are said to actively constitute relations of power and not simply to reflect them. Constitutive power is intrinsic to social interaction.

Conversation analysis Associated with ethnomethodology, conversation analysis takes a minute and detailed interest in the way that everyday interactions are ordered, produced and controlled. It has been widely used in positivistic research to document interactions. Topics of study have included the role of pauses in conversations and the negotiation of turn-taking and conversational topics in telephone conversations.

Discourse In common usage, a dialogue between speakers. In interpretive social research 'discourse' means 'that which can be described'; it is a broad term that refers to sets of conventions for talking or thinking about a given object or idea.

Emancipation The critical research stance is that discourses can be repressive. In its moderate form 'emancipation' refers to the critical research aim of promoting re-flexive awareness about the ways in which ideologies are formed and reproduced.

Ethnomethodology Refers to an approach to the sociology of everyday life pro-moted by Harold Garfinkel (1967). It focuses on how participants jointly produce a sense of everyday normality in social life and places great importance on the agency and social competence of individuals. Less emphasis is placed on the in-fluence of social structures and institutions over local interactions and practices.

Managerialist Managerialist research reflects and supports the apparent aims, given assumptions and taken-for-granted priorities and values of organisational manag-ers. It is usually positioned as an attempt to address or solve a managerial 'problem'.

Performative This refers to the distinction between language use as a referring device to indicate objects and concepts and as a social positioning device through which we signal motives or claim status. In other words, we *perform* social ac-complishments through language and other social practices.

Structural power The power to coerce and gain compliance through the implicit or actual threat of tangible or intangible sanctions. Structural power is extrinsic to social interaction since it reflects power relations that pre-exist a particular interaction.

Subjectivities Subjectivity refers to unreflexive personal consciousness. This sub-jectivity may appear to be private and unique but can be shown to be socially derived in important respects. We may absorb certain historical, linguistic and cultural practices and ideas so that they intimately form our values and assump-tions. We may take these values and assumptions as taken-for-granted and forget that, in fact, they were learned.

Chapter 10

Critical discourse analysis

Abstract

Critical discourse analysis is one of the most influential analytical approaches of critical and qualitative research. In this chapter, we offer a brief, practical introduction to doing discourse analysis in empirical research. The chapter outlines some of the theoretical principles of discourse analysis, especially the analytical emphasis on structure, function, action-orientation and variation in texts. The chapter concludes with some comments on the commonalities of interpretive approaches to qualitative research.

Chapter objectives

After reading this chapter students will be able to:

- outline the main theoretical influences in critical discourse analysis
- list the key assumptions in discourse analysis
- conduct a discourse analysis of text as part of an empirical study

Discourse, language and interaction

Discourse analysis focuses on the ways in which we construct our sense of social reality through language in interaction. Language is a major feature of discourse, but the term 'discourse' can refer to other interactional and representational practices in addition to language. 'Discourse' is referred to as 'a system of statements that construct an object' (Parker, 1992, p. 5). 'Discourse' is also described as anything that can be described, and hence can be represented as text; it therefore refers to both speech and writing (Stubbs, 1983). It is regarded by some authors as a broader concept still, referring to all genres in which someone 'organizes language to an audience' (Benveniste, 1971, p. 208). In its non-technical sense, discourse refers simply to conversation, but in social science discourse has a wider meaning, referring to many forms of social text. Some academics also refer to 'discourses' when they mean ways of talking or writing about something.

DOI: 10.4324/9781003432203-13

Discourse has become an important concept in marketing and consumer research (Bruce et al., 2011; Fitchett and Caruana, 2015; Skålén, Fougére and Fellesson, 2008; Thompson and Haytko, 1997; Thompson and Hirschman, 1995), particularly in analyses of constitutive power (Thompson, 2004). We draw on discourses or ways of speaking and writing about certain things, to articulate our experience and account for our actions and beliefs. These discourses, or ways of speaking and writing about certain things, become conventional, that is, taken-for-granted after a time. Foucault (1977) drew attention to the ideological character of discourses, meaning that discourses emerge under historical conditions and reflect relations of power that are then reproduced constitutively when the discourse becomes normalised and taken-for-granted.

The use of the term discourse in interpretive and critical social research implies that it is considered a central concept in understanding social, and also psychological, organisation. Discourses are ways of organising, describing and talking about certain events or things. They can be drawn upon by individuals to make sense of the world and to account for actions or events. We might also draw on certain discourses or 'ways of talking about' things to produce a sense of normality. We might adapt discourses to form our own strategies of social positioning and identity formation in local contexts. Studies of discourse focus on language as a major feature of constitutive social interaction.

The scope of discourse analytic research

The possible subjects of discourse analysis are as varied as the theoretical influences. The ways in which marketing managers construct their professional identity and work experiences through discourse have been studied by Ardley and Quinn (2014) and Ellis and Hopkinson (2010). Humphreys (2010) conducted a discourse analytic study of newspaper coverage of gambling and tracked its putative influence on the legitimacy of gambling. Moufahim et al. (2007) and Lim and Moufahim (2011) have studied the discourse of populist politics, while Ybema et al. (2009) used discourse analysis to explore how organisational identities are worked up using discursive strategies, as have Ellis et al. (2012). Ritson and Elliott (1999) combined discourse analysis with ethnography to study the ways in which school age adolescents produced a sense of identity within their group through their discourses about advertisements. As with most of the qualitative methods in this book, discourse analysis lends itself well to multi-method studies in combination with other research traditions, including ethnography, critical theory and phenomenology/existentialism. As a method of textual analysis, discourse analysis is essentially a thematic analysis of texts that is informed and guided by specific theoretical principles.

Discourse theory is operationalised in qualitative research through discourse analysis. Discourse analysis has been a significant development in organisational sociology (Fairclough, 1985, 2010) and management research (Alvesson et al., 2008; Burawoy, 1979; Ellis and Hopkinson, 2010; Morgan, 1992; Rod and Ellis, 2014) as well as in marketing and consumer research (Elliott, 1996; Lim and Moufahim, 2011; Moufahim et al., 2007; Roux and Belk, 2018; van Laer and Izberk-Bilgin, 2019). The techniques of discourse analysis may differ, but the notion of 'discourse' and the associated focus on the role of language and social practice in constructing social reality has become widely employed in critical marketing and management studies (e.g. Morgan, 1992). Critical discourse analysis (CDA) is seen as part of the post-structuralist movement in its focus on language and discourse as a site of contest and negotiation. Unlike postmodernism, poststructuralism can provide powerful techniques for empirical research through deconstruction (Stern, 1993) critical ethnography and CDA (Elliott and Ritson, 1997). Hackley et al. (2011) used discourse analysis in a study of young people's alcohol consumption practices, with reference to the influence of marketing and the public policy implications.

Discourse, then, refers broadly to the ways in which certain relations and phenomena are constituted through the ways in which they are represented in text and talk. Critical analyses of the discourses of marketing have been conducted applying differing intellectual traditions. For example, Skålén et al. (2008) conducted a critical discourse analytic study adapting Foucauldian influences, and Mautner (2016) has conducted extensive discourse analytic studies of marketing and consumption phenomena from a linguistics disciplinary perspective. Cook (2001) also used linguistics as a point of departure for a study of the discourse of advertisements. Hackley (2000) studied the discourse of advertising work in ad agencies using a version of discourse analysis adapted from qualitative social psychology (Potter and Wetherell, 1987; critical perspective in Burman and Parker, 1993; see van Dijk, 1984, 1985). Potter and Wetherell's (1987) social psychological version of discourse analysis is informed to varying degrees by other research traditions including *ethnomethodology*, semiotics and *conversation analysis*. Svensson (2007) and Alvesson (1998) also studied the discourses of advertising work, but from a more critically informed perspective.

Critical discourse analysis (CDA)

Foucauldian influences have been important in framing the use of the concept of discourse in management and organisation studies. Fairclough's (2010, 2014) CDA is probably the most influential version of discourse in organisational research, drawing on Foucauldian influences. For Foucault (1977), discourses embrace all the presuppositions, historically derived rules and institutions and social practices that make certain forms of representation possible (Mills, 1997). In this poststructuralist sense, discourses are the preconditions for everyday knowledge. The task of the critical researcher is to critically interrogate and unravel social phenomena so that the preconditions for their production become apparent. In other words, the task is to see how particular ways of seeing the world become accepted and 'normal'.

Outside management research, a focus on discourse has been used in ideology critique to explore, for example, how a particular scholarly discipline ('oriental studies') consolidated certain ways of understanding and thinking about colonialism (Said, 1978). Foucault (1977) famously explored the ways in which certain social groups acquired and sustained their own power over others by defining the terms of normality. 'Discursive closure' (Deetz, 1992) occurs where a given and accepted way of expressing things excludes or closes off alternatives. In this way particular discourses can be powerful in perpetuating particular ways of seeing the world. The idea of discourse, then, in ideology critique, becomes closely linked to ideology (Gramsci, 1971) in that discourses act as vehicles for the reproduction of, and perpetuation of, ideological norms.

Discourse is an important feature of the organisation of individual psychology because of the link between structural power in society and its constitutive manifestations in individual subjectivity. In other words, the ideological force of specific discourses leads us to internalise them unreflexively. Through our language and interactional practices, we may feel that we are asserting our individual sense of agency and realising our own 'personality' when in fact we are drawing on historically derived discourses that reproduce the power of other groups and sustain our own relative powerlessness (Edwards and Potter, 1992). Discourse analysis seeks to recover this sense of the history of certain forms of discourse as well as revealing the detailed process of how social life is produced in local contexts.

Doing discourse analysis: structure, function and variation in social texts

A social text such as a transcript of a depth interview or a set of written documents can be analysed for these three characteristics: structure, function and variation (see Figure 10.1). With regard to *structure*, the text is likely to display features that seem to recur. A person talking may use given strategies of accounting for events and actions, particular metaphors, tropes of speech, grammatical techniques or tone of voice that become evident on listening to the audio recording or reading and re-reading the text transcription. The same may be true of any kind of text: there are likely to be structural regularities of some kind, whether these are stylistic, thematic or grammatical. Very often, such structural characteristics are not evident on first listening or reading but become so after the text has been reflected upon and re-read over a period of time.

Once a text has been analysed for structural regularities, the researcher needs to reflect upon what rhetorical purpose they may serve, that is, what

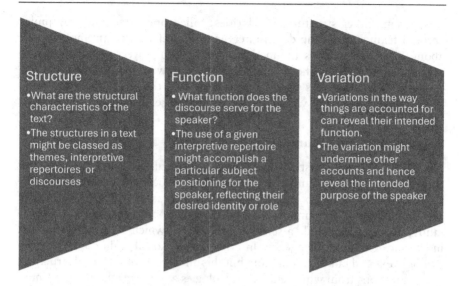

Structure
- What are the structural characteristics of the text?
- The structures in a text might be classed as themes, interpretive repertoires or discourses

Function
- What function does the discourse serve for the speaker?
- The use of a given interpretive repertoire might accomplish a particular subject positioning for the speaker, reflecting their desired identity or role

Variation
- Variations in the way things are accounted for can reveal their intended function.
- The variation might undermine other accounts and hence reveal the intended purpose of the speaker

Figure 10.1 Structure, function and variation in the discourse analysis of text

is their *function*. This is also sometimes called 'action-orientation' and refers to the performativity of words and text, the fact that representation is characterised by strategic motive as well as content. The idea of function in discourse reflects a tradition of linguistic philosophy that took as axiomatic that words do not merely refer to concepts or things, they *do* things as well (Austin, 1962). Language has a *performative* role in this sense. Speakers seek to accomplish certain social effects by their speech. If I am lecturing a class, I want to engage their interest by referring to theories and practices in my field. However, I also need to accomplish a professional role, that of lecturer. To this end, I try to sound plausible and authoritative as an academic researcher and lecturer. Performative speech-acts can also take tactical forms, such as when you ask someone a question not as a genuine query but as a social gambit at a party. In that context, you are not really interested in the answer, you simply want to strike up conversation and appear warm.

In discourse analysis, as in rhetorical analysis, what is said is important not only in itself, but in what it leaves unsaid (Antaki, 1994). That is, one kind of expression tends to omit or gloss over other, alternative expressions. In other words, in choosing to express something in one way, we also make a choice not to express it in others. For example, in a piece of the author's research (Hackley, 2000), one advertising agency's account team professional tended to account for actions and decisions in terms of a corporate way of doing things. It was 'the way we do things here'. They wanted to express that there was a company style and they conformed to it, although no one could express explicitly what it was. This way of accounting for actions and decisions was, among other structural regularities, called upon frequently by junior account team staff during depth interviews and referred to an implicit code about the agency's values and methods that new employees were expected to assimilate intuitively without being explicitly told what it is. By doing so successfully, new employees would demonstrate that they were the 'right' kind of people who would fit well with the culture of the agency.

Key themes and assumptions in discourse analysis

Box 10.1 lists characteristics of CDA. It lists these under four categories, but these categories overlap and leak into each other. The themes that characterise CDA include a focus on language and discourse as constitutive features of social interaction. This implies a social constructionist ontology but, importantly, it does not exclude a sense of the ways in which social structure and institutions circumscribe agency. In other words, social reality is worked up through text and talk in interaction, but this all occurs within social structures and institutions from which emanate ideologies and norms that may be internalised by speakers, and which may inform the speaker's sense of subjectivity.

Social constructionism is sometimes criticised by social theorists because they feel that it over-emphasises agency and underplays the influence of social structure and materiality on subjectivities. In CDA, the analysis of social texts embraces the context when it asks about the motives and interests behind variation in accounts and links these to aspects of materiality and/ or ideology. CDA also entails asking whose interests are served by certain discourses, in other words, what is the strategic intent behind social texts, how does it manifest, and in whose interests?

Interaction is another key concept in CDA. The assumption is that human psychology is inherently relational. We do not come into the world as blank sheets of paper, and we do not originate our thoughts and ideas – we get them from others, from social interaction. We may organise and experience them in ways that are unique to us, but we are not islands, our very subjectivities connect to other humans. The social world is produced in the spaces in between us. So, all discourse is seen in the light of interaction – all discourse is a rhetorical counterpoint to alternative possible ways of arranging those thoughts, words and/or ideas. Rhetorically, all communication is intended for an imaginary or actual receiver.

CDA focuses on text as the point of analysis, but it is important for the researcher to gain a sense of the ethnographic context that frames the text. Simply reading transcripts of interviews and focus groups will not allow the researcher to repair indexicality, that is, to understand deeply the meaning of every word, story, reference, pause, intonation and gesture. CDA is not just about the text, it entails interpreting the text in the light of what goes on in the whole context of the text. To this end, researchers who are fortunate enough to gain access to organisational settings in which to conduct research

Box 10.1 Features of critical discourse analysis

Themes

Focus on language and discourse as constitutive features of social interaction
Focus on ideology and the reproduction of relations of power through everyday talk and social practice
Performativity of language and social practice: words do things, they are more than their conceptual content, they can be used strategically to fulfil intended purposes
Effects are produced in interaction

Assumptions

Social constructionist ontology – social life is constituted through language, text and interaction
The possibility of agency is heavily circumscribed by social structures and institutions
Discourses (also called interpretive repertoires) as broad categories of speech, writing and representation carry ideological influences and preserve particular forms of understanding
We perform acts of social positioning and identity formation through our language and other interactional practices

Methods of data gathering

Qualitative methods that can generate descriptive text: depth interviews, ethnography, digital capture of talk and interaction, focus/discussion groups, analysis of published texts, e.g. media stories, advertisements, visual data, e.g. video, other forms of social text

Approach to data analysis

Seeking structure, function and variation in social texts: evidence of structure regarding recurring themes, tropes of speech, metaphors: evidence of variation in accounts: analysis of the rhetorical function of these positions and accounts in terms of the maintenance of particular meanings that have implications for social positioning and identity formation
Emphasis on revealing 'interpretive repertoires' or discourses that account for and justify particular ideas, actions or procedures, or subject positions
Ethnographic context is considered in order to repair indexicality
Consideration of materiality and the role of material objects as features of discourse, e.g. PowerPoint slides or books, clothing codes

interviews, should always take account of any informal data sources and make field notes of their impressions and thoughts. In another example from research in which the author was involved, a major study into young people and alcohol in the United Kingdom (Hackley et al., 2015), the study used discourse analysis as its primary method but also made use of ethnographic data. In addition, the research assistants who conducted the interviews and focus groups also carried out the transcription and took part in the data analysis meetings. In this way, the project authors sought to repair the indexicality of the transcripts through a fuller understanding of the context.

The 'interpretive repertoire'

In discourse analysis, researchers will sort and code the content of a text into themes, called 'discourses' or, following Potter and Wetherell's (1987) approach *interpretive repertoires*. This expression is used by Potter and Wetherell (1987) to mean a particular device or technique of accounting for and justifying actions or ideas. The way these authors use the term 'interpretive repertoire' usually refers to one specific linguistic device, or one arrangement of tropes and other expressive vehicles that seem to recur in the data set, while the term 'discourse' is more often used in poststructuralist research to refer to a collection of such devices that, together, reflect and reproduce a particular view of the world and justify certain positions or actions.

The interpretive repertoires (or discourses, if the researcher prefers) are the units or themes that structure the findings in the research report. The researcher will sort the various texts into interpretive repertoires that are essentially the key findings of the research. Each will be described in the research report, with examples from the transcribed data sets. The discussion section will elaborate on these interpretive repertoires with regard to the function they serve, mentioning any variation in usage that could underpin the intended function.

Variation in accounts

Function in social texts can often be revealed through the *variation* in accounts that people offer. Structural irregularities in social texts might be found as the text accounts for certain events or actions, perhaps for different purposes or to different audiences, or where the data set was generated in different contexts. The researcher can then use variations in accounts to speculate on the function such accounts might serve, perhaps in terms of subject positioning and the maintenance of a professional identity or social role. The performative dimension of language is key in this respect. The things that interviewees say can be seen as devices designed to accomplish certain social tasks, such as the social task of appearing a competent professional in an organisation. This does not imply that interviewees were not competent professionals. It simply acknowledges the self-evident truth that, in our various social roles, we must accomplish certain effects to be perceived as plausible and credible, and socially competent. For example, a TV newsreader might be a first rate journalist, but if they speak hesitantly with many pauses and stutters, they will not be perceived as credible. The successful maintenance of their professional identity as a TV newsreader, therefore, does not depend only on what they say, even if their grasp of issues and insightful analysis are impeccable. It also depends on the *how* they speak. Hence, the words they speak in a news broadcast have conceptual content, but they also *do* something – they accomplish a subject positioning for the speaker as a competent broadcasting professional.

The analysis of discourse, then, takes as its starting point the assumption that humans construct social life through language and social practice within a cultural setting replete with prevailing ideologies that derive from social structures and institutions. We are seen as autonomous individuals possessed of human agency, but we act within social structures, which sharply constrain our freedom and power to act in our own interests, and even sometimes constrain our ability to see where our own interests lie. The analysis of language and other practices of social interaction is central to critical research because language is said to be constitutive of social life, that is, language does not only refer to social reality: it actively constructs it, and it might obscure our own interests Critical research, then, strips back the taken-for-granted assumptions behind everyday discourse to try to see the cogs turning in the production of social interaction.

Variation in accounting practices does not necessarily imply that the speaker is disingenuous or lacking reflexive insight (although of course both are possibilities). The repertoires and discourses we draw upon to articulate our experiences and to account for our actions and beliefs are targeted both at others and at ourselves, in the sense that we seek to maintain a particular world view that seems coherent and consistent. However, we tend to be far less consistent than we like to think. In our talk and interaction, we are constantly in a notional dialogue with an imaginary interlocutor. In this sense, the psychological organisation of our subjectivity is rhetorical, and dialogic (Billig, 1987, 1988; see also Antaki, 1994; Antaki and Condor, 2014). In our talk and social practices, we construct subject positions that are designed to counter possible alternative versions, as we try to represent ourselves in a way that seems coherent and consistent with the identity and values we wish to project. In so doing, we try to accommodate or anticipate and counter the preconceptions of others, and our own wishes about our status and aims, in the positions we take and the things we say. This accommodation depends on our understanding of the social context of the interaction. We constantly interpret words as signs to understand what is meant (to construct meaning) in specific social contexts. The analysis of social texts can reveal this process of construction through structure, function and variation in accounts.

Discourse analysis and critical qualitative research

Discourse analysis was left to the end of the book because it exemplifies two key issues for qualitative data analysis. First, it emphasises the *performativity* of words and social practices when it seeks to understand function or action-orientation in social texts. Qualitative data sets should not be analysed merely for their content – to do so implies that qualitative data sets can be used in the same way as quantitative data sets are used for positivistic, realist research. For theoretically informed qualitative research that reaches a threshold of critical analysis, there must also be a critical appraisal of why that content is as it is. In other words, what is the strategic purpose of a piece of communication?

For example, does a media story carry an implicit political agenda? Does an interview passage defend the speaker against a possible attack on their sense of identity or their values? Does an advertisement promote implicit (or explicit) values or ideologies? This perspective on the strategic intent behind communication opens up channels of critical analysis that remain obscured if the focus falls merely on the content as it appears. For example, ways of expressing and articulating certain objects or ideas become habitual and un-reflexive, but might embody and reproduce relations of power and domination. In such instances, referring to the strategic intent of the communication does not necessarily imply any intended deceit, or even self-deceit, from the speaker or the source of the communication, but, rather, it alludes to the ideologies that are carried within discourses.

Another way of stating this is to look for sub-text. What is the story behind the story? How did the story get there, why is it placed where it is placed, and why is it expressed in the way it is expressed and not in other ways? What other, alternative version is it designed to counter?

Another, more commonplace, feature of qualitative research exemplified by discourse analysis is the fact that qualitative data sets are coded and sorted for themes, that is, the structure and content of the data set is examined to find recurring patterns. These patterns are resolved through coding and sorting into the themes that will structure the research report. This is a similar process in empirical studies that employ thematic analysis, grounded theory, ethnography or practice theory. In discourse analysis, the process is guided by the specific, theoretically grounded, concepts of structure, function and variation. Structure and function we have noted above, variation alludes to the social constructed character of memories and emotions. When we offer accounts of experiences or events, we are relying on our memory to reconstruct those events or experiences, and we construct them in a way that seems to present them, and us, in a way we deem acceptable. We may be far less consistent in our world views than we like to think, and critical discourse researchers are sensitive to variations in accounting practices, that is, subtle differences in the ways in which we might represent the same thing in differing contexts, to different audiences, or for different purposes. These variations in accounting practices reveal the motives and strategies, and sometimes the ideological influences, behind discourses. CDA, then, is a powerful theoretically informed approach to the interpretation of qualitative data sets.

We will now end the book with some comments about the commonality of qualitative research approaches.

Concluding comments

The commonalities of theoretically informed qualitative research

The book has tried to encompass some of the most influential and commonly used intellectual traditions for theoretically informed qualitative research in management and related areas, but there are others that may be equally useful. To take just a few examples, there are studies in cultural studies (e.g. Du Gay et al., 1997), ethnomethodology and conversation analysis (Garfinkel, 1967; Heritage, 1984), sociology (e.g. Ritzer, 2000), institutional theory (Scaraboto and Fischer, 2013) and communication, journalism and media studies (Bakir and McStay, 2018; McStay, 2010) that cover important topics that also fall within the scope of management, marketing and consumer research. The book has also cited many examples of work located in one discipline but reaches out across others, such as Schroeder's (2002) analysis of visual consumption in marketing by drawing on the discipline of art history, and the extensive use of ethnographic methods in studying cultures and sub-cultures of consumption (Belk et al., 1989; Schouten and McAlexander, 1995; Sherry et al., 2013). We have also made use of theoretical and methodological influences from a range of disciplines, including qualitative psychology, cultural anthropology, 'street' sociology and literary criticism.

One of the aims of the book is to promote not only plurality of research methods in business and management education, but also to promote interdisciplinarity. There is a tendency for subject areas taught in universities to become rather inward-looking. One of the great benefits of an appreciation of qualitative research methods is that it can help to highlight the commonalities and linkages between different methods and fields of social research. Qualitative methods, broadly, share many features – all are, after all, trying to make sense of 'messy' data sets, therefore all are, more or less, inductive (or abductive) methods that seek patterns, regularities, irregularities and structures in data sets. There is a vocabulary for qualitative research theory that may at times seem daunting and esoteric (although they should hold little fear if you can handle words like 'daunting' and 'esoteric') but, at the same time, qualitative research is an approach that can help us to access the most everyday and ordinary aspects of social life to reveal how, in fact, social life is a complex and multi-faceted construction. This complexity can be appreciated when qualitative social researchers stand back from the taken-for-granted understanding of everyday interactions to make the familiar, strange (Agar, 1996; De Yong et al., 2013), that is, to view the emic understanding of social phenomena from the etic standpoint.

There are many philosophical similarities between interpretive traditions. Semiotics, for example, can be seen as a 'phenomenological doctrine of consciousness' (Zeman, 1977, quoted in Mick, 1986, p. 199). In the sense that semiosis reflects apprehended reality, this may well be a notable area of commonality with phenomenological research. However, for C.S. Peirce, semiosis reflects the reality not of experience but of the world of signs. Furthermore, the interpretation placed on any given sign depends on a socially agreed code for many semioticians. Phenomenology, in contrast, seldom emphasises social agreement but, rather, focuses on private, apprehended experience. Ethnography has much in common with some strands of CDA, especially in the form of critical ethnography (Forester, 1992). However, traditionally, ethnography would seek to recreate the conditions of localised social life without necessarily offering a political critique of those conditions.

For all the many commonalities between qualitative social research methods, it is by no means a unified field and the differences in nuance between methods and intellectual traditions are important. As Chapter 5 emphasises, the theoretical framing of qualitative research projects is key to the overall coherence and quality of the project. The philosophical choices of research perspective are of crucial importance since they frame the questions that can be asked and presuppose the kinds of answers that can be offered.

The book has sought to encourage student researchers to reflect on their own and other's presuppositions about social research in marketing, management and consumer studies in order to make the conduct of research projects a creative and intellectually rewarding experience. The book is written from a conviction that the student research project can and should be such an experience and that it can also constitute a highly positive aspect of the student's academic and personal intellectual development.

As Rorty (1982) has remarked, choices between theories cannot be made solely on the basis of what theory is most efficient or correct. The choice should reflect questions such as 'What would it be like to believe that? What would happen if we did? What would I be committing myself to?' (p. 163). This book hopes to encourage students to investigate their own assumptions and to see where they lead in terms of research perspectives, methods and findings. In this regard, the book is conceived as a point of reference for the creative intellectual endeavours of student researchers, and it is hoped, a point of departure for many more such studies.

This chapter, then, has outlined the key principles of CDA, especially focusing on structure, function and variation in social texts. The chapter has discussed the critical potential of CDA at revealing deep assumptions about power and subjectivity. The chapter has located CDA at a nexus of various critical theoretical influences and, it has noted that CDA can be used alongside various forms of textual qualitative data. The chapter concluded with some comments about the common elements of interpretive, qualitative research methods.

Glossary

Function   In discourse analysis function refers to the intended purpose of speech-acts with regard to the social positioning they are intended to achieve.

Interpretive repertoire   A linguistic device, which accounts for and/or justifies a particular view of the world or specific acts.

Performativity   In this book, deriving from Austin's (1962) work on the ways in which words *do* things for the speaker as well as *say* things, in the sense that utterances may indicate desired or intended identity positioning, distancing from other subject positions, or other strategic intent. Performativity has been subsequently developed in complex renderings in poststructuralism, gender studies and anthropology.

Structure   In the discourse analysis of social texts researchers seek structural regularities characterised by tropes of speech, metaphors or ways of accounting for actions, ideas or decisions.

Variability   In social texts the accounts given to justify actions or ideas may vary in different circumstances. This variation may be revealing of the rhetorical function that it served in that version of events.

References

Agar, M. (1996) *The professional stranger*. London: Academic Press.

Akaka, M.A., Schau, H.J. and Vargo, S.L. (2022) 'Practice diffusion', *Journal of Consumer Research*, 48(6), pp. 939–969. https://doi.org/10.1093/jcr/ucab045

Akala (2019) *Natives: race and class in the ruins of empire*. London: Two Roads.

Alexander, J.C. and Smith, P. (2001) 'The strong program in cultural sociology: elements of a structural hermeneutics', in J. Turner (ed.) *The handbook of sociological theory*. New York, NY: Kluwer, pp. 135–150.

Alfakhri, D., Harness, D., Nicholson, J. and Harness, T. (2018). The role of aesthetics and design in hotelscape: a phenomenological investigation of cosmopolitan consumers. *Journal of Business Research*, 85, 523–531. https://doi.org/10.1016/j.jbusres.2017.10.031

Alsop, C.K. (2002) 'Home and away: self-reflexive auto-/ethnography', *Forum Qualitative Sozialforschung/Forum: Qualitative Social Research*, 3(3), Art. 10. http://nbn-resolving.de/urn:nbn:de:0114-fqs0203105

Althusser, L. (1971) *Lenin and philosophy and other essays*. London: New Left Books.

Alvesson, M. (1998) 'Gender relations and identity at work: a case study of masculinities and femininities in an advertising agency', *Human Relations*, 51(8), pp. 969–1005.

Alvesson, M. and Deetz, S. (2000) *Doing critical management research*. London: Sage.

Alvesson, M., Hardy, C. and Harley, B. (2008) 'Reflecting on reflexivity: reflexive textual practices in organization and management theory', *Journal of Management Studies*, 45(3), pp. 480–501.

Alvesson, M. and Kärreman, D. (2000) 'Taking the linguistic turn in organizational research', *Journal of Applied Behavioral Science*, 36(2), pp. 136–158.

Alvesson, M. and Skoldberg, K. (2000) *Reflexive methodology*. London: Sage.

Alvesson, M. and Willmott, H. (eds.) (1992) *Critical management studies*. London: Sage.

Antaki, C. (1994) *Explaining and arguing: the social organisation of accounts*. London: Sage.

Antaki, C. and Condor, S. (2014) *Rhetoric, ideology and social psychology: essays in honour of Michael Billig* (Explorations in Social Psychology). London: Routledge.

Appau, S. and Crockett, C. (2023) 'Wealth in people and places: understanding transnational gift obligations', *Journal of Consumer Research*, 49(6), pp. 1053–1073. https://doi.org/10.1093/jcr/ucac028

Ardley, B. (2009) *A phenomenological perspective on the work of the marketing manager: an analysis of the process of strategic planning in organisations*. Riga, Latvia: LAP Lambert Academic Publishing.

Ardley, B. (2011) 'Marketing theory and critical phenomenology: exploring the human side of management practice', *Marketing Intelligence & Planning*, 29, pp. 628–642. https://doi.org/10.1108/02634501111178668

Ardley, B. and Quinn, L. (2014) 'Practitioner accounts and knowledge production: an analysis of three marketing discourses', *Marketing Theory*, 14(1), pp. 97–114.

Armstrong, G. and Harris, R. (1991) 'Football hooligans: theory and evidence', *The Sociological Review*, 39(3), pp. 427–458. https://doi.org/10.1111/j.1467-954X.1991.tb00861.x

Arndt, J. (1985) 'On making marketing science more scientific: role of orientations, paradigms, metaphors, and puzzle solving', *Journal of Marketing*, 49(3), pp. 11–23.

Arnould, E.J. (1998) 'Daring consumer-oriented ethnography', in Stern, B.B. (ed.) *Representing consumers: voices, views and visions*. London: Routledge, pp. 85–126.

Arnould, E.J. and Thompson, C.J. (2005) 'Consumer culture theory (CCT) 20 years of research', *Journal of Consumer Research*, 31(4), pp. 868–882. https://doi.org/10.1086/426626

Arnould, E.J. and Thompson, C.J. (2018) *Consumer culture theory*. London: Sage.

Arnould, E.J. and Wallendorf, M. (1994) 'Market-orientated ethnography: interpretation building and marketing strategy formulation', *Journal of Marketing Research*, XXXI, pp. 484–504.

Arsel, Z. and Thompson, C.J. (2011) 'Demythologizing consumption practices: how consumers protect their field-dependent identity investments from devaluing marketplace myths', *Journal of Consumer Research*, 37(5), pp. 791–806. https://doi.org/10.1086/656389

Arvidsson, A. and Caliandro, A. (2016) 'Brand public', *Journal of Consumer Research*, 42(5), pp. 727–748. https://doi.org/10.1093/jcr/ucv053

Askegaard, S. and Linnet, J.T. (2011) 'Towards and epistemology of consumer culture theory: phenomenology and the context of context', *Marketing Theory*, 11(4), pp. 381–404.

Atanasova, A., Eckhardt, G.M. and Husemann, K.C. (2024) 'Liquid consumer security', *Journal of Consumer Research*, 50(6), pp. 1243–1264. https://doi.org/10.1093/jcr/ucad047

Austin, J. (1962) *How to do things with words*. London: Oxford University Press.

Ayer, A.J. (1936) *Language, truth and logic*. London: Penguin Books.

Bajde, D. (2013) 'Consumer culture theory (re)visits actor–network theory: flattening consumption studies', *Marketing Theory*, 13(2), pp. 227–242. https://doi.org/10.1177/1470593113477887

Baker, M. and Saren, M. (eds.) (2010) *Marketing theory: a student text*. 3rd edn. London: Sage.

Bakir, V. and McStay, A. (2018) 'Fake news and the economy of emotions: problems, causes, solutions', *Digital Journalism*, 6(2), pp. 154–175. https://doi.org/10.1080/21670811.2017.1345645

Banister, P., Burman, E., Parker, I., Taylor, M. and Tindall, C. (1994) *Qualitative methods in psychology: a research guide*. London: Sage.

Bardhi, F. and Eckhardt, G. (2017) 'Liquid Consumption', *Journal of Consumer Research*, 44(3), pp. 582–597. https://doi.org/10.1093/jcr/ucx050

Barthes, R. (1968) *Elements of semiology*, trans. A. Lavers, New York, NY: Hill and Wang.

Barthes, R. (1977) *Image – Music – Text*. London: Fontana.

Barthes, R. (2000) *Mythologies*. London: Vintage.

Bassiouni, D. and Hackley, C. (2016) 'Video games and young children's evolving sense of identity: a qualitative study', *Young Consumers*, 17(2), pp. 127–142. www.emeraldinsight.com/doi/abs/10.1108/YC-08-2015-00551

Bastrygina, T., Lim, W.M., Jopp, R. and Weissmann, M.A. (2024) 'Unraveling the power of social media influencers: qualitative insights into the role of Instagram influencers in the hospitality and tourism industry', *Journal of Hospitality and Tourism Management*, 58, pp. 214–243. https://www.sciencedirect.com/science/article/pii/S144767702400007X

Batat, W. (2023) "Experiential research as a methodological framework for studying consumer behaviors in phygital settings', *Qualitative Market Research*, 26(3), pp. 269–277. https://doi.org/10.1108/QMR-12-2022-0178

Beckman, S. and Elliott, R. (eds.) (2001) *Interpretive consumer research: paradigms, methodologies and applications.* Copenhagen: Copenhagen Business School Press, Handelshøjskolens Forlag.

Belk, R.W. (1988) 'Possessions and the extended self', *Journal of Consumer Research*, 15(2), pp. 139–168.

Belk, R. W. (ed.) (1991) *Highways and byways: naturalistic research from the consumer behaviour odyssey.* Provo, UT: Association for Consumer Research.

Belk, R.W. (1996) 'On aura, illusion, escape, and hope in apocalyptic consumption: the apotheosis of las vegas', in Brown, S., Carson, D., and Bell, J. (eds.) *Marketing apocalypse: eschatology, escapology and the illusion of the end.* London: Routledge, pp. 87–107.

Belk, R. W. (ed.) (2006) *Handbook of qualitative research methods in marketing.* New York, NY: Edward Elgar.

Belk, R.W. (2017) 'Qualitative research in advertising', *Journal of Advertising*, 46(1), pp. 36–47.

Belk, R.W., Caldwell, M., Devinney, T.M., Eckhardt, G.M., Henry, P., Kozinets, P. and Plakoyiannaki, E. (2017) 'Envisioning consumers: how videography can contribute to marketing knowledge', *Journal of Marketing Management*, 34(5–6), pp. 432–458. https://doi.org/10.1080/0267257X.2017.1377754

Belk, R. W., Fischer, E. and Kozinets, R. V. (eds.) (2012) *Qualitative consumer and marketing research.* London: Sage.

Belk, R.W., Sherry, J.F. and Wallendorf, M. (1988) 'A naturalistic inquiry into buyer and seller behaviour at a swap meet', *Journal of Consumer Research*, 14, pp. 449–470.

Belk, R.W., Wallendorf, M. and Sherry, J. (1989) 'The sacred and profane in consumer behaviour: theodicy on the odyssey', *Journal of Consumer Research*, 16, pp. 1–38.

Benhabib, S. (1992) *Situating the self: gender, community, and postmodernism in contemporary ethics.* New York, NY: Routledge.

Benveniste, E. (1971) *Problems in general linguistics.* Miami, FL: University of Florida Press.

Berger, P.L. and Luckman, T. (1966) *The social construction of reality.* London: Penguin.

Bergkvist, L., De Keyzer, F. and Buzeta, C. (2023) 'Perspectives: Replication is more than meets the eye', *International Journal of Advertising*, 43(3), pp. 580–599. https://doi.org/10.1080/02650487.2023.2245278

Bernays, E. (1928: 2004 reprint). *Propaganda.* New York: IG Publishing.

Bertrand, D. (1988) 'The creation of complicity: a semiotic analysis of an advertising campaign for Black and White Whiskey', *International Journal of Research in Marketing*, 4(4), pp. 273–289.

Bettany, S., Dobscha, S., O' Malley, L. and Prothero, A. (2010) 'Moving beyond binary opposition: exploring the tapestry of gender in consumer research and marketing', *Marketing Theory*, 10(1), pp. 3–28.

Beudaert, A., Mason, M. and Nau, J.P. (2023) 'The social model and consumers with disabilities research: Contributions, criticisms, and call for new perspectives',

Journal of Marketing Management, 40(5–6), pp. 481–511. https://doi.org/10.1080/0267257X.2023.2289379

Beverland, M.B., Fernandez, K.V. and Eckhardt, G.M. (2024) Consumer work and agency in the analog revival, *Journal of Consumer Research*, (in press), ucae003. https://doi.org/10.1093/jcr/ucae003

Billig, M. (1987) *Arguing and thinking: a rhetorical approach to social psychology*. Cambridge: Cambridge University Press.

Billig, M. (1988) 'Rhetorical and historical aspects of attitudes: the case of the British monarchy', *Philosophical Psychology*, 1, pp. 84–104.

Billig, M. (1989) 'Psychology, rhetoric and cognition', *History of the Human Sciences*, 2, pp. 289–307.

Billig, M. (1991) *Ideology and opinions*. London: Sage.

Bordieu, P. (1977) *Outline of a theory of practice*. Cambridge Studies of Social and Cultural Anthropology. Cambridge: Cambridge University Press.

Borgerson, J.L. and Schroeder, J.E. (2018) 'Making skin visible: how consumer culture imagery commodifies identity', *Body and Society*, 24(1–2), pp. 103–136.

Boylorn, R.M. and Orbe, R.P. (2021) *Critical autoethnography: intersecting cultural identities in everyday life*. London: Routledge.

Bradshaw, A. (2023) 'No surrender! Bono's 'Wemoirs', hiberno-philanthro-capitalism, and the Business School Conceit', *Journal of Customer Behaviour*, 22(3), pp. 10–16.

Bradshaw, A. and Haynes, P. (2023) 'The assemblage of British politics' breaking point', *Journal of Consumer Culture*, 23(4), pp. 971–989. https://doi.org/10.1177/14695405231160597

Bradshaw, A. and Scott, L. (2018) *Advertising revolution: the story of a song, from Beatles Hit to Nike Slogan*. UK: Repeater Books.

Braun, V. and Clarke, V. (2006) 'Using thematic analysis in psychology', *Qualitative Research in Psychology*, 3, pp. 77–101.

Brown, S. (1994) 'Marketing as multiplex: screening postmodernism', *European Journal of Marketing*, 28(8/9), pp. 27–51.

Brown, S. (1995) *Postmodern marketing*. London: International Thompson Business Press.

Brown, S. (1996) 'Art or science? Fifty years of marketing debate', *Journal of Marketing Management*, 12(4), pp. 243–267. https://doi.org/10.1080/0267257X.1996.9964413

Brown, S. (1998) 'What's love got to do with it: sex, shopping, and subjective personal introspection', in Brown, S., Doherty, A.M., and Clarke, B. (eds.) *Romancing the market*. New York, NY: Routledge, pp. 137–171.

Brown, S. (1999) 'Marketing and literature: the anxiety of academic influence', *Journal of Marketing*, 63, pp. 1–15. https://doi.org/10.2307/1251997

Brown, S. (2001) *Marketing – The retro revolution*. London: Sage.

Brown, S. (2005) *Writing marketing*. London: Sage.

Brown, S. (2006) *The marketing code*. London: Cyan Books and Marshall Cavendish.

Brown, S. (2012a) 'Wake up and smell the coffin: an introspective obituary', *Journal of Business Research*, 65(4), pp. 461–466.

Brown, S. (2012b) 'I have seen the future and it sucks: reactionary reflections on reading, writing and research', *European Business Review*, 24(1), pp. 5–19.

Brown, S. (2016a) 'Bow to stern: can literary theory plumb an unfathomable brand', *Marketing Theory*, 15(4), pp. 445–464. https://doi.org/10.1177/1470593115572670

Brown, S. (2016b) *Brands and branding*. London: Sage.

Brown, S. (2024) 'Is less, more?, *Journal of Customer Behaviour*, 23(1), pp. 1–6. https://doi.org/10.1362/147539224X17149185609967

Brown, S., Doherty, A. M. and Clarke, B. (eds.) (1998) *Romancing the market*. London: Routledge.

Brown, S., Hackley, C., Hunt, S.D., Marsh, C., O' Shaughnessy, J., Phillips, B.J., Tonks, D., Miles, C. and Nilsson, T. (2018) 'Marketing (as) rhetoric: paradigms, provocations, and perspectives', *Journal of Marketing Management*, pp. 1336–1378. https://doi.org/10.1080/0267257X.2018.1548799

Brownlie, D. (1997) 'Beyond ethnography', *European Journal of Marketing*, 31(3/4), pp. 264–284. https://doi.org/10.1108/03090569710162362

Brownlie, D. (2001) 'Interpretation as composition: debating modes of representation in marketing research', in Elliott, R.H. and Beckmann, S. (eds.) *Interpretive consumer research: paradigms, methodologies and applications*. Copenhagen: Copenhagen Business School Press, pp. 47–86.

Brownlie, D., Hewer, P. and Tadajewski, M. (eds.) (2013) *Expanding disciplinary space: on the potential of critical marketing*. London: Routledge.

Brownlie, D. and Saren, M. (1992) 'The four Ps of the marketing concept: prescriptive, polemical, permanent and problematical', *The European Journal of Marketing*, 26(4), pp. 34–47.

Brownlie, D., Saren, M., Wensley, R. and Whittington, R. (eds.) (1999) *Rethinking marketing: towards critical marketing accountings*. London: Sage.

Brown, S., Maclaran, P. and Stevens, L. (1996) 'Marcadia postponed: marketing, utopia and the millennium', *Journal of Marketing Management*, 12, pp. 671–683.

Brown, S. and Patterson, A. (eds.) (2000) *Imagining marketing: art, aesthetics and the Avante-Garde*. London: Routledge.

Brown, S. and Ponsonby-McCabe, S. (2022) 'Re-staging JCB: the show must go on', *Journal of Customer Behaviour*, 21(1–2), pp. 1–6.

Brown, S. and Reid, R. (1997) 'Shoppers on the verge of a nervous breakdown: chronicle, composition and confabulation in consumer research', Chapter 4 in Brown, S. and Turley, D. (eds.) *Consumer research: postcards from the edge*. London: Routledge, pp. 79–149.

Brown, S., Stevens, L. and Maclaran, P. (1999) 'I can't believe it's not Bakhtin! Literary theory, postmodern advertising, and the gender agenda', *Journal of Advertising*, 28(1), pp. 11–24. https://doi.org/10.1080/00913367.1999.10673573

Brown, S., Stevens, L. and Maclaran, P. (2017) 'Epic aspects of retail encounters: the Iliad of Hollister', *Journal of Retailing*, 94(1), pp. 58–72. https://doi.org/10.1016/j.jretai.2017.09.006

Bruce, B.C., Bruce, B.C., Higgins, C. and Mahoney, J.T. (2011) 'The discourse of management and the management of discourse', *International Journal of Strategic Change Management*, 3(1/2), pp. 141–154.

Bryman, A. (2012) *Social research methods*. Oxford: Oxford University Press.

Buchanan, I. (2021) *Assemblage theory and method*. London: Bloomsbury.

Burawoy, M. (1979) *Manufacturing consent*. Chicago, IL: Chicago University Press.

Burman, E. and Parker, I. (eds.) (1993) *Discourse analytic research*. London: Routledge.

Burrell, G. and Morgan, G. (1979: 2nd Edition, 2019) *Sociological paradigms and organisational analysis: elements of the sociology of corporate life*. London: Heinemann.

Campbell, C. (2018) *The romantic ethic and the spirit of modern consumerism – new extended edition*. London: Springer International Publishing.

Campbell, J. (2020, 3rd edition) *The hero with a thousand faces*. Joseph Campbell Foundation.

Canniford, R. and Shankar, A. (2013) 'Purifying practices: how consumers assemble romantic experiences of nature', *Journal of Consumer Research*, 39(5), pp. 1051–1069. https://doi.org/10.1086/667202

Capellini, B. and Yen, D.A. (2016) 'A space of one's own: Spatial and identity liminality in an online community of mothers', *Journal of Marketing Management*, *32(13–14)*, pp. 1260–1283. https://doi.org/10.1080/0267257X.2016.1156725

Carrigan, M. and Szmigin, I. (2004) 'Time, uncertainty and the expectancy experience: an interpretive exploration of consumption and impending motherhood', *Journal of Marketing Management*, *20(7–8)*, pp. 771–798. https://doi.org/10.1362/0267257041838755

Carrington, M.J. and Ozanne, J.L. (2022) 'Becoming through contiguity and lines of flight: the four faces of celebrity-proximate assemblages', *Journal of Consumer Research*, *48(5)*, pp. 858–884. https://doi.org/10.1093/jcr/ucab026

Carson, D., Gilmore, A., Perry, C. and Gronhaug, K. (2001) *Qualitative marketing research*. London: Sage.

Case, P. (1999) 'Remember re-engineering? The rhetorical appeal of a managerial salvation device', *Journal of Management Studies*, *36(4)*, pp. 419–442.

Castilhos, R.B. (2023) Class conflict and spatial domination in the Neoliberal City, *Journal of Consumer Research* (in press), ucad079. https://doi.org/10.1093/jcr/ucad079

Catterall, M. and Maclaran, P. (1997) 'Focus group data and qualitative analysis programs: coding the moving picture as well as the snapshots', *Sociological Research Online*, *2(1)*, pp. 1–9. https://doi.org/10.5153/sro.67

Catterall, M., Maclaran, P. and Stevens, L. (2000) *Marketing and feminism: current issues and research*. London: Routledge.

Catterall, M., Maclaran, P. and Stephens, L. (2001) *Marketing and feminism: current issues and research*. London: Routledge.

Chandler, D. (2002) *Semiotics for Beginners*. www.aber.ac.uk/media/Docu-ments/S4B/window.html.

Chang, H., Ngunjiri, F.W. and Hernandez, K.A.C. (2013) *Collaborative autoethnography*. Walnut Creek, CA: Left Coast Press.

Chatzidakis, A., Hakim, J., Litter, J. and Rottenberg, C. (2020) *The care manifesto: the politics of interdependence*. Verso Books.

Chatzidakis, A. and Maclaran, P. (2018) 'On critical collaborative videographies', *Journal of Marketing Management*, *34(5–6)*, pp. 509–517. https://doi.org/10.1080/0267257X.2018.1477820

Chatzidakis, A., Maclaran, P. and Varman, R. (2021) 'The regeneration of consumer movement solidarity', *Journal of Consumer Research*, *48(2)*, pp. 289–308. https://doi.org/10.1093/jcr/ucab007

Chowdhury, M.F. (2015) 'Coding, sorting and sifting of qualitative data analysis: debates and discussion', *Quality and Quantity*, *49(3)*, pp. 1135–1143. https://doi.org/10.1007/s11135-014-0039-2

Ciampa, I. and de Valck, K. (2024). Co-creative gift systems within digital platforms. *Psychology & Marketing*, 1–13. https://doi.org/10.1002/mar.22056

Cian, L. (2012) "A comparative analysis of print advertising applying the two main plastic semiotics schools: Barthes' and Greimas', *Semiotica*, *190*, pp. 57–79.

Clarke, I., Kell, I., Schmidt, R. and Vignall, C. (1998) 'Thinking the thought they do: symbolism and meaning in the consumer experience of the British Pub', *Qualitative Market Research: An International Journal*, *13*, pp. 132–144.

Contardo, I. and Wensley, R. (1999) 'The Harvard business school story: avoiding knowledge by being relevant', paper presented at the conference Re-organizing Knowledge, Transforming Institutions, Knowing, Knowledge and the University in the XXI Century, Amherst, September.

Cook, G. (2001) *The discourse of advertising*. London: Routledge.

Corso, J.J. (2014) 'What does Greimas's semiotic square really do?, *Mosaic: an Interdisciplinary Critical Journal*, *47(1)*, pp. 69–89. http://www.jstor.org/stable/44030128

Cova, B., Dalli, D., O'Donohoe, S. and Shankar, A. (2019) 'Fresh perspectives on interpretive consumer research', *Consumption Markets & Culture*, 22(3), pp. xi–xiii. https://doi.org/10.1080/10253866.2019.1625168

Cova, B. and Elliott, R. (2008) 'Everything you always wanted to know about interpretive consumer research but were afraid to ask', *Qualitative Market Research*, 11(2), pp. 121–129. https://doi.org/10.1108/13522750810864396

Crockett, D. and Wallendorf, M. (2004) 'The role of normative political ideology in consumer behavior', *Journal of Consumer Research*, 31(3), pp. 511–528. https://doi.org/10.1086/425086

Croft, R. (2013) 'Blessed are the geeks: an ethnographic study of consumer networks in social media, 2006–2012', *Journal of Marketing Management*, 29(5–6), pp. 545–561. https://doi.org/10.1080/0267257X.2013.787113

Cronin, A. (2018) *Public relations capitalism: promotional culture, publics and commercial democracy*. London: Palgrave Macmillan.

Crosby, E., McKeage, K., Rittenburg, T.L. and Adkins, N.R. (2023) 'Amplifying marginalised consumers' voices: a case for trauma-informed qualitative methodologies', *International Journal of Market Research*, 65(2–3), pp. 320–339. https://doi.org/10.1177/14707853221139576

Dam, C., Hartmann, B.J. and Brunk, K.H. (2024). Marketing the past: A literature review and future directions for researching retro, heritage, nostalgia, and vintage. *Journal of Marketing Management*, 1–25. https://doi.org/10.1080/0267257X.2024.2339454

Danesi, M. (1993) *Messages and meanings: an introduction to semiotics*. Toronto: Canadian Scholar's Press Inc.

Danesi, M. (2004) *Messages, signs and meanings, a basic textbook in semiotics and communication* (3rd edition), Toronto: Canadian Scholars Press.

Danesi, M. (2016) *The semiotics of emoji: the rise of visual language in the age of the internet (Bloomsbury advances in semiotics)*. London: Bloomsbury Academic.

Darley, J.M. and Batson, C.D. (1973) 'From Jerusalem to Jericho: a study of situational and dispositional variables in helping behavior', *Journal of Personality and Social Psychology*, 27, pp. 100–108.

Davis, A. (2013) *Promotional culture: the rise and spread of advertising, public relations, marketing and branding*. Cambridge: Polity Press.

De Yong, M., Kamsteeg, F. and Ybema, S. (2013) 'Ethnographic strategies for making the familiar strange: struggling with "distance" and "immersion" among Moroccan-Dutch students', *Journal of Business Anthropology*, 2(2), pp. 168–186. https://rauli.cbs.dk/index.php/jba/article/viewFile/4157/4577

Deetz, S. (1980) *Hermeneutics, Textuality, and Communication Research*, Seattle, WA, Summer Institute on Communication Theory. http://files.eric.ed.gov/fulltext/ED197419.pdf. Accessed 25 May 2014.

Deetz, S. (1992) *Democracy in an age of corporate colonization: developments in communication and the politics of everyday life*. Albany, NY: State University of New York Press.

DeLanda, M. (2006) Deleuzian social ontology and assemblage theory. in Fuglsang M. and Sorensen B.M. (eds.) *Deleuze and the social*. Edinburgh: Edinburgh University Press, pp. 250–267.

DeLanda, M. (2016) *Assemblage theory*. Edinburgh: Edinburgh University Press.

Deleuze, G. and Guattari, F. (1987) *A thousand plateaus*. Minneapolis: University of Minnesota Press.

Denzin, N.K. (2014) *Interpretive autoethnography*. 2nd edn. Thousand Oaks, CA: Sage.

Deshpandhe, R. (1999) 'Forseeing marketing', *Journal of Marketing*, 63, pp. 164–167.

Diwanji, V.S. (2023) 'Fuzzy-set qualitative comparative analysis in consumer research: a systematic literature review', *International Journal of Consumer Studies*, 47(6), pp. 2767–2789. https://doi.org/10.1111/ijcs.12889

Dobscha, S. (ed.) (2016) *Death in a consumer culture*. London: Routledge.

Dobscha, S. (2019) *Handbook of research on gender and marketing*. Cheltenham: Edward Elgar.

Dobscha, S. and Lee, N. (2014). "Introduction to the special section on interpretive consumer research", *European Journal of Marketing*, 48(5/6). https://doi.org/10.1108/EJM-03-2014-0174

Downes, D. and Rock, P. (1982) *Understanding deviance*. Oxford: Clarendon Press.

Drummond, K. (2018) *The road to wicked: the marketing and consumption of Oz, from Frank L. Baum to Broadway*. London: Palgrave Macmillan.

Eagleton, T. (2007) *Ideology*. London: Verso.

Easterby-Smith, M. and Malina, D. (1999) 'Cross-cultural collaborative research: toward reflexivity', *Academy of Management Journal*, 42(1), pp. 76–86.

Easterby-Smith, M., Thorpe, R., Jackson, P.R. and Jasperson, L. (2018) *Management and business research*. 6th edn. London, Sage.

Easterby-Smith, M., Thorpe, R. and Lowe, A. (1991) *Management research: an introduction*. 2nd edn., 2002. London: Sage.

Easton, G. and Aráujo, L. (1997) 'Management research and literary criticism', *British Journal of Management*, 8, pp. 99–106.

Eckhardt, G.M., Belk, R., Bradford, T.W., Dobscha, S., Ger, G. and Varman, R. (2021) 'Decolonizing marketing', *Consumption Markets & Culture*, 25(2), pp. 176–186. https://doi.org/10.1080/10253866.2021.1996734

Eco, U. (1976) *A theory of semiotics*. Bloomington: Indiana University Press.

Eco, U. (1984) *Semiotics and philosophy of language*. London: Palgrave Macmillan.

Eddo-Lodge, R. (2018) *Why I'm no longer talking to white people about race*. London: Bloomsbury.

Edgar, A. and Sedgwick, P. (1999) *Key concepts in cultural theory*. London: Routledge.

Edwards, D. and Potter, J. (1992) *Discursive psychology*. London: Sage.

Elam, K. (1988) *The semiotics of theatre and drama*. London: Routledge.

Elliott, R. (1994) 'Addictive consumption: function and fragmentation in postmodernity', *Journal of Consumer Policy*, 17(2), pp. 157–179.

Elliott, R. (1996) 'Discourse analysis: exploring action, function and conflict on social texts', *Marketing Intelligence and Planning*, 14(6), pp. 65–69.

Elliott, R. (1997) "Existential consumption and irrational desire', *European Journal of Marketing*, 31(3/4), pp. 285–296. https://doi.org/10.1108/03090569710162371

Elliott, R. (1998) 'A model of emotion-driven choice', *Journal of Marketing Management*, 14(1–3), pp. 95–108. https://doi.org/10.1362/026725798784959408

Elliott, R. and Gournay, K. (1996) 'Revenge, existential choice and addictive consumption', *Psychology and Marketing*, 3(8), pp. 753–768.

Elliott, R. and Jankel-Elliott, N. (2002) 'Using ethnography in strategic consumer research', *Qualitative Market Research: An International Journal*, 6(4), pp. 215–223. https://doi.org/10.1108/13522750310495300

Elliott, R. and Ritson, M. (1995) 'Practicing existential consumption: the lived meaning of sexuality in advertising', in Kardes, F.R. and Sujan, M. (eds.) *NA – Advances in consumer research*, volume 22. Provo, UT: Association for Consumer Research, pp. 740–745.

Elliott, R. and Ritson, M. (1997) 'Post-structuralism and the dialectics of advertising: discourse, ideology, resistance', Chapter 6 in Brown, S. and Turley, D. (eds.) *Consumer research: postcards from the edge*. London: Routledge, pp. 190–248.

Elliott, R. and Wattanasuwan, K. (1998) 'Brands as symbolic resources for the construction of identity', *International Journal of Advertising*, 17(2), pp. 131–144. https://doi.org/10.1080/02650487.1998.11104712

Ellis, C. (2009) *Revision: autoethnographic reflections on life and work*. Walnut Creek, CA: Left Coast Press.

Ellis, N., Fitchett, J., Higgins, M., Jack, G., Lim, M., Saren, M. and Tadajewski, M. (2011) *Marketing: a critical textbook*. London: Sage.

Ellis, N. and Hopkinson, G. (2010) 'The construction of managerial knowledge in business networks: managers' theories about communication', *Industrial Marketing Management*, 39(3), pp. 413–424. https://doi.org/10.1016/j.indmarman.2007.08.011

Ellis, N., Rod, M., Beal, T. and Lindsay, V. (2012) 'Constructing identities in Indian networks: discourses of marketing management in inter-organizational relationships', *Industrial Marketing Management*, 41(3), pp. 401–412.

Enck, S.M. and Morrissey, M.E. (2015) 'If orange is the new Black, I must be color blind: comic framings of post-racism in the prison-industrial complex', *Critical Studies in Media Communication*, 32(5), pp. 303–317.

Engel, J.F., Blackwell, R.D. and Miniard, P.W. (1990) *Consumer behaviour* (6th edition). London: Dryden Press.

Fairclough, N. (1985) 'Temporality in human action: an alternative to historicism and positivism', *American Psychologist*, 40, pp. 1179–1188.

Fairclough, N. (2010) *Critical discourse analysis: the critical study of language*. London: Routledge.

Fairclough, N. (2014) *Language and power*. 3rd edn. London: Routledge,

Featherstone, M. (1991) *Consumer culture and postmodernism*. London: Sage.

Feiereisen, S., Rasolofoarison, D., Russell, C.A. and Schau, H.J. (2021) 'One brand, many trajectories: narrative navigation in transmedia', *Journal of Consumer Research*, 48(4), pp. 651–681. https://doi.org/10.1093/jcr/ucaa046

Felix, R. and Fuat Fırat, A. (2019) 'Brands that "sell their soul": offshoring, brand liquefication and the excluded consumer', *Journal of Marketing Management*, 35(11–12), pp. 1080–1099. https://doi.org/10.1080/0267257X.2019.1604562

Firat, A. (1985) 'Ideology versus science in marketing changing the course of marketing, alternative paradigms for widening marketing theory', *Research in Marketing*, Suppl 2, pp. 135–146.

Firat, A., Dholakia, N. and Venkatesh, A. (1995) 'Marketing in a postmodern world', *European Journal of Marketing*, 29(1), pp. 40–56.

Firat, A. and Venkatesh, A. (1995a) 'Liberatory postmodernism and the re-enchantment of consumption', *Journal of Consumer Research*, 22(3), pp. 239–267.

Firat, A. and Venkatesh, A. (1995b) 'Postmodern perspectives on consumption', in Belk, R., Dholakia, N.R. and Venkatesh, A. (eds.) *Consumption and marketing, macro dimensions*. Cincinnati: South-Western College Publishing, pp. 234–265.

Fischer, E. and Guzel, G.T. (2023). The case for qualitative research. *Journal of Consumer Psychology*, 33, 259–272. https://doi.org/10.1002/jcpy.1300

Fiske, J.C. (1982) *Introduction to communication studies*. London: Methuen.

Fitchett, J. and Caruana, R. (2015) 'Exploring the role of discourse in marketing and consumer research', *Journal of Consumer Behaviour*, 14(1), pp. 1–12. https://doi.org/10.1002/cb.1497

Forester, J. (1992) 'Critical ethnography: on fieldwork in a Habermasian way', Chapter 3 in Alvesson, M. and Willmott, H. (eds.) *Critical management studies*. London: Sage, pp. 46–64.

Foster Davis, J. (2018) 'Selling whiteness? – A critical review of the literature on marketing and racism', *Journal of Marketing Management*, 34(1–2), pp. 134–177. https://doi.org/10.1080/0267257X.2017.1395902

Foucault, M. (1977) *Discipline and punish: the birth of the prison*, trans. A. Sheridan. New York, NY: Pantheon.

Foxall, G. (1995) 'Science and interpretation in consumer research: a radical behaviourist perspective', *European Journal of Marketing*, 29(9), pp. 3–99.

Fromm, E. (1941) *Escape from freedom*. New York, NY: Ishi Press International (2011 reprint).

Fry, D. and Fry, V.L. (1986) 'A semiotic model for the study of mass communication', in McLaughlin, M. (ed.) *Communication yearbook 9*. Beverly Hills: Sage, pp. 443–461.

Furusten, S. (1999) *Popular management books: how they are made and what they mean for organisations*. London: Routledge.

Gabriel, Y. (2017) 'Case studies as narratives: reflections prompted by the case of victor, the wild child of Aveyron', *Journal of Management Inquiry*, 28(4), pp. 403–408. https://doi.org/10.1177/1056492617715522

Gabriel, Y. and Lang, T. (2015) *The unmanageable consumer*. 3rd edn. London: Sage.

Gabriel, D. and Tate, S. A. (eds.) (2017) *Inside the Ivory Tower: narratives of women of color surviving and thriving in British Academia*. London: UCL Institute of Education Press.

Ganassali, S. and Matysiewicz, J. (2021) 'Echoing the golden legends: Storytelling archetypes and their impact on brand perceived value', *Journal of Marketing Management*, 37(5–6), pp. 437–463. https://doi.org/10.1080/0267257X.2020.1831577

Garfinkel, H. (1967) *Studies in ethnomethodology*. Englewood Cliffs, NJ: Prentice-Hall.

Gay, D., Hall, P., Janes, S., Mackay, L. and Negus, H. (1997) *Doing cultural studies: the story of the Sony Walkman*. London: Sage.

Geertz, C. (1973) *The interpretation of cultures*. London: Fontana Press.

Genette, G. (2010). *Paratexts: thresholds of interpretation*, J.E. Lewin (Trans.). Cambridge: Cambridge University Press.

Genette, G. and Maclean, M. (1991) 'Introduction to the paratext', *New Literary History*, 22(2), pp. 261–272. https://doi.org/10.2307/469037

Gergen, K. and Gergen, M. (1988) 'Narrative and the self as relationship', *Advances in Experimental Social Psychology*, 21, pp. 17–56.

Gerring, J. (2006) 'Single-outcome studies: a methodological primer', *International Sociology*, 21(5), pp. 707–734.

Ghaffari, M., Hackley, C. and Lee, Z. (2019) 'Control, knowledge, and persuasive power in advertising creativity: an ethnographic practice theory approach', *Journal of Advertising*, 48(2), pp. 242–249. https://doi.org/10.1080/00913367.2019.1598310

Giesler, M. (2024) 'Midrange, differential, meaningful, and multidisciplinary: reflections on *JCR*'s epistemic culture', *Journal of Consumer Research*, 51(1), pp. 204–209. https://doi.org/10.1093/jcr/ucae016

Giesler, M. and Thompson, C.J. (2016) 'A tutorial in consumer research: process theorization in cultural consumer research', *Journal of Consumer Research*, 43(4), pp. 497–508. https://doi.org/10.1093/jcr/ucw047

Gioia, D.A., Corley, K.G. and Hamilton, A.L. (2013) 'Seeking qualitative rigor in inductive research: notes on the Gioia methodology', *Organizational Research Methods*, 16(1), pp. 15–31.

Glaser, B.G. and Strauss, A.L. (1967) *The discovery of grounded theory*. Oxon: Routledge.

Goldman, W. (1983) *Adventures in the screen trade – A personal view of Hollywood* (2nd edition, first published 1983). New York, NY: Abacus.

Gollnhofer, J.F., Bhatnagar, K. and Manke, B. (2024) The discomfort of things! Tidying-up and decluttering in Consumers' homes, *Journal of Consumer Research*, ucae034. https://doi.org/10.1093/jcr/ucae034

Gollnhofer, J.F., Weijo, H.A. and Schouten, J.W. (2019) 'Consumer movements and value regimes: fighting food waste in Germany by building alternative object pathways', *Journal of Consumer Research*, 46(3), pp. 460–482. https://doi.org/10.1093/jcr/ucz004

Gould, S.J. (1991) 'The self-manipulation of my pervasive, perceived vital energy through product use: an introspective-praxis perspective', *Journal of Consumer Research*, 18(2), pp. 194–207.

Gould, S.J. (1995) 'Researcher introspection as a method in consumer research: applications, issues and implications', *Journal of Consumer Research*, 21(4), pp. 719–722.

Gould, S.J. (2008) 'An introspective genealogy of my introspective genealogy', *Marketing Theory*, 8(4), pp. 407–424. https://doi.org/10.1177/1470593108096543

Goulding, C. (2005) 'Grounded theory, ethnography and phenomenology', *European Journal of Marketing*, 39(3/4), pp. 294–308. https://doi.org/10.1108/03090560510581782

Goulding, C., Shankar, A. and Canniford, R. (2013) 'Learning to be tribal: facilitating the formation of consumer tribes', *European Journal of Marketing*, 47(5/6), pp. 813–832. https://doi.org/10.1108/03090561311306886

Goulding, C., Shankar, A., Elliott, R. and Canniford, R. (2009) 'The marketplace management of illicit pleasure', *Journal of Consumer Research*, 35(5), pp. 759–771.

Gramsci, A. (1971) *Selections from the prison notebooks*. New York, NY: International Publisher.

Grant, A., Canniford, R. and Shankar, A. (2024) Becoming nature: encounters in interspecies contact zones, *Journal of Consumer Research*, ucae032. https://doi.org/10.1093/jcr/ucae032

Gray, J. (2010) *Show sold separately. Promos, spoilers and other media paratexts.* New York: NYU Press.

Grayson, K. (1997) 'Narrative theory and consumer research: theoretical and methodological perspectives', *Advances in Consumer Research*, 24, pp. 67–70.

Grayson, K. and Shulman, D. (2000) 'Indexicality and the verification function of irreplaceable possessions: a semiotic analysis', *Journal of Consumer Research*, 27(1), pp. 17–30. https://doi.org/10.1086/314306

Greimas, A.J. (1988) *Maupassant: the semiotics of text*. John Benjamins Publishing Co.

Griffin, C., Bengry-Howell, A., Hackley, C., Mistral, W. and Szmigin, I. (2009) '"Every time I do it I absolutely annihilate myself": loss of (self)-consciousness and loss of memory in young people's drinking narratives', *Sociology*, 43(3), pp. 457–477.

Griffiths, J. and Follows, T. (2018) *98% pure potato – The origin of advertising account planning as told to us by its pioneers*. London: Unbound.

Gronhaug, K. (2000) 'The sociological basis of marketing', in Baker, M.J. (ed.) *Marketing theory: a student text*. London: Thompson Business Press.

Gruber, T., Szmigin, I., Reppel, A. and Voss, R. (2008) 'Designing and conducting online interviews to investigate interesting consumer phenomena', *Qualitative Market Research*, 11(3), pp. 256–274. https://doi.org/10.1108/13522750810879002

Gummeson, E. (2000) *Qualitative methods in management research*. London: Sage.

Gurrieri, L., Prothero, A., Bettany, S., Dobscha, S., Drenten, J., Ferguson, S. and Finkelstein, S. (2022). "Feminist academic organizations: challenging sexism through collective mobilizing across research, support, and advocacy." *Gender, Work & Organization*: 1–22. https://doi.org/10.1111/gwao.12912

Gurswitch, A. (1974) *Phenomenology and theory of science*. Evanston: Northwestern University Press.

Gutkind, L. (1996) *The art of creative nonfiction*. New York, NY: John Wiley & Sons.

Habermas, J. (1970) 'Knowledge and interest', in Emmett, D. and Macintyre, A. (eds.) *Sociological theory and philosophical analysis*. London: Palgrave Macmillan.

Hackett, P. M. W. (ed.) (2016) *Qualitative research methods in consumer psychology*. New York, NY and London: Routledge, pp. 105–117. ISBN 978-1-138-02349-9.

Hackley, A.R. (2021) The work of culture in Thai Theravāda Buddhist death rituals. in Minowa, Y. and Belk, R. (eds.) *Consumer culture theory in Asia: history and contemporary issues*. Routledge Frontiers in the Development of International Business, Management and Marketing. Taylor and Francis, pp. 138–155.

Hackley, C. (1998a) 'Mission statements as corporate communications: the consequences of social constructionism', *Corporate Communications: An International Journal*, 3(3), pp. 92–98.

Hackley, C. (1998b) 'Management learning and normative marketing theory: learning from the life-world', *Management Learning (Q1)*, 29(1), pp. 91–105.

Hackley, C. (1999) 'The communications process and the semiotic boundary', Chapter 9 in Kitchen, P. (ed.) *Marketing communications: principles and practice*. London: International Thomson Business Press, pp. 135–155.

Hackley, C. (2000) 'Silent running: tacit, discursive and psychological aspects of management in a top UK advertising agency', *British Journal of Management*, 11(3), pp. 239–254.

Hackley, C. (2001) *Marketing and social construction: exploring the rhetorics of marketed consumption*. London: Routledge.

Hackley, C. (2002) 'The Panoptic role of advertising agencies in the production of consumer culture', *Consumption, Markets and Culture*, 5(3), pp. 211–229.

Hackley, C. (2003a) 'Account planning: current agency perspectives on an advertising enigma', *Journal of Advertising Research (Q2/1)*, 43(2), pp. 235–246.

Hackley, C. (2003b) 'We are all customers now: rhetorical strategy and ideological control in marketing management texts', *Journal of Management Studies*, 40(5), pp. 1325–1352.

Hackley, C. (2003c) 'Divergent representational practices in advertising and consumer research: some thoughts on integration', *Qualitative Market Research: An International Journal Special Issue on Representation in Consumer Research*, 6(3), pp. 175–184.

Hackley, C. (2007) 'Auto-ethnographic consumer research and creative non-fiction: exploring connections and contrasts from a literary perspective', *Qualitative Market Research: An International Journal*, 10(1), pp. 98–108.

Hackley, C. (2009a) *Marketing – A critical introduction*. London: Sage.

Hackley, C. (2009b) 'Parallel universes and disciplinary space: the bifurcation of managerialism and social science in marketing studies', *Journal of Marketing Management*, 2(7–8), pp. 643–659.

Hackley, C. (2010) 'Theorizing advertising: managerial, scientific and cultural approaches', Chapter 6 in Maclaran, P., Saren, M., Stern, B.B. and Tadajewski, M. (eds.) *The Sage handbook of marketing theory*. London: Sage, pp. 89–107.

Hackley, C. (2016) 'Autoethnography in consumer research', Chapter 8 in Hackett, P.M.W. (ed.) *Qualitative research methods in consumer psychology*. New York, NY and London: Routledge, pp. 105–117.

Hackley, C. (2018) 'Advertising, marketing and PR: deepening mutuality amidst a convergent media landscape', Chapter 4 in Hardy, J., MacRury, I. and Powell, H. (eds.) *The advertising handbook (Media practice)*. 3rd edn. London: Routledge, pp. 58–74.

Hackley, C. (2019) 'Advertising practice and critical marketing', Chapter 11 in M. Tadajewski, M., Higgins, J. Denegri-Knott and R. Varman (eds.) *The Routledge companion to critical marketing studies*. London: Routledge, pp. 185–195.

Hackley, C. (2020). The discomfort of autoethnography in academic marketing research. Chapter 11 in Herrmann, A. (ed.) *The Routledge international handbook of organisational autoethnography*. New York: Routledge, pp. 176–187.

Hackley, C. (2022) 'Crap detecting. Autoethnographic reflections on critical practice in marketing pedagogy', *Journal of Marketing Management*, 39(1–2), pp. 20–31. https://doi.org/10.1080/0267257X.2022.2132754

Hackley, C. (2024) *But … How do you teach, business? A critical examination of the methods, ideology and influence of business and management studies and business schools*. Cheltenham: Edward Elgar.

Hackley, C., Bengry-Howell, A., Griffin, C., Mistral, W. and Szmigin, I. (2011) 'Young peoples' binge drinking constituted as a deficit of individual self-control in UK government alcohol policy', Chapter 15 in Candlin, C.N. and Crichton, J. (eds.) *Discourses of deficit*. Hampshire: Palgrave, Macmillan, Palgrave Studies in Professional and Organizational Discourse, pp. 293–310.

Hackley, C., Bengry-Howell, A., Griffin, C., Mistral, W., Szmigin, I. and Hackley, R.A. (2013) 'Young adults and "binge" drinking: a Bakhtinian analysis', *Journal of Marketing Management*, 29(7–8), pp. 933–949.

Hackley, C., Bengry-Howell, A., Griffin, C., Szmigin, I., Mistral, W. and Hackley, R.A. (2015) 'Transgressive drinking practices and the subversion of proscriptive alcohol policy messages', *Journal of Business Research*, 68(10), pp. 2125–2131. https://doi.org/10.1016/j.jbusres.2015.03.011

Hackley, C., Brown, S. and Hackley, R.A. (2012) 'The X-Factor enigma: Simon Cowell and the marketization of existential liminality', *Marketing Theory*, 12(4), pp. 451–469. https://doi.org/10.1177/1470593112457738

Hackley, J., Dixon, A., Royle, C., Moss, C., Brown, R. and Bell, T. (2024) "Seeing myself through someone Else's eyes": embodying the perfect nurturer in compassion focused therapy', *OBM Integrative and Complementary Medicine*, 9(1), p. 021. https://doi.org/10.21926/obm.icm.2401021

Hackley, C. and Hackley, R.A. (2015a) 'How the hungry ghost mythology reconciles materialism and spirituality in Thai death ritual', *Qualitative Market Research: An International Journal (Q2)*, 8(2), pp. 427–421.

Hackley, C. and Hackley, R.A. (2015b) 'Marketing and the cultural production of celebrity in the convergent media Era', *Journal of Marketing Management*, 31(5/6), pp. 461–477. www.tandfonline.com/doi/full/10.1080/0267257X.2014.1000940. Accessed 15 January 2015.

Hackley, C. and Hackley, A.R. (2019) 'Advertising at the threshold: paratextual promotion in the era of media convergence', *Marketing Theory*, 19(2), pp. 195–215. https://doi.org/10.1177/1470593118787581

Hackley, C. and Hackley, R.A. (2021) *5th edition advertising and promotion*. London: Sage.

Hackley, C. and Hackley, R.A. (2023) *Rethinking advertising a paratextual communication*. London: Edward Elgar.

Hackley, C., Hackley, R.A. and Bassiouni, D.H. (2018) 'Implications of the selfie for marketing management in the era of celebrity', *Marketing Intelligence and Planning*, 36(1), pp. 49–62. https://doi.org/10.1108/MIP-07-2017-0124

Hackley, C., Hackley, R.A. and Bassiouni, D.H. (2019) 'Imaginary futures: liminoid advertising and consumer identity', *Journal of Marketing Communications*, 27(3), pp. 269–283. https://doi.org/10.1080/13527266.2019.1694564

Hackley, C. and Kover, A. (2007) 'The trouble with creatives: negotiating creative identity in advertising agencies', *International Journal of Advertising*, 26(1), pp. 63–78.

Hackley, C., Tiwsakul, A. and Preuss, L. (2008) 'An ethical evaluation of product placement – A deceptive practice?, *Business Ethics – A European Review*, 17(2), pp. 109–120.

Hammer, M. and Champy, J. (1993) *Re-engineering the corporation: a manifesto for business revolution*. London: Nicholas Brealey.

Hammersley, M. and Atkinson, P. (1983) *Ethnography: principles and practice*. London: Routledge.

Harvey, D. (1989) *The condition of postmodernity: an enquiry into the origins of cultural change*. Oxford: Blackwell.

Hayward, K. and Hobbs, D. (2007) 'Beyond the binge: market-led liminalization and the spectacle of binge drinking', *The British Journal of Sociology*, 58(3), pp. 437–456.

Hearn, J. and Hein, W. (2015) 'Reframing gender and feminist knowledge construction in marketing and consumer research: missing feminisms and the case of men and masculinities', *Journal of Marketing Management*, 31(15–16), pp. 1626–1651. https://doi.org/10.1080/0267257X.2015.1068835

Heidegger, M. (1962) *Being and time*. Oxford: Basil Blackwell.

Hein, W. and O'Donohoe, S. (2014) 'Practising gender: the role of banter in young men's improvisations of masculine consumer identities', *Journal of Marketing Management*, 30(13–14), pp. 1293–1319. https://doi.org/10.1080/0267257X.2013.852608

Henderson, G.R., Hakstian, A.M. and Williams, J.D. (2016) *Consumer equality: race and the American marketplace* (Racism in American Institutions). Santa Barbara, CA: Praeger.

Heritage, J. (1984) *Garfinkel and ethnomethodology*. Cambridge: Polity Press.

Herrmann, A. (ed.) (2020) *The Routledge international handbook of organisational autoethnography*. London: Routledge.

Herrmann, A. (2022) 'The future of autoethnographic criteria', *International Review of Qualitative Research*, 15(1), pp. 125–135. https://doi.org/10.1177/19408447211049513

Hirschman, E.C. (1986) 'Humanistic inquiry in marketing research, philosophy, method and criteria', *Journal of Marketing Research*, 23, pp. 237–249.

Hirschman, E.C. (ed.) (1989) *Interpretive consumer research*. Provo, UT: Association for Consumer Research.

Hirschman, E.C. (1990) 'Secular immortality and the American ideology of affluence', *Journal of Consumer Research*, 17, pp. 344–359.

Hirschman, E.C. (1993) 'Ideology in consumer research, 1980 and 1990: a Marxist and feminist critique', *Journal of Consumer Research*, 19(4), pp. 537–555.

Hirschman, E.C. and Holbrook, M.B. (1992) *Postmodern consumer research: the study of consumption as text*. London: Sage.

Hirschman, E.C. and Stern, B.B. (1994) 'Women as commodities: prostitution as depicted in the Blue Angel, Pretty Baby, and Pretty Woman', in C.T. Allen and D.R. John (eds.) *NA – Advances in consumer research*, volume 21. Provo, UT: Association for Consumer Research, pp. 576–581.

Hoffman, D.L. and Novak, T.P. (2018) 'Consumer and object experience in the internet of things: an assemblage theory approach', *Journal of Consumer Research*, 44(6), pp. 1178–1204. https://doi.org/10.1093/jcr/ucx105

Holbrook, M.B. (1990) 'The role of lyricism in research on consumer emotions: skylark, have you anything to say to me?, *Advances in Consumer Research*, 17, pp. 1–18.

Holbrook, M.B. (1995) *Consumer research: introspective essays on the study of consumption*. London: Sage.

Holbrook, M.B. (2018) 'A subjective personal introspection essay on the evolution of business schools, the fate of marketing education, and aspirations toward a great society', *Australasian Marketing Journal*, 26(2), pp. 70–78.

Holbrook, M.B. (2024) 'What for art thou, marketing?, *Journal of Customer Behaviour*, 23(1), pp. 27–32.

Holbrook, M.B. and Grayson, M.W. (1986) 'The semiology of cinematic consumption: symbolic consumer behaviour in *Out of Africa*', *Journal of Consumer Research*, 13, pp. 374–381.

Holbrook, M.B. and Hirschman, E.C. (1982) 'The experiential aspects of consumption: consumer feelings, fantasies and fun', *Journal of Consumer Research*, 9, pp. 132–140.

Holbrook, M.B. and Hirschman, E.C. (1993) *The semiotics of consumption: interpreting symbolic consumer behaviour in popular culture and works of art*. New York, NY: Mouton de Gruyter.

Holbrook, M.B. and Shaughnessy, O. (1988) 'On the scientific status of consumer research and the need for an interpretive approach to studying consumer behaviour', *Journal of Consumer Research*, 15, pp. 398–403.

Holt, D.B. (1997) 'Poststructuralist lifestyle analysis: conceptualizing the social patterning of consumption in postmodernity', *Journal of Consumer Research*, 23(4), pp. 326–350. https://doi.org/10.1086/209487

Holt, D.B. (2002) 'Why do brands cause trouble? A dialectical theory of consumer culture and branding', *Journal of Consumer Research*, 29(1), pp. 70–90. https://doi.org/10.1086/339922

Holt, D.B. (2004) *How brands become icons – the principles of cultural branding*. Cambridge, MA: Harvard University Press.

Holt, D.B. and Cameron, D. (2010) *Cultural branding: using innovative ideologies to build breakthrough brands*. Oxford: Oxford University Press.

Holt, D.B. and Thompson, C.J. (2004) "Man-of-Action heroes: the pursuit of heroic masculinity in everyday consumption', *Journal of Consumer Research*, 31(2), pp. 425–40. https://doi.org/10.1086/422120

Horkheimer, M. and Adorno, T.W. (1944) *The dialectic of enlightenment*. New York, NY: Continuum.

Hudson, L.A. and Ozanne, J. (1988) 'Alternative ways of seeking knowledge in consumer research', *Journal of Consumer Research*, 14(4), pp. 508–521. https://doi.org/10.1086/209132

Huff, A.D., Humphreys, A. and Wilner, S. (2021) 'the politicization of objects: meaning and materiality in the U.S. Cannabis market', *Journal of Consumer Research*, 48(1), pp. 22–50. https://doi.org/10.1093/jcr/ucaa061

Humphreys, A. (2010) 'Semiotic structure and the legitimation of consumption practices: the case of casino gambling', *Journal of Consumer Research*, 37(3), pp. 490–510. https://doi.org/10.1086/652464

Humphreys, A. and Thompson, C.J. (2014) 'Branding disaster: reestablishing trust through the ideological containment of systemic risk anxieties', *Journal of Consumer Research*, 41(4), pp. 877–910. https://doi.org/10.1086/677905

Humphreys, A. and Wang, R.J.H. (2018) 'Automated text analysis for consumer research', *Journal of Consumer Research*, 44(6, April, pp. 1274–1306. https://doi.org/10.1093/jcr/ucx104

Hunt, S.D. (2003) *Controversy in marketing theory: for reason, realism, truth, and objectivity*. Armonk, NY: M.E. Sharpe, Inc.

Husemann, K. and Eckhardt, G.M. (2019) 'Consumer deceleration', *Journal of Consumer Research*, 45(6), pp. 1142–1163. https://doi.org/10.1093/jcr/ucy047

Husserl, E. (1931) *Ideas*. London: Allen & Unwin.

Husserl, E. (1970) *Logical investigations*. London: Routledge and Kegan Paul (first published 1900).

Hwang, J. and Park, H.Y. (2021) Hermeneutic phenomenological understanding of the inner journey of templestay. *Int J Environ Res Public Health*. 2021 Jul 23; 18(15):7830. https://doi.org/10.3390/ijerph18157830.

Hycner, R.H. (1985) 'Some guidelines for the phenomenological analysis of interview data', *Human Studies*, no. 8, pp. 279–303. www.depts.ttu.edu/education/our-people/Faculty/additional_pages/duemer/epsy_6305_class_materials/Hycne-R-H-1985.pdf.

Iser, W. (1972) 'The reading process: a phenomenological approach', *New Literary History*, 3(2), pp. 279–299.

Jankowicz, A.D. (1991) *Business research projects for students*. London: Chapman and Hall.

Jarzabkowski, P., Bednarek, R. and Lê, J.K. (2014) 'Producing persuasive findings: demystifying ethnographic text work in strategy and organization research', *Strategic Organization*, 12(4), pp. 274–287.

Jayasinghe, L. and Ritson, M. (2013) 'Everyday advertising context: an ethnography of advertising response in the family living room', *Journal of Consumer Research*, 40(1), pp. 104–121. https://doi.org/10.1086/668889

Johnson, P. and Duberley, J. (2003) 'Reflexivity in management research', *Journal of Management Studies*, 40(5), pp. 1279–1303. http://doi.org/10.1111/1467-6486.00380

Keith, R.J. (1960) 'The marketing revolution', *Journal of Marketing*, 24, pp. 35–38.

Kellogg, K., Orlikowski, W.J. and Yates, J. (2006) 'Life in the trading zone: structuring coordination across boundaries in post-bureaucratic organizations', *Organization Science*, 17(1), pp. 22–44.

Kelly, G.A., Lawlor, K. and Donohoe, O. (2005) 'Encoding advertisements: the creative perspective', *Journal of Marketing Management*, 21(5–6), pp. 505–528. https://doi.org/10.1362/0267257054307390

Kennedy, G. (1963) *The art of persuasion in Greece*. London: Routledge and Kegan Paul.

Kerin, R.A. (1996) 'In pursuit of an ideal: the editorial and literary history of the *Journal of Marketing*', *Journal of Marketing*, 60(1), pp. 1–13.

Khare, A. and Varman, R. (2017) 'Subalterns, empowerment and the failed imagination of markets', *Journal of Marketing Management*, 33(17–18), pp. 1593–1602. https://doi.org/10.1080/0267257X.2017.1403138

Knights, D. and Willmott, H. (2017) *Introducing organizational behaviour and management*. 3rd edn. London: Cengage Learning.

Knorr Cetina, K.D. and Mulkay, M. (eds.) (1983) *science observed: perspectives on the social study of science*. London: Sage.

Kotler, P. (1967) *Marketing management: analysis, planning and control*. Upper Saddle River: Prentice-Hall.

Kover, A.J., Goldberg, S.M. and James, W.L. (1995) 'Creativity vs effectiveness? An integrating classification for advertising', *Journal of Advertising Research*, 35(6), pp. 29–41.

Kozinets, R.V. (2008) 'Technology/ideology: how ideological fields influence consumers' technology narratives', *Journal of Consumer Research*, 34(6, April, pp. 865–881. https://doi.org/10.1086/523289

Kozinets, R.V. (2015) *Netnography – redefined.* 2nd edn. London: Sage.

Kozinets, R.V. (2019a) *Netnography – The essential guide to qualitative social media research.* 3rd edn. London: Sage.

Kozinets, R.V. (2019b) 'Consuming technocultures: an extended *JCR* curation', *Journal of Consumer Research*, ucz034. https://doi.org/10.1093/jcr/ucz034

Kozinets, R.V. and Kedzior, R. (2009) 'I, avatar: auto-netnographic research in virtual worlds', in M. Solomon and N. Wood (eds.) *Virtual social identity and consumer behavior.* Armonk, NY: M.E. Sharpe, pp. 3–19.

Kozinets, R.V., Scaraboto, D. and Parmentier, M.-A. (2018) 'Evolving netnography: how brand auto-netnography, a netnographic sensibility, and more-than-human netnography can transform your research', *Journal of Marketing Management*, *34(3–4)*, pp. 231–242. https://doi.org/10.1080/0267257X.2018.1446488

Kozinets, R.V., Sherry, J.F. Jr, Storm, D., Duhachek, A., Nuttavuthisit, K. and DeBerry-Spence, B. (2004) 'Ludic agency and retail spectacle', *Journal of Consumer Research*, *31(3)*, pp. 658–672.

Kuhn, T. (1970) *The structure of scientific revolutions.* Chicago, IL: University of Chicago Press.

Kunda, G. (1992) *Engineering culture: control and commitment in a high-tech corporation.* Philadelphia, PA: Temple University Press.

Kvale, S. (1983) 'The qualitative research interview: a phenomenological and a hermeneutical mode of understanding', *Journal of Phenomenological Psychology*, *14(2)*, pp. 171–196.

Labroo, A.A. and Patrick, V.M. (2009) 'Psychological distancing: why happiness helps you see the big picture', *Journal of Consumer Research*, *35(5)*, pp. 800–809.

Larsen, H.H., Mick, D.G. and Alsted, C. (1991) *Marketing and semiotics: selected papers from the Copenhagen symposium.* Copenhagen: Handelshøjskolens Forlag.

Larsen, G. and Patterson, M. (2018) 'Consumer identity projects', in O. Kravets, P. Maclaran, S. Miles, and A. Venkatesh (eds.) *Sage handbook of consumer culture.* London: Sage, pp. 194–213.

Latour, B. and Woolgar, S. (1979) *Laboratory life.* London: Sage.

Leach, E. (1976) *Culture and communication: the logic by which symbols are connected – An introduction to the use of structuralist analysis in social anthropology.* Cambridge: Cambridge University Press.

Letiche, H. (2002) 'Viagra(ization) or Technoromanticism', *Consumption, Markets and Culture*, *5(3)*, pp. 247–260.

Levitt, T. (1965) 'Exploit the product life cycle', *Harvard Business Review*, November. https://hbr.org/1965/11/exploit-the-product-life-cycle

Levy, S.J. (2006) 'History of qualitative research methods in marketing', in *Handbook of qualitative research methods in marketing.* Edward Elgar Publishing, pp. 3–18. https://doi.org/10.4337/9781847204127.00006; http://criticalmanagement.uniud.it/fileadmin/user_upload/Levy_in_Belk_2006.pdf

Levy, S.J. and Luedicke, M.K. (2013) 'From marketing ideology to branding ideology', *Journal of Macromarketing*, *33(1)*, pp. 58–66. https://doi.org/10.1177/0276146712459656

Lim, M. and Moufahim, M. (2011) 'Co-production and co-consumption: perspectives on immigration through a discourse analysis of voters' blogs in the 2010 general election', *Journal of Marketing Management*, *27(7–8)*, pp. 656–674. https://doi.org/10.1080/0267257X.2011.593539

Lisjak, M. and Ordabayeva, N. (2023) 'How political ideology shapes preferences for observably inferior products', *Journal of Consumer Research*, *49(6)*, pp. 1014–1031. https://doi.org/10.1093/jcr/ucac030

Loo, B.K. and Hackley, C. (2013) 'Internationalisation strategy of iconic Malaysian high fashion brands', *Qualitative Market Research: An International Journal (Q2)*, 16(4), pp. 406–420.

Lucarelli, A., Shahriar, H., Ulver, S. and Egan-Wyer, C. (2023). Research contributions in interpretivist marketing and consumer research studies: a kaleidoscopic framework. *Marketing Theory*, 0(0). https://doi.org/10.1177/14705931231202430

Luedicke, K., Thompson, C.J. and Giesler, M. (2009) 'Consumer identity work as moral protagonism: how myth and ideology animate a brand-mediated moral conflict', *Journal of Consumer Research*, 36(6), pp. 1016–1032. https://doi.org/10.1086/644761

Lupton, D. (2014) *Digital sociology*. London: Routledge.

Lyotard, J.F. (1984) *The postmodern condition: a report on knowledge*, trans. G. Bennington and B. Massumi. Minneapolis, MN: University of Minnesota Press.

MacInnis, D.J. and Folkes, V.S. (2010) 'The disciplinary status of consumer behavior: a sociology of science perspective on key controversies', *Journal of Consumer Research*, 36(6), pp. 899–914. https://doi.org/10.1086/644610

Maclaran, P. (2012) 'Marketing and feminism in historic perspective', *Journal of Historical Research in Marketing*, 4(3), pp. 462–469. https://doi.org/10.1108/17557501211252998

Maclaran, P. (2015) 'Feminism's fourth wave: a research agenda for marketing and consumer research', *Journal of Marketing Management*, 31(15–16), pp. 1732–1738. https://doi.org/10.1080/0267257X.2015.1076497

Maclaran, P. and Chatzidikas, A. (2022) *Gendered marketing: gendered management*. London: Edward Elgar.

Maclaran, P., Saren, M., Goulding, C., Elliott, R. and Catterall, M. (2007) *Critical marketing – Defining the field*. London: Routledge.

Maclaran, P., Stevens, L. and Kravets, O. (eds.) (2022) *The Routledge companion to marketing and feminism*. London: Routledge.

Magenta Research (2023) Exploring High Media Literacy Among Children and Adults: Discourse Analysis. Ofcom Report December https://www.ofcom.org.uk/siteassets/resources/documents/research-and-data/media-literacy-research/adults/high-media-literacy-among-adults-and-children/discourse-analysis/. Accessed June 2024.

Maguire, M. and Delahunt, B. (2017) 'Doing a thematic analysis: a practical, step-by-step guide for learning and teaching scholars', *AISHE-Journal*, 8(3). http://ojs.aishe.org/index.php/aishe-j/article/view/335

Mahoney, C. (ed.) (2015) *Critical perspectives on marketing and market research: health, food and social inequality*. London: Routledge.

Malinowski, B. (1922) *Argonauts of the Western pacific*. London: Routledge and Kegan Paul.

Mardon, R., Cocker, H. and Daunt, K. (2023) 'How social media influencers impact consumer collectives: an embeddedness perspective', *Journal of Consumer Research*, 50(3), pp. 617–644. https://doi.org/10.1093/jcr/ucad003

Mardon, R., Denegri-Knott, J. and Molesworth, M. (2023) "Kind of Mine, Kind of Not": digital possessions and affordance misalignment', *Journal of Consumer Research*, 50(2), pp. 255–281. https://doi.org/10.1093/jcr/ucac057

Marion, G. (2006) 'Research note: marketing ideology and criticism: legitimacy and legitimization', *Marketing Theory*, 6(2), pp. 245–262.

Martin, B.A.S. (2004) 'Using the imagination: consumer evoking and thematizing of the fantastic imaginary', *Journal of Consumer Research*, 31(1), pp. 136–149. https://doi.org/10.1086/383430

Martin, D.M. (2004) 'Humor in middle management: women negotiating the paradoxes of organizational life', *Journal of Applied Communication Research*, 32(2), pp. 147–170.

Martin, D.M., Schouten, J.W. and McAlexander, J.H. (2006) 'Claiming the throttle: multiple femininities in a hyper-masculine subculture', *Consumption, Markets and Culture*, 9(3), pp. 171–205.

Marx, K. and Engels, F. (2011: reprint of the 1939 edition) *The German ideology*. Martino Fine Books.

Mautner, G. (2016) *Discourse and management* (with contributions from Nick Ellis, Chris Hackley, Cliff Oswick and Ruth Wodak) Palgrave Critical Management Studies. London: Palgrave Macmillan.

McAlexander, J.H., Dufault, B.L., Martin, D.M. and Schouten, J.W. (2014) 'The marketization of religion: field, capital, and consumer identity', *Journal of Consumer Research*, 41(3), pp. 358–379.

McCarthy, E.J. (1960) *Basic marketing: a managerial approach* Richard D. Homewood, IL: Irwin Inc.

McCloskey, D.N. (1983) 'The rhetoric of economics', *Journal of Economic Literature*, 21(2), pp. 481–517. www.jstor.org/stable/2724987.

McCracken, G. (1986) 'Culture and consumption: a theoretical account of the structure and movement of the cultural meaning of consumer goods', *Journal of Consumer Research*, 13(1), pp. 71–84. https://doi.org/10.1086/209048

McCracken, G. (1989) 'Who is the celebrity endorser? Cultural foundations of the endorsement process', *Journal of Consumer Research*, 16(3, pp. 310–321. https://doi.org/10.1086/209217

McLeod, C., O'Donohoe, S. and Townley, B. (2009) 'The elephant in the room? Class and creative careers in British advertising agencies', *Human Relations*, 62(7), pp. 1011–1039.

McQuarrie, E.F. and Mick, D.G. (1992) 'On resonance: a critical pluralistic inquiry into advertising rhetoric', *Journal of Consumer Research*, 19(2), pp. 180–197. https://doi.org/10.1086/209295

McQuarrie, E.F. and Mick, D.G. (1996) 'Figures of rhetoric in advertising language', *Journal of Consumer Research*, 22(4), pp. 424–438. https://doi.org/10.1086/209459

McStay, A. (2010) 'A qualitative approach to understanding audience's perceptions of creativity in online advertising', *Qualitative Report*, 15(1), pp. 37–58.

Meamber, L. and Venkatesh, A. (1995) 'Discipline and practice: a postmodern critique of marketing as constituted by the work of Philip Kotler', in Stern, B. and Zinkhan, G.M. (eds.) *Enhancing knowledge development in marketing*, 6, pp. 248–253.

Merleau-Ponty, M. (1962a) *Experience and objective thought: the problem of the body*. New York, NY: Routledge.

Merleau-Ponty, M. (1962b) *Phenomenology of perception*. London: Routledge.

Merton, R.K. (reprint 2017) *Sociology of science and sociology as science*. New York, NY: Columbia University Press.

Metz, C. (1974) *Film language: a semiotics of the cinema*. New York, NY: Oxford University Press.

Mick, D.G. (1986) 'Consumer research and semiotics: exploring the morphology of signs, symbols and significance', *Journal of Consumer Research*, 13, pp. 180–197.

Mick, D.G. (1997) 'Semiotics in marketing and consumer research: balderdash, verity, pleas', Chapter 8 in Brown, S. and Turley, D. (eds.) *Consumer research: postcards from the edge*. London: Routledge, pp. 249–262.

Mick, D.G. and Buhl, C. (1992) 'A meaning-based model of advertising experiences', *Journal of Consumer Research*, 19, pp. 317–338.

Miles, C. (2013) 'Persuasion, marketing communication, and the metaphor of magic', *European Journal of Marketing*, 47(11/12), pp. 2002–2019.

Miles, C. (2014) 'The rhetoric of managed contagion: metaphor and agency in the discourse of viral marketing', *Marketing Theory*, 14(1), pp. 3–18.

Miles, C. and Nilsson, T. (2018) 'Marketing (as) rhetoric: an introduction', *Journal of Marketing Management, 34(15–16)*, pp. 1259–1271.

Mills, C.W. (1959) *The sociological imagination*. New York, NY: Oxford University Press.

Mills, S. (1997) *Discourse*. London: Routledge.

Mills, S., Patterson, A. and Quinn, L. (2015) 'Fabricating celebrity brands via scandalous narrative: crafting, capering and commodifying the comedian, Russell Brand', *Journal of Marketing Management, 31(5–6)*, pp. 599–615. https://doi.org/10.1080/0267257X.2015.1005116

Minowa, Y. and Belk, R.W. (2019) *Gifts, romance and consumer culture*. London: Routledge.

Minowa, Y., Maclaran, P. and Stevens, L. (2019) 'The femme fatale in vogue: femininity ideologies in Fin-de-siècle America', *Journal of Macromarketing*, pp. 1–17. https://doi.org/10.1177/0276146719847748

Minowa, Y., Visconti, L.M. and Maclaran, P. (2012) 'Researchers' introspection for multi-sited ethnographers: a xenoheteroglossic autoethnography', *Journal of Business Research, 65(4)*, pp. 483–489. https://doi.org/10.1016/j.jbusres.2011.02.026

Moeran, B. (1996) *A Japanese advertising agency: an anthropology of media and markets*. London: Routledge.

Moin, S.M.A., Hosany, S. and O'Brien, J. (2020) Storytelling in destination Brands' promotional videos, *Tourism Management Perspectives*, Vol 34 https://doi.org/10.1016/j.tmp.2020.100639

Moisander, J. and Valtonen, A. (2006) *Qualitative market research; A cultural approach*. London: Sage.

Molander, S., Ostberg, J. and Peñaloza, L. (2023) 'Brand morphogenesis: the role of heterogeneous consumer sub-assemblages in the change and continuity of a brand', *Journal of Consumer Research, 49(5)*, pp. 762–785. https://doi.org/10.1093/jcr/ucac009

Morgan, G. (1992) 'Marketing discourse and practice: towards a critical analysis', Chapter 7 in Alvesson, M. and Willmotts, H. (eds.) *Critical management studies*. London: Sage, pp. 136–158.

Morgan, G. and Smircich, L. (1980) 'The case for qualitative research', *Academy of Management Review, 5*, pp. 491–500.

Moufahim, M., Humphreys, M., Mitussis, D. and Fitchett, J. (2007) 'Interpreting discourse: a critical discourse analysis of the marketing of an extreme right party', *Journal of Marketing Management, 23(5–6)*, pp. 537–558. https://doi.org/10.1362/026725707X212829

Mumby-Croft, R. and Hackley, C. (1997) 'The social construction of market entrepreneurship: a case analysis in the UK fishing industry', *Marketing Education Review, 7(3)*, pp. 87–94.

Munro, R. (1997) 'Connection/disconnection: theory and practice in organizational control', *British Journal of Management, 8*, pp. 43–63.

Murray, J.B. and Ozanne, J.L. (1991) 'The critical imagination: emancipatory interests in consumer research', *Journal of Consumer Research, 18(2)*, pp. 129–144.

Murray, J.B., Ozanne, J.L. and Shapiro, J.L. (1994) 'Revitalising the critical imagination: unleashing the crouched tiger', *Journal of Consumer Research, 21*, pp. 559–565.

Nasiri, H., Kirillova, K. and Wassler, (2024). 'Beyond beauty: ugly and borderline tourism aesthetic experiences,' *Annals of Tourism Research, 105(C)*.

Nilsson, T. (2019) 'How marketers argue for business – Exploring the rhetorical nature of industrial marketing work', *Industrial Marketing Management, 80*, pp. 233–241. https://doi.org/10.1016/j.indmarman.2018.10.004

Nilsson, Y. (2015) *Rhetorical Business: A Study of Marketing Work in the Spirit of Contradiction*, Doctoral thesis, Lund, Lund University, Department of Service Management and Service Studies, p. 205. http://lnu.diva-portal.org/smash/record.jsf?pid=diva2%3A1095759&dswid=-402

Nøjgaard, M. (2023) 'The value-translation model of consumer activism: how consumer watchdog organizations change markets', *Journal of Consumer Research*, 49(6), pp. 967–986. https://doi.org/10.1093/jcr/ucac025

Norris, J. and Sawyer, R.D. (2012) 'Toward a dialogic methodology', in Norris, J., Sawyer, R.D. and Lund, D.E. (eds.) *Duoethnography: dialogic methods for social health and educational research*. Walnut Creek, CA: Left Coast Press, pp. 9–39.

Novak, T. and Hoffman, D.L. (2023) 'Automation assemblages in the internet of things: discovering qualitative practices at the boundaries of quantitative change', *Journal of Consumer Research*, 49(5), pp. 811–837. https://doi.org/10.1093/jcr/ucac014

Nuttall, P., Shankar, A., Beverland, M.B. and Hooper, C.S. (2011) 'Mapping the unarticulated potential of qualitative research stepping out from the shadow of quantitative studies', *Journal of Advertising Research*, 51(1), pp. 153–166. https://doi.org/10.2501/jar-51-1-153-166

O'Barr, W.M. (2006) Representations of masculinity and femininity in advertising. *Advertising & Society Review*, 7(2), Project MUSE. https://doi.org/10.1353/asr.2006.0028

O'Donohoe, S. (1994) 'Advertising uses and gratifications', *European Journal of Marketing*, 28(8/9), pp. 52–75. https://doi.org/10.1108/03090569410145706

O'Donohoe, S. (1997) 'Raiding the postmodern pantry: advertising intertextuality and the young adult audience', *European Journal of Marketing*, 3(34), pp. 234–253. https://doi.org/10.1108/03090569710162344

O'Guinn, T. and Faber, R.J. (1989) 'Compulsive buying: a phenomenological exploration', *Journal of Consumer Research*, 16(2), pp. 147–157. https://doi.org/10.1086/209204

O'Reilly, D. (2006) 'Commentary: branding ideology', *Marketing Theory*, 6(2), pp. 263–271. https://doi.org/10.1177/1470593106063986

O'Reilly, K. (2005) *Ethnographic methods*. London: Routledge.

O'Shaughnessy, J. (2009) *Interpretation in social life, social science, and marketing*. London: Routledge.

O'Shaughnessy, J. and Holbrook, M. (2015) 'Understanding consumer behaviour: the linguistic turn in marketing research', in Sheth, J. (ed.) *Legends in consumer behaviour: Morris b. Holbrook*. London: Sage.

O'Sullivan, S.R. (2016) 'The branded carnival: the dark magic of consumer excitement', *Journal of Marketing Management*, 32(9–10), pp. 1033–1058. https://doi.org/10.1080/0267257X.2016.1161656

Olsen, B. (2003) 'The revolution in marketing intimate apparel – a narrative ethnography', in de Waal Malefyt, T. and Moeran, B. (eds.) *Advertising cultures*. Oxford: Berg, pp. 113–138.

Olsen, B. (2016) 'Agency growing pains: ethnography in the 1980s', *Journal of Business Anthropology*, 5(1), pp. 89–104.

Olsen, B. and Gould, S. (2008) 'Revelations of cultural consumer lovemaps in Jamaican dancehall lyrics: an ethnomusicological ethnography', *Consumption, Markets and Culture*, 11(4), pp. 229–257.

Ots, M. and Nyilasy, G. (2017) 'Just doing it: theorising integrated marketing communications (IMC) practices', *European Journal of Marketing*, 51(3), pp. 490–510.

Parker, I. (1992) *Discourse dynamics: critical analysis for social and individual psychology*. London: Routledge.

Patterson, A. (2012) 'Social networkers of the world, unite and take over: a meta-introspective perspective on the Facebook brand', *Journal of Business Research*, 65(4), pp. 527–534.

Patterson, M. and Elliott, R. (2002) 'Negotiating masculinities: advertising and the inversion of the male gaze', *Consumption, Markets and Culture*, 21(3), pp. 231–249.

Peirce, C.S. (1953–66) *Collected papers*, Hartshorne, C., Weiss, P. and Burks, A.W. (eds.). Cambridge, MA: Harvard University Press.

Peirce, C.S. (1986) 'Logic as semiotic: the theory of signs', in Innis, R. E. (ed.) *Semiotics: an introductory reader*. London: Hutchinson.

Pelias, R.J. (2011) *Leaning: a poetics of personal relations*. Walnut Creek, CA: Left Coast Press.

Peters, T. and Waterman, R. (1982) *In search of excellence*. New York, NY: Harper & Row.

Pew (2023) *Racial disparities persist in many U.S. Jails*. Pew Trust. https://www.pewtrusts.org/en/research-and-analysis/issue-briefs/2023/05/racial-disparities-persist-in-many-us-jails

Phillips, B.J. and McQuarrie, E.F. (2004) 'Beyond visual metaphor: a new typology of visual rhetoric in advertising', *Marketing Theory*, 4(1/2), pp. 113–136. https://doi.org/10.1177/1470593104044089

Phillips, B.J. and McQuarrie, E.F. (eds.) (2008) *Go figure: new directions in advertising rhetoric*. New York, NY: M.E. Sharpe.

Phillips, J.M. and Reynolds, T.J. (2008) *Qualitative Market Research: an International Journal*, 12(1), pp. 83–99, 1352–2752. https://doi.org/10.1108/13522750910927232

Pielichaty, H. (2015) 'Festival space: gender, liminality and the carnivalesque', *International Journal of Event and Festival Management*, 6(3), pp. 235–250.

Pink, S., Horst, H., Hostel, J., Hjorth, L., Lewis, T. and Tacchi, J. (2016) *Digital ethnography: principles and practice*. London: Sage.

Potter, J. and Wetherell, M. (1987) *Discourse and social psychology*. London: Sage.

Pratt, M.L. (1992) *Imperial eyes: travel writing and transculturation*. London: Routledge.

Preece, C., Kerrigan, F. and O'Reilly, D. (2019) 'License to assemble: theorizing brand longevity', *Journal of Consumer Research*, 46(2), pp. 330–350. https://doi.org/10.1093/jcr/ucy076

Preece, C. and Rojas Gaviria, P. (2024) 'An ontology of consumers as distributed networks: A question of cause and effect', *Journal of Marketing Management*, 40(7–8), pp. 628–634. https://doi.org/10.1080/0267257X.2024.2346010

Puntoni, S., Schroeder, J. and Ritson, M. (2010) 'Meaning matters', *Journal of Advertising*, 39(2), pp. 51–64. https://doi.org/10.2753/JOA0091-3367390204

Puntoni, S., Vanhamme, J. and Visscher, R. (2011) 'Two birds and one stone', *Journal of Advertising*, 40(1), pp. 25–42. https://doi.org/10.2753/JOA0091-3367400102

Reed-Danahay, D.E. (1997) *Auto/Ethnography: rewriting the self and the social*. Oxford: Berg.

Relja, R., Ward, P. and Zhao, A.L. (2023). Three little words: a pragmatic qualitative method to understand modern markets. *International Journal of Market Research*, 0(0). https://doi.org/10.1177/14707853231219927

Reynolds, T.J. and Gutman, A. (1988) 'Laddering theory: method, analysis and interpretation', *Journal of Advertising Research*, 28(1), pp. 11–31.

Richardson, L. (2000) 'Writing: a method of inquiry', in Denzin, N.K. and Lincoln, Y.S. (eds.) *Handbook of qualitative research*. Thousand Oaks, CA: Sage, pp. 877–892.

Ritson, M. and Elliott, R. (1999) 'The social uses of advertising: an ethnographic study of adolescent advertising audiences', *Journal of Consumer Research*, 26(3), pp. 260–277.

Ritzer, G. (2000) *The McDonaldization of society* (New Century edition). Thousand Oaks, CA: Pine Forge Press, Sage.

Roberts, M. (2015) '"A big night out": young people's drinking, social practice and spatial experience in the "liminoid" zones of English night-time cities', *Urban Studies*, 52(3), pp. 571–588.

Roberts, S. (2012) 'The reception of my self-experimentation', *Journal of Business Research*, 65(7), pp. 1060–1066.

Rod, M. and Ellis, N. (2014) 'Using discourse analysis in case study research in business-to-business contexts', Chapter 21 in *Advances in Business Marketing and Purchasing*, pp. 77–99. https://doi.org/10.1108/S1069-096420140000021003

Roffe, J. (2015) The concept of assemblage and the case of markets. in Canniford R and Bajde D (eds.) *Assembling consumption: researching actors, networks and markets*. London: Routledge, pp. 42–55.

Rogers, C. (1945) 'The non-directive method as a technique for social research', *American Journal of Sociology*, 50, pp. 279–283.

Rogers, C. (1949) (2013 reprint) *Significant aspects of client-centred therapy*, Webb, D. (ed.) Creatspace Independent Publishing Platform.

Romero, F. (2019) Philosophy of science and the replicability crisis. *Philosophy Compass*, 14, p. e12633. https://doi.org/10.1111/phc3.12633

Rorty, R. (1982) *Consequences of pragmatism*. Minneapolis, MN: University of Minnesota Press.

Roux, D. and Belk, R. (2018) 'The body as (another) place: producing embodied heterotopias through tattooing', *Journal of Consumer Research*, ucy081. https://doi.org/10.1093/jcr/ucy081

Russell, C.A. and Schau, H.J. (2014) 'When narrative brands end: the impact of narrative closure and consumption sociality on loss accommodation', *Journal of Consumer Research*, 40(6), pp. 1039–1062. https://doi.org/10.1086/673959

Rust, L. (1993) 'Observations: parents and their children shopping together', *Journal of Advertising Research*, 33(4), pp. 65–70.

Said, E. (1978) *Orientalism*. London: Routledge and Kegan Paul.

Saldana, J. (2011) *Ethnotheatre: research from page to stage*. Walnut Creek, CA: Left Coast Press.

Salomonson, N. and Echeverri, P. (2024) 'Embodied interaction: A turn to better understand disabling marketplaces and consumer vulnerability', *Journal of Marketing Management*, 40(5–6), pp. 378–417. https://doi.org/10.1080/0267257X.2024.2303108

Sartre, J.P. (1943) *Being and nothingness*. London: Methuen (1958 edition).

Sartre, J.P. (1946) *Existentialism and humanism*, trans. P. Mairet. London: Methuen (1990 edition).

Sartre, J.P. (1963) *Search for a method*. New York, NY: Knopf.

de Saussure, F. (1915) *Course in general linguistics*, trans. W. Baskin. London: Fontana (1974 edition).

Scaraboto, D. and Fischer, E. (2013) 'Frustrated fatshionistas: an institutional theory perspective on consumer quests for greater choice in mainstream markets', *Journal of Consumer Research*, 39(6), pp. 1234–1257. https://doi.org/10.1086/668298

Schatzki, T.R. (1996) *Social practices: a Wittgensteinian approach to human activity and the social*. Cambridge, UK: Cambridge University Press.

Schatzki, T.R. (2002) *The site of the social: a philosophical account of the constitution of social life and change*. University Park: The Pennsylvania State University Press.

Schatzki, T.R. (2012) 'A primer on practices', in Higgs, J., Barnett, R., Billett, S., Hutchings, M. and Trede, F. (eds.) *Practice-based education perspectives and strategies*, volume 6. Rotterdam, The Netherlands: Sense, pp. 13–26.

Schau, H.J., Gilly, M.C. and Wolfinbarger, M. (2009) 'Consumer identity renaissance: the resurgence of identity-inspired consumption in retirement', *Journal of Consumer Research*, 36(2), pp. 255–277.

Schau, H.J. and Thompson, K. (2010) 'Betwixt and between: liminality and feminism in the twilight brand community', in Campbell, M.C., Inman, J. and Pieters, R. (eds.) *NA – Advances in consumer research*, vol. 37. Duluth, MN: Association for Consumer Research, pp. 89–93.

Schembri, S. and Latimer, L. (2016) 'Online brand communities: constructing and co-constructing brand culture', *Journal of Marketing Management*, 32(7–8), pp. 628–651. https://doi.org/10.1080/0267257X.2015.1117518

Schmitt, B., Joško Brakus, J. and Biraglia, A. (2022) 'Consumption ideology', *Journal of Consumer Research*, 49(1), pp. 74–95. http://doi.org/10.1093/jcr/ucab044

Schöps, J.D., Kogler, S. and Hemetsberger, A. (2019) '(De-)stabilizing the digitized fashion market on Instagram – Dynamics of visual performative assemblages', *Consumption Markets & Culture*. 10.1080/10253866.2019.1657099

Schouten, J. (1991) 'Selves in transition: symbolic consumption in personal rites of passage and identity reconstruction', *Journal of Consumer Research*, 17(4), pp. 412–425. https://doi.org/10.1086/208567

Schouten, J. (2023) 'Taking it to the streets: the making of a consumer ethnographer', *Journal of Customer Behaviour*, 22(4), pp. 33–43.

Schouten, J. and McAlexander, J.H. (1995) 'Subcultures of consumption: an ethnography of the new bikers', *Journal of Consumer Research*, 22(1), pp. 43–61. https://doi.org/10.1086/209434

Schroeder, J.E. (2002) *Visual consumption*. London: Routledge.

Schroeder, J.E. and Borgerson, J.L. (2015) 'Critical visual analysis of gender: reactions and reflections', *Journal of Marketing Management*, 31(15–16), pp. 1723–1731. https://doi.org/10.1080/0267257X.2015.1077883

Schutz, A. (1932) *The phenomenology of the social world*. London: Heinemann (1967 edition).

Schwartz-Shea, P. and Yanow, D. (2012) *Interpretive research design*. Oxfordshire: Routledge.

Scott, L. (1990) 'Understanding jingles and needledrop: a rhetorical approach to music in advertising', *Journal of Consumer Research*, 17, pp. 223–236.

Scott, L. (1994a) 'The bridge from text to mind: adapting reader-response theory to consumer research', *Journal of Consumer Research*, 21, pp. 461–480.

Scott, L. (1994b) 'Images in advertising: the need for a theory of visual rhetoric', *Journal of Consumer Research*, 21, pp. 252–273.

Sebeok, T. (1991) *A sign is just a sign*. Bloomington and Indianapolis: Indiana University Press.

Seregina, A. and Weijo, H.A. (2017) 'Play at any cost: how cosplayers produce and sustain their ludic communal consumption experiences', *Journal of Consumer Research*, 44(1), pp. 139–159. https://doi.org/10.1093/jcr/ucw077

Shankar, A. (2000) 'Lost in music? Subjective personal introspection and popular music consumption', *Qualitative Market Research: An International Journal*, 3(1), pp. 27–37.

Shankar, A., Elliott, R. and Goulding, C. (2001) 'Understanding consumption: contributions from a narrative perspective', *Journal of Marketing Management*, 17, pp. 429–453.

Shankar, A. and Goulding, C. (2001) 'Interpretive consumer research: two more contributions to theory and practice', *Qualitative Market Research: An International Journal*, 4(1), pp. 7–16.

Shepherd, S., Chartrand, T.L. and Fitzsimons, G.J. (2015) 'When brands reflect our ideal world: the values and brand preferences of consumers who support versus reject Society's dominant ideology', *Journal of Consumer Research*, 42(1), pp. 76–92. http://doi.org/10.1093/jcr/ucv005

Sherry, J.F. (1983) 'Gift giving in anthropological perspective', *Journal of Consumer Research*, 10(2). pp. 157–168. https://doi.org/10.1086/208956

Sherry, J.F. (1991) 'Postmodern alternatives: the interpretive turn in consumer research', in Robertson, T.S. and Kassarjian, H.H. (eds.) *Handbook of consumer behaviour*. Englewood-Cliffs, NJ: Prentice-Hall, pp. 548–591.

Sherry, J.F. (1995) 'Bottomless cup, plug-in drug: a telethnography of coffee', *Visual Anthropology*, 7(4), pp. 351–370.

Sherry, J.F. and Camargo, G. (1987) 'May your life be marvellous': English language labelling and the semiotics of Japanese promotion', *Journal of Consumer Research*, 14, pp. 174–188.

Sherry, J.F., McGrath, M.A. and Diamond, N. (2013) 'Discordant retail brand ideology in the *house of Barbie*', *Qualitative Marketing Research*, 16(1), pp. 12–37.

Sherry, J.F. and Schouten, J.W. (2002) 'A role for poetry in consumer research', *Journal of Consumer Research*, 29, pp. 218–234.

Sibai, O., Luedicke, M.K. and de Valck, K. (2024) Why online consumption communities brutalize, *Journal of Consumer Research*, ucae022. https://doi.org/10.1093/jcr/ucae022

Sinkovics, R.R., Richardson, C. and Lew, Y.K. (2015) 'Enhancing student competency and employability in international business through master's dissertations', *Journal of Teaching in International Business*, 26(4), pp. 293–317.

Skålén, P., Fougére, M. and Fellesson, M. (2008) *Marketing discourse: a critical perspective*. London: Routledge.

Skålén, P. and Hackley, C. (2011) 'Marketing-as-practice: introduction to the special issue', *Scandinavian Journal of Management*, 27(2), pp. 189–196. https://doi.org/10.1016/j.scaman.2011.03.004

Smith Maguire, J. (2010) 'Provenance and the liminality of production and consumption: the case of wine promoters', *Marketing Theory*, 10(3), pp. 269–282.

Spicer, A., Alvesson, M. and Kärreman, D. (2009) 'Critical performativity: the unfinished business of critical management studies', *Human Relations*, 62(4), pp. 537–560. https://doi.org/10.1177/0018726708101984

Spiggle, S. (1994) 'Analysis and interpretation of qualitative data in consumer research', *Journal of Consumer Research*, 21, pp. 491–503.

Spradley, J. (1980) *Participant observation*. New York, NY: Holt, Rinehart and Winston.

Stephens-Davidowitz, S. (2017) *Everybody lies – What the internet can tell us about who we really are*. London: Bloomsbury Publishing.

Stern, B.B. (1989) 'Literary criticism and consumer research: overview and illustrative analysis', *Journal of Consumer Research*, 16, pp. 34–46.

Stern, B.B. (1990) 'Literary criticism and the history of marketing thought: a new perspective on "reading" marketing theory', *Journal of the Academy of Marketing Science*, 18, pp. 329–336.

Stern, B.B. (1993) 'Feminist literary criticism and the deconstruction of Ads: a postmodern view of advertising and consumer responses', *Journal of Consumer Research*, 19, pp. 556–566.

Stern, B.B. and Schroeder, J. (1994) 'Interpretative methodology from art and literary criticism: a humanistic approach to advertising imagery', *European Journal of Marketing, 28(8)*.

Stern, B.B., Thompson, C. and Arnould, E. (1998) 'Narrative analysis of marketing relationship: the consumer's perspective', *Psychology and Marketing, 15(3)*, pp. 195–214.

Stubbs, M. (1983) *Discourse analysis: the sociolinguistic analysis of natural language.* Oxford: Basil Blackwell.

Sturge, G. (2019) *UK prison population statistics, briefing paper number CBP-04334,* 23 July 2019. House of Commons Library.

Svensson, P. (2007) 'Producing marketing: towards a social-phenomenology of marketing work', *Marketing Theory, 7(3)*, pp. 271–290. https://doi.org/10.1177/1470593107080346

Szmigin, I., Bengry-Howell, A., Griffin, C., Hackley, C. and Mistral, W. (2011) 'Social marketing, individual responsibility and the "culture of intoxication', *European Journal of Marketing (Q1, 45(5)*, pp. 759–779.

Szmigin, I. and Carrigan, M. (2001) 'Time, consumption and the older consumer: an interpretive study of the cognitively young', *Psychology and Marketing, 18(10)*, pp. 1091–1116.

Tadajewski, M. (2014) 'What is critical marketing studies? Reading macro, social, and critical marketing studies', in Varey, R. and Pirson, M. (eds.) *Humanistic marketing. Humanism in business series.* London: Palgrave Macmillan.

Tadajewski, M., Chelekis, J., DeBerry-Spence, B., Figueiredo, B., Kravets, O., Nuttavuthisit, K., Peñaloza, L. and Moisander, J. (2014) 'The discourses of marketing and development: towards "critical transformative marketing research"', *Journal of Marketing Management, 30(17–18)*, pp. 1728–1771. https://doi.org/10.1080/0267257X.2014.952660

Tadajewski, M., Higgins, M., Denegri-Knott, J. and Varman, R. (eds.) (2019) *The Routledge companion to critical marketing studies.* London: Routledge, pp. 185–195.

Tadajewski, M. and Maclaran, P. (2009) *Critical marketing studies.* London: Routledge.

Tanaka, K. (1994) *Advertising language: a pragmatic approach to advertisements in Britain and Japan.* London: Routledge.

Thaler, R.H. and Sunstein, C.R. (2008) *Nudge: improving decisions about health, wealth, and happiness.* New Haven, CT: Yale University Press.

Thomas, J. (1993) *Doing critical ethnography.* Newbury Park, CA: Sage.

Thomas, T.C. and Epp, A.M. (2019) 'The best laid plans: why new parents fail to habituate practices', *Journal of Consumer Research* (online early cite). https://doi.org/10.1093/jcr/ucz003

Thompson, C.J. (1997) 'Interpreting consumers: a hermeneutical framework for deriving marketing insights from the texts of consumers' consumption stories', *Journal of Marketing Research, 34(6)*, pp. 438–455.

Thompson, C.J. (2002) 'A re-inquiry on re-inquiries: a postmodern proposal for a critical-reflexive approach', *Journal of Consumer Research, 29(1)*, pp. 142–145. https://doi.org/10.1086/339926

Thompson, C.J. (2004) 'Marketplace mythology and discourses of power', *Journal of Consumer Research, 31(1)*, pp. 162–180. https://doi.org/10.1086/383432

Thompson, C.J. (2019) 'The "Big Data" myth and the pitfalls of "Thick Data" opportunism: on the need for a different ontology of markets and consumption', *Journal of Marketing Management, 35(3–4)*, pp. 207–230.

Thompson, C.J. and Coskuner-Balli, G. (2007) 'Countervailing market responses to corporate co-optation and the ideological recruitment of consumption communities', *Journal of Consumer Research, 34*, pp. 135–152. https://doi.org/10.1086/519143

Thompson, C.J. and Haytko, D.L. (1997) 'Speaking of fashion: consumers' uses of fashion discourses and the appropriation of countervailing cultural meanings', *Journal of Consumer Research*, 24(1), pp. 15–42. https://doi.org/10.1086/209491

Thompson, C.J., Henry, P.C. and Bardhi, F. (2018) 'Theorizing reactive reflexivity: lifestyle displacement and discordant performances of taste', *Journal of Consumer Research*, 45(3), pp. 571–594. https://doi.org/10.1093/jcr/ucy018

Thompson, C.J. and Hirschman, E.C. (1995) 'Understanding the socialized body: a poststructuralist analysis of consumers' self-conceptions, body images, and self-care practices', *Journal of Consumer Research*, 22(2), pp. 139–153. https://doi.org/10.1086/209441

Thompson, C.J., Locander, W.B. and Pollio, H.R. (1989) 'Putting consumer experience back into consumer research: the philosophy and method of existential phenomenology', *Journal of Consumer Research*, 17, pp. 133–147.

Thompson, C.J., Locander, W.B. and Pollio, H.R. (1990) 'The lived meaning of free choice: an existential – Phenomenological description of everyday consumer experiences of contemporary married women', *Journal of Consumer Research*, 17, pp. 346–361.

Thompson, C.J., Pollio, H.R. and Locander, W.B. (1994) 'The spoken and the unspoken: a hermeneutic approach to understanding the cultural viewpoints that underlie consumers' expressed meanings', *Journal of Consumer Research*, 21, pp. 431–453.

Thompson, C.J. and Tambyah, S.K. (1999) 'Trying to be cosmopolitan', *Journal of Consumer Research*, 26(3), pp. 214–241. https://doi.org/10.1086/209560

Thompson, C.J. and Ustunier, T. (2015) 'Women skating on the edge: marketplace performances as ideological edgework', *Journal of Consumer Research*, 42(2), pp. 235–265.

Tiwsakul, R.A. and Hackley, C. (2012) 'Postmodern paradoxes in Thai-Asian consumer identity', *Journal of Business Research*, 66(4), pp. 490–496. www.sciencedirect.com/science/article/pii/S0148296311000609

Tonks, D. (2002) 'Marketing as cooking: the return of the sophists', *Journal of Marketing Management*, 18, pp. 803–822.

Tumbat, G. and Belk, R.W. (2011) 'Marketplace tensions in extraordinary experiences', *Journal of Consumer Research*, 38(1), pp. 42–63. https://doi.org/10.1086/658220

Turner, V.W. (1967) *The forest of symbols: aspects of Ndembu ritual*. Ithaca and London: Cornell University Press.

Turner, V.W. (1969) *The ritual process: structure and anti-structure*. New Brunswick, NJ: Transaction Publishers, Rutgers, The State University.

Turner, V.W. (1974) 'Liminal to liminoid, in play, flow, and ritual: an essay in comparative symbology', *Rice University Studies*, 60(3), pp. 53–92.

Turner, V.W. (1982) *From ritual to theatre – The human seriousness of play*. New York, NY: PAJ Publications.

Turner, V.W. (1986) 'Dewey, dilthey and drama: an essay in the anthropology of experience', Chapter 2 in Turner, V.W. and Bruner, E.M. (eds.) *The anthropology of experience*. Chicago: University of Illinois Press.

Umiker-Sebeok, J. (ed.) (1987) *Marketing signs: new directions in the study of signs for Sale*. Berlin: Mouton.

Umiker-Sebeok, J., Cossette, C. and Bachand, D. (1988) 'Selected bibliography on the semiotics of marketing', *Semiotic Enquiry*, 8(3), pp. 415–423.

Urminsky, O. and Dietvorst, B.J. (2024) 'Taking the full measure: integrating replication into research practice to assess generalizability', *Journal of Consumer Research*, 51(1), pp. 157–168. https://doi.org/10.1093/jcr/ucae007

Üstüner, T. and Holt, D.B. (2007) 'Dominated consumer acculturation: the social construction of poor migrant women's consumer identity projects in a Turkish squatter', *Journal of Consumer Research*, 34(1), pp. 41–56. https://doi.org/10.1086/513045

van Dijk, T.A. (1984) *Prejudice in discourse: an analysis of ethnic prejudices in cognition and conversation.* Amsterdam: John Benjamins.

van Dijk, T.A. (ed.) (1985) *Handbook of discourse analysis* (vols. 1–4). London: Academic Press.

van Gennep, A. (1961) *The rites of passage.* Chicago: Chicago University Press.

van Laer, T., de Ruyter, K., Visconti, L.M. and Wetzels, M. (2014) 'The extended transportation-imagery model: a meta-analysis of the antecedents and consequences of consumers' narrative transportation', *Journal of Consumer Research,* 40(5, 1), pp. 797–817. https://doi.org/10.1086/673383

van Laer, T., Edson Escalas, J., Ludwig, S. and van den Hende, E.A. (2019) 'What happens in VegasSstays on Tripadvisor? A theory and technique to understand narrativity in consumer reviews', *Journal of Consumer Research,* 46(2), pp. 267–285. https://doi.org/10.1093/jcr/ucy067

van Laer, T. and Izberk-Bilgin, E. (2019) 'A discourse analysis of pilgrimage reviews', *Journal of Marketing Management,* 35(5), pp. 586–604. https://doi.org/10.1080/0267257X.2018.1550434

van Laer, T., Visconti, L.M. and Feiereisen, S. (2018) 'Need for narrative', *Journal of Marketing Management,* 34(5–6), pp. 484–496. https://doi.org/10.1080/0267257X.2018.1477817

van Mannen, J. (ed.) (1995) *Representation in ethnography.* Thousand Oaks, CA: Sage.

Varey, R. and Pirson, M. (2014) *Humanistic marketing.* London: Springer Link.

Varman, R., Belk, R.W. and Sreekumar, H. (2023) Post-colonial consumer respect and the framing of neocolonial consumption in advertising, *Journal of Consumer Research (in Press),* ucad063. https://doi.org/10.1093/jcr/ucad063

Varman, R., Saha, B. and Skålén, P. (2011) 'Market subjectivity and neoliberal governmentality in higher education', *Journal of Marketing Management,* 27(11–12), pp. 1163–1185. https://doi.org/10.1080/0267257X.2011.609134

Venkatesh, S. (2009) *Gang leader for a day.* New York, NY: Penguin.

Venkatraman, R., Ozanne, J.L. and Coslor, E. (2024) Stigma resistance through body-in-practice: embodying pride through creative mastery, *Journal of Consumer Research,* 2024, ucae015. https://doi.org/10.1093/jcr/ucae015

Villegas, D. (2018) 'From the self to the screen: a journey guide for auto-netnography in online communities', *Journal of Marketing Management,* 34(3–4), pp. 243–262. https://doi.org/10.1080/0267257X.2018.1443970

vom Lehn, D. (2014) 'Timing is money: managing the floor in sales interaction at street-market stalls', *Journal of Marketing Management,* 30(13–14), pp. 1448–1466. https://doi.org/10.1080/0267257X.2014.941378

Wallendorf, M. and Arnould, E.J. (1988) '"My favorite things": a cross-cultural inquiry into object attachment, possessiveness, and social linkage', *Journal of Consumer Research,* 14(4), 531–547. https://doi.org/10.1086/209134

Wallendorf, M. and Brucks, M. (1993) 'Introspection in consumer research: implementation and implications', *Journal of Consumer Research,* 20, pp. 339–359.

Watson, T.J. (1994) *In search of management: culture, chaos and control in managerial work.* London: Routledge.

Weijo, H.A., Martin, D.M. and Arnould, E.J. (2018) 'Consumer movements and collective creativity: the case of restaurant day', *Journal of Consumer Research,* 45(2), pp. 251–274. https://doi.org/10.1093/jcr/ucy003

Weinberger, M.F., Zavisca, J.R. and Silva, J.M. (2017) 'Consuming for an imagined future: middle-class consumer lifestyle and exploratory experiences in the transition to adulthood', *Journal of Consumer Research,* 44(2), pp. 332–360. https://doi.org/10.1093/jcr/ucx045

Wernick, A. (1991) *Promotional culture: advertising, ideology and symbolic expression*. London, Newbury Park: Sage.

Wetherell, M. and Potter, J. (1992) *Mapping the language of racism: discourse and the legitimation of exploitation*. New York, NY: Columbia University Press.

Williams Bradford, T. and Sherry, J.F. (2015) 'Domesticating public space through ritual: tailgating as vestaval', *Journal of Consumer Research*, 42(1), pp. 130–151. https://doi.org/10.1093/jcr/ucv001

Williamson, J. (1978) *Decoding advertisements: ideology and meaning in advertisements*. London: Marion Boyars.

Wilson, T. (2012) 'What can phenomenology offer the consumer?' *Qualitative Market Research*, 15(3), pp. 230–241. https://doi.org/10.1108/13522751211231969

Wilson, T. (2019) *Consumption, psychology and practice theories: A hermeneutic perspective*. London: Routledge.

Woermann, N. (2018) 'Focusing ethnography: theory and recommendations for effectively combining video and ethnographic research', *Journal of Marketing Management*, 34(5–6), pp. 459–483. https://doi.org/10.1080/0267257X.2018.1441174

Wohlfeil, M. (2018), *Celebrity fans and their consumer behaviour: autoethnographic insights into the life of a fan*, Routledge Interpretive Marketing Research Series No. 25, Basingstoke: Routledge.

Wohlfeil, M., Patterson, A. and Gould, S.J. (2019) 'The allure of celebrities: unpacking their polysemic consumer appeal', *European Journal of Marketing*. https://doi.org/10.1108/EJM-01-2017-0052

Wohlfeil, M. and Whelan, S. (2012) '"Saved" by Jena Malone: an introspective study of a consumer's fan relationship with an actress', *Journal of Business Research*, 65(4), pp. 511–519.

Wood, B. (1998) 'Stuart Hall's cultural studies and the problem of hegemony', *The British Journal of Sociology*, 49(3), pp. 399–414. https://doi.org/10.2307/591390

Woolgar, S. (1981) 'Interests and explanation in the social studies of science', *Social Studies of Science*, 11, pp. 365–394.

Woolgar, S. (1988) *Science: the very idea*. Chichester: Ellis Horwood, London, Tavistock.

Woolgar, S. (1989) 'The ideology of representation and the role of the agent', in Lawson, H. and Appignanesi, L. (eds.) *Dismantling truth: reality in the post-modern world*. London: Weidenfeld and Nicolson.

Wright, S. (1994) *Anthropology of organisations*. London: Routledge.

Yang, Y.N., Ozanne, J.L. and Phipps, M. (2024) Using cultural repertoires during unsettled times, *Journal of Consumer Research* (in press), ucae036. https://doi.org/10.1093/jcr/ucae036

Ybema, S., Keenoy, T., Oswick, C., Sabelis, I., Ellis, N. and Beverungen, A. (2009) 'Articulating identities', *Human Relations*, 62(3), pp. 299–322.

Yin, R.K. (2014) *Case study research design and methods*. 5th edn. Thousand Oaks, CA: Sage, 282 pages.

Zeman, J.J. (1977) 'Peirce's theory of signs', in Sebeok, T. (ed.) *A perfusion of signs*. Bloomington, IN: Indiana University Press, pp. 22–39.

Zhao, X. and Belk, R.W. (2008) 'Politicizing consumer culture: advertising's appropriation of political ideology in China's social transition', *Journal of Consumer Research*, 35(2), pp. 231–244. https://doi.org/10.1086/588747

Zwick, D. (2018) 'No longer violent enough? Creative destruction, innovation and the ossification of neoliberal capitalism', *Journal of Marketing Management*, 34(11–12), pp. 913–931. https://doi.org/10.1080/0267257X.2018.1536076

Index

Printed in the United States
by Baker & Taylor Publisher Services